TRADE
YOUR WAY TO
FINANCIAL
FREEDOM

TRADE YOUR WAY TO FINANCIAL FREEDOM

SECOND EDITION

VAN K. THARP

McGraw-Hill
New York Chicago San Francisco Lisbon London
Madrid Mexico City Milan New Delhi
San Juan Seoul Singapore Sydney Toronto

The McGraw-Hill Companies

5 6 7 8 9 0 FGR/FGR 0 9 8

ISBN 13: 978-0-07-147871-7
ISBN 10: 0-07-147871-X

This book is printed on acid-free paper.

Library of Congress Cataloging-in-Publication Data

Tharp, Van K.
Trade your way to financial freedom, / by Van K. Tharp.—2nd ed.
p. cm.
Includes index.
ISBN 0-07-147871-X (alk. paper)
1. Finance, Personal. 2. Stocks. I. Title.
HG179.T452 2007
332.024—dc22 2006020425

This book is dedicated to my wife, Kalavathi Tharp.
Kala provides a very special spark in my life.
Without that spark and her tremendous love,
this book would not be possible.

CONTENTS

PART TWO

CONCEPTUALIZING YOUR SYSTEM

Chapter 4

Steps to Developing a System 69

Chapter 5

Selecting a Concept That Works 97

FOREWORD

Let me start by saying that *Trade Your Way to Financial Freedom* is required reading for all of my new traders. Of all of Dr. Van Tharp's published books, this one gives the essence of his teachings from his workshops and home study courses. My name is Chuck Whitman, and I am the CEO of Infinium Capital Management, a proprietary trading firm located in the Chicago Board of Trade. We currently have 90 employees, trade on 15 different exchanges, and trade underlying instruments and options on all asset classes. I have personally purchased many copies of this book, but before I get into that, let me tell you about my experiences with Van Tharp.

I first became aware of Van's teachings in 1998, when one of my mentors, Bruce, obtained two of Van's home study courses, the *Peak Performance Course for Traders and Investors* and the *Developing a Winning System That Fits You* Course. Later, Bruce also attended one of Van's System seminars, and he came back telling me how impressed he was with the material and the quality of students that had attended the seminar.

At that time, I was in the midst of one of the most difficult periods of trading of my career. Ironically, 1997 was one of my most successful trading years, and in 1998 I had decided to commit myself to becoming absolutely the best trader I could be. However, the only approach I knew was to "do more" so I could hit my new revenue goal, and needless to say, I was overtrading and battling huge profit and loss swings in my account. In the fall of 1998, I put on a large trade that conceptually was a great trade. However, I mismanaged the trade, and it quickly spiraled into one of the largest losses of my career. Looking back at it now, I'd made many mistakes, and this is according to Van's definition of a mistake which is "not following my rules." I had not done any scenario planning before the trade, and I found myself in a position with a terrible reward-to-risk ratio. Furthermore, as I battled the loss,

I responded emotionally and did everything I could to prevent it. It's what Van calls the "loss trap." Instead of just taking a small loss, I struggled with it, trying to avoid it. And the more I struggled with the loss, the worse it became. And the bigger it got, the more I wanted to avoid it and not take it. Eventually, the loss became too painful and I liquidated the trade. The moment I was out of the trade, I made a vow that I was going to learn from what I had been through and make sure I would never repeat it. It turned out to be a major turning point in my trading career.

I started on my evaluation of myself to discover what I could do to improve as a trader. As a result, I decided to borrow the first book of the *Peak Performance Course* from Bruce, and I found a chapter in there on the "loss trap." I could see myself in the story and how I had responded to that difficult trade. All the mistakes I had made on that trade and how I approached my trading in general were described in that chapter. I was hooked. I immediately ordered myself a personal copy of the course.

In January 1999, I had knee surgery, and I was required to be off my feet for 10 weeks. At the time I was a floor trader, so I was planning to test some of my "off-the-floor" trading ideas. I also started working through the *Peak Performance Course*, and I quickly decided that the best use of my time would be to clear my head from the markets and focus on my trading psychology. Early in the course, Dr. Tharp had said that the exercises you didn't want to do were probably the ones you needed to do the most. As a result, I committed to doing every single exercise in the course, working at it every day for four to six hours for 10 weeks. And, in my opinion, I emerged from that process a trader with a totally different psychology that has served as the foundation of my trading ever since.

At that same time, I decided to attend one of Dr. Tharp's workshops. It was given by Van and Robert Kiyosaki of *Rich Dad, Poor Dad* fame. That seminar changed my beliefs about wealth and wealth creation as radically as the *Peak Performance Course* had changed my psychology. I'm really glad to see that Dr. Tharp has incorporated a little of that material into this new edition of *Trade Your Way to Financial Freedom* by defining *financial freedom* in the preface. I learned that wealth was an idea, not a finite resource as was taught in my economics classes. I realized that I was the biggest factor in my success and that time was more valuable than money. From that point on, I started to act on faith, and I made decisions that revolved around increasing my productivity and learning. If I could spend money to improve my productivity and give me more time to learn, I would do it. Shortly after that workshop, I returned to trading with a new perspective on trading and wealth. I made more money in the next four months than I had made in my entire career.

After that period, I backed off my trading, doing it instead on more of a part-time basis, and I started to work on a lifelong dream that I had, which was to build my own trading firm and become an upstairs speculator. I spent the next two years learning, researching, and building the plan of how I wanted to trade. As I built this plan, I used many of Van's principles as the foundation. I read this book and his other published book at the time, *Financial Freedom through Electronic Day Trading*. I took several more of Van's workshops, and I adopted five key principles around which I built my firm. Four of those principles I learned from Van. I have kept the principles consistent and in the order Van teaches them as well. Here they are:

1. *Psychology.* You could have the best opportunities and resources in the world but if your psychology is flawed, you won't make it. We operate on the belief that we create and manifest our own realities. If we think the world has problems, then we manifest those beliefs in what we see. But if we think the world is abundant, then we find lots of evidence to show that it is. We place the most amount of focus in this area from how we hire new employees to how we teach them and how we grow. And in this new edition of *Trade Your Way to Financial Freedom*, you'll find that principle throughout the book. You are responsible for the results you get, which means that you are in charge of your trading. When you get results that you don't like, you made a mistake in some way, and you can fix that mistake.
2. *Position sizing.* You could have the best trading plan, information, and execution systems, but if you bet too big, you'll blow out. As Van points out in this new edition, a low-risk idea is an idea that's traded at a risk level that allows you to survive the worst-case contingencies in the

long term, so that you can achieve the long-term expectancy of the system. This is one of the real keys to trading success, and you should read this book, several times, just to make sure that you understand this point. You are going to have losses, and it's important to limit the damage of those losses to achieve optimal compounded returns. Position sizing is one of the most important aspects of trading yet so few people teach it. It's that part of your system that helps you achieve your objectives. Make sure you really let that sink in as you read this book.

3. *Market selection.* This principle is my addition, although it's part of Dr. Tharp's model given in Chapter 4. The market you trade is far more important than how you trade. I've seen this principle operating throughout my trading career. In the late 1990s, early 2000s there were stock options guys making enormous amounts of money, yet they had no idea what they were doing. A few short years later, some of these same traders were approaching me for jobs as clerks with our firm. In contrast, I saw some great traders make a solid living slugging it out in bad markets. If they were in some of the busy markets, they would have been legends. This confirmed my belief. Find the busiest, most volatile markets and focus on those. As John Paul Getty used to say, "Go where the oil is!" I'm really glad to see that Dr. Tharp has added a chapter to this new edition on assessing the big picture, and then finding markets and strategies that fit the big picture.
4. *Exits.* The key to making money in the markets is in how you exit the market. You must limit your losses by knowing when you are wrong and pulling the trigger on your bad trades. This is discussed extensively in Chapter 10. You must also know how to manage a winner and let it optimally run. This is discussed extensively in Chapter 11. Some of the greatest traders I know and have watched were masters at admitting they were wrong, exiting the position without ego, and doing it in a way that no one even knew they were getting out of the market.
5. *Entries.* In Chapter 9, you learn that you can enter the market randomly and still make money. Dr. Tharp even

> talks about his random entry system and shows you how to make money with it. If you have a sound psychology that allows you to trade without ego; a positive expectancy system, which is produced by making sure that your losses are kept to a minimum (Van calls this "making sure your losses are 1*R* or less"), and trading for excellent reward-to-risk ratios (which Van calls "having your winners be large multiples of your initial risk"); and trade in the best market, using position sizing to meet your objectives, then your entry just isn't that important. These principles are discussed throughout this new edition of *Trade Your Way to Financial Freedom.*

These principles are the core of my business, and I teach them to all new recruits and to the employees of my firm. These principles are in sharp contrast to the following beliefs that are held by most of the general trading public:

- You have to pick the right stock. If you haven't made any money, you probably picked the wrong stock. Contrast this belief with Principle 5 above.
- You should be fully invested at all times, and diversification is involved in controlled risk. Contrast this belief with Principle 2.
- When you lose money in the market, it is probably because you are a victim of the market or your broker or advisor. Contrast this with Principle 1.

As a result, the general trading public is primarily focused on picking the right stocks at the right time and they ignore what's really important for success. That's why this book is so important.

In Chapter 2 you'll learn why success is so elusive to so many people—it's because of all the biases they have in their decision making. Dr. Tharp calls these "judgmental heuristics." And, ironically, the people who know about them use them to try to predict the market. In contrast, we've adopted Van's idea that most people lose because they are inefficient decision makers, so why not make ourselves more efficient.

As I mentioned earlier, *Trade Your Way to Financial Freedom* is required reading for my new traders. It gives insight into all of

Van's other work that I have found so valuable. This book will help you learn how to develop a trading system that fits your beliefs and helps you to achieve your objectives. If you read it again and again, you'll gain even more insight into the five key principles I use to run my company.

I would not have had the success and blessings I have had or had the opportunity to share them with so many others in the building of my firm if it had not been for the philosophies that Dr. Tharp taught me. I believe it was God's plan that I ran into Dr. Tharp and had the chance to learn from him. I have seen these philosophies put to the test over and over again as I have built my firm. They are the principal reason my firm has become extremely successful.

I hope you too learn the wonderful lessons from this book and use them to trade more profitably and to live your life more purposefully.

Chuck Whitman
Chief Executive Officer
Infinium Capital Management
Chicago, Illinois

BECOMING FINANCIALLY FREE THROUGH THIS BOOK

First, I'd like to comment on the title, which includes the words "financial freedom" in it. Many people thought that the words "financial freedom" made the title a bit too commercial. Jack Schwager even wrote a comment on the first edition that said, "While I can't promise you financial freedom, I can promise you a book filled with sound trading advice and lots of ideas you can use to develop your *own* trading methodology. And, if you don't think that's enough, then you really need this book."

So what is financial freedom? The first section of my book *Safe Strategies for Financial Freedom* is devoted to this topic. I won't repeat that discussion here, but I will summarize it.

Financial freedom is really a new way to think about money. Most people think they win the money game by having the most money and the most toys. This rule has been set up by other people to mislead you. If you follow it, someone else besides you will win the money game. The reason is that only one person in the world can have the most money, and even if you think billionaire status qualifies, it still means that your chances of winning the game are very slim.

If you think having the most toys wins the game, then you'll probably end up in debt because, after all, you can buy any toy now if the down payment and the monthly payments are low enough. However, doing this ultimately relegates you to a world of huge consumer debt and a life of financial slavery in which financial freedom (as I mean it) continues to move farther and farther away.

Financial freedom, to me, means adopting a different set of money rules to win the game of money. And if you follow those rules, become committed to the goal, and learn from your mistakes, then I can promise you financial freedom through this book. Financial freedom means that your money working for you makes more money than you need to meet your monthly expenses. For example, if your expenses are $5,000 per month, and your money working for you makes you $5,000 or more each month, then you are financially free.

Trading and investing make up one of the many ways that you can have your money working for you. I believe if you can develop a methodology through this book that doesn't require a lot of work to maintain (that is, it doesn't require more than a few hours each day) and that can generate enough money to meet your monthly expenses, then you are financially free. For example, if you have a $300,000 account and you make $60,000 (that is, 20 percent) each year trading that account and it takes you only a few hours each day to do that, then you are financially free. That doesn't mean that you won't spend hundreds, or even thousands, of hours building the foundation for your financial freedom. It also doesn't mean that you can avoid working on yourself yet continue to maintain that level of return. It does mean, however, that financial freedom is possible once you lay that foundation.

YOU TRADE ONLY YOUR BELIEFS

This book was originally published in 1999. Since then, numerous people have told me that it totally changed their thinking about trading, investing, and approaching the markets.

My understanding has always been that you cannot trade the markets. Instead, you trade your *beliefs* about the market. For example, if you believe that the market is going to go up (or generally that it goes up in the long run) and you believe that trend following works, then you might adopt a trend-following approach to buy stocks that are going up. However, if you believe that the market is overvalued and likely to go down, then you might have trouble buying stocks that are going up because doing so conflicts with your beliefs.

Everything that I said in the first edition of this book reflected my beliefs about the markets and what was necessary for trading success at the time that I wrote the book. However, beliefs are not reality. Instead, they are your filters to reality. I've acknowledged that for a long time, and I've continually said that what I teach reflects the most useful beliefs that I now have about the market and trading success.

Over the years, I occasionally run across beliefs that seem to help people even more. And in the seven years that have elapsed since the first edition of this book was published, I've adopted many new, more useful beliefs. As a result, even though most of the core concepts have *not* changed from the first edition, enough things have changed that I can help people even further with this new edition of the book.

Here are a few of the major changes that reflect my current beliefs:

- I believe that all trading systems should reflect the big picture. In 1999, we were nearly at the end of a great secular bull market that had begun in 1982. In 1999, you could buy any high-tech stock and hang on to it for six months and perhaps double your money. However, secular bull markets are followed by secular bear markets such as the one that began in 2000. These tend to last for as long as 20 years, so people need strategies that take advantage of these macro tendencies to make good profits. The bear market isn't bad news. It just requires a different focus to make money in it.
- My model for developing a trading system that fits you has evolved slightly over the last six years, and I've included the changes in this book.
- Although most of the concepts in the first edition are timeless, my perspective on them is not. As a result, I've changed my emphasis in this second edition to what I believe works best now.
- My explanation of expectancy in the first edition of this book was slightly misleading and definitely confusing. I changed it in my other books, *Financial Freedom through Electronic Day Trading* and *Safe Strategies for Financial Freedom*, and I've also made sure that it is crystal clear in this book as well.
- I now strongly believe that systems can be thought of as distributions of *R* multiples that they generate, which

you'll understand better as you read the book. When you understand this, your perspective on trading systems will totally change.

- Because systems can be thought of as distributions of *R* multiples, it's also possible to use those distributions to simulate what your future results might be like. And even more importantly, such simulations will tell you how to position size your system to meet your objectives. I've placed a strong emphasis on this topic in this new edition.

In addition, there are many small but significant changes in this edition that will help you become a much better trader or investor. I hope you benefit as much from the second edition as many people have claimed to have benefited from the first.

Van K. Tharp, Ph.D.
August 2006

PREFACE TO THE FIRST EDITION

A number of my clients have asked me not to include certain sections in this book with the admonishment of "You're giving away too much." Yet my job is to coach traders and investors to achieve peak performance. Every available tool is important in attempting to do that because so much misinformation exists in the literature that the average person will constantly be led astray.

Most of the misinformation is not deliberate. People want to be led astray. They constantly ask the wrong questions. For example,

- What's the market going to do now?
- What should I buy now?
- I own XYZ stock. Do you think it's going to go up? (If you say no, then they'll ask someone else until they find a person who agrees with their opinion.)
- Tell me how I can get into the market and be "right" most of the time.

And those selling information get rewarded by giving them the answers they want.

In April 1997, I did a two-day seminar in Germany. Toward the end of the seminar, I gave the participants the choice between doing an exercise dealing with self-sabotage (which all of them needed) and asking me questions. Although I believe that working on yourself is the most important thing you can do, they voted to ask questions. Guess what the first question asked of me was: "Dr. Tharp, what's your opinion about what the U.S. stock market will do for the rest of 1997?" This was despite my best efforts over the past two days to explain to them why such questions were unimportant. And hopefully, by the time you finish this book, you'll understand why.

When people move beyond questions on what to buy to questions about "how?" they still ask the wrong questions. Now the question becomes something like this:

> What criteria should I use to enter the market in order to be right most of the time?

There is a large industry available to give you the answer to such questions. Hot investment books are filled with entry strategies that the author claims to be 80 percent reliable or to have the promise of big gains. A picture tends to be worth a thousand words, so each strategy is accompanied by a graph in which the market just took off. Such "best-case" pictures can sway a lot of people and sell a lot of books. They also sell a lot of newsletters and a lot of trading systems. Unfortunately, they don't help that many people.

At an investment conference in 1995, a well-known speaker on the futures markets talked about his high-probability entry signals. The room was packed as he carefully explained what to do. Toward the end of the talk, one person raised his hand and asked, "How do you exit the market?" His response, albeit facetiously, was, "You want to know all my secrets, don't you?"

At another conference about a year later, the keynote speaker gave an hour talk before 600 people on high-probability entry techniques. Everyone listened eagerly to every word. Nothing was said about exits except that one should keep a tight stop and pay close attention to money management. After the talk, this particular speaker sold $10,000 worth of books in about a half-hour period because people were so excited that such high-probability entry techniques were the answer.

At the same conference, I spoke about position sizing—the key factor in determining one's profits. Thirty people listened to the talk, and about four of them purchased a book having to do with that particular topic. People gravitate toward the things that don't work. It's human nature.

Such stories could be repeated in conference after conference. Everyone will flock to a talk on high-probability entry signals or the software that they believe will tell them what to buy right now. And fewer than 1 percent will learn anything significant. However, talks featuring the most important keys to making real money, those on position sizing and your personal psychology, will have few people in attendance.

Even the software programs dealing with the markets have the same biases built into them. These products typically are loaded with indicators that can help you perfectly understand why markets did what they did in the past. Why wouldn't they? Those indicators are formed from that past data about which they are predicting prices. If you could do that with futures prices, the software would be wonderful. However, the reality is that you cannot predict prices in this manner. But it does sell a lot of software. And the software does answer the question that most people have: "What should I buy now?"

I might be leaning on a lot of sacred cows before I finish this book. The reason is that you can learn the real secrets to the market only if you pay attention to what really works. If your attention is elsewhere, you are not likely to find any secrets. However, this book simply contains my beliefs and opinions. It is filled with the kind of information that will help you really improve your performance as a trader or investor. Search it out and you will take a giant leap forward in your ability to make money consistently.

Van K. Tharp, Ph.D.
June 1998

ACKNOWLEDGMENTS

This book is a product of 25 years of thinking about markets, studying hundreds of great traders and investors, and coaching many more to greatness by helping them apply some of the principles you'll find in this book. The first edition has been an inspiration to thousands of traders. And if this new edition helps thousands more, even those I have never met, it will have been worth the effort.

During the 25 years I've spent in this field, numerous people have helped shape the thinking that has gone into this book. I can acknowledge only a few of those people by name. However, everyone who contributed in any way has my deepest thanks and appreciation.

Tom Basso has been a great contributor to my thinking and my life. Tom was a guest speaker at more than a dozen of my seminars and several of our professional trader schools. Tom has also contributed several sections to this book.

Ray Kelly was one of my earliest clients. I watched him evolve from a tough, Irish floor trader whose favorite saying used to be "My way or the highway!" into someone who would freely give his time to inner-city high school kids just to convince them to start to take responsibility for their lives, and who later ran a spiritual retreat in California. Ray was one of the best traders I've known and a great teacher as well. He presented at many of our seminars and wrote the arbitrage section of this book. Ray passed away since the first edition of this book was published. He was special and I miss him greatly.

I'd like to thank Chuck Whitman for writing the foreword to this book. Chuck's been part of my Super Trader program, and I used to consult with him regularly on the phone regarding system ideas. Chuck's not only been one of my best clients, he's also evolved into a model trader.

Chuck LeBeau helped me make the link from the famous traders' axiom "Cut your losses short and let your profits run" to the importance of exits. Think about it: Cutting losses short is all about aborting losses, exits. Letting profits run is all about exits as well. The entire axiom is about exits. Chuck's persistence in driving home this point has been very valuable to me. Chuck is frequently a guest speaker at our advanced systems seminar.

I'd also like to thank D. R. Barton. Over the last 15 years, I've watched D.R. transform himself from an engineer into a trader-teacher and a great contributor to our workshops. D.R. wrote the band trading section in the concepts chapter and thus has the honor of having contributed to all three of the books I've published through McGraw-Hill.

Kevin Thomas, Jerry Toepke, and Louis Mendelsohn all contributed great sections to the concepts chapter. Their work is very insightful and helpful. I deeply appreciate their contributions. Kevin was the first person to join my Super Trader program, and he now trains traders in London.

I'd also like to acknowledge Chuck Branscomb. When Chuck first came to our workshops, he thought he had a great system, when he really had no system at all—just some entry signals. Over the years, I watched him evolve into a very knowledgeable systems trader. He is also a great example of how solid "intuition" about the market evolves out of solid systems trading. Chuck is a former editor of our newsletter, and in that capacity he helped me coin such concepts as *R* multiples that have been included in this book.

Both Frank Gallucci and Chris Anderson helped me develop software that has shown me the importance of using simulation to determine the appropriate position-sizing algorithm to meet one's objectives in trading. In addition, I'd also like to acknowledge John Humphreys who incorporated all of my suggestions about position sizing and enabled me to see the millions of possibilities that now exist for various algorithms.

I'd like to thank my staff at IITM for their support in completing this book. Cathy Hasty was a great help in laying out the book in its original format with the graphics. Becky McKay helped me tremendously with the second edition of this book with proofreading and chapter editing. I had only a few months to get the second edition done, and I couldn't have done it without you, Becky. I am also grateful to Ana Walle and Tamika Williams, who assisted and supported me in a variety of different ways on this project. And I want to especially thank Melita Hunt for inspiring me to write this second edition of the book. Melita spearheaded the project and played the most critical role in handling details with my publisher, McGraw-Hill, which made this second edition possible.

I'd like to thank my editors at McGraw-Hill who made this second edition possible. They include Jeanne Glasser, the acquisition editor, and Jane Palmieri, the editing manager. In addition, I'd like to thank Marci Nugent who caught many of the errors that always creep into the manuscript.

To the best of my knowledge, *position sizing* was never used as a trading term prior to the first edition of this book. Since the publication of the first edition, it has virtually replaced *money management* as the word that best describes the most critical aspect of your trading system—the topic of "how much." To all of you who have adopted the term, whether you credited this book or not, I extend my thanks because by doing so you have taken much of the confusion out of this most important aspect of trading.

I'd also like to acknowledge all of the great traders I've had the privilege to work with over these many years. Many of you have made millions of dollars in profits in your trading career following the concepts contained in this book. Whether you helped me understand the concepts better or helped me prove to others that these concepts work, I extend to you my deepest gratitude.

Last, I'd like to thank the three people I love most—my wife Kalavathi, my son Robert, and my niece Nanthini. You are all my inspiration. Thank you for being there.

PART ONE

The Most Important Factor in Your Success: You!

The objectives of this book are twofold:

1. To help you in your search for the secrets of the Holy Grail and at the same time,
2. To help you in your search for a winning trading system that's right for you.

There is a critical assumption in both of these objectives: that you are the most important factor in your performance. Jack Schwager, after writing two books for which he interviewed some of the world's top traders, concluded that the most important factor in their success was that they each had a trading system that was right for them. I'd like to take that assumption one step further. You cannot design a system that is right for you unless you know something about yourself.

As a result, the first part of this book is about self-discovery and moving yourself to a point from which it's possible for you to do market research. I've included a chapter on the psychological essence of successful trading (what the Holy Grail is really all about), a chapter on judgmental heuristics, and a chapter on setting your personal objectives.

CHAPTER 1

The Legend of the Holy Grail

> We have only to follow the hero's path, and where we had thought to find an abomination, we shall find a god. And where we had thought to slay another, we shall slay ourselves. Where we had thought to travel outward, we will come to the center of our own existence. And where we had thought to be done, we will be with all the world.
>
> *Joseph Campbell,*
> The Power of Myth (page 51)

Let me tell you a secret about the market. You can make big money by buying breakouts that go beyond a normal day's range of price movement. These are called *volatility breakouts*. One trader is famous for making millions with volatility breakouts. You can do it too! You can make a bundle! Here's how you do it.

First, you take yesterday's price range. If there's a gap between yesterday and the day before, then add the gap into the range. That's called the *true range*. Now, take 40 percent of yesterday's true range, and bracket today's opening price by that amount. The upper value is your buy signal, and the lower value is your sell signal (that is, for selling short). If either value is hit, get into the market, and you'll have an 80 percent chance of making money. And over the long run, you'll make big money.

Did that particular pitch sound interesting to you? Well, it has attracted thousands of speculators and investors alike. And while there's some truth to the pitch—it can be a basis for making big money in the market—it's certainly not a magic secret to success. Many people could go broke following that advice because it's only part of a sound methodology. For example, it does not tell you

- How to protect your capital if the market goes against you
- How or when to take your profits
- How much to buy or sell when you get a signal
- What markets the method is designed for and if it works in all markets
- When the method works and when it fails miserably

Most importantly, you must ask yourself, when you put all of those pieces together, does the method fit you? Is it something you'd be able to trade? Does it fit your investment objectives? Does it fit your personality? Can you tolerate the drawdowns or the losing streaks it might generate? Does the system meet your criteria for feeling comfortable trading it, and what are those criteria?

This book is intended to help traders and investors make more money by learning more about themselves and then designing a methodology to fit their own personality and objectives. It is intended for both traders and investors because both of them attempt to make money in the markets. The trader tends to have a more neutral approach—being willing to both buy and sell short. The investor, in contrast, is looking for an investment that can be purchased and held over a longer period of time. Both of them are looking for a magic system to guide their decision making—the so-called Holy Grail system.

The journey into finding the profits available in the markets usually starts another way. In fact, the typical investor or trader, in preparing to trade, goes through an evolutionary process. At first he gets hooked on the idea of making a lot of money. Perhaps some broker gives him a pitch about how much money he can make playing the market. I've heard a radio advertisement in North Carolina that goes something like this:

> Do you know where real money is made year after year? It's all in the agricultural sector—people have to eat. And when you consider the weather we've been having lately, there's likely to be a shortage. And that means higher prices. And for just a small investment

> of $5,000, you can control a lot of grain. You'll make a small fortune if grain moves just a few pennies in your favor. Of course, there are risks in this sort of recommendation. People can and do lose money. But if I'm right about what I'm saying, just think how much money you can make![1]

(I've heard similar pitches for various other commodities and, these days, even for currency trading.)

Once the trader has committed his initial $5,000, he's hooked. Even if he loses it all—and in most cases he will—he'll still retain the belief that he can make big money playing the markets. "Didn't Hillary Clinton turn $1,000 into $100,000? If she can do it, then I certainly can do it."[2] As a result, our investor will spend a great deal of time trying to find someone to tell him what to buy and sell in his quest to determine the hot prospect.

I don't know many people who have made money consistently following other people's advice. There are exceptions, but they are very rare. In time, the people who have followed other people's advice and have consequently lost their capital get discouraged and drop out of the picture.

Another pitch that really seems to get people is the newsletter pitch. That typically goes something like this: "If you had followed our guru's advice, you would have made 320 percent on XYZ, 220 percent on GEF, and 93 percent on DEC. And it's not too late. You can get our guru's picks for each of the next 12 months for only $1,000." As you'll learn from both the expectancy chapter and the position sizing chapter, one could easily have gone broke following such a guru's advice because we know nothing about his or her downside or even the expectancy of his or her system.

I once heard this pitch from an options trading guru: "If you had followed my advice on every trade last year, you would have turned $10,000 into $40,000." Now does that sound impressive? It does to most people, but what he really meant was if you had risked $10,000 on every trade recommendation made, then at the end of the year, you would have been up by $40,000. In other words, if your risk per trade was 1*R* (where *R* is short for risk), then you would have been up by 4*R* at the end of the year. Believe me when I say that 99 percent of the trading systems you'll probably develop will give you better performance than this one. Nevertheless, people fork out the $1,000 for the guru's advice because the pitch suggests a 400 percent return rather than a 4*R* return. That is, they do until they decide that perhaps they should ask a better question.

A few people miraculously move onto the next phase, which is "Tell me how to do it." Suddenly, they go on a wild search for the magic methodology that will make them a lot of money. This is what some people call the "search for the Holy Grail." During the search, our trader is looking for anything that will provide her with the secrets to unlocking the universe of untold riches. Typically, people in this phase go to lots of seminars in which they learn about various methods such as this one:

> Now this is my chair pattern. It consists of at least six bars in a congestion range followed by a seventh bar that seems to break out of the congestion. Notice how it looks like a chair facing to the left? See what happens on this chart after a chair pattern occurred—the market just zoomed up. And here's another example. It's that easy. And here's a chart showing how much profit I made with the chair pattern over the last 10 years. Look at that: $92,000 profit each year from just a $10,000 investment.

Somehow, when these investors actually try to use the chair system, that $10,000 investment turns into large losses. (You'll learn the reasons for these losses later in this book.) Such setbacks notwithstanding, these investors simply go looking for yet another system. And they continue in this losing cycle until they are finally broke or they learn the real meaning behind the *Holy Grail metaphor*.

THE HOLY GRAIL METAPHOR

In trading circles, one frequently hears: "She's searching for the Holy Grail." Typically this means that she's searching for the magic secrets of the market that will make her rich—the secret rules that underlie all markets. But are there such secrets? Yes, there are! And when you really understand the Holy Grail metaphor, you will understand the secrets of making money in the market.

Several books such as Malcolm Goodwin's *Holy Grail* deal with the topic of the Holy Grail metaphor.[3] Beyond the Grail romances themselves, the metaphor has been used extensively throughout history, and most Westerners instantly recognize something described as a "Grail quest" as very significant. Scholars have used the term to mean all types of things, from blood feuds to searches for everlasting youth. Some scholars consider a "Grail quest" to be a search for perfectionism, enlightenment, unity, or even direct communion with God. The investor's "search for the Holy Grail" has been framed within the context of those other quests.

Most investors believe that there is some magic order to the markets. They believe that a few people know about it and that those few are making vast fortunes from the market. These believers are constantly trying to discover the secrets so that they too can become wealthy. Such secrets exist. But few people know where to find them because they are where one would least expect the secrets to be.

As you complete more and more of this book, you'll really understand the secrets of making money in the markets. And as those secrets are revealed to you, you'll begin to understand the real meaning of a "Grail quest."

According to one interesting Grail account, there is an ongoing war in heaven between God and Satan. The Grail has been placed in the middle of the conflict by neutral angels. Thus, it exists in the midst of a spiritual path between pairs of opposites (such as profits and losses). Over time this territory of concern has become a wasteland. Joseph Campbell says that the wasteland symbolizes the inauthentic life that most of us lead.[4] Most of us typically do what other people do, following the crowd and doing as we're told. Thus, the wasteland represents our lack of courage to lead our own life. Finding the Holy Grail represents finding the means to escape the wasteland—which means leading our own life and thereby attaining the ultimate potential of the human psyche.

Investors who follow the crowd might make money during long trends, but overall they'll probably lose, while the investors who are thinking and acting independently will usually make money. What's holding back the crowd followers? They ask others for advice (including their neighbors) rather than thinking independently and designing a method that fits them. Most investors have a strong desire to be right about every trade, and so they find some hot entry technique that gives them a feeling of control over the market. For example, you can require that the market totally do your bidding before you enter it. Yet real money is made through intelligent exits because they allow the trader to cut losses short and let profits run. Making intelligent exits requires that the trader be totally in tune with what the market is doing. In summary, people make money in the markets by finding themselves, achieving their potential, and getting in tune with the market.

There are probably hundreds of thousands of trading systems that work. But most people, when given such a system, will not follow it. Why not? Because the system doesn't fit them. One of the secrets of successful trading is finding a trading system that fits you. In fact, Jack Schwager, after interviewing enough "market wizards" to write two books, concluded that the most important characteristic of all good traders was that they had found a system or methodology that was right for them.[5] So part of the secret of the Holy Grail quest is in following your own unique way—and thus finding something that really fits you. But there is still a lot more to the Holy Grail metaphor.

> People make money in the markets by finding themselves, achieving their potential, and getting in tune with the market.

Life starts out in the neutral position between profits and losses—it neither fears losses nor desires profits. Life just is, and that's represented by the Grail. However, as a human being develops self-awareness, fear and greed also arise. But when you get rid of the greed (and the fear that comes from lacking), you reach a special unity with everything. And that's where great traders and investors emerge.

Joseph Campbell, the late, great scholar and leading expert on myths, says:

> Suppose the grass were to say, "Well, for Pete's sake, what's the use if you keep getting cut down this way?" Instead, it keeps on growing. That's the sense of the energy at the center. That's the meaning of the image of the Grail, of the inexhaustible fountain of the source. The source doesn't care what happens once it gives into being.[6]

One of the Grail legends starts out with a short poem that states: "Every act has both good and evil results." Thus every act in life has both positive and negative consequences—profits and losses, so to speak. The best we can do is to accept both while leaning toward the light.

Think about what that means for you as an investor or trader. You're playing a game of life. Sometimes you win and sometimes you lose, so there are both positive and negative consequences. To accept both the positive and the negative, you need to find that special place inside of you in which you can just be. From that vantage point, wins and losses are equally a part of trading. That metaphor, to me, is the real secret of the Holy Grail.

If you haven't found that place in yourself, then it's very hard to accept losses. And if you cannot accept the negative consequences, you'll never succeed as a trader. Good traders usually make money on less than half their trades. If you can't accept losses, then you are not likely to want to get out of a position when you know you are wrong. Small losses are more likely to turn into giant ones. More importantly, if you cannot accept that losses will occur, then you cannot accept a good trading system that will make a lot of money in the long run but might lose money 60 percent of the time.

To accept both the positive and the negative, you need to find that special place inside of you in which you can just be. From that vantage point, wins and losses are equally a part of trading.

WHAT'S REALLY IMPORTANT TO TRADING

Almost every successful investor that I have encountered has realized the lesson of the Holy Grail metaphor—that success in the markets comes from internal control. This is a radical change for most investors. Internal control is not that difficult to achieve, but it is difficult for most people to realize how important it is. For example, most investors believe that markets are living entities that create victims. If you believe that statement, then it is true for you. But markets do not create victims; investors turn themselves into victims. Each trader controls his or her own destiny. No trader will find success without understanding this important principle at least subconsciously.

Let's look at some facts:

- Most successful market professionals achieve success by controlling risk. Controlling risk goes against our natural tendencies. Risk control requires tremendous internal control.
- Most successful speculators have success rates of 35 to 50 percent. They are not successful because they predict prices well. They are successful because the size of their profitable trades far exceeds the size of their losses. This requires tremendous internal control.
- Most successful conservative investors are contrarians. They do what everyone else is afraid to do. They buy when everyone else is afraid, and they sell when everyone else is greedy. They have patience and are willing to wait for the right opportunity. This also requires internal control.

Investment success requires internal control more than any other factor. This is the first step toward trading success. People who dedicate themselves toward developing that control are the ones who will ultimately succeed.

Let's explore internal control, the key to trading success, from another perspective. When I've had discussions about what's important to trading, three areas typically come up: psychology, money management (that is, position sizing), and system development. Most people emphasize system development and deemphasize the other two topics. More sophisticated people suggest that all three aspects are important but that psychology is the most important (about 60 percent), position sizing is the next most important (about 30 percent), and system development is the least important (about 10 percent). This is illustrated in Figure 1.1. These people would argue that internal control would fall only into the psychological sector.

A good trader once told me that his personal psychology did not enter into his trading at all because everything he did was automated. I responded, "That's interesting, but what if you decide not to take one of your signals?" He responded, "That would never happen!" About six years later this trader went out of business as a professional trader because his partner did not take a trade. That trade would have made them very profitable for the year because it

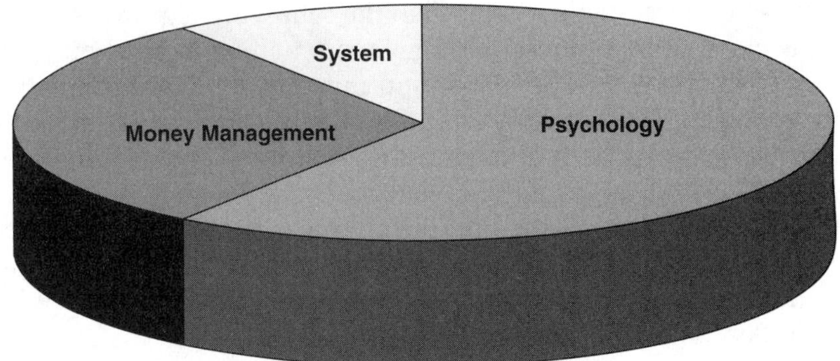

Figure 1.1 Ingredients of trading

was a huge winner, but they'd had so many losses in that particular area that his partner decided not to take it.

A great trader once told me that he taught a college course in trading (in the late 1970s) that lasted 10 weeks. He spent the first week of class teaching basic information about trading. He then spent another week teaching the class Donchian's 10–20 moving average crossover system. However, he needed the remaining eight weeks of the class to convince people to use the system that he had taught—to get them to work on themselves enough to accept the losses that it (or any other good trading system) would generate.

I've argued for a long time that trading is 100 percent psychology and that psychology includes position sizing and system development. The reason is simple: We are human beings, not robots. To perform any behavior, we must process information through the brain. Behavior is required to both design and to execute a trading system. And to duplicate any behavior, one must learn the ingredients of that behavior. That is where the science of modeling comes into play.

MODELING MARKET GENIUSES

Perhaps you have had the experience of attending a workshop conducted by an investment expert who explains his success secrets. For example, I just told you about a class that one of the world's greatest traders taught on trading in the early 1970s. He spent the first two weeks teaching the class a method that would have made them very rich (at the time) and then the following eight weeks getting the class to the point where they were willing to apply it.

Like the people in the class, you may have been impressed in some workshop you attended by the expert's presence and skills. You may have left the workshop full of confidence that you could make money using his methods. Unfortunately, when you tried to put his secrets into practice, you may have discovered that you weren't much wiser than you were before the workshop. Something didn't work, or somehow you just couldn't apply what you had learned.

Why does this occur? The reason is that you do not structure your thinking in the same manner as the expert. His mental structure, the way he thinks, is one of the keys to his success.

When others teach you how they approach the markets, chances are they only superficially teach you what they actually do. It's not that they mean to deceive you. It's just that they really do not understand the essential elements of what they do. And even if they did, they would probably have trouble transferring that information to someone else. This leads people to assume that perhaps you must have a certain "gift" or type of talent to be successful in the markets. Many people, as a result, become discouraged and leave the markets because they believe that they do not have the talent. But talent can be taught!

I believe that if at least two people can do something well, then the skill can be taught to most other people. The key to teaching the skill is to model it first. Over the last 20 years, the science of modeling has emerged almost as an underground movement. That movement comes out of a technology developed by Richard Bandler and John Grinder called *neuro-linguistic programming* (NLP, for short).

> If at least two people can do something well, then the skill can be taught to most other people.

NLP seminars usually just cover the trail of techniques left behind by the modeling process. For example, when I give a seminar, I usually just teach the models I've developed from modeling top traders and investors. However, if you take enough NLP classes, you eventually begin to understand the modeling process itself.

I've modeled three primary aspects of trading plus the process of developing wealth. The first model I developed is on how to be a great trader-investor and master the markets. Essentially, the steps to developing such a model involve working with a number of great traders and investors to determine what they do in common. If you attempt to model one person, you will find a lot of idiosyncrasies that are unique to that person. But if you model the common elements of a number of good traders and investors, then you find what's really important to the success of all of them.

For example, when I first asked my model traders what they did, they told me about their methodology. After interviewing about 50 traders, I discovered that none of them had the same methodology. As a result, I concluded that their methods were not a secret to their success except that their methods all involved "low-risk" ideas. Thus, one of the ingredients that all these traders had was the ability to find low-risk ideas. I'll define a low-risk idea later in the next chapter.

Once you discover the common elements to what they do, then you must discover the real ingredients of each common task. What are the beliefs that enable them to master the markets? How do they think so that they can effectively carry out those tasks? What are the mental strategies necessary to do the task (that is, the sequence of their thinking)? What are the mental states necessary to perform the task (for example, commitment, openness)? These ingredients are all psychological, which is another reason that I believe trading (or anything else for that matter) is 100 percent psychology.

The last step in determining if you've successfully developed an accurate model is to teach the model to others and determine if they get the same results. The trading model I've developed is part of my Peak Performance Home Study Course.[7] We also teach the model in our Peak Performance Workshop. And we've been able to create some amazingly successful traders, thus verifying the model.

The second model I developed is on how great traders and investors learn their craft and how they do their research. That's the topic of this book. Most people consider this to be the nonpsychological part of trading. The surprise is that the task of finding and developing a system that is right for them is purely a mental one. You must discover your beliefs about the market so that your system will fit those beliefs. You must know yourself well enough to develop your personal objectives and a system that fits those objectives. And you must work on your system until you are comfortable trading it. You must know your criteria for comfort. Most people have many biases against doing it well. To overcome those biases, most people need to take some steps in their personal development. I generally find that the more therapeutic work an individual has done, the easier it is for that individual to develop a system he can successfully trade.

One of your primary tasks in beginning the search for the right trading system is to find out enough about yourself that you can design a system that will work for you. But how do you do that? And once you find out enough about yourself, how do you find out what will work for you?

The third model I developed is on how great traders determine their position size throughout a trade. The topic of money management is talked about by every great trader. There have even been a few books on money management, but most of them talk about one or more of the results of money management (that is, controlling risk or getting optimal profits) rather than the topic itself. Money management is essentially that part of your system that determines your position size—that answers the question "how much?" throughout the trade. I've chosen to call this topic "position sizing" throughout the remainder of this book to eliminate possible confusion that might arise. And since the first edition of this book, many of you have also adopted that term.

As is true in other areas of trading, most people are doomed to do all of the wrong things in terms of position sizing because of psychological biases that they have. For example, as I was writing the first edition of this book in 1997, I was on a speaking tour of eight Asian cities. In each city, it was clear that most of the audience did not understand the importance of position sizing. Most of them were institutional traders, and many of them didn't even know how much money they were trading or even how much money they could lose before they lost their jobs. Consequently, they had no way to adequately determine how big or small their positions should be.

To help my audiences understand this idea, I've had them play a game to illustrate the importance of position sizing. But when I finished talking, no one asked me, "Dr. Tharp, what should I do in terms of position sizing in my situation?" Yet almost all of them could make great strides in their trading by asking that question and getting an appropriate answer.

You'll learn the key elements of position sizing in this book because it is an essential part of system development. However, the presentation of the entire model is in another one of my books, *The Definitive Guide to Expectancy and Position Sizing*.[8]

The fourth model I developed is on wealth. As I already mentioned in the beginning of this chapter, most people lose the money game because they follow someone else's rules for how to win the game. They believe that the person with the most money or the most toys wins the game. Perhaps you win when you become a millionaire or a billionaire. But if that's the case, most people lose.

Or perhaps you win if you have the most toys or the best toys. And if you play the game right, you can buy each toy now if the down payment and the monthly payments are low enough. Well, if you follow that rule, you'll be led down the path of financial slavery as you acquire more and more consumer debt. Today, the average American is spending more than he or she makes for the first time since the Great Depression. And it is all done through borrowing. Thus, we're clearly losing the money game.

My solution to this is to adopt new rules. Financial freedom occurs when your passive income (income that comes in when your money works for you) is greater than your monthly expenses. Thus, if you need $5,000 per month to live on, you become financially free when your passive income is greater than $5,000 per month. It's that easy, and anyone with enough desire and commitment can do it. I've described the procedures in detail in my third book, *Safe Strategies for Financial Freedom*.[9]

In this book, I want to focus more on trading as a method of developing passive income. If you can generate enough income through trading or investing to meet your monthly expenses, and if the process requires only a few hours of your time each day, then I'm willing to call that income "passive income." And through this process you can be financially free.[10] Although you may have to spend several years learning the business of trading and developing a business plan and systems that fit your plan, once that is complete, you could be financially free by my definition. I've seen many people do it, and if you have the commitment and the desire to work on yourself as the key ingredient in your success, then you can do it too.

I have divided this book into three primary parts: Part One is about self-discovery and moving yourself to a point where it's possible for you to do market research. Chapter 2 is on judgmental heuristics, and Chapter 3 is on setting your personal objectives. I've deliberately made Part One a short section so that you won't get too impatient with me for not giving you what you probably think is the "meat" of the topic of system development. The reason I've put this self-discovery material first is because it is critical to your success in developing your system.

Part Two deals with my model for system development. It covers concepts behind market systems, and I've invited various experts to write the sections behind those concepts. Part Two also deals with expectancy—one of those key ideas that everyone should understand. Few people who are actively involved in the markets even know what *expectancy* means. Even fewer people understand the implications of designing a system around expectancy. Thus, you may find it important to study this section carefully. I've also included a new chapter on understanding the big picture because that understanding is critical to developing your system.

Part Three covers the various parts of a system. These include setups, entry or timing techniques, stop-loss exits, profit-taking exits, and, one of the critical parts, position sizing.

Part Four is about how to put it all together. It includes a chapter on how seven different investors approach the markets. It also includes a chapter on how to evaluate your system, using some newsletters as examples, and a chapter on position sizing. The chapter that concludes this book includes everything else you need to think about to be a great trader.

NOTES

1. These words are my best recollection of the text of the commercial, but the actual words were probably somewhat different.
2. My comments about the former first lady's trading simply reflect my opinion. You can decide for yourself if she really was so "lucky" when you read the chapter on position sizing.

3. Malcolm Goodwin, *The Holy Grail: Its Origins, Secrets and Meaning Revealed* (New York: Viking Studio Books, 1994). This book discusses nine Holy Grail myths that appeared in the 30-year span between AD 1190 and 1220.
4. Joseph Campbell (with Bill Moyers), *The Power of Myth* (New York: Doubleday, 1988).
5. Jack Schwager, *Market Wizards* (New York: New York Institute of Finance, 1988).
6. Campbell, *The Power of Myth.*
7. Van K. Tharp, *The Peak Performance Course for Traders and Investors* (Cary, N.C.: International Institute of Trading Mastery, 1988–2006). Call 919-466-0043 for more information, or go to www.iitm.com. This is my model of the trading process, presented in such a way as to help you install the model in yourself.
8. Van K. Tharp, *The Definitive Guide to Expectancy and Position Sizing* (Cary, N.C.: International Institute of Trading Mastery). Call 919-466-0043 for details, or go to www.iitm.com.
9. Van K. Tharp, *Safe Strategies for Financial Freedom* (New York: McGraw-Hill, 2004).
10. This must be a consistent return for you to count it as passive income. For example, if you are up 30 percent one month, 20 percent the next, down 25 percent the next, down 15 percent the next, and up 60 percent the next, I'd be reluctant to count any of it as passive income because it is not consistent and you cannot rely upon it.

CHAPTER 2

Judgmental Biases: Why Mastering the Markets Is So Difficult for Most People

> We typically trade our beliefs about the market, and once we've made up our minds about those beliefs, we're not likely to change them. And when we play the markets, we assume that we are considering all of the available information. Instead, our beliefs, through selective perception, may have eliminated the most useful information.
>
> *Van K. Tharp, Ph.D.*

You now understand that the search for the Holy Grail system is an internal search. This chapter will help you in that search by helping you take the first step, that of becoming aware of what might be holding you back. And the miracle is that when you have such awareness and accept that you are in charge of your life, then you also have the ability to change.

Overall, a basic source of problems for all of us is the vast amount of information we must process regularly. French economist George Anderla has measured changes in the rate of information flow with which we human beings must cope. He has concluded that information flow doubled in the 1,500 years between the time of Jesus and Leonardo da Vinci. It doubled again by the year 1750 (that is, in about 250 years). The next doubling took only about 150 years to the turn of the century. The onset of the computer age reduced the doubling time to about 5 years. And, with today's computers offering electronic bulletin boards, DVDs, fiber optics, the Internet, and so on, the amount of information to which we are exposed currently doubles in about a year or less.

Researchers estimate that humans, with what we currently use of our brain potential, can take in only 1 to 2 percent of the visual information available at any one time. And for traders and investors the situation is at an extreme. A trader or investor, looking at every market in the world simultaneously, could easily have about a million bits of information coming at him or her every second. Many traders have two to four computer screens operating simultaneously. And since there are usually some markets open around the world at all times, the information flow does not stop. Some misguided traders actually stay glued to their trading screens, trying to process as much information as possible for as long as their brain will permit.

The conscious mind has a very limited capacity to process information. Even under ideal conditions, that limited capacity is between 5 and 9 chunks of information at a time. A "chunk" of information could be one bit, or it could be thousands of bits (for example, a chunk could be the number 2 or the number 687,941). For example, read the following list of numbers, close the book, and then try to write them all down:

6, 38, 57, 19, 121, 212, 83, 41, 917, 64, 817, 24

Could you remember all the numbers? Probably not because human beings can consciously process only 7 plus or minus 2 chunks of information. Yet we have millions of bits of information coming at us every second. And the current rate of information availability is now doubling every year. How do we cope?

The answer is that we generalize, delete, and distort the information to which we are exposed. We generalize and delete most of the information—"Oh, I'm not interested in the stock market." That one sentence takes about 90 percent of the information available on the markets, generalizes it as "stock market information," and then deletes it from consideration.

We also generalize the information we do pay attention to by being selective: "I'm going to look at only the daily bar charts on markets that meet the following criteria." We then have our computers sort the data according to those criteria so that an incredible amount of information is suddenly reduced to several lines on a computer screen. Those few lines are something we can process in our conscious minds.

Most traders and investors then distort the generalized information that remains by representing it as an indicator. For example, we don't just look at the last bar. Instead, we think the information is much more meaningful in the form of a 10-day exponential moving average or a 14-day RSI or a stochastic, or a band or trendline, and so on. All of these indicators are examples of distortions. And what people trade are "their beliefs about the distortion"—which may or may not be useful beliefs.

Psychologists have taken a lot of these deletions and distortions and grouped them together under the label "judgmental heuristics." They are called "judgmental" because they affect our decision-making process. They are called "heuristics" because they are shortcuts. They allow us to sift through and sort out a lot of information in a short period of time. We could never make market decisions without them, but they are also very dangerous to people who are not aware that they exist and who are also unaware that they use them. They affect the way we develop trading systems and make decisions about the market.

The primary way most people use judgmental heuristics is to preserve the status quo. We typically trade our beliefs about the market, and once we've made up our minds about those beliefs, we're not likely to change them. And when we play the markets, we assume that we are considering all of the available information. Instead, we may have already eliminated the most useful information available by our selective perception.

Interestingly, Karl Popper points out that progress in knowledge results more from efforts to find fault with our theories than from efforts to prove them.[1] If his theory is true, then the more we tend to realize our beliefs and assumptions (especially about the market) and disprove them, the more success we are likely to have making money in the market.

The purpose of this chapter is to explore how such judgmental heuristics or biases affect the process of trading or investing. First, we'll cover biases that distort the process of system development. Most of the biases covered fall into this category. However, some of them affect other aspects of trading as well. For example, the gambler's fallacy affects trading system development because people want systems that don't have losing long streaks, but it also affects how the system is traded once it is developed.

Next, we'll cover biases that affect how you test trading systems. For example, one gentleman, when exposed to some of the information contained in this book, claimed that it is full of controversy and that key elements were left out. Those statements, however, were just projections coming from him. There is no conflict within the material presented in this book—it's just information. Thus, if you perceive such controversy, it is because that controversy is coming from you. In addition, some steps that most people do in system development are left out, but they are left out intentionally because my research shows that they are not important or they are more of a hindrance (than a help) to the development of a good system.

Last, we cover a few biases that might affect how you trade the system you've developed. Although this is a book about doing trading system research, the biases included here are important because you need to consider them when you are doing your research before you actually start trading. I've deliberately kept this part of the chapter to a minimum, however, because those biases are covered in much more detail in my home study course for traders and investors.

BIASES THAT AFFECT TRADING SYSTEM DEVELOPMENT

Before you think about trading systems, you have to represent market information in such a way that your brain can cope with the available information. Look at the chart in Figure 2.1. It illustrates a typical bar chart, which is how most people think about market activity. A daily bar chart, as shown in the illustration, takes a day's worth of data and summarizes it. That summary includes, at most, four pieces of information—the open, the close, the high, and the low.

Japanese candlestick charts make the information a little more obvious and also give you visual information about whether the market generally moved up or down. As shown in Figure 2.2, the

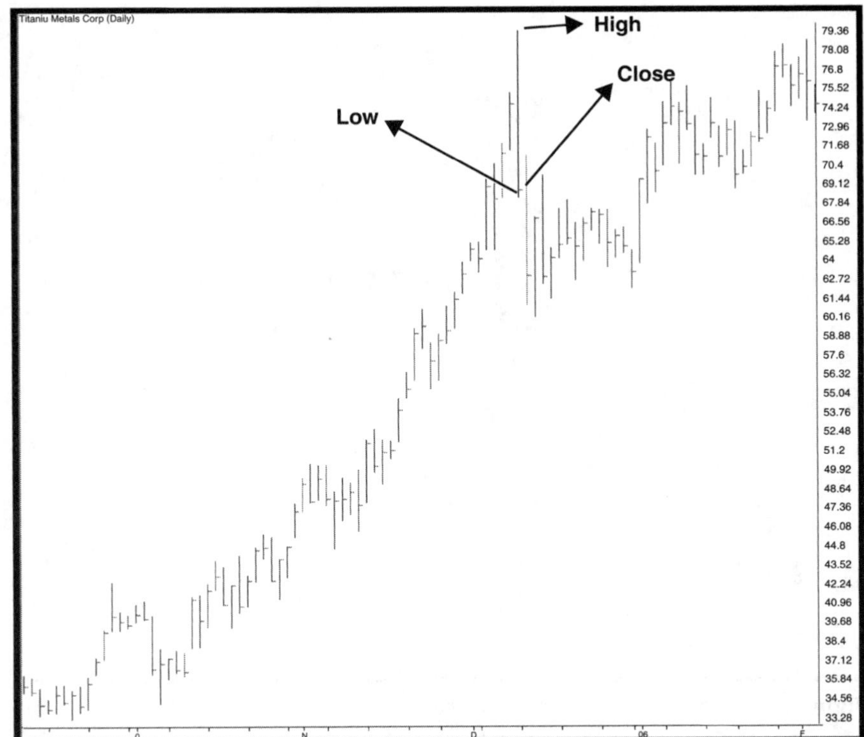

Figure 2.1 A simple bar chart

fat part of the bar (the body) represents the difference between the open and the close, whereas the extreme tails (the wicks) represent the high and the low. Candlesticks are generally solid if the market goes down and clear if it goes up, making it easier to see what happened.

Representativeness Bias

The two daily bar charts in Figures 2.1 and 2.2 are good examples of the first heuristic, which everyone uses, called the *law of representation*. What it means is that people assume when something is assigned to represent something, it really is what it is supposed to represent. Thus, most of us just look at the daily bar and accept that it represents a day's worth of trading. In reality, it's just a line on a

Figure 2.2 Japanese candlestick chart

piece of paper—no more and no less. Yet, you probably have accepted that it is meaningful because

- You were told it was meaningful when you first started studying the markets.
- Everybody else uses daily bars to represent the markets.
- When you purchase data or get free data, they are typically in daily bar format.
- When you think about a day's worth of trading, you typically visualize a daily bar.

The bar chart in Figure 2.1 and the candlestick chart in Figure 2.2 only show you three things. First, they show the range of prices that occurred throughout the day. Second, they show a little bit about how prices moved—they moved from the open to the close (plus some variation for the high and the low). And third, the Japanese candlesticks make the overall movement that day clear through the shading.

What doesn't a typical daily bar show you? A daily bar doesn't show you how much activity occurred. It doesn't show you how much activity occurred at what price. It doesn't show you when during the day the underlying commodity or equity was at a given price (except at the beginning or the end). Yet this information might be useful to traders or investors. You can get some of this information by lowering your time frame and looking at five-minute bars or tick charts. But wait: Wasn't the purpose of the daily bar chart to reduce the information flow so you are not overwhelmed?

There is a lot of other information that might be useful to traders that is not shown in the daily bar chart. In the case of futures, did the transactions involve opening up new contracts or closing out old ones? What kinds of people were doing the trading? Did a handful of floor traders trade with each other all day long, trying to outguess and outmaneuver each other? How much of the activity was in the form of a single unit (100 shares of stock or a single commodity contract)? How much of the activity was in large units? How much was bought or sold by large investors? And how much was bought and sold by mutual fund portfolio managers or managers of large commodity funds? How much was bought or sold by hedgers or big companies?

And there is a third class of information that is not represented in the daily bar chart—who's in the market. For example, how many people are currently holding long or short positions? What is the size of their positions? That information is available, but it is generally not easily accessible. The various exchanges, with the kind of computers available today, could store and report information like this each day:

> The price moved from 83 to 85. There are 4,718 investors holding long positions, and the average position size is 200 units. During the day, long positions increased by a total of 50,600 units. There are 298 investors holding short positions with an average position size of 450 units. Short positions increased by 5 units. The top 100 positions are held by the following people and their position is . . . [followed by a listing].

Perhaps, you're saying, "Yes, I'd like to know who owns what and how large their positions are." Well, if you had that information, would you know what to do with it? Would it be any more meaningful? Probably not—unless you have some beliefs that would allow you to trade it.

The daily bar chart also does not give you any statistical probabilities—given that *X* happens, what is the likelihood of *Y*? You can use historical data to determine the likelihood of *Y*, but only if variable *X* (and *Y*, for that matter) is contained in your data. But what if *X* or *Y* is interesting but not contained in your data?

Finally, there is another, critical type of information that is not included in a simple daily bar—psychological information. That information involves the strength of conviction of the long positions and the short positions. When would various traders be likely to liquidate and at what price? How will they react to various news items or price movements? And how many people are sitting on the outside of the market with the belief that it is going up or the belief that it is going down? Are they likely to convert those beliefs into market positions and under what conditions? And if they did, at what price and how much money are they likely to have behind them to back their positions? But even if you had this information, do you have beliefs that would help you make money from it?

Until now, you've probably thought that a daily bar chart really was the market. Remember, all you're really looking at is a single line on your computer or chart book. You are assuming that it represents the market. You might call it a generalization about the market's activity in a given day, but that is the best you can call it. The scary thing is that a daily bar, which is at best summary information, is typically the raw data that you manipulate to make your decisions.

The scary thing is that a daily bar, which is at best summary information, is typically the raw data that you manipulate to make your decisions.

I hope that you're beginning to understand why judgmental heuristics are important to you as a trader—and all I've given you is just one example of one heuristic, the tendency we have to assume that a bar chart really represents a day's worth of market activity.

You could just trade bar charts. But most people want to do something with their data before they trade, so they use indicators. Unfortunately, people do the same thing with market indicators. They assume they are reality rather than just attempts to represent something that might occur. RSI, stochastics, moving averages, MACD, and so on—all seem to take on a reality, and people forget they are merely distortions of raw data that are assumed to represent something.

For example, think about the technical concept of support levels on a chart. Originally, technicians observed that once prices dropped to a certain area on the chart, they seemed to bounce back. That area was then assumed to be a level at which a lot of buyers were willing to buy and thus "support" the price of the stock. Unfortunately, many people treat words like *support level* and *resistance level* as if they were real phenomena rather than simply concepts that represent relationships that people have observed in the past.

I've previously talked about the representativeness bias in the sense that people tend to judge something by what it "looks like" as opposed to what its probability rate is. This is especially important in terms of using a trading system or trading signal. Have you considered probability rate information in developing your trading system or assessing the validity of your signals? That is, do you consider the percentage of time that your predicted outcome follows your signal? Probably not, because I don't know 1 trader in 1,000 who does that—even though I tell people about it constantly. What this means is that most people don't even test their systems or know the expectancy of their systems (see Chapter 7).

Now let's discuss a few more biases. We'll determine what these additional biases might do to your thinking about the markets and trading system development.

Reliability Bias

A bias related to the representation bias is the assumption that our data are reliable—that they really are what they are supposed to be. With respect to the daily bar chart, we just commonly assume that it represents a day's worth of data. It looks like a day's worth of data so that's what it must be. However, many data vendors combine day data and night data, so is it really a day's worth of data? And what about the accuracy of the data?

Seasoned traders and investors know that gauging data reliability is one of the worst problems that traders can have. Most data vendors are fairly accurate with respect to daily bar charts, but when you start using tick data, 5-minute bars, 30-minute bars, and so on, accuracy goes out the window. *Thus, if you are testing a system based on 5-minute bars, most of your results (good or bad) could have more to do with inaccurate data rather than real expected results.*

Look at the story in the sidebar about the problems one can have with data. It's a personal story from Chuck Branscomb that appeared in one of our newsletters.

Once you've read the story, you can understand how most people accept a lot more about the market than is true. All is not as one would expect. And when you think you have a good system, you could simply have poor data that makes it look good. Conversely, you might think that you have a bad system when you really have poor data that makes a good system look bad.

But let's assume that you are accepting the fact that daily bar charts really do represent the market. You wish to accept that generalization and trade it. That's fine, but let me show you how many more biases probably creep into your thinking.

A PERSONAL STORY FROM CHUCK BRANSCOMB

I trade a portfolio of 16 futures markets using a system of my design. I use portfolio trading system software to run my system code against daily data to generate orders each night. The basic entry and exit rules are programmed into a real-time software program so that I am alerted when I have taken a position in a market.

On July 10, 1995, I had correctly placed all of my entry and exit orders for the portfolio prior to the open. Shortly after the Chicago currency markets opened, the real-time software alerted me to a long entry in the Canadian dollar. I was shocked since I hadn't even generated an order for the Canadian dollar that day. I just stared at the screen for a few seconds in disbelief. Having mentally rehearsed being shocked by an unexpected market occurrence, I automatically fell into my rehearsal scenario: take a deep breath, relax all my muscles from forehead to toe while exhaling, and create a systematic process of checking for errors from highest to lowest probability.

It took just a couple of minutes to find that the low for the previous day was different between the data I had downloaded for my portfolio software to run against versus that collected by my real-time software. A quick check of the previous day's tick data confirmed my suspicion: the data the portfolio system used were invalid. I quickly edited the database manually and reran the program. It now generated an entry order. I glanced at the screen to see that the market had now rallied well above my entry point. I had feelings of frustration running through me, but I calmly inputted the information from the program into my portfolio manager spreadsheet to size the position. Looking at the screen, I saw the market up yet another 5 ticks now that I had the order ready. My reaction at that point was totally automatic and focused: I called my trade desk and placed an order to enter the position at the market.

This whole process consumed about 10 minutes' time during which the Canadian dollar rallied further and further away from my intended entry price. Fortunately, mental rehearsal saved me from second-guessing what to do. My trading objectives include not *ever* missing a trade entry since I have no idea when a monster move may be evolving. Missing out on a substantial winning trade is far worse than simply taking a small loss. When I knew I should be in that market already, the phone call was an automatic, focused response. For the type of trading that I do, it was the right thing to do. I have no use for *hoping* the market will come back to the entry point or second-guessing whether to follow through on the entry.

This occurrence marked the need for me to create a procedure that would force a disciplined checking of daily data for each futures contract. Up to that point, I thought that I was doing a sufficient job of screening daily data. I had caught many errors in the past, but I now knew that I needed to create yet more work for myself each day to ensure that I could trade my business plan as designed.

From *Market Mastery*, July 1996, Vol. 1(2), pp. 2–3.

Lotto Bias

The lotto bias relates to the increased confidence people have when they, in some way, manipulate data—as if manipulating that data is somehow meaningful and gives them control over the market. Now that you've accepted the daily bar chart as your way of representing the market, you must either trade daily bars or manipulate them in some way until you feel confident enough to trade them. But of course the data manipulation itself often can and will give you this increased confidence.

A perfect example of how this illusion of control works is the state-run lottery game called *lotto*. When you play lotto, you get to pick some numbers (usually six or seven of them), and if you happen to hit all of them, you become an instant millionaire. People really like to play the lotto game (even logical people who understand the odds). Why? Because the prize is so big and the risk is so small (a dollar ticket is small compared with the size of the prize) that people are drawn to play. It doesn't matter to them that the odds are so stacked against them that if they bought a million tickets (each with different numbers), they still would not be likely to win. Your chance of winning $1 million in a state-run lottery is about 1 in 13 million (and the odds are much worse if you expect to win more).

The big prize for such a small amount of money is also a heuristic, but it's not the lotto bias. The lotto bias is the illusion of control that people get when they play the game. *People think because they get to pick the numbers that their odds of success are somehow improved.* Thus, some people might suspect that if they picked the numbers in their birthday and their anniversary, it might improve their chances for winning. For example, some years ago a man won the jackpot in the Spanish national lottery. He won it because of his interpretation of his dream. It seems that he dreamt about the number 7 for 7 straight nights. Since he mistakenly thought that 7 times 7 was 48, he selected a ticket with the numbers 4 and 8 on it.

Others, rather than using their dreams, consult with psychics or astrologers. In fact, you can purchase all sorts of advice to help you win the lotto. Some people who have analyzed the numbers thinking they can predict subsequent numbers are quite willing to sell you their advice. Others have their own lotto machines and believe that if they generate a random sequence of numbers, it might just correspond to what the state-controlled lotto machine might select. They are also willing to sell you advice. And if some guru or astrologer claims to have several jackpot winners (a distinct possibility if the person has enough followers), then many more people will be attracted to that person. People will do anything to find the magic numbers.

If this seems a little familiar, it should be. This is exactly what occurs in speculative markets. People believe they can make a quick dollar by picking the right numbers. Picking the right numbers, in the case of speculators and investors, means that they simply want to know what to buy and when. The most important question the average person wants to know is, "What should I buy right now that will make me a fortune?" Most people would rather have someone tell them what to do.

People do everything they possibly can to figure out what to do right now. They buy software that picks numbers and analyzes tendencies. Brokers have found that if they help them pick numbers, by reading off entry points on radio and television shows, thousands of people will want their advice. If you are known to publicly give advice, no matter how accurate (or inaccurate) that advice is, people will consider you an expert. In addition, there are plenty of gurus who are good at promoting and are more than happy to tell people in their newsletters what to buy and when. And of course, astrologers and fortune tellers also play a role in this process.

Some people get the notion that perhaps they would be better off on their own. Consequently, they become fascinated by entry signals that they perceive to be synonymous with a complete trading system. You get a sense of control with entry signals because the point at which you choose to enter the market is the point at which the market is doing exactly what you want it to do. As a result, you feel as though you have some control—not just over your entry but over the market. Unfortunately, once you are in a position in the market, the market is going to do whatever it wants to do, and you no longer have any control over anything except your exits.

I'm amazed at what people consider a trading system! For example, one gentleman visited me from Australia some years ago. He'd been talking with various experts all over the United States about what kind of trading systems work. At dinner one night, he told me what he'd learned and showed me the "guts" of the various systems he'd discovered so that I could give him my blessing. He had some great ideas. Yet all of his trading systems, as he relayed them to me, had to do with entry techniques. In fact, the only thing he described about each trading system was the entry. My comment was that he was on the right track, but if he'd now spend at least as much time working on his exits and position sizing, then he'd really have a good system.

Most people believe that they have a trading system if they have some sort of entry point that makes them money. As you'll learn later in this book, there are as many as 10 components to a professional trading system, and the entry signal is probably the least important. Nevertheless, most people just want to know about entry.

I was a speaker at an international conference on technical analysis of futures and stocks in Malaysia in 1995. There were about 15 speakers from the United States, and we got rated on our performance. The speakers with the highest ratings talked mostly about entry signals. And the one speaker who talked about the various components of a trading system, and whose talk was therefore very valuable, received much lower ratings.

I attended one of the more highly rated talks. The speaker was a brilliant trader who was up about 76 percent in his account in 1994 with only a 10 percent drawdown. Yet what he talked about were mostly signals for picking changes in a trend. He presented six to eight such signals in his talk and mentioned something about exits and money management when people asked him. Later, I asked him if he traded all of those signals. His response was, "Of course not! I trade a trend-following signal. But this is what people want to hear, so I give it to them."

One of my clients, upon reading this, made the following observation: "I have always felt that this 'lotto bias' is a way of dealing with the anxiety of not feeling in control. Most people would rather pretend to be in control (and be wrong) than feel the anxiety of having no control over the environment in which they must exist. The big step is in realizing that 'I have control over my actions.' And that is enough!"

This bias is so powerful that people frequently do not get the information they need to prosper in the market. Instead, they get what they want to hear. After all, people typically make the most money giving people what they want rather than giving them what they need. This book is an exception to that rule. And, hopefully, there will be a number of such exceptions in the future.

Law of Small Numbers

The pattern shown in Figure 2.3 could represent another bias for some people. There are four days in which the market does nothing (within the first five days shown), followed by a big rise. If you

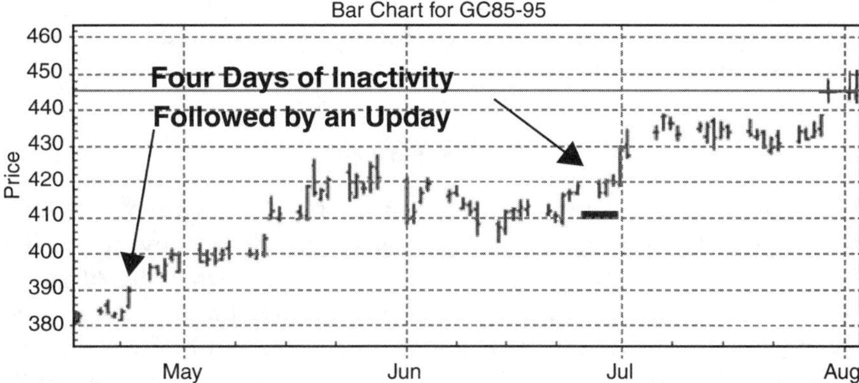

Figure 2.3 Sample pattern that tends to attract people to the market and to entry signals

peruse some chart books, you might find four or five examples like that. The law of small numbers says that it doesn't take many such cases for you to jump to a conclusion. For example, let's enter the market when we have four days in a narrow range followed by a big jump in prices.

In fact, my observation is that most people trade by following the patterns they observe in a few well-chosen examples. If you see a pattern like the one shown in Figure 2.3, followed by a large move, then you assume that the pattern is a good entry signal. Notice that all four biases discussed so far have entered into this decision.

The following quote from William Eckhardt really describes this bias well:

> We don't look at data neutrally—that is, when the human eye scans a chart, it doesn't give all data points equal weight. Instead, it will focus on certain outstanding cases, and we tend to form our opinions on the basis of these special cases. It's human nature to pick out the stunning successes of a method and to overlook the day-in, day-out losses that grind you to the bone. Thus, even a fairly careful perusal of the charts is prone to leave the researcher with the idea that the system is a lot better than it really is.[2]

Scientific research knows about this kind of bias. Even the most careful researcher will tend to bias his or her result toward his or her hypothesis. That's why scientists have *double-blind tests*—tests in which the experimenter does not know which group is the experimental group and which group is the control group until the experiment is over.

Conservatism Bias

Once we have a trading concept in mind, the conservatism bias takes over: we fail to recognize, or even see, contradictory evidence. The human mind is quick to see the few outstanding examples of moves that work while avoiding or ignoring examples that don't work. For example, if you looked at a lot of data, you might find that the pattern in Figure 2.3 was followed by a large move 20 percent of the time. The rest of the time nothing significant happened.

Most people totally ignore the contradictory evidence, despite the fact that it is overwhelming. However, after seven or eight losses in a row, they suddenly begin to be concerned about the validity of their trading system without ever determining how many losses could occur.

If the move that occurs 20 percent of the time is large enough, then it is still tradable—but only if you are careful to cut losses short during the 80 percent of the moves when nothing happens. But, of course, that points out the importance of the lotto bias. If you just concentrate on the pattern, you probably won't make money.

The implication of this bias is that people search out what they want, and expect, to see in the market. Most people, as a result, are not neutral with respect to the market, and they cannot go with the flow. Instead, they are constantly searching for what they expect to see.

Randomness Bias

The next bias influences trading system development in two ways: First, economists and many investors tend to assume that the market is random—that prices tend to move according to random chance. Second, people make erroneous assumptions about what such randomness, if it exists, might mean.

One reason people like to pick tops and bottoms is that they assume the market can, and will, turn around at any time. Basically, they assume that the market is random. Indeed, many academic researchers still hold the belief that the market is random.[3] But is that assumption correct? And even if the assumption is correct, could people trade such a market?

The market may have characteristics of randomness, but that does not mean it is random. For example, you can generate a series of bar charts using a random number generator. When you look at those bar charts, they look like bar charts. But this is an example of the representativeness bias, and "looking like random" is not "being random." These kinds of data are unlike market data because the distribution of prices in the market has extreme tails that you could never predict from normally distributed random prices. Why? When you look at market data, the sample variability just gets larger and larger as you add more data. The 80-point drop in the S&P that occurred on October 19, 1987, within a decade of the inauguration of the S&P futures contract, would be difficult to predict from a random number series. It might occur once in 10,000 years, but that event occurred in our lifetime. Moreover, it has happened again. On October 27, 1997, the S&P had a drop of 70 points, and on the next day, it had a daily range of 87 points. Similarly, the Nasdaq had several huge one-day drops during 2000 to 2002.

The fact that market price distributions tend to have an infinite variance, or nearly so, suggests that more extreme scenarios than you might imagine are right around the corner. As a result, any derived estimate of risk will be significantly underestimated. And unfortunately, most people take way too much risk in the market. When a market wizard like Tom Basso claims that risking as much as 3 percent of your equity on a single position is being a "gunslinger," it suggests that most people are really crazy in the amount of risk they take.

Even if the markets were random, people fail to understand randomness. When a long trend does occur in a random sequence, people assume that it is not random. They develop theories to suggest that it is something other than a long series in a random sequence. This tendency comes from our natural inclination to treat the world as if everything were predictable and understandable. As a result, people seek patterns where none exist and assume the existence of unjustified causal relationships.

One consequence of the randomness bias (and the lotto bias) is that people tend to want to pick tops and bottoms. We want to be "right" and have control over the market, and we project our ideas onto the market. The result tends to be a belief that we can pick tops and bottoms. This seldom occurs in the life of a trader or an investor. Those who attempt to do it are doomed to many experiences of failure.

Need-to-Understand Bias

The need-to-understand bias enters into how most people develop trading systems. They totally ignore the randomness element. In fact, they don't even consider position sizing as part of their system.

One of my clients, Joe, claimed that he had the most difficulty with the market when he got into a position and got confused. As a result, I asked him a number of questions. "How often are your positions winners?" His response was that he was right about 60 percent of the time. "When you get confused, how often do you come out a winner?" This time his response was that he almost never came out a winner when he got confused. I then said, "Since your system isn't much above chance, you probably don't understand that much about the markets anyway. But when you clearly are confused, you should just get out." He agreed it was probably a good idea.

When you think about Joe's trading system, however, he really didn't have one. Why? Joe was so concerned about understanding every aspect of the market that he didn't have clearly defined exit signals that told him (1) when he should get out to preserve his capital and (2) when he should take his profits.

Most people still need to make up elaborate theories about what is going on in the markets. The media are always trying to explain the market even though they know nothing about the market. For example, when the Dow Jones plunges over 100 points, the next day the newspapers are filled with numerous explanations. Here's what you might read in your local paper:

> A late Wednesday warning from the Federal Reserve that it might raise interest rates unnerved investors Thursday. Stocks plunged, especially building companies, on fears of an industry-wide earnings slowdown. In today's market climate, investors seem to be particularly nervous whenever they think interest rates might rise. Investors

> are also concerned about the impact of what is going on in the Middle East. Any sign of trouble and investors start to get very nervous.

The next day the Dow Jones Industrials might go up more than 100 points. You'll probably read something like the following:

> Wall Street, which was getting nervous over a potential interest rate hike, shook off the rumor and plunged into the market again as the Dow Jones Industrials rose over 100 points. R. P. Jinner, of H.P. Mor Securities commented, "Earnings have been so good recently that investors seem to easily shrug off potentially damaging news."[4]

The need-to-understand bias becomes even more elaborate when it comes to trading system design. People manipulate daily bars in any number of strange ways and then develop strange theories to explain the market based upon those manipulations. The resulting theories then take on a life of their own, but they have little basis in reality. For example, what is the rational basis for the Elliott Wave theory? Why should the market move in three legs one way and two legs the other?

Are you beginning to understand why the task of trading system development is so full of psychological biases? My experience is that most people will not be able to deal with the issues that come up in trading system design until they've solved some of their personal psychological issues dealing with fear or anger. Furthermore, some people don't even want to resolve such issues—in fact, some people probably skipped this section just to get to the real material on system development.

BIASES THAT AFFECT HOW YOU TEST TRADING SYSTEMS

Our next set of biases affect the testing of trading systems. Most people never encounter these biases because they never get to the point of testing systems. Actually, the conservatism bias, discussed earlier in this chapter, would stop most people from ever testing a system. And more importantly, most people never get to the point where they even have a testable system. However, for those who do get to this point, the result of these next biases can be insidious.

Degrees-of-Freedom Bias

A *degree of freedom* is a parameter that yields a different system for every value allowed. For example, a moving average based on 10 days will yield different results from a moving average based on 24 days. Thus, the length of a moving average represents 1 degree of freedom. People tend to want as many degrees of freedom as possible in their systems. The more indicators you add, the better you can describe historical market prices. The more degrees of freedom you have in a system, the more likely that system will fit itself to a series of prices. Unfortunately, the more a system fits the data upon which it was developed, the less likely it will be to produce profits in the future.

System development software (most of it, that is) really encourages the degrees-of-freedom bias. Give a system developer enough leeway and that person will have a system that perfectly predicts the moves in the market and makes thousands of dollars on paper—with certain historical markets, that is. Most software allows people to optimize to their hearts' content. Eventually, they will end up with a meaningless system that makes a fortune on the data from which it was obtained but performs miserably in real trading.

Most system development software is designed to cater to this bias. People want to know the perfect answer to the markets. They want to be able to predict the markets perfectly. As a result, you can buy software now for a few hundred dollars that will allow you to overlay numerous studies over past market data. Within a few minutes, you can begin to think that the markets are perfectly predictable. And that belief will stay with you until you attempt to trade the real market instead of the historically optimized market.

No matter how much I mention this bias, most of you will still give into it. You'll still want to optimize your systems as much as possible. As a result, let me give you several precautions in such optimization. First, understand the concept you are using so well that you will not even feel that you need to optimize. The more you understand the concept you are trading, the less need you have to do historical testing.

Second, I would strongly suggest that you imagine various scenarios that might happen in the market. For example, you might imagine the next war, a nuclear terrorist attack, the adoption of the euro as the world's reserve currency, the adoption of a common currency in Asia, China joining Japan to become a common power, or an unemployment report that jumps 120 percent. Some of these ideas might seem wild, but if you can understand how your system concept would handle these events if they actually happened, then you understand your concept very well.

No matter how much traders and investors learn about the dangers of overoptimization, they still want to optimize. Thus, I strongly recommend that you not use more than 4 or 5 degrees of freedom in your system. So if you use two indicators (1 degree of freedom each) and two filters in your complete system, that's probably all you can tolerate. Filters and indicators you might consider are discussed extensively later in this book.

Postdictive Error Bias

People use postdictive errors when they use information in their testing that would actually be available only after the fact. This kind of error is very common in system testing. It is easy to make. For example, in some software, unless you are careful, you can use today's data in your testing, which is always a postdictive error—imagine the value of being able to use today's close to predict what prices will do today. That's a postdictive error.

Sometimes these errors are quite subtle. For instance, since the highest prices in your data are nearly always followed by lower prices, it's quite possible to sneak high prices into a trading rule so that the rule works great—but only postdictively.

When you are testing data, if your results seem too good to be true, they probably are. You probably got those results through postdictive errors.

Bias of Not Giving Yourself Enough Protection

When you design a system, your goal should be to design a system that produces low-risk ideas. My definition of a low-risk idea is this:

> A methodology with a long-term positive expectancy and a reward (overall return) to risk (maximum peak-to-trough drawdown) ratio

> with which you can live. That methodology must be traded at a position sizing level (usually based on a percentage of equity) that will protect you from the worst possible conditions in the short run while still allowing you to achieve the long-term expectancy of the system.

The bias that most people have is that they do not trade at a position sizing level that is low enough to protect them from such worst-case scenarios in the short run. Most people cannot, and do not, anticipate all possible events that might affect their systems. Consequently, in any worthwhile trading or investing methodology, you must have all kinds of backups to protect you when you're in a trade that's going against you.

If you ask the average person, "How will you get out of a bad trade if it really goes against you?" he or she has no answer. Most people just don't have the backup protection they should have. More importantly, they trade at way too high a level. If you have $50,000 and are trading five or more different futures contracts simultaneously, then you are probably trading at too high a risk level. If you are a day trader and you get margin calls, then your risk level is way too high. That risk level may get you high rates of return, but it will eventually bankrupt your account. Think about the protection bias. Paying attention to this bias alone could preserve much of the equity that you currently have in your account.

BIASES THAT AFFECT HOW YOU TRADE YOUR SYSTEM

Let's assume that you have gone through a system, thoroughly tested it, and determined it to be something you can trade. Unfortunately, there are still more biases that tend to cause people to override their systems.

You want maximum performance, so there is always a temptation to override your trading system. The few times you have done something to override your system and improve your performance really stand out in your mind. You tend to forget the times that didn't work and the day-in, day-out slippage (that is, the cost of trading) that have affected your bottom line.

If you don't have a trading system, then numerous biases affect your trading. However, several key biases come into play even when you have the best of systems. Let's take a look at these biases that tend to cause people to override their systems.

Bias of the Gambler's Fallacy

The gambler's fallacy is a natural consequence of the randomness bias. The gambler's fallacy is the belief that when a trend is established in a random sequence (or in the market, for that matter), the trend could change at any time. Thus, after four consecutive up days in the market, we expect a down day. Even people who are well-respected researchers of the market suffer from this bias. For example, Larry Williams, in my opinion, shows this bias in the following quote: "After you have had three or four losing trades in a row, the probability of the next trade being not only a winner but a substantial winner is way in your favor."[5]

When you understand what's involved in winning, as do professional gamblers, you'll tend to bet more during a winning streak and less during a losing streak. However, the average person does exactly the opposite: he or she bets more after a series of losses and less after a series of wins.

Ralph Vince once did an experiment with 40 Ph.D.s.[6] They were asked to play 100 trials of a simple computer game in which they would win 60 percent of the time. They were each given $1,000 in play money and told to bet as much or as little as they wished on each of the plays. None of the Ph.D.s knew about position sizing (that is, the effect of bet size on the performance of such a game).

How many of them made money? Only 2 of the 40 participants had more than their original $1,000 at the end of the game—or 5 percent. But had they bet a constant $10 per bet, they would have ended up with about $1,200. And if they had bet optimally for achieving the maximum gain (which was to risk 20 percent of their new equity each time—an approach not advocated by this author), they would have ended up with about $7,490 (on average).

What happened? The participants tended to bet more after an adverse run and less after a favorable run. Let's say the first three bets are losers, and you bet $100 each time. Now you are down to $700. You think, "Since I've had three losses in a row and the odds are 60 percent in my favor, I'm sure it's time for a win." As a result, you bet $400. But you suffer another loss. Your stake is down to $300, and your chances of making it back are almost nonexistent.

The gambler's fallacy bias enters into how most people develop trading systems, how they size their positions, and how they trade. They totally ignore the randomness element. They look for certainty and trade their systems as if they had it, not giving themselves enough protection. Thus, they don't even consider position sizing as part of their system.

Conservative-with-Profits-and-Risky-with-Losses Bias

Perhaps the number 1 rule of trading is to cut your losses short and let your profits run. Those who can follow this simple rule tend to make large fortunes in the market. However, most people have a bias that keeps them from following either part of this rule.

> Consider the following example in which you must pick one of two choices. Which would you prefer: (1) a sure loss of $9,000 or (2) a 5 percent chance of no loss at all plus a 95 percent chance of a $10,000 loss?

Which did you pick, the sure loss or the risky gamble? Approximately 80 percent of the population picks the risky gamble in this case. However, the risky gamble works out to a bigger loss (that is, $\$10,000 \times 0.95 + 0 \times 0.05 = \$9,500$ loss—which is larger than the sure $9,000 loss). Taking the gamble violates the key trading rule—cut your losses short. Yet most people continue to take the gamble, thinking that the loss will stop and that the market will turn around from here. It usually doesn't. As a result, the loss gets a little bigger, and then it's even harder to take. And that starts the process all over again. Eventually, the loss gets big enough that the gambler becomes forced to take it. Many small investors go broke because they cannot take losses.

> Now, consider another example. Which would you prefer: (1) a sure gain of $9,000 or (2) a 95 percent chance of a $10,000 gain plus a 5 percent chance of no gain at all?

Did you pick the sure gain or the risky gamble? Approximately 80 percent of the population picks the sure gain. However, the risky gamble works out to a bigger gain (that is, $10,000 $\times$ 0.95 + 0 $\times$ 0.05 = $9,500 gain—which is larger than the sure gain of $9,000). Taking the sure gain violates the second part of the key rule of trading—let your profits run.

Once they have a profit in hand, most people are so afraid of letting it get away that they tend to take the sure profit at any sign of a turnaround. Even if their system gives no exit signal, it is so tempting to avoid letting a profit get away that many investors and traders continue to lament over the large profits they miss as they take sure small profits.

These two common biases are well stated in the old saying: "Seize opportunities, but hold your ground in adversity." The good trader had better use the adage: "Watch profit-taking opportunities carefully, but run like a deer at the first sign of adversity."

My-Current-Trade-or-Investment-Must-Be-a-Winner Bias

What makes all these problems come to the forefront is the overwhelming desire of human beings to make current positions (those you have right now) work out. What happens? First, when you have a losing position, you'll do anything to nurse it along, hoping it will turn around. As a result, losing trades tend to become even bigger. Second, people take profits prematurely in order to make sure those profits remain profits.

Why? People have an overwhelming desire to be right. Over and over again, I hear traders and investors tell me how important it is for them to be right when they make a market prediction or, even worse, when they invest their money in the market.

I once worked with a client who published a daily fax that gave predictions for a particular commodity. Big traders all over the world subscribed to his fax because his accuracy was outstanding. He was known worldwide for his accuracy. However, despite the fact that his accuracy was outstanding, his ability to trade that commodity was rather poor. Why? Because of the need to be right. Once a person makes a prediction, the ego becomes involved in it, making it difficult to accept anything that happens in the process of trading that seems to differ from your prediction. Thus, it becomes very difficult to trade anything that you publicly predict in any way.

SUMMARY

The amount of information to which the average individual is now exposed doubles every year. Consciously, however, we can only process about 7 chunks of information before it is lost. As a result, we have developed a number of shortcuts or heuristics to help us cope with the vast amount of information to which we are exposed. These heuristics are useful under most circumstances, but their implications for traders and investors are so strong that my belief is that the average person has no probability of making money in the markets unless he or she deals with them. I've divided these heuristics into three types of biases that are summarized below.

Biases That Affect Trading System Development

Representation bias. People assume that when something is supposed to represent something, that it really is what it is supposed to represent. Thus, we assume that the daily bar chart is the market or that our favorite indicator is the market. Instead, we need to keep in mind that the representation is just a shortcut for presenting a lot of information, or even worse, a distortion of that information.

Reliability bias. People assume that something is accurate when it may not be. For example, market data that you use in your historical testing or that come to you live are often filled with errors. Unless you assume that errors can and do exist, you may make lots of mistakes in your trading and investing decisions.

Lotto bias. People want to control the market, and so they tend to focus on entry, where they can "force" the market to do a lot of things before they enter. Unfortunately, once they enter, the market is going to do what the market is going to do. *And the golden rule of trading "Cut your losses short and let your profits run" has nothing to do with entry and everything to do with exits.*

Law-of-small-numbers bias. People tend to see patterns where none exist, and it takes only a few well-chosen examples to convince someone that a pattern has meaning. When you combine this bias with the conservatism bias (below), you have a very dangerous situation.

Conservatism bias. Once you believe you have found such a pattern and become convinced that it works (by means of a few well-chosen examples), you will do everything you can to avoid evidence that it does not work.

Randomness bias. People like to assume that the market is random and has many tops and bottoms that they can trade easily. Yet the markets are not random. Distributions of prices show that markets over time have infinite variance, or what statisticians call "long tails" at the end of the bell curve. Furthermore, people fail to understand that even random markets can have long streaks. As a result, top and bottom fishing is the most difficult type of trading there is.

Need-to-understand bias. We attempt to make order out of the market and find reasons for everything. This attempt to find order tends to block our ability to go with the flow of the markets because we see what we expect to see rather than what is really happening.

Biases That Affect How You Test Trading Systems

Degrees-of-freedom bias. We want to optimize our systems, and we believe that the more we manipulate the data to fit history, the more we know about trading well. Instead, you are much better off understanding how your concept (that you are using to trade or invest) works and doing only a minimum amount of historical testing.

Postdictive error bias. We can inadvertently use data in system development that, in real-life trading, will not yet have occurred. For example, if you factor today's close into your analysis, then you will probably do very well in your testing—especially when you tend to exit before the close.

Not-giving-yourself-enough-protection bias. People fail to consider that position sizing and exit strategies are a key part of trading. Consequently, they often put too much of their capital at risk in a given trade.

Biases That Affect How You Trade Your System

Gambler's fallacy bias. People assume that the probability goes up for a win after a long losing streak or up for a loss after a long winning streak.

Conservative-with-profits-and-risky-with-losses bias. People want to take profits quickly and give their losses some room. This gives them the illusion of being right, but what they are really doing is cutting their profits short and letting their losses run.

My-current-trade-or-investment-must-be-a-winner bias. This bias may be at the root of all other biases. Yet being right has little to do with making money.

NOTES

1. Karl Popper, *Objective Knowledge: An Evolutionary Approach* (Oxford: Clarendon Press, 1972).
2. Jack Schwager, "William Eckhardt: The Mathematician," *The New Market Wizards: Conversations with America's Top Traders* (New York: HarperCollins, 1992), p. 114.
3. For example, Burton G. Malkiel, *A Random Walk Down Wall Street*, 8th ed. (New York: Norton, 2004).
4. These stories were made up, but they are typical examples of what you might read to explain the action of the market.
5. Larry Williams, *The Definitive Guide to Futures Trading*, Vol. II (Brightwaters, N.Y.: Windsor Books, 1989), p. 202.
6. Ralph Vince, "The Ralph Vince Experiment," in *Technical Trader's Bulletin*, eds. David W. Lucas and Charles LeBeau (March 1992), pp. 1–2.

CHAPTER 3

Setting Your Objectives

> The crowd, the world, and sometimes even the grave step aside for the man who knows where he's going, but pushes the aimless drifter aside.
>
> *Ancient Roman saying*

Now you understand that the search for the Holy Grail is an internal search. In addition, you should have some idea of what might be holding you back. Now it's time to decide what you want. Sam requested a 10-minute consultation with me because he just couldn't seem to get results he was happy with. I said yes, so we met at O'Hare Airport in Chicago at the end of one of my business trips. The conversation went something like this:

What can I help you with, Sam?
Well, I just don't think my trading results are on track.

What does "on track" mean?
I'm not happy with my results.

What are your goals for trading in the market this year?
Well, I really don't have any goals.

What would you like to accomplish in the market this year?
(*After a long pause*) I'd like to buy my wife a car out of my trading profits.

Okay. What kind of car are we talking about? A Rolls-Royce? A Mercedes? A Lexus? A pickup truck? What do you want to buy her?
Oh, an American car—one that sells for about $15,000.

Great. When would you like to buy this car?
September. In about three months!

Fine. How much money do you have in your trading account?
About $10,000.

So you want to make 150 percent in your account in about three months?
Yes, I guess that's right.

Do you realize that 150 percent return in three months is equivalent to an annual rate of return of almost 1,000 percent?
No, I didn't.

How much are you willing to lose in your account in order to make that much?
I don't know. I really haven't thought about it.

Are you willing to lose $5,000?
No, I couldn't do anything like that. That's way too much.

Are you willing to lose $2,500? That's 25 percent.
No, that's still too much. Maybe 10 percent.

So you want to make 150 percent in the market in three months, and you're only willing to take a 10 percent risk in the process?
Yes.

Do you know of any trading method that will consistently give you a reward-to-risk ratio of 15 to 1?
No.

I don't know of any either. Three-to-one is usually a very good reward-to-risk ratio.

Although there are many trading and investing methods that make good money, I don't know of any that meet those requirements. However, most beginning traders and investors with small amounts of money are constantly giving themselves similar expectations—expectations that they are unlikely to meet.

DESIGNING OBJECTIVES: A MAJOR PART OF YOUR SYSTEM WORK

I once worked with a man whose job was to give money to budding commodity trading advisors (CTAs). Part of his job was to assess the various systems that these CTAs had developed, and many people considered him to be one of the world's experts in system development.

One day I said to him, "If you could give any particular suggestion to traders who are trying to come up with a new system, what would it be?" His response was, "To spend at least 50 percent of the system development time working out objectives." He said that objectives were a critical part of any system, and yet few people bother to spend time working on them. If you're going to develop a system for trading or investing in the market, then decide exactly what it is you want to accomplish before you begin.

Your objectives are a critical part of your system. How can you develop a trading system if you have no idea what it's supposed to do? Similarly, how can you go somewhere when you have no idea where you are going? You just can't do it. So you need to decide what you want to accomplish first. Once you've done that, you can decide if your goals are realistic. If they are, then you can develop a trading system to accomplish those goals.

I took my friend's advice to heart when we did our first workshop, "How to Develop a Winning Trading System to Fit You." A major portion of that workshop was devoted to objectives. However, so many people grumbled over including objectives as part of the workshop that we now require workshop participants to complete the objectives section prior to the workshop.

Typical comments included "What does this have to do with trading in the markets?" "This is private material; I don't want to spend class time talking about my equity or anything like that." None of them seemed to realize that if they didn't spend time on their objectives, they wouldn't really be able to develop a system that "fit" them. They needed to assess themselves for strengths and weaknesses; for time, resources, capital, and skills; and for what it was they were trying to accomplish. What kind of returns did they want to make? What kind of drawdowns were they willing to tolerate in order to make those returns? This is one of the real keys in our search for the Holy Grail.

TOM BASSO ON OBJECTIVES

Tom Basso was a guest speaker at the first three system development workshops that we did. During those workshops, I frequently interviewed him on his objectives in order to demonstrate how one should approach this portion of the task. Tom was kind enough to volunteer to do another of those interviews for this book.

Tom Basso was the president of Trendstat, Inc., located in Scottsdale, Arizona. He was a professional money manager who was qualified both as a CTA and as a registered investment advisor (RIA). He was also a private investor in that he invested his own money in his funds.

Tom was interviewed by Jack Schwager in his book *The New Market Wizards* at my suggestion. Schwager then named him "Mr. Serenity," and he considers him his best personal role model out of all the market wizards he interviewed. Basso is also one of the most logical, organized people I have ever met. As a result, I thought you might like to learn how Tom thinks about trading system development.

The first part of the objectives exercise involves taking a self-inventory of your time, money, skills, and other resources. Tom's answers are in italics:

> **Tom, how much capital do you have?**
> *We currently have about $95 million under management.*[1]
>
> **How much money do you need to live on each year?**
> *About $80,000.*
>
> **How much of that must come out of your trading profits?**
> *None of it. I get a salary through Trendstat.*

I ask that question in order to determine what percentage of one's trading capital the person needs to make in order to just survive. This is important just to determine if it's reasonable. For example, those who need to make 30 percent or more just to survive are putting themselves in a rather untenable position, plus giving little opportunity for the trading capital to grow.

I frequently get people who have about $100,000 of trading or investment capital, but they need about $50,000 to live on each year. In my opinion, they are putting themselves in a very difficult position. They might believe they can make 100 percent every year, and perhaps they can. But if they start out with a 30 percent drawdown—which is quite possible—their situation becomes very tenuous at best. That's why it's best to think about these situations before you get into them. Obviously, none of these things is a problem for Tom Basso.

Part 1. Self-Assessment

Tom, how much time during the day do you have to devote to trading? [This is important because the amount of time you have available almost dictates the kind of trading system you must develop. Those who have a full-time job and just look at the markets in the evening must, quite obviously, find a fairly long-term system to use.]

I've got about six hours each day, but that time is mostly involved in managing our trading business.

When you are trading, how many distractions can you expect to have?

Many.

So obviously, you need a trading methodology that allows you to deal with those distractions.

Yes.

How much time do you expect to devote to developing your trading system, to doing your personal psychological work, and to working on your business plan for trading?

In my case, I've already put in a lot of time over the last 20 years. However, we're always planning and doing research. I put in however much time it takes.

What are your computer skills? What skills do you need before you begin this trading venture?

I'm very good with computers. I custom programmed all of Trendstat's early models myself. However, at this time I have a fully automated office and a staff of full-time programmers. My job is simply to look for inefficiencies and see to it that the staff takes care of them.

What do you know about statistics?

I understand and can use simple statistics. In addition, I'm familiar with some multivariate statistics.

How would you rate your market knowledge? [Here you should include knowledge of trading mechanics, what moves the markets, how to execute orders effectively at low cost, which trading indicators you might need, and so on.]

I have extensive experience in options, futures, stocks, bonds, mutual funds, cash currencies. I am very familiar with trade mechanics and low-cost execution. I also have my own perception of how the markets work.

What are your psychological strengths and weaknesses, especially in terms of trading system development?

I am very strategic and patient, and I believe those qualities are useful in developing long-term strategies for trading. I'm self-confident, which gives me a lot of psychological strength in trusting the systems we develop. In terms of weaknesses, I guess I'm always trying to get a lot done—perhaps too much. Sometimes that can distract me from my primary mission as a trader.

How about your strengths and weaknesses in terms of personal discipline?

I am fairly good at discipline. I have no problems following a system.

Do you tend to get compulsive (that is, do you get caught up in the excitement of trading), do you have personal conflicts (that is, do you have a history of conflicts in your family life, at your job, or during past trading experience), or do you have any emotional issues that constantly crop up, such as fear or anger?

I certainly don't think of myself as compulsive. I don't find trading exciting at all. It's just a business to me. I look at trading as an interesting brain tease.

I don't think I have any conflicts. My family life is reasonably stable. In addition, I rarely get angry or frustrated. I used to get tense from time to time. But I learned something in one of your workshops about what happens first when I get tense. In my case, my fingers got tense first. As soon as I became consciously aware of it, I automatically went into a relaxation state. And now it's so automatic for me that I don't even notice it.

Based on your personal inventory, what do you need to learn, accomplish, or solve prior to beginning trading? How will you do that?

I think my personal inventory was and is quite strong. I'm able to trade well.

I hope, for those of you who have a lot of things to overcome, this inventory will be an eye-opener. You really need to think about all of these things before you start developing a trading system. Why? Because the essence of a good trading system is to find one that best fits you!

Part 2. Defining Your Objectives

This section is probably the most important part of developing a trading system. Until you know where you want to go, you can never get there. As a result, a major portion of the time you spend in developing a trading system should be directed to developing objectives.

Objectives probably should be treated differently for individual traders and investors than for those who are managing money. Since Tom fills both roles, I asked him both sets of questions. First, here are the questions for individual traders and investors.

A. Objectives for Individual Investors and Traders

What is your advantage or edge in trading? What is the particular concept that you are trading that gives you an advantage? [If you don't know, various concepts are discussed in detail in Chapter 5.]

Strategic thinking is our edge because so many people don't do that. We also have an edge in terms of patience and detachment. Most people are neither patient nor detached. Computer programming is also an edge. Most people don't take it to the level that we do. Long-term automated trend following is the outflow of the edge.

How much money do you have personally? How much of that money could you afford to lose? For example, most funds stop trading at 50 percent. How about you? How much risk can you afford to take on a given trade?

I have several million dollars, and I could afford to lose 25 percent of that comfortably. All of my money is in our trading program, and we're only risking between 0.8 to 1.0 percent per trade. However, if I were trading on my own, I'd go to 1 percent to 1.5 percent. I think 2 to 3 percent risk would push the envelope for me, partially because I could be in up to 20 markets at a time.

How much money do you need to make each year? Do you need to live off that money? What if you don't make enough to live off it? Can you make more than you need to live off of so that your trading capital can grow? Can you stand regular withdrawals from your trading capital to pay your monthly bills?

My income comes from my salary at Trendstat, so I don't need anything from my trading income. Trading income is simply a second income for me.

I know this doesn't pertain to you, but I'll ask anyway because it's one of the standard questions under objectives. Are you being realistic, or are you expecting to trade like the best trader in the world? For example, suppose you have a very good system that is right half the time and gives you profits that are twice as large as your losses. In that system, just by chance, you could still easily have 10 losses in a row. Your system is still working as expected, but you could easily have 10 losses in a row. Could you tolerate that?

I think I'm quite realistic about the returns and the risk. I also know about 10 losses in a row. I've gone through that in the past, so I know that it is to be expected.

Do you have the time to trade short term?

I have about six hours each day to devote to trading. The rest of my time is devoted to specific business or personal commitments. I don't plan to trade short term so that's not a problem.

How much social contact do you need?

I don't need much, but I do enjoy it.

Can you work by yourself day after day? Do you need one or two other people around, or do you need a lot of other people around? How much do those other people influence you?

I have a full staff of people at Trendstat, but I don't need that. I can easily work by myself. Those people don't influence me at all in terms of the early development of our trading models.

In summary, what do you expect to make each year as a percentage of your trading capital?

About 20 to 40 percent.

What risk level are you willing to tolerate in order to achieve that?

About half the potential gain, so the maximum loss would be 20 percent in a year.

What is the largest peak-to-trough drawdown you are willing to tolerate?

About 25 percent.

How will you know your plan is working, and how will you know when it's not working? What do you expect from your system in various kinds of markets? Trending? Consolidating? Highly volatile?

I plan everything. I set up worst-case scenarios, and we run through them just as an exercise. I have specifications on the best case and the worst case for each scenario. Thus, when something comes along, I've usually planned for it and have a range of expectancy. If the results fall within that range, then I know everything is as planned. If the results fall outside of that range, then I know that something needs to be fixed. We'll then step in and study what went wrong.

Generally, I expect a 40 percent return at the best and a 10 percent return at the worst, with average returns of 15 to 25 percent. We also expect worst-case drawdowns of 25 percent.

I remember one year I had a return greater than 40 percent. I'm glad that happened because I was outside the extremes of our parameters. What it told me is that our risk was too great and that we could also be outside the range on the downside. As a result, we went in and cut down our risk so that the worst case on the downside couldn't happen.

B. Objectives for Trading Advisors

Now let's do the objectives for you as a trading manager. What kind of clients do you want? Retail clients? A few good friends? Several pool operators placing money with you? Very sophisticated traders?

We want balanced clients that have reasonable objectives. My objective here is to remain one of the top 100 firms by size, so we'll take the kinds of clients who'll get us there. We have both retail and institutional clients. In some ways they are different and in other ways they are the same, but both types are fine with us.

What are your clients like? What are their goals? What kind of service do you provide for them? For example, by putting their money with you, are they attempting a special type of diversification?

Our clients are definitely looking for diversification. We provide that with four different programs that strive for returns in the 10 to 20 percent range with lower drawdowns. We're looking for returns of 20 percent with 10 percent drawdowns. Our clients know that so that's what they're getting in terms of their goals.

Since you are trading clients' money, how much risk can they tolerate? When would they be likely to withdraw their money?

They expect risk in the 5 to 10 percent range. Any drawdown that is over 15 percent or that lasts over a year is deadly—lots of clients would fire us.

For that matter, how much gain can they tolerate before they get too excited?

Gains over 25 percent definitely get noticed. We don't want to be too high, or clients tend to draw a straight line to the moon and then expect that kind of performance to continue.

What kind of fees do you charge? In other words, what is the total amount extracted from the client's account each quarter or month? What kinds of returns will you have to make in order to be able to satisfy a client who is subject to those fees?

We charge a management fee of 2 percent and an incentive fee of 20 percent. Our clients are happy with those fees as long as they can make their 15 to 20 percent returns after fees and they are not too uncomfortable with the drawdowns.

What is your trading capacity? How do you expect to achieve it? What do you expect to do when you achieve it? How will that change your trading?

Our capacity is about $1 to $2 billion. We expect to achieve it by our current policy of marketing to banks, large-pool operators, and high-net-worth individuals. When we reach it, we'll simply turn away new money. As we grow, our trading needs to be continually consolidated at fewer trading desks.

What's the worst thing that can happen in terms of your client relationship? How can you prepare for that so that it will not occur?

The worst thing that can happen to a client is a surprise. We make sure that doesn't happen by educating our clients. I even wrote a book to prepare them, Panic Proof Investing.[2]

How will you handle a large infusion of new capital or a large withdrawal?

A large infusion of new capital is planned in our programs. Large withdrawals are easily handled by the software we've developed.

As you can tell, Tom Basso has carefully planned every little detail of his trading program. That's why an exercise like this one is so important. It gets you thinking about issues you probably would not have thought about had you not done the exercise.

Part 3. Trading Ideas

The last section gets specifically into how you want to trade. It has to do with ideas about markets, entry, exit, and money management—the specifics of your trading plan.

Tom, what kind of markets do you want to trade? Is it appropriate to specialize? Do you want to trade only liquid markets, or are there some illiquid markets you'd like to trade?

I'm a generalist, not a specialist. There are 20 futures markets that I trade, 15 cash currency markets, and 30 mutual funds.

All of them are very liquid because I concentrate on only liquid markets. If I didn't concentrate on these liquid markets, then we'd have a very small capacity—not the several billion we're shooting toward.

What beliefs do you have about entering the markets? How important do you believe entry to be?

Entry is probably the least important component of my trading. I want to enter the market when there is a change of trend. At that very instant—when the trend changes—the reward-to-risk ratio is the best it will be for the rest of the trade.

Given your goals in terms of returns and drawdowns, what kind of initial risk stop do you want? If it's close, will you be able to get right back into the market so that you will not miss a move?

Stops, in my opinion, should be a violation of the reason why I wanted to get into the trade in the first place. And, yes, I always have a way to get back into the trade.

My stop is a function of the market and what it's doing. It's only indirectly related to risk—unless the risk is too big for me to even take a position. I control risk as part of my position sizing, which I suspect you'll ask about later on in this interview.

How do you plan to take profits? Reversal stops? Trailing stops? Technical stops? Price objectives? Contrary to popular opinion, much of your emphasis should be in the area of stops and exits.

I don't limit the amount I can make in a trade. My philosophy is to let my profits run. If I ever find a trade that keeps going in my direction so that I never have to get out, great!

I use trailing or technical stops. Once those are hit, I'm out of the position.

What do you do in terms of position sizing?

I set up a portfolio of instruments to be traded at set risk and volatility limits as a percent of equity. I monitor the amount of initial risk and volatility and keep them at set limits. In addition, I keep the ongoing risk and volatility at fixed percentages of my equity. As a result, I always know how much fluctuation can occur in my portfolio overnight and it's well within my sleeping limits.

Perhaps now you can understand why planning your objectives is so important to developing a trading system. If you do, then I've done my job in this chapter. The rest of this chapter gives you the opportunity to answer the same questions for yourself.

It's easy to take a few minutes to answer the questions (and some of you won't even do that). However, what is critical is to really take the time to think about the issues raised by these questions. That's why this section should be 50 percent of the task of preparing to trade.

SETTING YOUR OWN OBJECTIVES

Part 1: Self-Assessment

How much time during the day do you have to devote to trading? [This is important because the amount of time you have available almost dictates the kind of trading system you must develop. Those who have a full-time job and just look at the markets in the evening must, quite obviously, find a fairly long-term system to use.]

When you are trading, how many distractions can you expect to have?

How much time do you expect to devote to developing your trading system, to doing your personal psychological work, and to working on your business plan for trading?

What are your computer skills? What skills do you need before you begin this trading venture?

What do you know about statistics?

How would you rate your market knowledge? [Here you should include knowledge of trading mechanics, what moves the markets, how to execute orders effectively at low cost, any trading indicators you might need, and so on.]

What are your psychological strengths and weaknesses, especially in terms of trading system development?

How about your strengths and weaknesses in terms of personal discipline?

Do you tend to get compulsive (that is, do you get caught up in the excitement of trading), do you have personal conflicts (that is, do you have a history of conflicts in your family life, at your job, or during past trading experience), or do you have any emotional issues that constantly crop up, such as fear or anger?

Based on your personal inventory, what do you need to learn, accomplish, or solve prior to beginning trading? How will you do that?

You really need to think about all of these things before you start developing a trading system. Remember, the essence of a good trading system is to find one that best fits you!

Part 2. Defining Your Objectives

This section is probably the most important part of developing a trading system. Until you know where you want to go, you can never get there. As a result, a major portion of the time you spend in developing a trading system should be in terms of developing objectives.

Objectives for Individuals

What is your advantage or edge in trading? What is the particular concept that you are trading that gives you an advantage? [If you don't know, various concepts are discussed in detail in Chapter 5. Think about the issues and then answer the question.]

How much money do you have personally? How much of that money could you afford to lose? For example, most funds stop trading at 50 percent. How about you? How much risk can you afford to take on a given trade?

How much money do you need to make each year? Do you need to live off that money?

What if you don't make enough to live off it? Can you make more than you need to live off of so that

your trading capital can grow? Can you stand regular withdrawals from your trading capital to pay your monthly bills?

Are you being realistic, or are you expecting to trade like the best trader in the world? For example, suppose you have a very good system that is right half the time and gives you profits that are twice as large as your losses. In that system, just by chance, you could still easily have 10 losses in a row. Your system is still working as expected, but you could easily have 10 losses in a row. Could you tolerate that?

Do you have the time to trade short term?

How much social contact do you need?

Can you work by yourself day after day? Do you need one or two other people around, or do you need a lot of other people around? How much do those other people influence you?

In summary, what do you expect to make each year as a percentage of your trading capital?

What risk level are you willing to tolerate in order to achieve that?

What is the largest peak-to-trough drawdown you are willing to tolerate?

How will you know your plan is working, and how will you know when it's not working? What do you expect from your system in various kinds of markets? Trending? Consolidating? Highly volatile?

Objectives for Trading Managers

Now let's do the objectives for those of you who want to be a trading manager.

What kind of clients do you want? Retail clients? A few good friends? Several pool operators placing money with you? Very sophisticated traders? Institutional clients?

What are your clients like? What are their goals? What kind of service do you provide for them? For example, by putting their money with you, are they attempting a special type of diversification?

Since you are trading clients' money, how much risk can they tolerate? When would they be likely to withdraw their money?

For that matter, how much gain can they tolerate before they get too excited?

What kind of fees do you charge? In other words, what is the total amount extracted from the client's account each quarter or month? What kinds of returns will you have to make in order to be able to satisfy a client who is subject to those fees?

What is your trading capacity? How do you expect to achieve it? What do you expect to do when you achieve it? How will that change your trading?

What's the worst thing that can happen in terms of your client relationship? How can you prepare for that so that it will not occur? How will you deal with client problems or problem clients?

How will you handle a large infusion of new capital or a large withdrawal?

Part 3. Trading Ideas

The last section gets specifically into how you want to trade. It has to do with ideas about markets, entry, exit, and money management—the specifics of your trading plan.

What kind of markets do you want to trade? Is it appropriate to specialize? Do you want to trade only liquid markets, or are there some illiquid markets you'd like to trade?

Do you want any conditions to set up before you enter the market? If so, what are those conditions? [Tom did not answer this question, but you might find it useful to answer it.]

What beliefs do you have about entering the markets? How important do you believe entry to be?

Given your goals in terms of returns and drawdowns, what kind of initial risk stop do you want? If it's close, will you be able to get right back into the market so that you will not miss a move? [In other words, discuss what kind of stop loss you plan to have.]

How do you plan to take profits? Reversal stops? Trailing stops? Technical stops? Price objectives? Contrary to popular opinion, much of your emphasis should be in the area of stops and exits.

What do you do in terms of position sizing? [Write down any specific ideas you may have here.]

These are about the most important topics you need to think about.

NOTES

1. From the time this interview was finished, Trendstat's assets under management grew to over a half-billion dollars. However, Tom has since retired as a professional money manager, and he spends his time enjoying his retirement.
2. Tom Basso, *Panic Proof Investing* (New York: Wiley, 1994).

PART TWO

Conceptualizing Your System

The purpose of Part Two is to help you conceptualize your system and then build the groundwork necessary to construct it. Part Two consists of four chapters. Chapter 4 presents the critical steps that are necessary for developing a system that fits you. It represents years of work studying the world's best traders and investors to determine exactly how they do their research.

Chapter 5 presents a synopsis of some of the various concepts that you might use in your trading system. I've asked some extremely knowledgeable people to contribute to this chapter; plus I've added my own sections. Read through the different concepts and determine which concept appeals to you the most. You might even adopt several of them.

Chapter 6 presents my understanding of the big picture. I believe that whatever system you develop must take the big picture into account and be adaptable as the big picture changes. For example, you might have had a trend-following system that only bought high-technology stocks in 1998, and you thought you were going to become very rich and successful. However, if that was your system, then everything turned upside down in 2000.

Chapter 7 presents the concept of expectancy. *Expectancy* refers to how much you will make with your trading system per dollar risked. Few traders or investors really understand expectancy, and yet it is one of the most important topics in this entire book.

CHAPTER 4

Steps to Developing a System

There must be a map or model of the data, which shows the zone to be navigated and upon which is marked the best route.

David Foster, Ph.D.

It's very useful to believe that if several people can do something well, then the skill can be copied, or modeled, and taught to someone else. This belief is what *neuro-linguistic programming* (NLP), or the science of modeling, is all about. To develop a good model, you need to find several people who can do what you are modeling well. You then need to interview those people to find out what they do in common. These are the key tasks involved in making the model.[1] It's very important to find out what they do *in common*. If you don't, you'll simply discover the idiosyncrasies of the people involved, which usually are not that important.

I've worked with hundreds of outstanding traders and investors in a coaching role over the past 25 years. During that time, I've had the opportunity to learn how to conduct trading research from these experts. The steps are quite clear and easy to do. This chapter is a synopsis of the model I've developed through these associations. In addition, we've improved the model since the last edition of this book.

1. TAKE AN INVENTORY

The first key step is to take an inventory of yourself—your strengths and weaknesses. To have market success, you must develop a system that is right for you. In order to develop such a system, you must take a careful self-inventory—of your skills, your temperament, your time, your resources, your strengths, and your weaknesses. Without taking such an inventory, you cannot possibly develop a methodology that's right for you.

Among the questions you need to consider:

- Do you have strong computer skills? If not, then do you have the resources to hire someone who does or who can help you to become computer proficient?
- How much capital do you have? How much of that is risk capital? You must have enough money to trade or invest with the system you develop. Lack of sufficient funds is a major problem for many traders and investors. If you don't have sufficient funds, then you cannot practice adequate position sizing. This is one of the essential ingredients to a successful system that most people ignore.
- How well can you tolerate losses?
- How are your math skills? And what's your level of understanding of statistics and probability?

There are many important issues that you should contemplate. For example, consider what time constraints you have. If you have a full-time job, think about using a long-term system that requires you to spend only about a half-hour each night looking at end-of-day data. Stop orders are then given to your broker for the next day. Trading such a system doesn't take much time, so it's quite appropriate to use if you don't have much time. In fact, many professionals who spend all day with the markets still rely on long-term systems that use only end-of-day data.

Let's look at another issue you should consider. Are you going to be in the market with your own money or someone else's? When you trade for other people, you have to deal with the impact of their psychology on your trading, which could be quite substantial. For example, what would your trading be like if you had to deal with clients who were always complaining to you about something?

Say you are a money manager, and after two losing months, your client withdraws her money. You then have three winning months, and the client decides to reinvest with you. After you have another two losing months, she again withdraws. She decides to wait until you get really hot in the markets, and after five winning months, she puts her money back in. You have, again, two losing months. The result of all this is a client who is continually losing while you, as a money manager, have made a lot of money. But the wear and tear that she will have experienced could also affect you and your trading, especially if she complains a lot.

I'd also recommend that you take a thorough inventory of your personal psychology. You should spend a lot of time thinking about the questions asked in the self-inventory in Chapter 3 on managing client money and think about your answers. Did you just give a quick answer, or did you give an accurate assessment of what you believe and feel? In addition, did you just answer the questions, or did you put a lot of thought into each answer before you put it down on paper? Compare your answers with Tom Basso's answers so that you can compare yourself with a top professional money manager.

In addition to the questions in Chapter 3, as part of the self-inventory you do, ask yourself the very important question, "Who am I?" The answer to that question is the basis for everything else you do, so think about it seriously.

For example, I've been working with a large trading firm, and early in 2006 the president of the firm canceled his monthly consulting call with me. He said he was changing what he was doing and needed to sort out some important things in his mind. Well, after reading his e-mail, it was clear to me that he was readdressing the question "Who am I?" In his particular case, he had been (1) the CEO of the company, (2) the head of a trading group, and (3) one of the best traders in the group. The answer he arrived at led him ultimately to disband his trading group to focus more on his own trading because his self-inventory helped him decide that role number 2 did not suit him.

To adequately answer the "Who am I?" question, I would strongly suggest that you write down all of your beliefs about yourself. Sit down with several sheets of paper and start writing free-flowing notes about yourself. Who are you really and what do you believe? When you've written down about 100 beliefs, you'll have a pretty good idea.

Here are a few of the beliefs one of my clients wrote down:

- I'm a full-time professional who has several hours each day to commit to being the best trader I can be.
- I am totally committed to becoming a full-time trader within the next 12 months.
- I am a short-term trader for my personal account and a very long-term trader for my retirement account.
- I believe I can make 50 percent or better in my short-term trading account, while I'm only trying to outperform the market in my retirement account.

Those are just a few of the beliefs about himself that he wrote, but hopefully you can begin to see from them how they shape everything else. Now it's time for you to write down your beliefs about yourself.

2. DEVELOP AN OPEN MIND AND GATHER MARKET INFORMATION

One of the three-day workshops that we conduct is called Developing a Winning System That Fits You. And we also have an audio series on that topic from a prior workshop. Most people learn a great deal from that workshop or audio series, but sometimes people don't learn enough until they've addressed some of their psychological issues first. For example, some people seem totally closed to what we are trying to teach. They have their own ideas about what they want, and they are just not open to a general model for improving their methodology—much less to specific suggestions on how they should change. And the interesting thing is that the people who are most closed to the ideas presented are usually people who need the material the most.

Thus, the first part of step 2 in the system development model is to develop a completely open mind. Here are some suggestions for doing that.

First, you need to understand that just about everything you've ever been taught—including every sentence you've read so far in this book—consists of beliefs. "The world is flat" is a belief, just as is the statement "The world is round." You might say, "No, the second statement is a fact." Perhaps, but it is also a belief—with a lot of important meaning in each word. For example, what does *round* mean? Or for that matter, what does *world* mean?

Anything that seems to be a fact is still relative and depends upon the semantics of the situation. Its factuality depends on some assumptions you are making and the perspective you are bringing to the situation—all of which are also beliefs. You'll become a lot less rigid and much more flexible and open in your thinking if you consider "facts" to be "useful beliefs" that you've made up.

The reality that we know consists solely of our beliefs. As soon as you change your beliefs, then your reality will change. Of course, what I've just said is also a belief. However, when you adopt this belief for yourself, you can begin to admit that you don't really know what is real. Instead, you just have a model of the world by which you live your life. As a result, you can evaluate each new belief in terms of its "utility." When something conflicts with what you know or believe, think to yourself, "Is there any chance that this is a more useful belief?" You'd be surprised at how open you'll suddenly become to new ideas and new input. One of my favorite quotations is the following from Einstein: "The real nature of things, we shall never know, never."

> Keep in mind the following: You don't trade or invest in markets—you trade or invest according to your beliefs about the markets.

Thus, part of the necessity of having an open mind is the requirement to determine just your beliefs about the market. When you are not open, they don't seem like "beliefs"—they just seem like "what is." Trading "an illusion," which everyone does, is particularly dangerous when you don't know it. And you may be deluding yourself extensively with your beliefs.

Charles LeBeau, a veteran trader of 40 years, says that when he started to design trading systems for the computer, he had hundreds of beliefs about the market. Most of those beliefs did not stand up to the rigors of computerized testing.

When your mind is open, start reading about the markets.[2] I strongly recommend almost any book written by Jack Schwager.

However, start with *Market Wizards* and *The New Market Wizards*. They are two of the best books available on trading and investing. Two other books by Schwager, *Fundamental Analysis* and *Technical Analysis*, are also excellent.

Computer Analysis of the Futures Market, by Charles LeBeau and David Lucas, is one of the best books available on the systematic process of developing a trading system. Indeed, I've learned a lot from reading that book and from conducting regular workshops with Chuck. I'd also recommend Perry Kaufman's book *Smarter Trading*; Cynthia Kase's book *Trading with the Odds*; and William O'Neil's book *How to Make Money in Stocks*. Tushar Chande's book *Beyond Technical Analysis*[3] is also good in that it gets the reader to think about concepts that are beyond the scope of this volume.

The suggested readings will give you the appropriate background required to develop useful beliefs about the markets that will support you in the game ahead of you. They will answer a lot of the pressing questions about trading that might be cluttering your mind. More detailed information about these books is provided in the Recommended Readings at the end of this book.

Once you've completed this reading list, write down your beliefs about the market. Every sentence in this book represents one or more of my beliefs. You may want to find the ones you agree with having to do with the market. They will be a good starting point for your task of finding your beliefs about the market. This step will prepare you for subsequent tasks you will have to tackle in exploring the markets and developing your own system for making a lot of money. This study of the markets you will have done and the list of your beliefs that your study will have generated (you should write down at least 100 of them) will probably become the basis for a trading system that fits you. At the very least, your list will make a good starting point. Look at each part of a trading system, as described in this book, and make sure that you've listed your beliefs about each of them.

As you read this book, make a note of what you agree with and what you disagree with. There is no right or wrong, just beliefs and the meaning and amount of energy you attach to them. Doing this exercise will tell you a lot about your beliefs. For example, I gave a manuscript of this book to ten traders for their comments. What I got back simply reflected their beliefs. Here are some examples:

- I would argue that position sizing is part of your system, not a separate system.
- Indicators are not distortions of chart data but rather derivations.
- There are a lot of flaws in expectancy because of judgmental heuristics such as "curve fitting," "data mining," and the long-term data problem.
- I don't believe that catastrophic events are predictive except that they might increase or decrease market volatility and/or value. Thus, designing a system that adapts to changing volatility is the key.
- A bad trade is not a losing trade, but one which didn't meet my entry criteria that I took anyway.
- I don't believe that reliability (win rate) has anything to do with your entry. Instead, it has to do with your exits.
- When you say we're in a secular bear market, you will create a psychological bias for your readers. You don't have a crystal ball.
- You say the markets move sideways 85 percent of the time. I think the estimate is high—it's probably 50 to 75 percent of the time.

The people with these beliefs each wanted me to make changes in the book to reflect their beliefs. Instead, I chose to keep my beliefs and just inform you that you might have beliefs that conflict with mine. Just make sure that your belief is useful for you. What's really important is to recognize your beliefs because you will only trade a system that fits your beliefs.

3. DETERMINE YOUR MISSION AND YOUR OBJECTIVES

You cannot develop an adequate system for making money in the market unless you totally understand what you are trying to accomplish in the markets. Thinking about your objectives and getting them clearly in mind should be a major priority in your system development. In fact, it probably should occupy 20 to 50 percent of your time in designing a system. Unfortunately, most people totally ignore this task or just spend a few minutes doing it. To see if you're spending adequate attention on determining your objectives, start by recalling how much time you spent working on the exercise in Chapter 3.

Give Chapter 3 a lot of time and a lot of thought. The chapter contains a detailed questionnaire for you to fill out. If you took only15 to 30 minutes to answer the same questions I asked Tom Basso, then you are probably not doing an adequate job. Establishing objectives is one of the tasks that most people want to avoid, but if you want to develop a great system for trading or investing, then you must give this task sufficient attention. Remember how important it is to keep an open mind? Doing an adequate job with your objectives is part of being open.

4. DETERMINE THE CONCEPT THAT YOU WANT TO TRADE

In my experience as a trading coach, only certain concepts work. So your next step is to familiarize yourself with the various concepts that work and decide which of them you wish to focus on. I've devoted an entire chapter to explaining these various concepts, but I'll briefly outline them here.

Trend Following

This concept assumes that markets, at times, tend to *trend* (that is, they move up or down for a fairly long period of time). If you can spot when the trend starts and capture much of the move, then you can make a lot of money as a trader. However, to be a trend follower, you must be able to buy what's going up and sell what's going down. And if it's been going up for a while, so much the better—you still must be able to buy it if you want to trade this particular concept. However, all trend followers must ask themselves the following questions:

- How will I spot my trends? How will I know a market is trending?

- Will I be trading trends on the upside and the downside?
- What will I do when the market goes sideways (which tends to be about 85 percent of the time, according to many estimates)?
- What will my entry criteria be?
- How will I handle corrections?
- How will I know when the trend is over?

Figure 4.1 shows a great example of a trend. You can see that if you can spot such trends early enough, you have a tremendous potential for making a lot of money. Tom Basso does an excellent job of describing trend following as a concept in Chapter 5.

Figure 4.1 Papa John's Pizza: A clear example of an upward trending stock

Band Trading

The second concept that people can successfully trade is *band trading*. Here we make the assumption that the markets we are trading are somewhat range bound. Such markets go up for a limited period of time until they reach the top of the range. These markets then turn down for a limited period of time until they reach the bottom of the range. Figure 4.2 shows an example of a range-bound market that you could use to trade bands.

Notice that in the particular instance of the stock selected, Linear Technology Corp., you could do quite well selling whenever the price touched and then penetrated the upper band. Similarly, you could do quite well buying whenever the price touched and then penetrated the lower band. However, the common issues always arise. How do you determine the bands? I just drew them in after the fact, but there are mathematical formulas to make them more objective. How do you close out a position, especially since the price does not always touch the opposite band? And what if the band you are using breaks down?

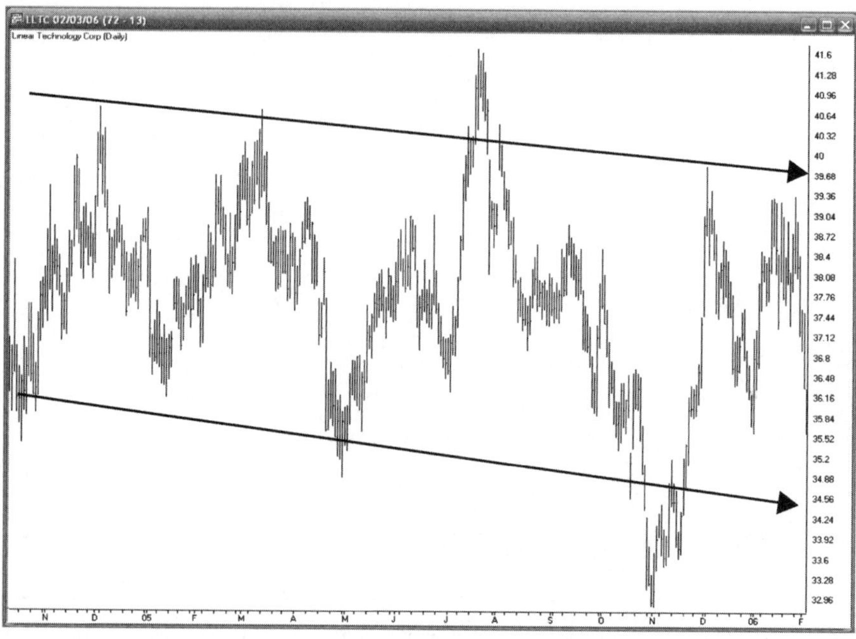

Figure 4.2 A range-bound market for band trading

If you can spot such a range-bound market, then your objective would be to sell at the top of the range and buy at the bottom of the range. And if you like this particular concept, then the primary questions you must ask yourself are the following:

- How do I find range-bound markets to buy?
- Will my bands work in a trending market?
- How do I define the range? For example, should I use fixed or static bands?
- What are my entry criteria?
- What if my band breaks down? How will I exit?
- Do I exit at the other end of the band and under what criteria?

D. R. Barton does an excellent job of discussing band trading in Chapter 5.

Value Trading

Value trading centers on some definition of value. You buy stocks or commodities that are undervalued and sell them when they are overvalued. When you adopt this approach, the key questions you must ask yourself are the following:

- How do I define value?
- When is something undervalued?
- What are my criteria for buying something that is undervalued?
- What are my criteria for selling something that is overvalued?

Many fundamentalists and portfolio managers use some form of value trading.

Arbitrage

Arbitrage occurs when you are able to buy something at a low price in one place and sell it for a higher price in some other place. These discrepancies usually occur because of some temporary loophole in the law or in the way the marketplace works. For example, one of my clients recently discovered that you could buy a seat on the Chicago Board of Trade (CBOT) for about $3 million, but he could sell the various components of the seat for $3.8 million. That's a 27 percent built-in profit on each transaction. It's an easy surefire trade. However, easy trades usually have their downfall. In this case, to purchase the Chicago Board of Trade seat required that he also purchase Chicago Board of Trade stock. He was required to keep the stock six months before selling it. Thus, if the stock were to drop 27 percent during the six months he was required to hold it, then it would negate all of his profits. Thus, like most arbitrage trades, there is some risk.

The key questions you must ask yourself when arbitrage is your niche are the following:

- What areas of the market do I need to search to find loopholes?
- What exactly is the loophole, and how can I best take advantage of it?
- What are the risks?
- How long will the loophole last, and how will I know it's over?

Many floor traders, especially those using options, conduct various forms of arbitrage. In addition, the few day traders who have survived since 2000 have survived by finding good arbitrage situations. The late Ray Kelly does an excellent job of discussing arbitrage in his section of Chapter 5.

Spreading as a Concept

Another technique used by market makers and options traders is spreading. *Spreading* is somewhat related to arbitrage in that it requires that you usually buy one thing and sell something else, hoping you have the relationship right. For example, most trading of foreign currency is a form of spreading because you become long (that is, you own it and profit if it goes up) in one currency against another (that is, you profit if it goes down).

The key questions you must ask yourself as a spreader are the following:

- What do I think might move?
- What can I short against that move to hedge my risk?
- Is there a limit to my profit (as there is with some options spreads)?
- How will I know if I'm wrong?
- Or if I'm right, how will I know the move is over?

Kevin Thomas, the first person to join my Super Trader program, writes about spreading in Chapter 5.

Other concepts included in Chapter 5 that you might also select from are *seasonals* (taking trades at some particular time period that is most appropriate for a market move) and deciding that there is some secret order to the universe. I don't know of any other trading concepts besides these, but this is still a wide range of concepts from which you can select one or two.

5. DETERMINE THE BIG PICTURE

I've been coaching traders since 1982, and during this time I've seen many market cycles. When I first started coaching, most of my traders were futures traders and options traders. This was interesting considering that I was starting right at the beginning of the huge secular bull market in stocks.

During the 1980s most of my clients continued to be futures traders, although the futures markets tended to be dominated by big CTAs. And then trends in futures toward the end of the decade (as inflation quieted) tended to be small. And I noticed that, gradually, all of these traders were moving toward trading foreign exchange.

Later, in the mid-1990s, I started to get a lot of equity traders as clients. This peaked in March 2000 when over 70 people attended our Stock Market Workshop. At that time, one bartender in the local hotel where we were giving such workshops remarked, "Perhaps we should attend Dr. Tharp's stock market workshop." However, the other bartender responded, "No, I could teach that workshop."

Such things usually happen at market extremes, and you know what happened in 2000. Now, in 2006, I'm finding that about half of our clients are again futures traders. So our clients clearly move in cycles, gravitating toward the hot market—perhaps at the wrong time. As a result, I now think it's critical to make part of your system development an assessment of the big picture. Several non-correlated systems that fit the big picture would make up a great trading business plan. In addition, you might develop several more systems to use should the big picture change.

I believe that this step is critical, so I've devoted a new chapter in this book to helping you assess the big picture. In addition, I write a monthly update on the big picture in my free e-mail newsletter *Tharp's Thoughts.*

6. DETERMINE YOUR TIME FRAME FOR TRADING

Your sixth task is to decide how active you want to be in the market. What is your time frame for trading? Do you want to have a very long-term outlook, probably making a change in your portfolio only once a quarter? Do you want to be a stock trader who holds positions for a year or longer? Do you want to be a long-term futures trader whose positions last one to six months? Do you want to be a swing trader who might make several trades each day with none lasting more than a few days? Or do you want the ultimate in action—being a day trader who makes 3 to 10 trades each day that are closed by the end of the day so that you have no overnight risk?

Table 4.1 shows the advantages and disadvantages of long-term trading. Long-term trading or investing is simple. It requires little time each day and has minimal psychological pressures each day—especially if you take advantage of your free time to work or spend time with your hobbies. You can typically use a fairly simple system and still make a lot of money if you adequately size your positions.

I think the primary advantage of long-term trading or investing is that you have an infinite profit opportunity (theoretically at least) on each position in the market. When you study many of the people who've gotten rich through investments, you'll find that in many instances wealth builds up because people have bought many stocks and just held on to them.[4] One of the stocks turns out

TABLE 4.1

The Advantages and Disadvantages of Long-Term Trading

Advantages	Disadvantages
No need to watch the market all day—you can use stops or options to protect yourself.	You can be whipsawed by intraday market moves each day.
Psychological pressure of the market is lowest in this type of system.	You can have large equity swings on a single position.
Transaction costs are low.	You must be patient.
It only takes one or two trades to make your whole year profitable.	It usually has a reliability (number of winning trades) of less than 50 percent.
You could have an expectancy (see Chapter 7) well over a dollar per dollar risked.	Trades tend to be infrequent, so you must capitalize by trading many markets.
You can use a simple methodology to make a lot of money.	It requires a lot of money to participate if you want to trade big liquid futures markets.
You theoretically have an infinite profit opportunity with each trade or investment.	If you miss one good trading opportunity, it can turn a winning year into a losing year.
Costs of data and equipment are minimal.	

to be a gold mine—turning an investment of a few thousand dollars into millions over a 10- to 20-year period.

The primary disadvantage of long-term trading or investing is that you must be patient. For example, you might not get a lot of opportunities, so you must wait for them to come along. In addition, once you're in a position, you must go through fairly extensive equity swings (although you can design something that minimizes them) and have the patience to wait them out. Another disadvantage of longer-term trading is that you generally need more money to participate. If you don't have enough money, then you cannot adequately size your positions in a portfolio. In fact, many people lose money in the markets simply because they don't have enough money to practice the type of trading or investing that they are doing.

Shorter-term trading (which might be anything from day trading to swing trading of one to five days) has different advantages and disadvantages. These are illustrated in Table 4.2. Read through the list and then compare it with the long-term table. Once you've done so, you can then decide for yourself what best fits your personality.

I once met a short-term foreign-exchange trader who made about six trades a day. No trade would last more than a day or two. However, the fascinating thing about what he was doing was that his gains and losses were about equal and he made money on 75 percent of his trades. This is a fantastic trading methodology. He had $500,000 to trade with and a $10 million credit line with a bank. When you understand position sizing, as discussed later in this book, you'll realize that this system comes as close to the Holy Grail as anything in existence. He could easily make a hundred million each year with that system and the capital he has.[5]

However, that's not the case with most short-term systems. Most of them seldom have a reliability much higher than 60 percent,

TABLE 4.2

The Advantages and Disadvantages of Short-Term Trading

Advantages	Disadvantages
Most day traders get many opportunities each day.	Transaction costs are still high and can add up. For example, in my own active account, transaction costs for last year amounted to about 20 percent of the initial value of the account.
This type of trading is very exciting and stimulating.	Excitement usually has nothing to do with making money—it's a psychological need!
If you have a methodology with an expectancy of 50 cents or more per dollar risked, you may never have a losing month—or even week.	Profits are limited by time, so you may need to have a reliability well over 50 percent to make money. However, I've seen some notable exceptions to this rule of thumb.
You don't have overnight risk in day trading, so there is little or no margin required even in big markets.	Data costs are very high because most short-term traders need live quotes.
High-probability entry systems, which most people want, work with short-term trading.	Many high-probability entries can have losses that are bigger than the gains.
There's always another opportunity to make money.	Short-term systems are subject to the random noise of the markets.
Transaction costs have come down so significantly that they are no longer prohibitive.	The short-term psychological pressures are intense.

and their gains are usually smaller than their losses—sometimes even leading to a negative expectancy.[6] Sometimes one big loss can ruin the whole system and psychologically devastate the trader. In addition, the psychological pressures of short-term trading are intense. I've had people call me who say something like this:

> I make money almost every day, and I haven't had a losing week in almost two years. At least until now. Yesterday, I gave back all the profits I had made over the last two years.

Keep that in mind before you decide that short-term trading is for you. Your profits are limited. Your transaction costs are high. Most importantly, the psychological pressures could destroy you. Nevertheless, my belief is that the largest profit percentages are made by active short-term traders who really have their psychology together. I've seen short-term traders who could make as much as 50 percent or more per month (on small amounts of money such as a $50,000 account) when they were very in tune with the market and themselves.

7. DETERMINE THE ESSENCE OF YOUR TRADING AND HOW YOU CAN OBJECTIVELY MEASURE IT

What is the key idea that you've observed? The first part of your idea should tell you the conditions under which the move occurs. How can you objectively measure that part of the idea? Typically, your answer to this question will give you two elements of your system: the setup conditions that you might want to use and the timing or entry signal. These topics are discussed extensively later in this book.

Your setup and timing signal are important for the reliability of your system—how often will you make money when such a move occurs? This should be tested independently from all of the other components of your system.

LeBeau and Lucas in their book, cited earlier, have an excellent method for testing such signals. What they do is determine the reliability (that is, the percentage of time it is profitable) of the signal after various time periods. You might try an hour, the end of the day, and after 1, 2, 5, 10, and 20 days. A random system should give you an average reliability of about 50 percent (that is, generally between 45 and 55 percent). If your concept is any better than random, then it should give you a reliability of 55 percent or better—especially in the 1- to 5-day time periods. If it doesn't do that, then it is no better than random, no matter how sound the concept seems to be.

When you do your entry testing, if entry reliability is your objective, then the only thing you are looking at is how often it is profitable after the selected time periods. You have no stops, so that is not a consideration. When you add stops, the reliability of your system will go down because some of your profitable trades will probably be stopped out at a loss. You also do not consider transaction costs (that is, slippage and commissions) in determining its reliability. As soon as you add transaction costs, your reliability will go down. You want to know that the reliability of your entry is significantly better than chance before these elements are added.

Some ideas seem so brilliant when you first observe them. You might find that you have a hundred examples of great moves. Your idea is common to all of them. As a result, you get very excited about it. However, you also must consider the false-positive rate. How often is your idea present when there is not a good move? If the false-positive rate is very high, then you don't have a great concept, and it might not be much better than chance.

One precaution you should keep in mind in using this kind of testing is that reliability is not the only consideration in your system. If your entry idea helps you capture giant moves, then it may be valuable.

Some people would argue that I've neglected an important step in system development: optimization. However, optimization really amounts to fitting your idea to the past. The more you do this, the less likely your system is to work in the future. Instead, I believe that you should work toward *understanding* your idea as much as possible. The more you understand the real nature of your edge, the less historical testing you will have to do.

I believe that you should work toward *understanding* your idea as much as possible. The more you understand the real nature of your edge, the less historical testing you will have to do.

8. DETERMINE WHAT YOUR INITIAL 1*R* RISK WILL BE

An important part of your idea is to know when it is not working. Thus, the next step is to understand the effect of adding a protective stop.[7] *Your protective stop is that part of your system that tells you when to get out of a trade in order to protect your capital.* It is a key portion of any system. It's that point at which you should get out in order to preserve capital because your idea doesn't seem to be working. The way you'll know your idea is not working depends upon the nature of your idea.

For example, suppose you have some theory that says there is "perfect" order to the market. You can pinpoint market turning points to the day—sometimes to the hour. In this case, your concept would give you a setup that is the time at which the market is supposed to move. Your entry signal should be a price confirmation that the market is indeed moving, such as a volatility breakout (as discussed in Chapter 9). At this point, you need a stop to tell you that your idea isn't working. What might you select? What if the market exited the time window without your making a significant profit? Then you'd probably want to get out because you didn't predict the turning point that was the reason for your entry. Or you might consider the average daily price range (such as the average true range) of the last 10 days to be the amount of noise in the market. If the price moved against you by that amount (or some multiple of that amount), you might want to get out.

Examples of protective stops are discussed extensively in Chapter 10. Read that chapter in detail, and pick one (or more) that best fits your idea. Or perhaps your idea leads to a logical stop point that isn't discussed in that chapter. If so, then use that logical stop point.

Think about what you are trying to accomplish with your entry. Is it fairly arbitrary? Do you think a major trend should be starting? If so, then you'll probably want to give the market lots of room so that the trend will develop. Thus, you'll want to use a very wide stop.

On the other hand, perhaps your idea is very precise. You expect to be wrong a lot, but when you are right, you don't expect to lose money on the trade. If that is the case, then you can have very close stops that don't lose much money when they are executed.

Once you've decided on the nature of your stop, add your stop plus transaction fees (that is, estimated slippage and commissions) to the calculations you did in the previous step and redo them. You'll probably find a significant drop in the reliability of your entry signal when you add in these values. For example, if your initial reliability was 60 percent, it will probably drop to 50 to 55 percent when you add your stop and the transaction costs to each trade.

At this stage of the process you've now determined what your initial risk, or *R*, will be for every trade you make. This is a huge step for you because you can now think of your profits as some multiple of your initial risk (or *R* multiples). For example, most good traders believe they should never take a trade unless it gives them a potential reward that is at least three times the size of their potential risk (3*R*). You'll learn later in this book that every system is really defined by the *R*-multiple distribution of the profits and losses it generates.

9. ADD YOUR PROFIT-TAKING EXITS AND DETERMINE THE *R*-MULTIPLE DISTRIBUTION OF YOUR SYSTEM AND ITS EXPECTANCY

The third part of your system should tell you when the move is over. As a result, the next step is to determine how you will take your profits. Exits are discussed extensively in Chapter 11, where you'll learn about what exits are most effective. Read through that chapter and determine what exits best fit your concept. Think about your personal situation—what you're trying to accomplish, your time frame for trading, and your idea—before you select your exit.

Generally, if you're a long-term trader or investor who is trying to capture a major trend or enjoy the rewards of long-term fundamental values, then you want a fairly wide stop. You don't want to be in and out of the market all the time if you can help it. You'll only make money on 30 to 50 percent of your positions, so you want your gains to be really big—as much as 20 times your average risk. If this is the case, your exits should be designed to capture some big profits.

On the other hand, if you are a day trader or scalper who is in and out quickly, then you'll want fairly tight stops. You expect to be right on better than 50 percent of your positions—in fact, you must be because you are not in the market long enough for huge rewards. Instead, you're looking for small losses with a reward-to-risk ratio of about 1. However, it is possible to make money 50 to 60 percent of the time, have your losses at minimal levels, and still capture a few trades that will give you big profits.

Overall what you are looking for when you add in your exits is to make the expectancy on your system as high as possible. *Expectancy* is the mean *R* multiple of your trading system. Or stated another way, it's the average amount of money you'll make in your system per trade—over many, many trades—per dollar risked. The exact formula for expectancy, plus the factors that go into it, are discussed extensively in Chapter 7. At this point in the model, however, your goal is simply to produce as high an expectancy as possible. You are also looking for as much opportunity as possible to trade (within a limited time frame) to realize that expectancy.

In my opinion, expectancy is controlled by your exits. Thus, the best systems have three or four different exits. You'll need to test the ones you select one at a time. You'll probably want to select them logically, based on your trading and/or investing idea. However, you'll want to test them with everything in place (up to this point) to determine what they do to your expectancy.

Once you determine your expectancy, look at your system results trade by trade. What is the makeup of the expectancy? Is it mostly made up of a lot of 1:1 or 2:1 reward-to-risk ratio trades? Or do you find that one or two really big trades make up most of the expectancy? If it's long term and you don't have enough contribution from big trades, then you probably need to modify your exits so that you can capture some of those big trades.[8]

10. DETERMINE THE ACCURACY OF YOUR *R*-MULTIPLE DISTRIBUTION

At this point you have the essence of a trading system because you should be able to determine the *R*-multiple distribution of that system. In other words, look at all of your historical profit and loss results. What does that distribution look like? Are your losses 1*R* or less, or do you tend to have losses that are bigger than 1*R*? What do your profits look like as a function of your initial risk? Do you have some occasional 20*R* trades? Or even 30*R* trades? Or do you have many 2*R* and 3*R* gains? What's the nature of the *R*-multiple distribution that you've produced?

You might have a lot of biases that influence your initial determination of your expectancy. As a result, you now need to determine the accuracy of your *R*-multiple distribution by trading it in real time with a very small size. What if you traded with 1 to 10 shares of stock or a single commodity contract? What kind of *R*-multiple distribution would you get doing that? Is it similar to the one you worked out theoretically or through historical testing? Does it have a good expectancy?

You also need to know what kind of *R*-multiple distribution your trading system produces in each kind of market. For example, markets can go up, down, or sideways. They can do so quietly or in a volatile manner. If you combine those elements, we now have six different types of markets:

- Up quiet
- Up volatile
- Sideways and quiet
- Sideways and volatile
- Down quiet
- Down volatile

You should know what to expect from your system in each of those types of markets. And this means a minimum of 30 *R* multiples from completed trades from each of those markets. And if you don't have that kind of data, then you at least need a theoretical understanding of how your system will perform in each of those markets before you begin trading. Will your system work in down volatile markets? Most systems, except for a few options systems, will not work in sideways, quiet markets. But you need to know that for sure.

11. EVALUATE YOUR OVERALL SYSTEM

Once you have a system, you need to determine how good it is. There are several ways you can do that.

The most naive way to determine how good your system may be is through its *win rate*. Here you'd decide that the system that wins most of the time will be the best system. However, in Chapter 1 on judgmental biases, we've already shown that you could have a system that's right 90 percent of the time and still lose money if you trade it enough. Thus, the win rate is not the best measure.

There are much better methods you can use to determine the quality of your system:

- The expectancy of the system. Isn't a system that produces an average gain of 2.3*R* per trade better than a system that produces an average gain of only 0.4*R*? Well, the answer is "Sometimes."
- How about the expected gain in terms of *R* at the end of a fixed time period? What if system 1 produces 20*R* in gains at the end of the month while system 2 produces 30*R*? Isn't system 2 better? Again the answer is "Sometimes" because it also depends on the variability of your system. For example, the system that produces an average gain of 30*R* might have a negative expectancy 30 percent of the time, while the system that produces an average gain of 20*R* might never have a negative expectancy.

Once you determine the accuracy of your system, and you know how it will perform in various kinds of markets and how it will perform compared with other possible systems, then it is time to work on meeting your objectives. And the way you will meet your objectives is through position sizing.

12. USE POSITION SIZING TO MEET YOUR OBJECTIVES

Your expectancy is a rough estimate of the true potential of your system. Once you develop an adequate system, then you need to determine what algorithm you will use to size your positions. Position sizing is the most important part of any system because it is through position sizing that you will meet your objectives or meet ruin. Position sizing is that part of your system that helps you meet your objectives.

How much size will you put on in any one position? Can you afford to even take a single position (that is, one share of stock

> Position sizing is the most important part of any system because it is through position sizing that you will meet your objectives or meet ruin. Position sizing is that part of your system that helps you meet your objectives.

or one futures contract)? These questions are keys to being able to achieve your objectives—whether you desire a triple-digit rate of return or a smooth equity curve. If your position-sizing algorithm is inappropriate, you will go bust no matter how you define "going bust" (whether it's losing 50 percent of your capital or all of it). But if your position-sizing techniques are well designed for your capital, your system, and your objectives, then you can generally meet your objectives.

Chapter 14 of this book discusses a number of position-sizing models that you may want to consider in the design of your system. Once you have defined your objectives and developed a high-expectancy system, you can use these models to accomplish your objectives. However, you need to apply and test various position-sizing models until you find something that perfectly fits what you want to accomplish.

13. DETERMINE HOW YOU CAN IMPROVE YOUR SYSTEM

The next task in developing your system is to determine how you can improve it. Market research is an ongoing process. Markets tend to change according to the character of the people who are playing them. For example, right now the stock market is dominated by professional mutual fund managers. However, of the 7,000 plus managers, fewer than 10 of them have been around long enough to have seen the prolonged bear markets that occurred in the 1970s. In addition, the futures market is dominated by professional CTAs—most of whom have trend-following strategies that they employ using very large amounts of money. In another 10 to 20 years, the markets might have quite different participants and thus take on a different character.

Any system with a good, positive expectancy generally will improve its performance if more trades are taken in a given period of time. Thus, you can usually improve performance by adding independent markets. In fact, a good system will perform well in many different markets, so adding many markets simply gives you more opportunity.

In addition, performance can usually be improved by adding noncorrelated systems—each with its own unique position-sizing model. For example, if you have a major trend-following system with a very short-term system that takes advantage of consolidating markets, then you'll probably do very well when you combine them. The hope is that your short-term system will make money when there are no trending markets. This will lessen the impact of any drawdowns produced by the trending system during these periods, or perhaps you might even make money overall. In either case, your performance will be better because you will move into trends with a higher capital base.

14. MENTALLY PLAN FOR YOUR WORST-CASE SCENARIO

It's important to think about what your system could do under a variety of circumstances. How will you expect your system to perform in all types of market conditions—highly volatile markets, consolidating markets, strong trending markets, very thin markets with no interest? You won't really know what to expect from your system unless you understand how it's likely to perform under each possible market condition.

Tom Basso was fond of telling students in our system workshop to think about their system this way:

> Imagine what it's like to take the other side of each trade. Pretend you just bought it (instead of sold it) or pretend that you just sold it (instead of bought it). How would you feel? What would your thinking be like?

This exercise is one of the most important exercises you can do. I strongly recommend that you take it seriously.

You also need to plan for every possible catastrophe that might come up. For example, how would your system perform should the market have a 1- or 2-day price shock (that is, a very large move) against you? Think about how you could tolerate an unexpected, once-in-a-lifetime move in the market, like a 500-point drop in the

Dow (it has happened twice in 10 years!) or another crude oil disaster as we saw during the Gulf War in Kuwait. Because of the current commodities boom, oil is now as high as $70 per barrel. What if world demand pushes it to $150 per barrel? How will that affect you and your trading? What if we have large inflation again to wipe out our debt? What would happen to your system if currencies were stabilized by linking them to gold and you were a currency trader? Or what if a meteor lands in the middle of the Atlantic and wipes out half of the population of Europe and the United States? Or what about more mundane things such as your communications being shut down or your computers being stolen?

You have to think about what the worst possible scenario could be for your system and how you would handle it. Brainstorm and determine every possible scenario you can think of that would be disastrous for your system. When you have your list of disasters, develop several plans that you can implement for each one. Plan your response in your mind and rehearse them. Once you've established your actions in the event of an unexpected calamity, your system is complete.

NOTES

1. There is a lot more to modeling excellence than just finding out what the key tasks are. You need to find the components of each task, and you need to be able to install the model in other people. We've been able to accomplish this with the system development model. However, the topic of model development would be an entire book by itself.
2. The references to all of these books are given in the Recommended Readings at the end of the book.
3. Chande's book is very good, but I don't agree with all his conclusions, especially when he starts testing portfolios and developing conclusions about position sizing.
4. These people may have purchased a dozen low-capitalization stocks. Eleven may turn out to be worthless, while one turns into a new giant. Because the stocks were largely ignored, the owner neither gets rid of the losers before they become worthless nor finds out about the winner until it is worth a lot of money.
5. Somehow fate is often cruel to people with such a great system. In this person's case, he could not trade size. Nor was it possible for him to

fix his problem psychologically because he did not believe that he had anything to do with the problem. In fact, at this point he cannot trade at all because he's nervous and he believes that his stomach is stopping him from trading. Thus, in my opinion, he doesn't understand the real meaning behind a Holy Grail system—finding yourself in the market.

6. One of my clients has developed a day-trading system based on gains being significantly larger than losses. His system has a reliability rate of less than 50 percent, yet it nets him tremendous rates of return. This shows that there are other ways to conceive of short-term systems.
7. The word *stop* is used here because most people execute such stops by putting in a stop order in the market. This means "Execute my order as a market order once it reaches that price."
8. If you are looking at your expectancy based on the results of real trading (that is, what you have been doing in the market), then a low expectancy (15 cents per dollar risked or less) could be due to psychological problems such as not following your system or panicking and taking profits too early.

CHAPTER 5

Selecting a Concept That Works

The more you understand the concept you are trading, how it might behave under all sorts of market conditions, the less historical testing you need to do.

Tom Basso

My estimate is that fewer than 20 percent of the people trading the markets have a system to guide their trading or investing. Of those who do, most are just using predefined indicators and don't understand the concepts behind their system. As a result, I asked a number of experts to write about the concepts that they trade. This is not an exhaustive discussion of the various concepts you might trade. It is just a sampling. Your goal in reading this chapter should be to think about each concept and determine if it fits your personality and your beliefs. The concept that fits will be the one you have the most success trading. But you must understand your concept thoroughly before you develop a system using it.

While I was writing the first edition of this book, I received a phone call from an expert on chaos theory. He said that he had been following my work for many years. He believed that I had a lot of integrity but that I was very wrong about systems. He said that it was ridiculous to assume that any sort of system was possible—instead, it was all about luck and individual psychology. I said that I agreed with him if he were defining *system* as just an entry technique. Instead, I said, one had to develop a methodology with a positive expectancy[1] through stops and exits in order to make psychology and position sizing meaningful.

Most people try to find a high-probability entry signal as their system. They typically have no concept of an exit or of adequate position sizing. This usually leads to a trading methodology with a negative expectancy. In contrast, people who understand the role that exits and position sizing play in systems can be quite satisfied with an entry system that produces only 40 percent winners. I think my caller was a little stunned, but he then went on to say that I was wrong: "People cannot develop any sort of expectancy based on past data," he said.[2] Yet interestingly enough, this person had still written a book about how to make "big" money from the market through understanding chaos theory.

I found the conversation quite interesting. I thought that I was one of the most open people around because I come from the viewpoint that *you can trade ANY concept as long as you have a positive expectancy.* What I learned is that even this basic assumption about being able to trade any concept with a positive expectancy is still an assumption—an assumption that forms the basis for my thinking about systems. As I've said before, we can trade only through our beliefs. Keeping that assumption in mind, let's look at a few trading concepts that are used by many traders and investors.

TREND FOLLOWING

I've contacted some great traders (and wonderful friends) to write about these various concepts. You've already met Tom Basso, since he was interviewed in Chapter 3. Tom and I have done about 20 workshops together, and I can testify from personal experience that he is the most balanced trader I have ever met. Although Tom is now retired, when he was trading, he was the most mechanical trader I've ever met. Everything in his office was computerized. Even the trading orders went out to the broker via computer-generated fax. Tom traded two computerized trend-following systems, so I thought he was the most logical choice to write on trend following.[3]

Tom Basso: The Philosophy of Trend Following

Many successful investors fall into a group called *trend followers*. In the following discussion I will attempt to describe what trend following is all about and why investors should be interested in using these general principles in their investing endeavors.

Let's break down the term *trend following* into its components. The first part is *trend*. Every trader needs a trend to make money. If you think about it, no matter what the technique, if there is not a trend after you buy, then you will not be able to sell at higher prices. You will take a loss on the trade. There must be a trend up after you buy in order to sell at higher prices. Conversely, if you sell first, then there must be a subsequent trend down for you to buy back at lower prices.

Following is the next part of the term. We use this word because trend followers always wait for the trend to shift first, then they "follow" it. If the market is moving down and then indicates a major shift to the upside, the trend follower immediately buys that market. In doing so, the trader follows the trend.

"Let your profits run. Cut your losses short." This old trader's axiom describes trend following perfectly. Trend-following indicators tell the investor when the direction of a market has shifted from up to down or from down to up. Various charts or mathematical representations of the market are used to measure the current direction and observe the shift. Once in a trend, the trader sits back and enjoys the ride, as long as the trend keeps going in the trader's direction. This is "letting profits run."

I once heard a new investor questioning a very successful trend follower. The trend follower had just bought some foreign currency contracts, and the novice asked, "Where's your objective on this trade?" The trend follower wisely answered, "To the moon. I've never had one get there yet, but maybe some day . . ." That tells a lot about the philosophy of trend following. If the market cooperates, the trend follower would get into the trade as soon as the market met his or her criteria for "trending" and would stay in it for the rest of his or her life.

Unfortunately, the trend usually ends at some point. As a result, when the direction shifts, then the cutting-losses-short aspect of the axiom should come into play. The trader, sensing that the direction of the market has shifted against the position, immediately liquidates. If the position is ahead at that point, then the trader has made a profit. If, at the time, the position is behind, then the trader has aborted the trade, preventing a runaway loss. Either way, the trader is out of a position that is currently going against him or her.

The Advantage of Trend Following

The advantage of trend following is simple: you will never miss a major move of any market. If the market you are watching turns from a down to an up direction, any trend-following indicator must flash a buy signal. It's just a question of when. If it's a major move, you will get the signal. The longer term the trend-following indicators are, the lower the transaction costs—a definite advantage of trend following.

Strategically, the investor must realize that if he or she can get onboard a major move in almost any market, the profits from just one trade can be substantial. In essence, one trade can make your whole year. Thus, the reliability of one's strategy can be far below 50 percent and you'll still show a profit. This is because the average size of one's winning trades is so much greater than the size of one's losing trades.

The Disadvantage of Trend Following

The disadvantage of trend following is that your indicator cannot detect the difference between a major profitable move and a short-lived unprofitable move. As a result, trend followers often get whipsawed as signals immediately turn against them, resulting in small losses. Multiple whipsaws can add up, creating concern for the trend follower and tempting him or her to abandon the strategy.

Most markets spend a large amount of time in nontrending conditions. Trending periods could be as little as 15 to 25 percent of the time. Yet the trend follower must be willing to trade in these unfavorable markets so as not to miss the big trend.

Does Trend Following Still Work?

Absolutely! First, if there were no trends, there would be no need for organized markets. Producers could sell to the marketplace without worrying about having to hedge to protect themselves. End users would know that they could obtain the products they need at a reasonable price. And people would buy shares of companies purely for the income from dividends. Thus, should trends disappear for any length of time, those markets would probably cease to exist.

Second, if there were no trends, you could expect a fairly random distribution of price changes. Yet if you look at the distribution of price changes over time in almost any market, you'll see a very long tail in the direction of large price changes. This is because there are abnormally large price changes that you'd never expect to see by chance over a given period of time. For example, the S&P futures market opened in 1982, and within five years it had a price move that you might expect to see once every hundred years. These abnormally large price changes over a short period of time are what make trend following work, and you see them all the time.

Is Trend Following for Everyone?

Trend following is probably one of the easiest techniques for the new trader or investor to understand and use. The longer term the indicators, the less that total transaction costs will affect profits. Short-term models tend to have difficulty overcoming the costs of many transactions. Costs include not only commissions but also slippage on the trades. The fewer trades you make, provided you have the patience for it, the less you spend in transaction costs and the easier it is for you to make a profit.

There are numerous examples where trend following is not appropriate. Floor traders who are scalping ticks are not likely to use a trend-following concept. Hedging investors may find it more risky to hedge their risk by using trend-following indicators than by choosing some form of passive economic hedge approach. Day traders may find it difficult to use trend-following models. When day trading, you cannot let profits run due to the time limits of day trading. The day simply ends, forcing the trader to liquidate the position.

If trend following fits your personality and your needs, then give it a try. There are many examples of successful traders and investors who consistently use this time-tested approach to the markets. With the economic world becoming more unstable, there are constantly new trends for the trend follower to exploit.

Editor's Comments

Trend following is probably the most successful technique for trading or investing of all the concepts discussed. In fact, almost all the system models presented later in this book work because of trend following. As Basso points out, the biggest problem with it is that markets don't always trend. However, this is generally not a problem for people who play the stock market. There are thousands of stocks that you can trade—on either the long or the short side. If you are willing to go both long and short, then there are always good trending markets.

The difficulty many people have with the stock market is that (1) there are times when few stocks are trending up so that the best opportunities are only on the short side; (2) people don't understand shorting so they avoid it; (3) the exchange regulators make it difficult to short (that is, you have to be able to borrow the stock to short and you have to short on an uptick); and (4) retirement accounts typically prohibit shorting. Nevertheless, if you plan for short selling, then it can be very lucrative under the right market conditions.

FUNDAMENTAL ANALYSIS

I've asked another friend, Charles LeBeau, to write the section on fundamental analysis. LeBeau is well known as a former editor of a great newsletter entitled the *Technical Traders Bulletin.* He is also a coauthor of an excellent book, *Computer Analysis of the Futures Market.* Chuck is a talented speaker, and he frequently gives talks at investment conferences. And he has been a guest speaker at many of our How to Develop a Winning Trading System That Fits You workshops. Chuck is now retired and lives near Sedona, Arizona. When he was an active trader, he was a commodity trading advisor (CTA), and later on he had his own hedge fund.[4]

You might wonder why I asked Chuck, who has such an extensive technical background, to write about fundamental analysis.

Chuck used to lecture about fundamental analysis for a major university, and he also ran a discretionary fundamentally based trading system for Island View Financial Group. In Chuck LeBeau's words, "I prefer to think of myself as a trader who is willing to use the best tools available to get the job done."

Charles LeBeau: Introduction to Fundamental Trading

Fundamental analysis, as it applies to futures trading, is the use of actual and/or anticipated relationships of supply and demand to forecast the direction and magnitude of future price changes. There may be more precise and detailed definitions, but this brief overview is intended to be about the benefits and practical applications of fundamental analysis.

Almost all traders mistakenly assume that they must be either fundamentalists who rely solely on supply-demand analysis or technicians who ignore fundamentals entirely and make their decisions based solely on price action. Who forces us to make such unnecessary and illogical either-or decisions about how best to trade? If you ever have two or more good ideas, you will almost certainly be better off if you do them all rather than falling into the either-or trap.[5]

Fundamental analysis has a distinct advantage over technical analysis in the area of determining price objectives. Correctly interpreted, technical indicators can give you direction and timing, but they will fall short in giving you any indication of the magnitude of the anticipated price movement. Some technicians claim that their methods give them price objectives, but after 40 years of trading, I have yet to find any technical methods that were valid at forecasting price objectives. However, there is no question that good fundamental analysis can help you determine approximate profit objectives. By employing fundamental price targets, you should have a general idea of whether you want to take a quick, small profit or hold for a major long-term price objective. As limited as the accuracy of fundamental price targeting might be, having even a general idea of the magnitude of the profit you are expecting is a big advantage in successful trading.

Fundamental analysis does have definite limitations. The results of the best possible fundamental analysis will be painfully imprecise. If you do everything right, or better yet, rely on the sophisticated analysis of a true fundamental expert, you might be able to conclude that a particular market will probably make a "big" move in an upward direction at some vague time in the future. At its best, fundamental analysis will tell you only the direction and general magnitude of future price movements. It will rarely tell you when the price movement will begin or exactly how far prices will travel. However, knowing the direction and general magnitude of future price changes is certainly critical information that can be invaluable to a trader. Our logical combination of fundamental and technical analysis will supply several important pieces of the trading puzzle—with position sizing (covered elsewhere in this book) being the missing piece.

How to Employ Fundamental Analysis

Let's deal with the practical aspect of successfully employing fundamental analysis. The suggestions that follow are based upon many years of actual trading with fundamentals and are not necessarily listed in order of importance.

Avoid Doing Your Own Fundamental Analysis Even If You Have Some Highly Specialized Training I've been trading futures for 40 years and frequently lecture on fundamental analysis to graduate students at a major university, yet I wouldn't think of doing my own fundamental analysis. True fundamental experts, who are much better qualified than you or I, are devoting full time to this task, and their conclusions are readily available at no cost.

Start looking around to find qualified experts whose fundamental analysis is available to the public. Call the major brokerage firms and ask them to put you on their mailing lists. Get a trial subscription to *Consensus* and read all the analyses. Pick out the ones you like and weed out the weaker sources. Look for analysts who are willing to make helpful forecasts and don't beat around the bush all the time. Remember that you only need one good source of fundamental information for each market. If you get input from too many sources, you will receive conflicting input and become confused and indecisive.

News and Fundamental Analysis Are Not the Same Thing Fundamental analysis *predicts* price direction, while news *follows* price direction. When I was a senior executive at a major commodity firm, the media would often phone me after the markets had closed and ask why a particular market had gone up or down that day. If the market had gone up, I would give them some bullish news that had come to my attention. If the market had gone down, I would give them some bearish news. There is always plenty of bullish and bearish news floating around the markets each day. *What gets reported in the papers is whatever "news" happens to correlate with the direction of the prices for that day.*

You will also observe that pending news will move a market longer and further than actual reported news. The anticipation of bullish news can support a market for weeks or even months. When the bullish news is eventually reported, the market may well move in the opposite direction. That's why the old adage of "Buy the rumor, sell the fact" seems to work so well. (Of course, the same logic applies to bearish news as well.)

Be Careful about Reacting to Fundamental Reports For example, let's assume that a crop report has just been released showing that the soybean crop is going to be 10 percent smaller than it was last year. At first glance this might seem to be very bullish because the supply of beans was being reduced substantially. But if the traders and analysts involved in this market had expected the report to show 15 percent fewer beans, the prices might decline severely on the "bullish" report. *Before you can analyze the bullishness or bearishness of a report, you have to be aware of what the expectations are and put the report into the context of the expectations.* Also, don't judge the bullishness or bearishness of a report by the initial reaction. Give the market some time to digest the news. You will often find that the first reaction to a report is either overdone or incorrect.

Look for Markets That Are Encountering Rising Levels of Demand Demand is the motivator that makes for long sustained uptrends that are easy to trade for big profits. *Demand-driven markets are the markets where you can make long-term trades that produce unusually high levels of profitability.* Of course, markets will also rise because of supply shortages, but you will often find that price rallies motivated by supply concerns tend to be short lived and the long-term price forecasts in these supply-shortage markets are generally overestimated. *Look for demand-driven markets to trade.*

Timing Is Important, So Be Patient with Your Fundamental Scenario The best fundamental analysts seem to be able to forecast price trends much more easily than most market participants. Of course, this is an advantage if you are careful about your timing. However, if you are impulsive and enter the market too soon, you can lose a great deal of money over the short run. Be patient and let your technical indicators tell you when the market is beginning to trend in the direction it should. Remember, the goal is not to be the first to have the correct forecast. The goal is to make money and keep your risk under control. *You may have to wait weeks or even months to take advantage of an accurate fundamental forecast.* Acting too soon could easily turn an accurate forecast into a losing trade.

Many Forecasts of Major Price Changes Fail to Materialize for One Reason or Another If you have done a good job of finding accurate sources of fundamental information on a broad group of markets, you might expect to become informed of 8 to 10 forecasts of a major price change in a typical year. Of these forecasts, only 6 or 7 are likely to occur. But if you can manage to get positioned in half of those in a timely fashion and then do a good job of letting the profits run, you should have an extremely profitable year.

Be Decisive and Willing to Take Your Share of Losses Don't be afraid to chase after markets that are moving with big fundamental potential. Many traders, fundamental or technical, lack the nerve or discipline to get into a market once it has started running. It is human nature to want to get in at more favorable prices and to postpone your entry waiting for a pullback that may never come. You must have confidence and the courage to take action promptly. The best analysis, fundamental or technical, is worthless in the hands of an indecisive "trader." If in doubt, start with a small position and then add to it later.

I hope this brief introduction to fundamental analysis has provoked an idea or two and perhaps convinced you that fundamental analysis might have a place in your trading plan. If so, I would strongly urge you to learn more about this topic. The best book, in my opinion, on the topic is entitled *Schwager on Futures: Fundamental Analysis*[6] by Jack Schwager. Anyone interested in using fundamentals in trading should find this well-written book extremely helpful.

Editor's Comments

Chuck LeBeau's comments apply primarily to futures trading and could be used in the methodology developed by Gallacher that is presented later in this book. If you are a stock market trader or investor, look at the value section presented next. In addition, two systems that involve fundamentals will be presented later for your consideration—William O'Neil's CANSLIM system and Warren Buffett's business model. Buffett's model is almost totally fundamental, while O'Neil's model relies on fundamentals for setups.

VALUE TRADING

Value trading is one of the major methods used by portfolio managers to trade the stock market. Basically, your goal is to buy when something is undervalued and sell it when it's at fair value or when it is overvalued. If you are willing to short stock, you can also short it when it is overvalued and buy it back when it reaches fair value or becomes undervalued. Many people do the former and few do the latter. I chose to write this section myself as I trade the "value concept" in the retirement funds I manage for my company.

What Works in Value Investing

Many of the greatest investors in the history of the stock market would probably call themselves "value traders." The list would include Warren Buffett and his mentor Benjamin Graham. It would also include such luminaries as Sir John Marks Templeton and great investors such as Michael Price, Mario Gabellio, John Neff, Larry Tisch, Marty Whitman, David Dreman, Jim Rogers, and Michael Steinhardt—just to name a few. All of these masters are the same in that they emphasize value. Yet all of them are different because they define value a little bit differently. In this brief section on value investing, I will touch on the ideas that I believe work and the ideas that I believe do not work. I'd also like to add a few precautions that, in my opinion, will make any form of value investing more successful.

First, let's talk about what works. What works all the time in value investing, assuming you have a little patience, is buying something at a huge discount to what it is worth. But, of course, the key question you must ask yourself is how you determine worth. In my book *Safe Strategies for Financial Freedom*, I talk extensively about one of Benjamin Graham's famous techniques for making money—*Graham's number technique*. In this case, value is really simple: What's the liquidation value of the company? If you were to sell all of the company's assets within the next year, how much could you get for it? You can actually find this information when you look up a company at Yahoo or *BusinessWeek*. It's called the *company's current assets*. If you took the company's current assets and subtracted its total debt, then you'd have a great idea about what the company is worth if you liquidated it within the next year.

Now what if you determined that a company's liquidation value is $10 per share and also discovered that company's stock is currently selling for $7 per share? That's what I call a *value play*. You can actually buy the stock at 70 cents on the dollar based upon the company's liquidation value. That's real value, and those stocks tend to be easy to find when the market is depressed. For example, when we were writing *Safe Strategies for Financial Freedom* in April 2003, we found a list of four stocks that made it through our screening. The market was starting to turn, so we were able to look at those same stocks nine weeks later on June 20—just before the book was to go to press. Nine weeks later those four stocks were up 86.25 percent while the S&P 500 was up only 15 percent over the same time period. However, I want to point out that this occurred at the bottom of a bear market decline and there have not been many stocks meeting these criteria since that time.

Finding stocks that are selling at a substantial discount to their liquidation value is an extreme form of value trading. There are other methods. For example, you could screen stocks that list assets on their books at an extreme discount to the true value. This could be done with land values, for example. What if a company lists its land assets at $1,000 per acre while the actual value is $50,000 per acre? If you can find such discounts, then you know you also have a highly undervalued stock. For example, several companies that own lots of land that they discount on their books include St. Joe (owns 3 percent of Florida carried on its books at $2 per acre), Alexander and Baldwin (owns Hawaiian land carried on its books at $150 per acre), and Tejon Ranch (has huge land holdings carried on its books at $25 per acre). Basically, if you buy these companies, you are buying land at almost nothing compared to what it is worth.[7]

How to Improve What Works

One clear technique to improve value trading for any investor is to observe the following precaution: Never buy an undervalued stock when it is going down. For example, if you find a stock selling at 70 percent of its liquidation value, you don't necessarily want to buy it the next day. Yes, it's a cheap stock, but it's cheap because people are selling it for various reasons. That could continue for some time in the future. And just because it is undervalued today doesn't mean that it won't be more undervalued in two or three months.

Instead, let the stock prove itself. Get some indication from the market that the downtrend is over. I will never buy a value stock unless it has proven itself to me. At minimum, I want my stock to have formed at least a two-month base, meaning that it has stayed in the same price range for two months. Even better, I'd prefer a stock to be going up for at least two months before I buy it. Now a pure value investor might get very upset at this idea, saying, "You could have gotten it cheaper!" That's true, but we used that concept when we bought our value stocks in April 2003. Had we bought them much earlier, we could have held them for a year or more with no gains. It's your choice, but remember that you trade only your beliefs about the markets, and you must determine whether or not your beliefs are useful.

Incidentally, if you use this concept of letting the market prove itself, you have a huge advantage over most portfolio managers who do value investing. The large portfolio manager might be purchasing millions of dollars' worth of stock, and his purchase of the stock might have a significant impact on the price of the stock. As a result, he does not dare wait until the price starts going up. However, if you are only purchasing a small amount of the stock (that is, fewer than 10,000 shares), then you can afford to wait until the stock starts to move up. In fact, your clue may be that the big institutional investors have started to move into the stock you've discovered.

What Doesn't Work in Value Investing

Wall Street pays stock analysts huge salaries to try to determine when something is undervalued. These analysts look at things like future products that will be introduced, the potential market for those products, and what selling that product could do for the company's price in the next year. They sift through piles and piles of fundamental data in order to make forecasts about future earnings. And based on these forecasts of future earnings, they can then say, "This stock is undervalued" or "This stock is overvalued."

In my many years of experience as a trading coach, I've seen no evidence that this approach works. Most analysts are just guessing at many of the variables they look at. They say that company officials lie to them. But even if that didn't happen, there is still no evidence (in my opinion) that their forecasts about future earnings are that meaningful in terms of the future performance of the stock. So if you want my advice, don't play this game of value investing. It's not a real measure of value.

BAND TRADING

Markets only trend about 15 percent of the time. So what do you do the other 85 percent of the time? You could not trade or you could find a strategy that works most of the time in most markets. One such strategy is band trading. D. R. Barton teaches our short-term trading workshops (Swing Trading and Day Trading) and has been involved with using band trading for some time. D.R. even writes a newsletter based on a band trading technique that he has developed and tested.[8] Consequently, I thought he'd be a good choice to write this section.

D. R. Barton, Jr.: An Overview of Band Trading

Traders and investors are often interested in a methodology that is effective across most market conditions. Band trading (also known as *range trading*) is one strategy that works in a great majority of market environments. We'll describe those conditions in detail below. But first, let's define *band trading* and look at the market beliefs that make band trading effective.

A band trading strategy attempts to buy at the bottom of a trading range and sell at the top of the range. Band trading is based on the belief that the market moves much like a rubber band or a spring—stretching to a certain point and then pulling back. This type of action is easy to see and understand in a sideways market. The second half of the chart in Figure 5.1 shows price moving in a

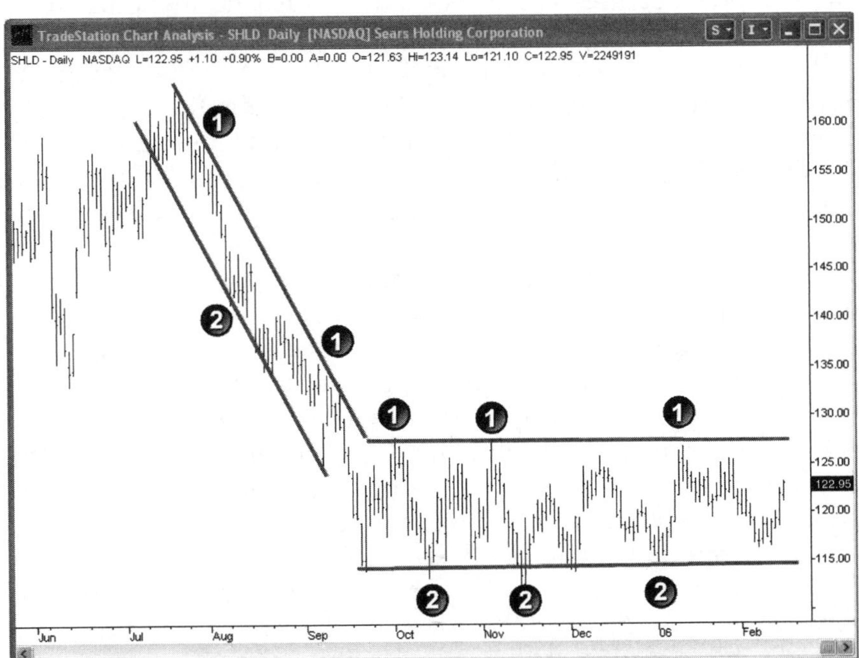

Figure 5.1 Illustrates both a trending band and a consolidation band

distinct sideways channel. Price moves to the top of the range (point 1), retraces to the bottom of the range (point 2), and then repeats the cycle (1 to 2 to 1).

While using bands for sideways markets is fairly well known, fewer folks know that band trading can be very effective in trending markets as well. Even when trending, markets rarely move straight up or straight down. More common is the "three steps up, two steps back" action that characterizes most trends. Looking again at Figure 5.1, you can see that price is clearly in a downtrend early in the chart. However, we can still observe the same pattern of price movement that we saw in the sideways market: up to the top band (point 1), down to the lower band (point 2), and repeat back down to the lower band at point 2. This behavior of stretch and retrace, stretch and retrace gives us a repeatable action in the market that we can exploit.

Join the Bands: How Bands Are Defined

Trading ranges can be represented visually and mathematically by three broad categories: channels, static bands, and dynamic bands. Channels are typically defined by a single price at the upper channel and another at the lower channel. These two channels remain stationary until they are redefined. An example is the well-known *Donchian channel* that uses the high of the last *x* number of days as the upper channel and the low of the last *x* number of days as the lower channel. A channel only changes when a new high or low is made.

Static bands consist of an upper and lower band, and each of these bands is drawn a set distance from a central (or basis) line. This type of band configuration is also called an *envelope*. Figure 5.2 shows the most common static band or envelope setup: a simple moving average with upper and lower bands drawn at a user-defined percentage above and below the moving average line (the chart shows a 20-day simple moving average, SMA, with bands drawn at 5 percent of price above and below the SMA).

Dynamic bands start out the same as static bands—with a basis line (typically an SMA). But with dynamic bands, the distance between the basis line and the upper and lower bands varies—most typically as a function of current volatility. The most common type of dynamic bands is *Bollinger Bands*, named for their originator, John

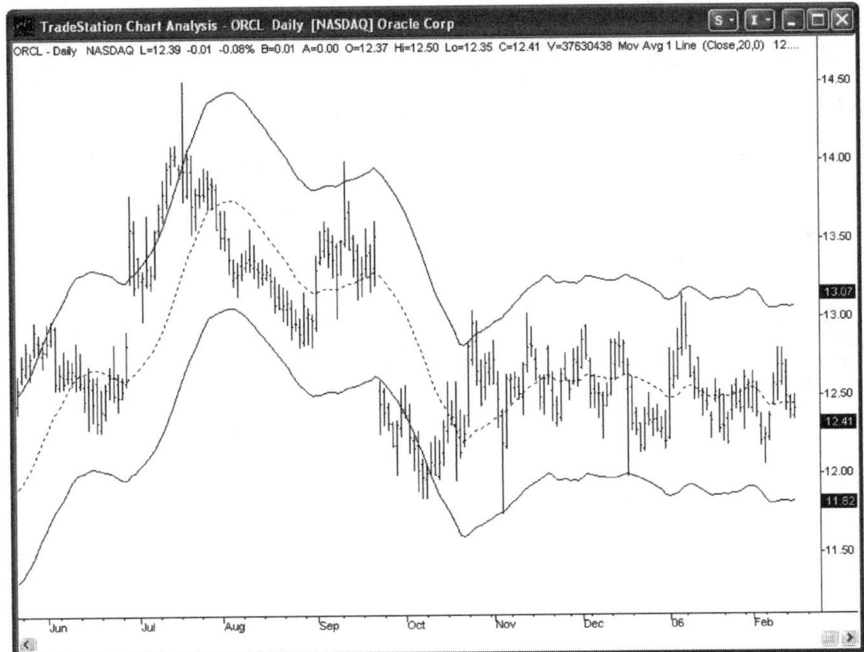

Figure 5.2 An example of static moving average bands: 20-day simple moving average bands at ± 5 percent

Bollinger. Figure 5.3 shows a set of Bollinger Bands using the default settings: the basis line represented by a 20-day simple moving average, with the upper and lower bands drawn 2 standard deviations above and below the basis line. (The *standard deviation* is a statistical measure that is commonly used to quantify volatility.) Another common type of dynamic band uses average true range (ATR) to vary the upper and lower band distance from the basis line.

Figure 5.3 shows how Bollinger Bands adjust as volatility expands or contracts. Note how close together the bands are in times of low volatility (point 1) and how the bands widen when volatility expands (point 2).

How to Trade Using Bands

I have seen all three types of bands used effectively in trading systems. I personally write a newsletter based on using adaptive

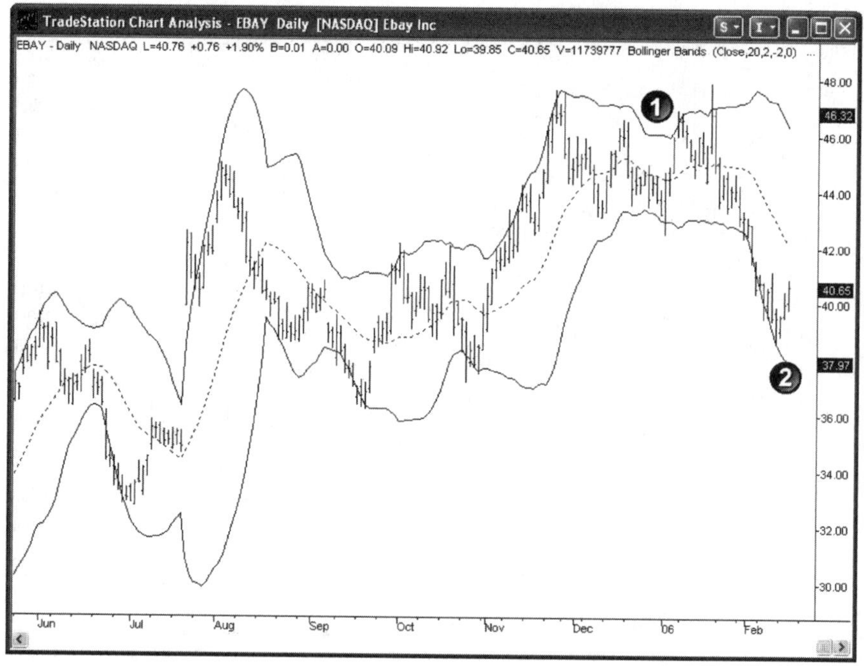

Figure 5.3 Bollinger Bands as an example of dynamic bands

dynamic bands (though not Bollinger Bands) that has both tested well and traded well in real time. Here are some guidelines for trading using bands.

Whether you use static or dynamic bands, setting the width of the bands is a large part of the art and science of band trading. There are trade-offs in selecting the band width: using a one-size-fits-all parameter, such as a 5 percent moving average envelope, ensures against curve fitting test parameters. But using 1 percentage for both volatile and less volatile instruments can lead to overtrading the volatile markets and undertrading the less volatile ones. Using an optimized band width for each market would almost certainly lead to overoptimized parameters that are not very robust in real-time trading. A useful compromise might be to find an optimum value for a sector of stocks or group of commodities with similar volatility.

You can make a band trade entry in two ways: pure countertrend entries or retracement entries. In a pure countertrend entry, you would sell (or short) the stock or commodity at the first touch of the upper band, or buy it after a touch of the lower band. In the retrace option, you would wait and enter after a prescribed retracement back into the channel between the bands after a band had been touched or penetrated. The key question you must ask yourself here is, "Do I want the position to be moving in my favor before I enter into my band trade?"

Once you are into a band trade, you ideally want to hold the position until it moves to the other band. Then you'd actually reverse your position. And in the ideal world, you'd watch the price go up, selling at the upper band, and then down, buying at the lower band. You'd have a profitable long trade, followed by a profitable short trade, followed by a profitable long trade, and so on. You'd have a nice stream of uninterrupted profits.

However, the world is not ideal, and band traders have to ask themselves all of the following questions:

- What if the bands are never touched?
- What if the bands break down and stop being accurate?
- What if the price goes in my direction after entry, but doesn't come near the other band?
- And what if the price goes right through the band and keeps going?

Wise band traders must deal with all of these issues. And they do so by having a thorough understanding of the concept they are trading. You need to understand how your concept should work and when you are wrong. You need to understand the nature of the band and what to do if the band concept you are trading stops working. And you need to understand all of the worst-case scenarios that could happen when you are band trading. If you understand all of this, then you can take the concept and develop it into a methodology that really fits you.

The Strengths and Weaknesses of Band Trading

Band trading can be the foundation of your trading toolbox or a useful complement to other strategies. To wrap up this section, let's look at the pros and cons of band trading.

Strengths of Band Trading Band trading is effective in many more market conditions than trend-following strategies. It works in up, down, and sideways markets as long as there is enough volatility to produce a usable band. This, along with more frequent opportunities to trade, allows a successful band trader to produce a smoother, less volatile equity curve than a trend follower. Therefore, band traders can often use more aggressive position-sizing strategies and have a lower account equity requirement to successfully implement their strategy.

Weaknesses of Band Trading Band trading requires entries that are countertrend in nature. You sell after a move up and buy after a move down. This is very difficult for many trend followers. There are some stocks and commodities that do not trend very well and make poor trend-following candidates. Likewise, there are those that have ranges that are too tight for band trading or do not trade well in ranges (they frequently extend far past bands, for example). These can be identified only through experience and/or backtesting.

Editor's Comments

Band trading typically gives you lots of trading opportunities, and it is excellent for short-term traders. Thus, if you like (1) lots of trading activity, (2) selling highs, and (3) buying lows, then some form of band trading might be right for you.

If you look at the charts, you'll see many examples that work very well and many examples that do not work at all. Your job as a band trader would be to (1) maximize the good trades and (2) minimize the losing trades by either filtering them out or reducing their impact through your exits. But those are topics for later in this book because they are important for any system you might develop.

SEASONAL TENDENCIES

In my opinion, Moore Research Center, Inc., located in Eugene, Oregon, is the leading center for research on seasonal tendencies in the market. It specializes in computerized analysis of futures, cash, and stock prices. Since 1989 it has published a monthly report with studies on specific futures complexes that go all over the world. It also does great research on probabilistic tendencies in the market. As a result, I approached Steve Moore about doing this chapter. Steve said that the center had a specialist for communicating with the public—Jerry Toepke, the editor of Moore Research Center Publications. Jerry has authored many articles and has spoken at several conferences.[9] Some of the graphs in this section are a bit old, but the points being illustrated are still valid and that's what's important.

Jerry Toepke: Why Seasonals Work

The seasonal approach to markets is designed to anticipate future price movement rather than constantly reacting to an endless stream of often contradictory news. Although numerous factors affect the markets, certain conditions and events recur at annual intervals. Perhaps the most obvious is the annual cycle of weather from warm to cold and back to warm. However, the calendar also marks the annual passing of important events, such as the due date for U.S. income taxes every April 15. Such annual events create yearly cycles in supply and demand. Enormous supplies of grain at harvest dwindle throughout the year. Demand for heating oil typically rises as cold weather approaches but subsides as inventory is filled. Monetary liquidity may decline as taxes are paid but rise as the Federal Reserve recirculates funds.

These annual cycles in supply and demand give rise to seasonal price phenomena—to a greater or lesser degree and in a more or less timely manner. An annual pattern of changing conditions, then, may cause a more or less well-defined annual pattern of price responses. Thus, *seasonality* may be defined as a market's natural rhythm, the established tendency for prices to move in the same direction at a similar time every year. As such, it becomes a valid principle subject to objective analysis in any market.

In a market strongly influenced by annual cycles, seasonal price movement may become more than just an effect of seasonal cause. It can become so ingrained as to be nearly a fundamental condition in its own right—almost as if the market had a memory of its own. Why? Once consumers and producers fall into a pattern, they tend to rely on it, almost to the point of becoming dependent on it. Vested interests then maintain it.

Patterns imply a degree of predictability. Future prices move when anticipating change and adjust when that change is realized. When those changes are annual in nature, a recurring cycle of anticipation and realization evolves. This recurring phenomenon is intrinsic to the seasonal approach to trading, for it is designed to anticipate, enter, and capture recurrent trends as they emerge and to exit as they are realized.

The first step, of course, is to find a market's seasonal price pattern. In the past, weekly or monthly high and low prices were used to construct relatively crude studies. Such analysis might suggest, for instance, that cattle prices in April were higher than in March 67 percent of the time and higher than in May 80 percent of the time. Computers, however, can now derive a daily seasonal pattern of price behavior from a composite of daily price activity over several years. Properly constructed, such a pattern provides historical perspective on a market's annual price cycle.

The four primary components of any cycle are (1) its low point, (2) its rise, (3) its high point, and (4) its decline. When translated into a seasonal price pattern, those components become a seasonal low, a seasonal rise, a seasonal high, and a seasonal decline. A seasonal pattern, then, graphically illustrates an established tendency for market prices to anticipate recurring annual conditions of greatest supply–least demand, increasing demand–decreasing supply, greatest demand–least supply, and decreasing demand–increasing supply. From this pattern one may begin to better anticipate future price movement.

Consider the seasonal pattern that has evolved (1982–1996) for heating oil deliverables in January as shown in Figure 5.4. Demand, and therefore prices, is typically low during July—often the hottest month of the year. As the industry begins anticipating cooler weather, the market finds increasing demand for future inventory—exerting upward pressure on prices. Finally, the rise in prices tends to climax even before the onset of the coldest weather as anticipated demand is realized, refineries gear up to meet the demand, and the market focuses on future liquidation of inventory.

Figure 5.4 January heating oil No. 2 (NYM), 15-year seasonal (1982–1996)

The other primary petroleum product encounters a different, albeit still weather-driven, cycle of demand as exhibited in the seasonal pattern (1986–1995) for August gasoline as shown in Figure 5.5. Prices tend to be lower during the poorer driving conditions of winter. However, as the industry begins to anticipate the summer driving season, demand for future inventory increases and exerts upward pressure on prices. By the official opening of the driving season (Memorial Day), refineries then have enough incentive to meet that demand.

Seasonal patterns derived from daily prices rarely appear as perfect cycles. Even in patterns with distinct seasonal highs and lows, seasonal trends in between are subject to various, sometimes conflicting, forces before they are fully realized. A seasonal decline may typically be punctuated by brief rallies. For example, even though cattle prices have usually declined from March–April into June–July, they have exhibited a strong tendency to rally in early May as retail grocery outlets inventory beef for Memorial Day barbecues. Soybean prices tend to decline from June–July into October's harvest, but by Labor Day the market has typically anticipated a frost scare.

Figure 5.5 August unleaded regular gas (NYM), 10-year seasonal (1986–1995)

Conversely, a seasonal rise may typically be punctuated by brief dips. For example, future uptrends are regularly interrupted by bouts of artificial selling pressure associated with first notice day for nearby contracts. Such liquidation to avoid delivery can offer opportunities both to take profits and then to enter or reestablish positions.

Therefore, a seasonal pattern constructed from daily prices can depict not only the four major components of seasonal price movement but also especially reliable segments of larger seasonal trends. Recognizing fundamental events that tend to coincide with these punctuations can provide even greater confidence in the pattern.

Consider the seasonal price pattern that has evolved (1981–1995) for September Treasury bonds as shown in Figure 5.6. The U.S. government's fiscal year begins October 1, increasing liquidity and easing borrowing demands somewhat. Is it merely coincidental that the tendency for bond prices to rise from then also tends to culminate with personal income tax liability for the calendar year?

Figure 5.6 30-year T-bonds (CBT), September, 15-year seasonal (1981–1995)

Is the seasonal decline into May a reflection of the market anticipating tighter monetary liquidity as taxes are paid? Notice the final sharp decline beginning—surprise!—April 15, the final date for payment of U.S. income taxes. Does liquidity tend to increase sharply after June 1 because the Federal Reserve is finally able to recirculate funds?

Take a close look at the typical market activity surrounding December 1, March 1, June 1, and September 1—dates of first delivery against Chicago Board of Trade futures contracts on debt instruments. Finally, notice the distinct dips during the first or second week of the second month of each quarter—November, February, May, and August. Bond traders know that prices tend to decline into at least the second day of a quarterly Treasury refunding—at which time the market gains a better sense of the three-day auction's coverage.

Consider also the pattern for November soybeans as shown in Figure 5.7 as it has evolved in the 15 years (1981–1995) since Brazil became a major producer with a crop cycle exactly opposite that in the Northern Hemisphere. Notice the tendency for prices to work

Figure 5.7 November soybeans (CBT), 15-year seasonal (1981–1995)

sideways to lower in the "February break" as U.S. producers market their recent harvest and Brazil's crop develops rapidly. By the time initial notices of delivery against March contracts are posted, the fundamental dynamics for a spring rally are in place—the Brazilian crop is "made" (realized), the pressure of U.S. producer selling has climaxed, the market anticipates the return of demand as cheaper river transportation becomes more available, and the market begins focusing attention on providing both an incentive for U.S. acreage and a premium for weather risks.

By mid-May, however, the amount of prime U.S. acreage available in the Midwest for soybeans is mostly determined and planting gets under way. At the same time, Brazil begins marketing its recent harvest. The availability of these new supplies and the potential of the new U.S. crop typically combine to exert pressure on market prices. The minor peaks in late June and mid-July denote the tendencies for occasional crop scares.

By mid-August, the new U.S. crop is "made" (realized), and futures can sometimes establish an early seasonal low. However, prices more often decline further into October's harvest low—but only after rallying into September on commercial demand for the first new-crop soybeans and/or concerns over early crop-damaging frost. Notice also the minor punctuations (decline and rally) associated with the first notice day for July, August, September, and November contracts.

Such trading patterns do not repeat without fail, of course. The seasonal methodology, as does any other, has its own inherent limitations. Of immediate practical concern to traders may be issues of timing and contraseasonal price movement. Fundamentals, both daily and longer term, inevitably ebb and flow. For instance, some summers are hotter and dryer, and at more critical times, than others. Even trends of exceptional seasonal consistency are best traded with common sense, a simple technical indicator, and/or a basic familiarity with current fundamentals to enhance selectivity and timing.

How large must a valid statistical sample be? Generally, more is better. For some uses, however, "modern" history may be more practical. For example, Brazil's ascent as a major soybean producer in 1980 was a major factor in the nearly 180-degree reversal in that market's trading patterns from the 1970s. Conversely, relying solely on deflationary patterns prevalent in 1985–1991 could be detrimental in an inflationary environment.

In such historic transitions, a time lag in the relevancy of recent patterns may occur. Analyzing cash markets can help neutralize such effects, but certain patterns specific to futures (such as those that are delivery- or expiration-driven) can get lost in translation. Thus, both sample size and the sample itself must be appropriate for their intended use. These may be determined arbitrarily, but only by a user who is fully cognizant of the consequences of his or her choice.

Related issues involve projecting into the future with statistics, which confirm the past but do not predict in and of themselves. The Super Bowl–winner/stock market–direction "phenomenon" is an example of statistical coincidence because no cause-and-effect relationship exists. However, it does raise a valid issue: When computers sift only raw data, what discoveries have meaning? Is a pattern that has repeated, for instance, in 14 of the last 15 years necessarily valid?

Certainly, patterns driven by fundamentals inspire more confidence, but to know all relevant fundamentals in every market is impractical. When one properly constructs seasonal patterns, one may typically find trends that have recurred in the same direction between specific dates with a great degree of past reliability. A "cluster" of such historically reliable trends, with similar entry and/or exit dates, not only reduces the odds of statistical aberration but also implies recurring fundamental conditions that, presumably, will exist again in the future and affect the market to one degree or another and in a more or less timely manner.

A seasonal pattern merely depicts the well-worn path a market itself has tended to follow. It is a market's own consistency that provides the foundation for why seasonals work.

Editor's Comments

Some people are promoting seasonal information that, in my opinion, has no meaning. This usually takes the form of information such as: The price of X has moved higher in 13 of the last 14 years on April 13. Computers will always find correlations of this nature, and some people will want to trade on the basis of them. However, trade a seasonal pattern without a logical cause-and-effect relationship behind it only at your own risk. The results of the January 2006 Super Bowl, for example, predicted an increase in the stock market for 2006.[10] Would you have wanted to trade that?

SPREADING

Kevin Thomas was one of the more successful floor traders on the London International Financial Futures and Options Exchange (LIFFE) before it became an electronic exchange. Kevin was also the first person to complete our two-year Super Trader program. At the time this section was written, Kevin was trading mostly spreads on the floor. When I originally interviewed Kevin for one of my newsletters, he talked extensively about spreads. Consequently, I thought he was the logical person to write about the concept of spreading for this book. Kevin used the terms Eurodollars (meaning dollars traded in London) and Euromarks (meaning deutsche marks traded in London) because those are the contracts he used to trade. Some of the charts in this section reflect what Kevin used to trade when the exchange had active floor traders, but I've elected to keep them, even though they represent instruments that are no longer traded, because they still illustrate educational information about spreading.

Kevin Thomas: Introduction to Spreading

Spreads can be used in the futures market to create positions that behave like long and short positions. These types of synthetic positions are well worth considering. They have several advantages over outright trading—a lower risk profile and a much lower margin requirement. In addition, some spreads can be charted like any other market.

For instance, in Eurodollars one could be long a nearby contract and short a contract a year further out, and this artificial position would take on the characteristics of a short position for only the spread margin rate. This type of spread is called an *intercontract spread*, and it can be used in markets that have liquid forward contracts. However, the behavior of the spread varies from market to market.

In interest rate futures, trading *calendar spreads* (spreading a nearby contract versus a forward contract) is a common strategy depending on your view of short-term interest rates. If you think rates are going to rise, then you would buy the nearby contracts and sell the forward contracts. More contract months between the two means more responsiveness and volatility of the spread. A spread between June and September of the same year is likely to be less volatile than a spread between September this year and September next year. The example in Figure 5.8 illustrates this.

Figure 5.8 shows the movement of the spread between September 1996 Euromarks and September 1997 Euromarks. I have drawn trendlines and included a 14-day RSI on the spread. Notice that there was a divergence at point *A* and a breakout at point *B*. This was a signal that short-term interest rates were about to rise. By being long the spread, you could have participated in the down move in the market that was coming. Notice that the spread then moved 76 ticks from the low to the high of the move.

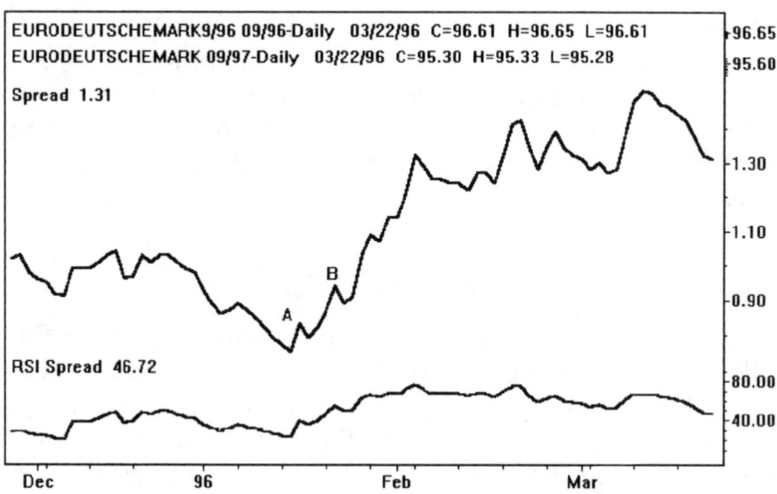

Figure 5.8 Nearby- (bottom) and distant-calendar spreads (Graph done by Kevin Thomas with SuperCharts by Omega Research, Inc.)

Figure 5.9 Movement in individual months (Graph done by Kevin Thomas with SuperCharts by Omega Research, Inc.)

The charts in Figure 5.9 show how the individual months moved over the same period. Notice that the movement of the spread was in fact a good leading indicator of what was about to happen in the individual months. In addition, the move in the spread was more than the down move in September 1996 and about 75 percent of the down move in September 1997. The margin for the spread is 600 Euromarks per unit compared with 1,500 Euromarks for a straight futures position.

Such spread trading is a concept that is popular among floor traders because it enables them to participate in a position that has a lower risk profile than an outright futures position and has a good potential for profit. Once a spread position has been taken, then it can be treated like any other position you would have. Trend-following and position-sizing models can be applied.

By using spreads, you can create relationships that may not be available otherwise. *Currency cross rates*, for example, are spreads that can be created using International Monetary Market (IMM) currencies such as the deutsche mark versus the yen. This creates one of the most actively traded relationships in the world but one you wouldn't think about if you just thought in terms of dollars or pounds. Another widely traded example would be trading cash bonds against bond futures, which is called *basis trading*.

> By using spreads, you can create relationships that may not be available otherwise.

Another common strategy used in these markets is a *butterfly spread*, which is the difference between two spreads that share a common month (for example, long September 1, 1996, short December 2, 1996, and long March 1, 1997). Butterfly spreads are very expensive to trade because of the commission costs for an off-floor trader. However, a floor trader in such a market as Eurodollars or Euromarks can utilize this strategy because of the lower commissions and his or her market-maker edge. The strategy usually has a very low risk with a very high expectation of making a profit. The floor trader, because he or she is trading two spreads, is often able to scratch (that is, meaning to break even) one spread and make a tick on the other or may scratch the whole butterfly spread.

Commodities also lend themselves to intercontract spreading. Let's assume that you predict that copper prices are going to rise because of a supply shortage. If that is the case, then you would buy the nearby contract and sell the forward. This occurs because in times of shortages, nearby prices will rise above forward, creating a phenomenon called *backwardation.*

Always bear in mind when trading commodities that physical delivery is part of the contract specifications. *Cash-and-carry* is a strategy that can be used in trading metals—both base and precious—when they are in good supply. The idea is to take delivery of the metal in a warehouse and redeliver it at a future date if the return (the increase in price) will exceed the interest rate for that period of time. If the interest rate is more than the return or the return ends up being negative, then the strategy is not worth doing.

Intermarket spreading is another spread trading idea worth doing. Here you simply trade different markets against each other, such as the S&P versus the T-bonds, currency cross rates, gold versus silver, and so on. Indeed, Van has included a new section on intermarket analysis in this chapter, and John Murphy has devoted a whole book (*Intermarket Technical Analysis*) to the topic.[11] The basic idea is that you would use such spreads because you believe that the relative move of the two markets is probably your best trading idea.

There are numerous forms of other spreads that you can look at, including (1) spreading options contracts and (2) arbitrage, covered later in this chapter. Both of these are complete trading art forms by themselves. Spread trading can be as simple or as complex as you like, but it is definitely worth investigating.

Editor's Comments

All the previous concepts can be used with spreading. The advantage of spreading is simply that you can trade a relationship that was not tradable before. When you buy gold, for example, you are really buying the relationship between gold and your currency. The relationship will go up if either your currency goes down in value with respect to gold or gold goes up in value with respect to your currency. For example, in 2003 we seemed to have a rise in the price of gold. However, gold went up in 2003 only because the U.S. dollar went down and we were looking at gold prices in U.S. dollars. In contrast, the gold move in 2006 was in all currencies. Gold is actually going up while the dollar is going up.

A spread simply sets up another relationship that you can trade. It could be a stock priced in dollars or euros, or even the relationship between gold and oil prices.

ARBITRAGE

Ray Kelly was a close personal friend and one of my earliest clients. He was also a great teacher and one of the best traders I've known. From the time I finished working with him in 1987 until early 1994, Ray averaged returns of 40 to 60 percent each year. He accomplished that partially by having only one losing month, a mere 2 percent loss, during that entire period. Ray later retired to become a traders' coach and to run a spiritual retreat center in Southern California. He has since passed away, and I find myself thinking of him often. Ray's section is full of great humor and a great understanding of how the markets really work, so please read it and think of him with a smile as I do.

Ray Kelly: Arbitrage—What It Is and How It's Implemented

When people ask me what I do for a living and I say "arbitrage," I see the same blank stare that I often use myself when I lift the hood of my car engine or someone utters the word "calculus." Mothers gather their children to them, and men eye me with suspicion.

If you can overcome your fear of the "A" word for about 10 minutes, I guarantee that you will understand not only the essence of arbitrage but also the way it affects your everyday life. If you begin to "arb-think," you will see opportunities in every facet of your life that you previously had ignored. Your knowledge will secure you from having to excuse yourself for the punch bowl at the next cocktail party when someone says "those arb guys." You will be considered one of the intellectuals at the party, and people will stare at you in admiration—all because you invested 10 minutes in reading this section of the book.

Arbitrage is done by entrepreneurs in almost every business. The dictionary defines *arbitrage* as "the buying of bills of exchange in one market and selling them in another." It also describes a *woman* as a "female human being." Both of these definitions are true, but they don't capture the essence of the word in total. Arbitrage is the magic of discovery. It is the art and science of delving into minute detail to the point of being obnoxious. It is the process of looking at every part of a situation as if it were a diamond slowly turning on a pedestal so you can observe all of its facets and see them as unique rather than the same. It belongs to those of you who love to solve the impossible riddle.

Arbitrage is the magic of discovery. It is the art and science of delving into minute detail to the point of being obnoxious. It is the process of looking at every part of a situation as if it were a diamond slowly turning on a pedestal so you can observe all of its facets and see them as unique rather than the same. It belongs to those of you who love to solve the impossible riddle.

Edwin Lefèvre, in the book *Reminiscence of a Stock Operator*,[12] describes what happened in the early 1920s with the advent of the telephone. All stock quotes from the New York Stock Exchange were sent out by teletyping houses that we now know as bucket shops. It was very similar to off-track betting. The shops allowed a person to know a quote and then place an order to buy or sell. The difference was that the shop owner was the bookie or regional specialist, and rather than call the exchange, he would book the trade himself. For example, the ticker would say Eastman Kodak trades for 66½. The customer would say "Buy 500 shares," and the shop owner would confirm the purchase and take the other side of this transaction.

A smart fellow with a phone finally figured out that the phone was faster than the Teletype operator on the floor of the New York Stock Exchange. He would transact some small trades to establish a presence with the shop but always kept in contact with a cohort by phone in times of volatility. If bad news came out, he may have found that Eastman Kodak, while on the tape at 66½, was actually 65 at the post in New York. Consequently, he would sell to the shop owner as much as he could at 66½ and buy it back through his friend on the floor in New York at 65. Thus, he made a sure $150 for every hundred shares. Over time, this clever fellow hired others to trade at the bucket shops and put many of them out of business. Eventually, the remaining bucket shops got their own phones.

Is this action unscrupulous, or is it a way to more efficiently price a marketplace? Is it unscrupulous for the shop owner to book the trades himself rather than put them in the name of the person who actually buys the stock? The important thing to remember is that economics per se does not have a moral code. It simply is. People ascribe "good" and "bad" or "right" and "wrong" to various practices. The shop owner feels that the actions of the arb player are wrong. The New York broker loves the increased commission business and loves the arb player.

The important thing to remember is that economics per se does not have a moral code. It simply is . . . Economics is neutral to the emotions of the players. It says, "If there is money on the table, it belongs to the person who picks it up."

Arb players themselves feel that since the phone is open to everyone, they are only implementing something that any clever person could figure out. They do not feel an obligation to negate their cleverness by spelling everything out to those who could eventually figure it out for themselves. Over time, there are always actions of others to stop the arbs or to join in and make the opportunity less profitable. Economics is neutral to the emotions of the players. It says, "If there is money on the table, it belongs to the person who picks it up."

When I was a teenager, I did my first arb. I lived in a wealthy neighborhood, although I was broke. My dad kept getting "free" credit cards in the mail. One day in the 1960s we had a blizzard as we do now and then in the Midwest. I lived across from a hardware store, and I knew that it had a snowblower for sale for $265. It was a beast of a blower! I could see that even the snowplows couldn't get to the rich folks' houses.

I also noticed an unopened letter with a Towne and Country Credit Card on my father's desk. My name and my father's are the same, so I took it. (This is what is called *risk arbitrage*.) I bought the snowblower with the credit card when the store opened at 7 a.m. I did 11 long driveways by 8 p.m. that night and made $550. The next morning at 7 a.m., I sold the snowblower back to the guy in the store for $200. He gave me back the credit card slip, and I gave him the slightly used snowblower, which was still in great demand. I netted $485 and felt like the cat that ate the canary!

A few years ago I was approached for advice by a man who had 3,000 shares of stock. He had an opportunity to buy more shares through the company at a discount. This was a chance to buy a $25 stock for $19. Even though the amount of stock he could buy was small, it still seemed like a good opportunity.

I had been on the Chicago Board Options Exchange (CBOE) for 25 years and could not find any comparable investments. As a result, I told him it was a good deal and called the company to find out more about its dividend reinvestment plan. I also found out that other companies had similar plans and that the brokerage community was starting to participate in these plans.

I wondered, "How are they doing this? If they bought a million shares, they would be able to reinvest only the amount of the dividend, and the interest on the purchase would wipe out the profit." They also would have huge market risk. However, I saw others doing the trade, and I became obsessed with finding out how it was done. Some people were obviously making money. I dug through records, talked to margin clerks, and watched the trades that took place before the dividend payout dates. Slowly, the picture became clearer. I eventually solved the problem of what looked like a mathematical loser. However, I didn't have enough capital to do it myself, so I went through the painful and agonizing steps to find a company in the securities business that was not doing it and would not steal it from me once I explained it to the people there. That was a long process.

An arbitrager must find a company that is willing to look beyond the obvious—that's where the opportunity lies. Lawyers are usually a formidable wall of resistance. Lawyers for institutions are paid to investigate, and the status quo is normally hard to change. If something goes wrong, they are blamed. But if things drag out, the attorneys get paid anyway. If there is a little twist in the path, they are not paid to find another way, but just to tell you that the one you are on won't work. They do not like being pressed for specifics, nor do they like quick answers. That is their charm. On the other hand, once you get through the process, you become part of the status quo (at least, for a little while).

Arbitrage is usually time-sensitive. Once certain opportunities are discovered, competition usually lowers the profits, and regulators eventually plug the once overlooked loophole. This time frame is usually referred to as "the window." A company that has a dividend reinvestment plan, for example, may say, "We meant this plan only for small investors." The arbitrager may respond that the intentions of the company are not part of the legal text of its plan. The company, in turn, will usually seek remedy through legislation or by changing its plan. In either case, the arbitrage opportunity pointed to a flaw in the economics of the company's "intent." The arb player is paid by that flaw.

The institutions I have presented ideas to over the years have a problem called "infrastructure." Large companies are broken into divisions that manage specific parts of their business. In the securities area, one group may handle customer accounts, another will handle stock lending, another will handle proprietary trading, and so on. Each division has its own profit goals and what is called a hurdle rate. The *hurdle rate* is a computation of the minimum return the division head will accept to entertain a business proposal.

The CEO will usually turn management over to the division head. The problem here is that the economy (and the opportunity) doesn't care about the corporation's structure. What is perhaps efficient from a corporate viewpoint may leave inefficiencies that are accepted as a cost of doing business. Since it is anathema for one corporate division head to peek into another manager's area, these inefficiencies are rarely addressed quickly, if at all.

In a specific and actual situation, I presented one major brokerage firm with a strategy that returned 67 percent on capital net after my percentages were taken out. Unfortunately, I needed three divisions of the company to accomplish this. Each of these divisions had a 30 percent hurdle rate. None of them would take less because it weakened the individual division's overall picture even though it greatly enhanced the overall return to the company. During almost two years of negotiation the return went from 67 percent down to 35 percent. There were literally tens of millions of dollars of potential profit at stake. The company never did a trade, and to my knowledge all the same managers still work there.

Once you get through the infrastructure and gain credibility with a firm, there are other problems. The troops in the trenches get irritated because nothing you do is normal. They are always asked to do things somewhat differently for me than they do for their regular customers. We insist on minute-to-minute concentration on little, seemingly innocuous procedures.

For example, if a trade is executed on the New York Stock Exchange, I can negotiate a fixed ticket charge of say $150 regardless of the size of the trade. I cannot help my client negotiate with the Securities and Exchange Commission on its 0.003 percent charge on the sale of the stock. This seems to be a small amount of money. But on a $100 million trade, the amount is $3,333.33. To me, that is a lot of money.

A brokerage firm cannot charge the U.S. government. It simply passes the charge on to the customer, and such charges go unchallenged. Yet if my client were to do 1,000 of these $100 million trades each year, the government charge would be over $3 million. Once again the economy of the opportunity does not concern itself with the intransigence of policy—even from the U.S. government. Yet if I suggest to my client that should she transact her trade in Toronto rather than the United States, she would save this fee, be reasonably free from questioning by governmental authorities, and not get any notoriety domestically, the client loves me. The clerk who has to process these trades, however, doesn't love me at all. I have upset his day with what he sees as trivia. If I were to cut him in on 10 percent of the saved fee, the light would dawn quickly. But the more I disclose information to people, the quicker the advantage goes away.

Eventually, others will figure out what I am doing and find a way to cut themselves in on the profit. This is called *reverse engineering*. Some firms have whole divisions that dedicate themselves to watching the street and uncovering strategies. It's my belief that this process is a critical part of price discovery in the economic system. The arbitrager points out, in a way that can't be ignored or pushed back by bureaucracy, some miscalculation or misperception. In many cases, it forces institutions to look at situations they would otherwise ignore.

I am still dumbfounded by all the precautions that securities firms and banks seem to take—yet they still come up with billion dollar snafus. The process of strategy approval is so rigorous that the arbitrage players who do the trading have no incentive to help their own corporations in risk evaluation. The arbitragers almost invariably wind up in an adversarial role by the nature of their business. The integrity of the trader should be heavily considered in all aspects of the trader's life. Integrity seems to be the last line of defense of most trading companies.

In conclusion, the case could be made that there is no stability to a career in arbitrage since everything always changes—the loopholes close and the profits become smaller. On the other hand, you can realize that everything in life changes constantly, and accepting that change is to live a grand adventure. You can realize that errors and miscalculations are part of the human condition. They are how we learn and grow. Your mission, through arbitrage, is to correct inefficiencies whether people want you to or not. You get paid to correct errors. Your job is to pick apart the strategy or concept of someone else piece by piece. If you don't find anything, which is usually the case, you simply move on to another strategy or concept. The way you view things, your frame of reference, determines your view of arbitrage.

Your mission, through arbitrage, is to correct inefficiencies whether people want you to or not. You get paid to correct errors. Your job is to pick apart the strategy or concept of someone else piece by piece. If you don't find anything, which is usually the case, you simply move on to another strategy or concept.

The arbitrager's success is determined by his or her commitment to go the extra distance. Arbitrage is the cleanser of inefficiency. It keeps me from being a spectator. After all, there are only two places you can be in life—on the playing field or in the stands. I prefer to be on the playing field.

Editor's Comments

In essence, most trading and investing is a form of arbitrage—looking for inefficiencies in the market. Arbitrage keeps prices in line and really allows markets to be somewhat orderly. Ray Kelly's form of arbitrage, however, is the purest application of arbitrage. It's almost a license to print money, but for a limited period of time.

If you are really serious about being a professional trader, then I strongly agree that you continually look for such opportunities. Each opportunity, when found and exploited properly, could be worth millions of dollars to you.

INTERMARKET ANALYSIS

In the last edition of *Trade Your Way to Financial Freedom,* I included a section by Lou Mendelsohn on neural networks. However, neural networks is really not a trading concept but rather a method of analyzing the markets. As a result, I elected to drop that section from this edition. What might be considered a concept, however, is what neural networks can do, and that is to show the relationships between markets. And that might be considered a concept for trading. Furthermore, given my belief that the economy is now becoming a global economy, understanding the relationships between markets is becoming more and more important. Louis Mendelsohn is also an expert on intermarket analysis, so I requested that he write a new section on this interesting topic.[13]

Louis B. Mendelsohn: Intermarket Analysis

If you look at a restaurant menu and see filet mignon priced at $27.95, you may decide that's a bit too expensive for your taste. So you choose the lamb chops at $21.95 or maybe even the chicken at $15.95.

Welcome to the world of intermarket analysis. Knowingly or not, you are probably making the same types of choices every day that corporate executives make when they decide whether to heat their offices or factories with natural gas or heating oil (if they have the flexibility to choose). Or farmers make when they look at input costs and market prices in determining whether to plant corn or soybeans. Or investors make when they analyze returns from small-caps compared to big-caps or from one market sector versus another or between international and domestic stocks.

No Isolated Markets

No individual market operates in a vacuum, especially in today's global, 24-hour, electronically traded marketplace where one market is quickly influenced by what happens in other related markets. While many traders look backward at historical prices to gauge how a market's past behavior might suggest how that market will play out in the future, they also need to look sideways to detect the impact that prices in other markets have on the price of the market they are trading.

Intuitively, most traders know that markets are interrelated and that a development that affects one market is likely to have repercussions in other markets. However, many individual traders still limit themselves to using single-market analysis tools and information sources that have been around since the 1970s when I first started in this industry.

Although there has long been general awareness of intermarket relationships, the difficulty is in quantifying these relationships in terms that traders can use in making their decisions. My research since the mid-1980s has focused on developing a quantitative approach to implement intermarket analysis. It is neither a radical departure from traditional single-market technical analysis nor an attempt to replace it.

Intermarket analysis, in my opinion, is just an expansion of traditional single-market technical analysis, given the global context of today's interdependent economies and financial markets. Especially in markets such as foreign exchange, which provide the pricing basis for other markets, you have to adopt an approach that incorporates intermarket analysis in one way or another. An important aspect of my ongoing research involves analyzing which markets have the most influence on each other and determining the degree of influence these markets have on one another.

"Hurricaneomics," a concept that I coined in 2005, is a perfect example of the interconnectedness of events and markets and how nothing can be looked at in isolation. The spate of hurricanes that hit the Gulf Coast and Florida in 2005 did not simply cause local damage to the economy of those regions. On the contrary, hurricaneomic effects will ripple throughout the world economy for months and years to come, impacting the energy markets, agricultural markets, construction industry, the federal deficit, interest rates, and, of course, the forex market. Hurricaneomic analysis goes hand in hand with intermarket analysis in looking at events such as natural disasters and their effects on the global financial markets.

Discovering Market Impacts

Research in my ongoing development of VantagePoint Intermarket Analysis Software began when it was first introduced in 1991. That research indicates that, if you want to analyze the value of the euro versus the U.S. dollar (EUR/USD), for instance, you not only have to look at euro data but also at the data for other related markets to find hidden patterns and relationships that influence the EUR/USD relationship:

- Australian dollar/U.S. dollar (AUD/USD)
- Australian dollar/Japanese yen (AUD/JPY)
- British pound
- Euro/Canadian dollar (EUR/CAD)
- Gold
- Nasdaq 100 Index
- British pound/Japanese yen (GBP/JPY)
- British pound/U.S. dollar (GBP/USD)
- Japanese yen

The intermarket relationships among various currencies may be rather obvious, but the impact of stock indices, U.S. T-notes, or crude oil prices on a forex pair may seem like more of a reach. But research has shown that these related markets do have an important influence on a target forex market and can provide early insights into the forex market's future price direction.

Some analysts like to perform correlation studies of two related markets, measuring the degree to which the prices of one market move in relation to the prices of the second market. Two markets are considered perfectly correlated if the price change of the second market can be forecasted precisely from the price change of the first market. A perfectly positive correlation occurs when both markets move in the same direction. A perfectly negative correlation occurs when the two markets move in opposite directions.

This approach has its limitations because it compares prices of only one market to another and does not take into account the influence exerted by other markets on the target market. In the financial markets and especially the forex markets, a number of related markets need to be included in the analysis rather than assuming that there is a one-to-one cause-effect relationship between just two markets.

Nor do the correlation studies take into account the leads and lags that may exist in economic activity or other factors affecting markets such as forex. These calculations are based only on the values at the moment and may not consider the longer-term consequences of central bank intervention or a policy change that takes some time to play itself out in the markets.

Inverse Factor

In some cases, it is the inverse correlation that is most significant, especially for markets such as gold or oil that are priced in U.S. dollars in international trade. A chart comparing the price of gold and the value of the U.S. dollar (see Figure 5.10) illustrates that when the value of the U.S. dollar declines, not only do foreign currencies rise but gold prices also rise. Studies on data from the last few years have shown a negative correlation between gold and the dollar of more than minus 0.90—that is, they almost never move in tandem but almost always move in opposite directions.

Figure 5.10 Inverse relationship between gold and the U.S. dollar

On the other hand, the value of EUR/USD versus gold prices shows a high positive correlation—that is, the value of the euro and gold prices often go hand in hand, suggesting these markets are both beneficiaries when funds are flowing away from the U.S. dollar (see Figure 5.11).

If you see a trend or price signal on a gold chart, it may be a good clue for taking a position in the forex market, where a price move may not have started to occur yet. Or vice versa: a forex move may tip off a gold move.

Because of crude oil's standing in world business and commerce, it is another key market to monitor because anything that affects its supply or distribution is likely to produce a response in other markets. That's why terrorist attacks or natural disasters such as Hurricane Katrina that threaten the normal flow of oil supplies often cause an immediate response in forex and other markets.

Although these are the kinds of shocks that make market analysis difficult for any trader, the more typical scenario usually involves subtle movements taking place in intermarket relationships that hint a price change may be coming. If you are not doing some form of intermarket analysis, you probably are not going to pick up on these relationships and the effects they have on related markets, as those clues are hidden from obvious view.

Figure 5.11 Direct relationship between gold and the euro

Multimarket Effect

Markets are dynamic, constantly shifting, and evolving. When you try to examine the multiple effects of 5 or 10 related markets simultaneously on a target market going back on 5 or 10 years of data to find recurring, predictive patterns, methods such as linear correlation analysis and subjective chart analysis fall short as trend and price forecasting tools.

Market interrelationships cannot be ferreted out with single-market analysis tools. Anyone who is serious about trading needs to make the commitment to get the right tools from the start. Of course, no matter what you spend or what tools you use, nothing is 100 percent correct. Even the best tool can give you only mathematical probabilities, not certainties. But your tools don't need to be perfect to give you a trading edge.

If you have analytical tools that can help you identify the recurring patterns within individual markets and between related global markets, you've got all you need to have a leg up on other traders. This insight into price activity over the next few trading days can give you added confidence and discipline to adhere to your trading strategies and enable you to pull the trigger at the right time without self-doubt or hesitation.

Of course, market analysis shouldn't be limited to intermarket relationships. In today's world of speedy telecommunications and sophisticated trading techniques, you should use an approach that I call *synergistic market analysis*, which combines technical, intermarket, and fundamental approaches. That includes traditional tools that fit your trading style as well as taking advantage of information now available on the Internet.

Editor's Comments

In the next chapter I'm going to be talking about mental scenario trading, which means understanding the impact that the big picture has on your trading ideas. We will be talking about the big picture and how you can use that to help you in your trading. The concept that markets are related is basically the same thing. How can you trade the dollar without knowing the impact of the euro, gold, oil, and interest rates, just to name a few of the significant variables? Well, you can do so just by looking at prices and trading value, bands, trends, and so on. However, wouldn't it be to your advantage to know what to expect as a result of what was going on with other markets as well? That is the power of intermarket analysis.

THERE'S AN ORDER TO THE UNIVERSE

The idea that there is an order to the universe is extremely popular. People want to understand how the markets work, so it is most appealing to them to find some underlying structure. They believe, of course, that once you know the underlying structure, you can predict market movements. In many cases, such theories are even more exact because they attempt to predict market turning points. This naturally appeals to the psychological bias that most people have of wanting to be right and to have control over the markets. As a result, they want to catch market turning points. In addition, it's a highly marketable idea to sell to the public. There are a number of theories involving market order, including Gann, Elliott Wave, astrological theories, and so on.

I elected to write this part of the chapter myself because (1) someone who is an expert in one market-orderliness theory is not necessarily an expert in another, and (2) the experts seemed to be more concerned with proving (or disproving) their theories than with the issue of whether or not the concept is tradable. Since I believe that almost any concept is tradable, I thought it would be easier for me to discuss the concepts in general terms and then indicate how one might trade them.

Basically, there are three types of concepts that presume some order to the markets. All these concepts function to predict turning points in the market. I am making some gross oversimplifications in discussing them, so I ask the indulgence of any experts in the various concepts described.

Human Behavior Has a Cycle

The first concept assumes that the markets are a function of human behavior and that the motives of human beings can be characterized by a certain structure. The most well-known structure of this type is the Elliott Wave theory. Here one assumes that the impulses of fear and greed follow a distinct wave pattern. Basically, the market is thought to consist of five up waves followed by three corrective waves. For example, the major upthrust of the market would consist of five waves up (with waves 2 and 4 being in the opposite direction) followed by three waves down (with the middle wave being in the opposite direction). Each wave has a distinct characteristic, with the third major wave in the series of five being the most tradable. However, the theory gets much more complex because there are waves within waves. In other words, there are Elliott Waves of different magnitudes. For example, the first wave of the major movement would consist of another whole sequence of five waves followed by three corrective waves. Elliott, in fact, decided that there were nine categories of magnitude of waves, ranging from the Grand Supercycle to the subminuette waves.

Certain rules aid the Elliott Wave theoretician in making decisions about the market. There are also variations to the rules in that waves may be stretched or compressed and there are some pattern variations. The nature of those rules and variations is beyond the scope of this discussion, *but the rules do allow you to arrive at market turning points that are tradable.* In other words, the task is to determine which wave series was responsible for any given turning point.

Physical Systems Influence Human Behavior in Predictable Patterns

The second concept of order in the markets is based on the aspects of physical systems in the universe. The logic of looking at physical systems is based on the following assumptions: (1) market movements are based on the behavior of human beings; and (2) human beings are influenced, both physically and emotionally, by the various physical systems and the energy they put out; therefore, (3) if there are patterns to those physical energies, then they should have strong predictable effects on markets.

For example, scientists have shown that there are regular cycles to sunspots. Sunspots are actually a release of electromagnetic energy from the sun and can have profound effects on the earth.

Large amounts of sunspot activity will cause huge amounts of charged particles to be trapped in the earth's magnetosphere. This seems to protect the earth from some of the harmful effects of the sun. In addition, the most intense periods of sunspot activity, as one might expect if this theory were true, seem to correlate with the high points in civilization. (See reference note 15.) We're currently in one! In contrast, low periods of sunspot activity seem to correlate with what might be termed declines in civilization. Obviously, if such a theory is valid and if sunspot activity is predictable, then one would expect sunspot activity to have a strong effect on what happens in the market.

There are numerous attempts to correlate and predict markets based upon major physical systems such as the activity of the sun. It is very easy to put together enough best-case examples to prove to others—or yourself—that these theories are correct. I've seen it happen hundreds of times because there is a simple perceptual bias that will convince people of certain relationships from just a few well-chosen examples. Nevertheless, there is a big difference between theory and reality.

John Nelson—a radio propagation specialist—was able to predict six-hour intervals of radio propagation quality at 88 percent accuracy. He did so by using planetary alignments. Several market researchers have taken the dates of the worst storms from 1940 through 1964 and run statistics on the percent change in the Dow Jones Industrial Average (DJIA) from minus 10 days to plus 10 days from the onset of the storms. They find that the DJIA shows a statistically significant decline from 2 days before the storm until 3 days after the storm. And during a new moon or a full moon, the effect is amplified even more. However, during much of this time the stock market was in a bear market when there was already a downward bias.[14]

On March 5, 1989, a massive X-ray flare, lasting 137 minutes, erupted on the sun's surface. It overloaded the sensors on the equipment monitoring it; and in the region from which it occurred, a cluster of sunspots were clearly visible. On March 8 a solar proton flow began, and a large quantity of these ions began flowing toward the earth on a solar wind, lasting until March 13. Monitors of the earth's magnetism in the Shetland Islands registered a change in magnetism of as much as 8 degrees per hour (with the normal deviation being only 0.2 degree). There were huge surges in power lines, telephone lines, and cable networks. Radio and satellite communications were badly affected. Transformers overloaded in Canada, and over a million people were suddenly left without electricity. Yet this particular flare was by no means a spectacular event in solar terms.

The solar flare between March 5 and March 13, 1989, was small in terms of what the sun is capable of, but it was the largest recorded in this century—bigger than any of the storms reported by Nelson. So the question obviously is, "What effect did it have on the markets?" The answer, as best I can tell, was that it had no effect at all.

In a book written by Francois Masson in 1979[15] entitled *The End of Our Century*, the author predicted that a sunspot activity and a stock market peak would occur in 2000. And indeed, the peak in sunspot activity occurred in April 2000. However, Masson claimed there was a 16-year cycle to sunspot activity, while scientists now believe it to be 11 years. Furthermore, we'd expect the low in sunspot activity to occur in 2006, so would this be a start of an economic boom? I personally don't think so. However, if you are really interested in understanding solar cycles better, you might look at *The 23rd Cycle* by Sten Odenwald.[16] This phenomena is shown in Figure 5.12 taken from NASA.

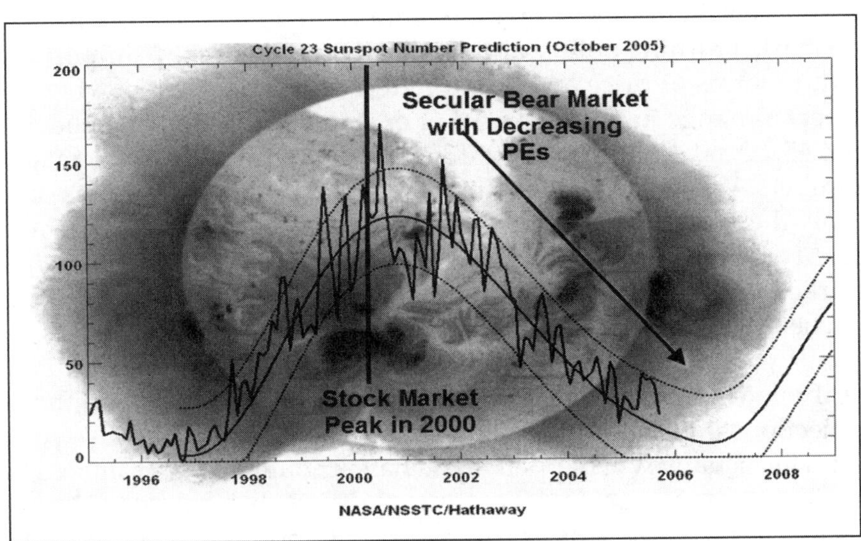

Figure 5.12 A graph of sunspot activity

Despite some evidence to the contrary, let us assume that there is some rhythm to the activity of these physical entities and that it does have a slight effect on the markets. Perhaps, for example, it raises the odds of being "right" about a market change from 48 to 52 percent. That's about the same odds that a card counter at blackjack gets in Las Vegas, and the casinos kick out card counters. As a result, the physical system explanation of order in the markets is also a tradable one.

There's a Mysterious Mathematical Order to the Universe

The third concept relating to orderliness in the markets searches through mathematics in order to find the answers. It asserts that certain "magic" numbers, and the relationships among the numbers, influence the markets. For example, Pythagoras is rumored to have taught in an ancient "mystery school" that all the principles of the universe were based on mathematics and geometry. Furthermore, certain "magical" societies and sects seem to carry this notion forward. The work of W. D. Gann, as currently promoted by many of his followers, is based on mathematical orderliness.

Mathematical orderliness theories make two key assumptions: (1) that certain numbers are more important than others in predicting market turning points, and (2) that these numbers are important both in terms of price levels and in terms of time (that is, when to expect a change in the market). For example, suppose you believed that 45, 50, 60, 66, 90, 100, 120, 135, 144, 618, and so on, were magic numbers. What you'd do is find "significant" tops or bottoms and apply these numbers to them—looking at both time and price. You might expect, for example, a 0.50, a 0.618, or a 0.667 correction in the market. In addition, you might expect your target price to be reached in 45 days or 144 days or some other magic number.

If you have enough magic numbers, you can figure out and verify a lot of projections after the fact. You can then extend those projections into the future, and some of them might actually work out. This usually will happen if you have enough magic numbers to work with in your arsenal. For example, if you have at least 33 people in a room, your odds are quite good of finding two people with the same birthday. That doesn't necessarily mean, however, that the common date is a magic number, although some people might jump to that conclusion.

Let's assume that such numbers do exist. Let's also assume that they are not perfect, but they do increase the reliability of your predictions beyond chance. For example, with magic numbers you might predict that the Dow Jones Industrial Average should make a major turn on July 23. You estimate that the reliability of your prediction is 55 percent. If you have that kind of edge, then you have a tradable event.

Some of these magic numbers are called *Fibonacci numbers*. I've seen some pretty amazing correlations when Fibonacci retracements are placed on the chart. For example, 0.667, 0.618, and 0.5 do seem almost "magical" in predicting turning points. However, there is also a nonmathematical explanation for this. If enough people believe in the power of magic numbers, then they will achieve a magic just from people's faith in them. Remember that you can trade only your beliefs about the market.

Conclusion

What do these three concepts about orderliness in the markets have in common? They all predict turning points. Turning points, in most cases, tend to give traders information about when to enter the market. In some cases, they also give profit objectives and a clue about when to get out of the market. You'll learn in Chapter 9 that it's possible to make money with a trading system in which the entry is totally random. As a result, if any prediction method gives you a better-than-chance expectation of predicting the market, you could have some advantage in trading it.

How should one trade such predictions? First, you could use the expected target date (with whatever time variance you are willing to give it) as a filter for entry. Thus, if your method predicts a market turn on July 23 with a possible variance of one day, then you should look for an entry signal between July 22 and July 24.

Second, you must look for the market to tell you that it is making the move you expect before you enter. The move itself should be your trading signal, not the time at which you expect the move to occur. The simplest way of trading it would be to look for a volatility breakout signal during the window in which you expect a move.

For example, suppose the average daily price range (measured by the average true range) for the last 10 days has been 4 points. Your signal might be 1.5 times this range, or 6 points. As a result, you would enter on a 6-point move from yesterday's close. You would then use appropriate stops, exits, and position sizing to control the trade. These are discussed in subsequent chapters.

The keys to trading such concepts of orderliness in a profitable way are the same as the keys to trading any concept properly. First, you need good exits to preserve your capital when your concept does not work and to create a high payoff when it does. Second, you need to size your positions appropriately to be able to meet your trading objectives. Thus, even if such concepts increase your accuracy by 1 percent, you can still trade them profitably. However, if you deemphasize the prediction part of such systems (thus giving up your need to be in control and to be right) and concentrate on exits and position sizing, you should do quite well.

SUMMARY

The purpose of this chapter was to introduce you to a few of the many different concepts that you can use to trade or invest in the market, depending on your beliefs. Each of these concepts could give you an edge, but none of these concepts will help you make money unless they are combined with all of the other significant factors that are contained within this book, such as having an initial stop, having exits, understanding your system as a distribution of *R* multiples, or using position sizing to meet your objectives. All of these topics will be covered later in this book and must be integrated with whatever concepts you elect to trade as your primary "style" of investing.

None of these concepts, in my opinion, is more valid (or valuable) than any other. In addition, I'm not expressing any personal preferences for any of these concepts. My point in including this chapter is simply to show you how many different ideas there are.[17]

- Tom Basso started out with the discussions by talking about trend following, and he simply expressed the viewpoint that the markets occasionally move in one direction for a long time or trend. These trends can be captured and form the basis for a type of trading. The basic philosophy is to find a criterion to determine when the market is trending, enter the market in the direction of the trend, and then exit when the trend is over or the signal proves to be false. It's an easy technique to follow, and it makes good money if you understand the concepts behind it and follow it consistently.

- Chuck LeBeau discussed the next concept, fundamental analysis. This is the actual analysis of supply and demand in the market, and many academics think it is the only way one can trade. The concept typically does give you a price objective, but your analysis (or some expert's analysis) may have no relationship to what prices actually do. Nevertheless, some people trade fundamental data quite well, and this is another option for you to consider. Chuck gives seven suggestions for you to follow if you wish to follow this concept. Generally, a trend supported by fundamentals is much stronger than a trend with no fundamental reason behind it. Mostly, Chuck discusses fundamental analysis only as it applies to the futures markets, not as it applies to equities. That is covered in the value section.
- Next I covered the idea of value investing in which you buy what you believe to be undervalued and sell what you believe to be overvalued. It's a simple concept used by many people who are considered market geniuses. However, the key question is, "How do you determine value?" This section discusses the methods that work and the methods that do not work and also offers some tips to improve your performance if you like value investing.
- D. R. Barton covered band trading. If you believe that a market tends to be range bound and that the range is wide enough to trade, then band trading offers you the perfect solutions. This concept works well for short-term traders and for people who dislike buying high and selling low. D.R. discusses the advantages and disadvantages of band trading as well as providing a brief description of the types of bands traded.

- Jerry Toepke discussed the concept of seasonal tendencies. Seasonal analysis is based on the fundamental qualities of certain products to be higher priced at some times during the year and lower priced at other times. The result is a concept that combines both the supply-and-demand analysis of fundamental analysis and the timing value of trend following. It's another way to play the markets if you ensure that there is a valid reason for any seasonal tendencies that you find.
- Kevin Thomas, a former floor trader on the LIFFE exchange, talked about spreading. The advantage of spreading is that you are trading relationships between products instead of the products themselves. As a result, new opportunities are available that could not come to you any other way. Kevin gives some wonderful examples of spreads in his discussion.
- Arbitrage, presented by Ray Kelly in a very humorous and artful way, is looking for opportunities that have a very narrow window of opportunity. While the window is open, the opportunity is like "free money." However, sooner or later the window shuts, and then the arb player must find new opportunities. Ray gives many examples of such windows and gives some humorous stories of his frustrations in trying to capture some of them.
- Lou Mendelsohn covered the topic of intermarket analysis, the idea that one market might be influenced by many other markets. If you can begin to understand how those markets are related, then you may have an edge in understanding price changes in the market in which you are interested in trading.
- The final concept presented was a synopsis of several theories that claim to understand some magic order to the markets. There are three types of order concepts: (1) based on waves of human emotion, (2) based on large physical events influencing human behavior, and (3) based on mathematical order. Many of them may have little or no validity, but people trade them because they believe they work. Furthermore, if enough people believe something

will work, then the concept becomes "real" and does work. As a result, these concepts can be traded profitably—just as random entry can be traded profitably, as you'll learn in the entry chapter. In this last discussion, you learned how to take one of the order concepts (if one of them appeals to you) and use it to your advantage. Such concepts are probably excellent for people who feel that they must know how markets work before they can commit themselves to trade.

NOTES

1. Expectancy will be discussed extensively in Chapter 7. It is one of the most important topics that you need to understand as a trader or investor.
2. The CFTC requires that commodity trading advisors include a statement in their advertisements and disclosure documents that says that past results do not reflect upon future results.
3. Tom Basso is now retired from trading and spends his time having fun. However, when he wrote this section, in 1996, he was an active money manager. He still can be reached by e-mail at tom@trendstat.com.
4. Chuck LeBeau is also retired. You can reach Chuck LeBeau at clebeau2@cableone.net.
5. I don't want to get off on a tangent discussing how to make life's decisions; that's a subject more suitable to one of Dr. Tharp's enjoyable workshops. The point is that you can easily and successfully combine fundamental and technical analysis in your trading.
6. Jack Schwager, *Schwager on Futures: Fundamental Analysis* (New York: Wiley, 1996).
7. A newsletter that concentrates on finding this sort of recommendation is *Extreme Value,* which is available at www.stansberryresearch.com. This is not a recommendation for the newsletter. However, this newsletter is among the letters that are analyzed as systems later in the book.
8. D. R. Barton can be reached at 302-731-1551 or at drbarton@ilovetotrade.com. I was not able to evaluate the *R* multiples of this newsletter prior to publication of this edition.

9. Moore Research Center, Inc., can be reached at 1-800-927-7257 or at www.mrci.com.
10. An old correlation that is right better than 80 percent of the time says that if an old AFL team (Denver being one) wins the Super Bowl, then the market will go down. If an old NFL team wins, then the market will go up. Obviously, this predictor totally fell apart in 1998. An old AFL team won the 1998 Super Bowl, and you also know how much the market went up in 1998–1999. In 2000 and 2001 an old NFL team won, and you know how much the market fell in those years.
11. John Murphy, *Intermarket Technical Analysis* (New York: Wiley, 1986).
12. Edwin Lefèvre, *Reminiscence of a Stock Operator* (New York: Wiley Investment Classics, 2006; first published in 1923).
13. Louis B. Mendelsohn is president and chief executive officer of Market Technologies, LLC, in Wesley Chapel, Florida, and the developer of VantagePoint Intermarket Analysis Software. He also is involved in a free educational Web site at www.TradingEducation.com. He can be reached through www.Tradertech.com.
14. This information came from an Internet posting by Greg Meadors and Eric Gatey. The dates of the worst storms were March 23, 1940; August 4, 1941; September 18, 1941; October 2, 1942; February 7, 1944; March 27, 1945; September 23, 1957; April 24, 1960; July 15, 1960; August 30, 1960; November 12, 1960; April 14, 1961; and September 22, 1963. See www.mindspring.com/edge/home.html.
15. For references to this theory, go to www.divinecosmos.com/index.php?option = com_content&task= category§ionid=6&id=26&Itemid=36
16. Sten F. Odenwald. *The 23rd Cycle: Learning to Live with a Stormy Star* (New York: Columbia University Press, 2001).
17. I haven't included a number of concepts, such as scalping, statistical trading, hedging, and so on, simply because doing so would turn this chapter into a lot more than it was intended to be. I have included most of the major concepts that most people trade.

CHAPTER 6

Trading Strategies That Fit the Big Picture

For every dollar added to [America's] GDP, there are now 4 dollars added to indebtedness. This is the worst performance in terms of credit expansion in history and of course in comparison to any other country.

Dr. Kurt Richebächer, Economics Lecture, November 2005

When I wrote the first edition of this book, I left out one style of trading that I called *mental scenario trading*. My experience of it was that it was an art form practiced by some of the best investors and traders. For example, I would describe *Market Wizards* Bruce Kovner and Jim Rogers with the label "mental scenario traders." And the best way I could describe what they did was to say that they kept up with everything going on in the world and through that knowledge developed great ideas to trade. Jim Rogers has said about mental scenario trading, "How can you invest in American Steel without understanding what is going on in Malaysian palm oil? . . . It is all part of a big, three-dimensional puzzle that is always changing."[1]

I've never modeled a mental scenario trader, so I haven't talked much about it in my books and courses. But my thoughts about mental scenario trading have also changed since the first edition of this book. I believe that everyone, at minimum, should keep track of the big picture and trade two or three systems that develop from the patterns that seem to emerge. For example, here are a few of my beliefs about the big picture. Once again realize these are just my beliefs, my filters for reality and your beliefs might be different:

- I believe that emerging nations will be consuming increasingly greater quantities of raw resources.
- I also believe that the United States is in the beginnings of a secular bear market during which such issues as our massive debt and the retirement problems of the baby boomers must play out.
- I believe the United States has probably reached its peak as a world power and will decline in the long term. I'm just being realistic here because throughout history this happens to every great nation.
- Given that scenario, I believe that the United States must endure at minimum a general devaluation of the dollar (best-case scenario) and perhaps a fairly strong inflation, which will really erode the purchasing power of the dollar. We could see a Dow of 40,000 with the dollar worth about 5 cents in today's purchasing power. And, just in case you thought I was predicting a great boom in the stock market, that translates to a Dow of 2,000 in terms of 2006 dollars.

These beliefs lead me to want to focus on certain trading ideas:

- Be careful about the U.S. dollar and the U.S. stock market over the long term.
- Expect great trading opportunities in global stock markets over the long term.
- Expect great trading opportunities in gold, oil, and commodities in general over the long term.
- Focus on consumable assets (such as timber) over equities (such as General Motors). Collectibles also will probably do very well over the next 10 to 15 years.

I will discuss some of these ideas (and others) in more detail in this chapter. My reason for discussing them is to give you an example of laying out a big-picture scenario. My big picture may not be the same as yours, but reading mine may give you some questions and ideas that you might want to focus on in your own big-picture planning. Furthermore, when you do lay out your big picture, you should have a way to measure it and update its progress.

I now recommend that all of my clients develop a business plan in which they play out their own long-term scenarios for trading. In that plan you must ask yourself, "What do you think the big picture will be over the next 5 to 20 years?" And the answer to that question will help you focus on the markets to trade and the type of trading you might want to do.

> . . . what I'm suggesting is that everyone do some form of mental scenario thinking as the basis for your trading.

As I was laying out my version of the big picture for you, it suddenly dawned on me that *what I'm suggesting is that everyone do some form of mental scenario thinking as the basis for your trading*. At one level, you can focus on the big picture as I just did and come up with markets that you want to concentrate on with some expectation of the type of results you can get. Or, as an alternative, you can drill down into the big picture on a regular basis and become more and more of a mental scenario trader-investor.

You basically have a choice: If you want to be a good trader-investor, then I suggest that you focus broadly on the big picture to get an idea of the types of markets you want to concentrate on and how you might want to trade them. If this is your choice, then you probably need to gather some data weekly (or at least monthly) to refresh your big-picture scenario. Doing so will help you know if (1) your beliefs need to be changed or (2) if you were totally wrong about one aspect of the big picture or even all of it.

On the other hand, you might want to gather more and more ideas and information about the big picture to the point that doing so is a part of your daily routine. When you do this, specific trading ideas will develop that you'll want to act on. And, if this is your style, then in my opinion, you've become a mental scenario trader-investor.

So let's look at where you are in your development as a trader-investor. At this point you should have a list of your beliefs about yourself and the market. And from Chapter 5 you should have some idea of the concepts and edges that most appeal to you. Now I'd like to encourage you, at minimum, to think about developing systems that fit with the big picture as you see it and to develop some monthly measurements that will help you keep up with changes that might occur in the big picture.

This chapter, just like all of the other chapters, reflects my beliefs that I've found useful in my trading and in helping me to be a top trading coach. I'm going to be talking about the big picture as I see it today in late 2006. *This is just to give you an example of big-picture thinking. Your beliefs about the big picture might be totally different. Furthermore, my beliefs in the future might be totally different as new developments unfold.* However, if things change, I have a method of monitoring the market for data that would cause me to think differently about what might be going on in the world. You need that as well. *You'll also need to understand that while some aspects of the big picture imply a crisis, every crisis is also an economic opportunity.*

You'll also need to understand that while some aspects of the big picture imply a crisis, every crisis is also an economic opportunity.

THE BIG PICTURE AS I SEE IT

When looking at the big picture today, I believe that several primary factors must be considered. First, the debt situation in the United States is absolutely horrific with the total government debt equaling about $125,000 per person in the United States. Second, I believe we're currently in a secular bear market that started in 2000 and could easily last until 2020. That doesn't mean that stock prices will go down, but it does mean that stock valuations, measured by price-to-earnings ratios, will go down. Third, we're becoming a global economy with former third-world countries like China and India now becoming significant economic players. The fourth key factor in the big picture, at least for Americans, is the impact on the stock market of the large-portfolio managers. Right now they support the major stock averages, such as the S&P 500. But when baby boomers start to retire in 2010, there will probably be a net redemption for many years, and this will have a negative impact on the major averages. The fifth key factor in the big picture is to be aware of changes in taxes, policy, regulations, and so on that could change the entire economic picture. The government generally does what it can do to fix problems by using short-term solutions, but such solutions are chosen usually at the expense of future generations. And the final key is that people are very inefficient when it comes to money decisions, but this is good news for you. You can actually become efficient. There are probably other keys that you may want to consider in your mental scenario planning, but those are my major ones.

My reason for reviewing my beliefs about the big picture is simply to give you a starting point. The key issues you come up with could be entirely different.

FACTOR 1. THE U.S. DEBT SITUATION

In 1983 the United States was the largest creditor nation in the world. Two years later, we became a debtor nation for the first time since 1914. And now, in 2006, we are the largest debtor nation in the history of the world. In 1993, Rep. James Traficant, Jr. (Ohio), made the following comments to the floor of the House of Representatives:

> Mr. Speaker, we are here now in chapter 11. Members of Congress are official trustees presiding over the greatest reorganization of any Bankrupt entity in world history, the U.S. Government. We are setting forth hopefully, a blueprint for our future. There are some who say it is a coroner's report that will lead to our demise.[2]

I can remember when the U.S. debt hit a trillion dollars in 1980. I kept thinking "How can it get any higher?" Well, it's now much higher, and we don't seem that much worse off, so perhaps it can go on forever. But can it? I decided to take a look at a graph of the U.S. debt of the past 100 years, and that graph is shown in Figure 6.1. It's not a pretty picture.

In 1900 our debt was about $2.1 billion. It goes from $2.6 billion to $16 billion in 1920 after the formation of the Federal Reserve. The debt begins to take off in 1950 after the expenses of World War II, supported by the U.S. dollar being adopted as the reserve currency of the world. It takes off again in 1980 after the expenses of the

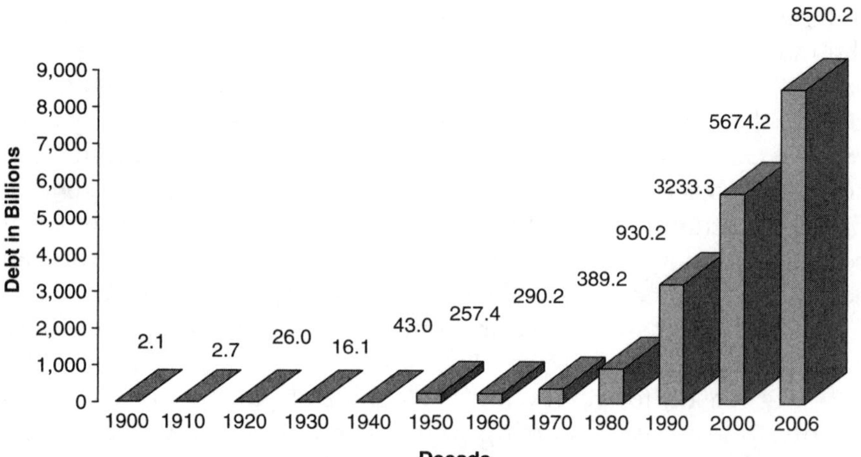

Figure 6.1 The official U.S. debt by decade since 1900

Vietnam War and the United States' refusal to redeem dollars for gold. But since that time, it's gotten totally out of control, and by 2006, which is not a full 10 years from 2000, the official debt is $8.5 trillion. We could easily see our official debt at $15 trillion by 2010. Furthermore, this graph does not include future entitlements such as Social Security, which the government includes when it now estimates our total debt at $67 trillion. In fact, the St. Louis Federal Reserve sponsored a study by Dr. Laurence J. Kotlikoff that now says that the U.S. government is bankrupt.[3]

We currently have a balance of payments problem to the tune of $750 billion per year, with about $200 billion of that going directly to China. This means that the United States is spending about $750 billion more each year with other countries than it is exporting to other countries. Already, foreign countries hold about $3 trillion in U.S. debt instruments. They seem to be willing to do this because the U.S. consumer supported the growth of the world economy during the 1990s. But it took decades for foreign governments to accumulate $3 trillion in U.S. debt. With our current balance of payments now at $750 billion per year, it will only take four years to double the commitment that foreigners must hold of our debt. What happens if they decide they don't want our debt anymore? They are sort of in a catch-22 situation. If they decide they don't want our debt, then the dollar will dramatically shrink in value and the debt they hold will be worth even less. And if the dollar shrinks dramatically, it will be almost impossible for them to sell more of their products to "toy-hungry" U.S. consumers. Already the Italian government has sold off U.S. debt instruments as part of its official government reserves and replaced them with British pounds.

U.S. Corporate Debt

Furthermore, the debt problem is not just due to the U.S. government. U.S. corporations have taken on massive debt over the years. My friend Steve Sjuggerud in May 2002, when the Nasdaq was down 70 percent from its all-time high, discovered that the debt of all Nasdaq companies in the United States was $2.3 trillion. If we take away the two biggest stocks (Microsoft and Intel), then you have a picture in which the entire Nasdaq was worth $2 trillion with a debt of $2.3 trillion. That's a little like buying a $200,000 house with a $230,000 mortgage. The Nasdaq decided to stop publishing this data right after Steve first reported it. The bottom line is the debt situation of U.S. corporations is not good.

In the last chapter I mentioned how we look at the value of U.S. corporations. We take the current assets (that is, what the corporation is worth if we liquidated everything within the next year) and subtract from that number its total debt. Why don't you try doing this for about 10 to 15 major U.S. corporations? Try some big household names like General Electric, Boeing, Google, Microsoft, or IBM, plus some stocks you might pick randomly out of the newspaper. For about 70 percent of them or more, you'll find that this number is negative. What does that mean? U.S. corporations have way too much debt and are in trouble.

U.S. Consumer Debt

And now let's look at the U.S. consumer debt, lest you think that the U.S. consumer is any different than the U.S. government and U.S. corporations. U.S. consumer debt has reached staggering levels, going well over $2.2 trillion by 2006. This is up from $1.3 trillion in

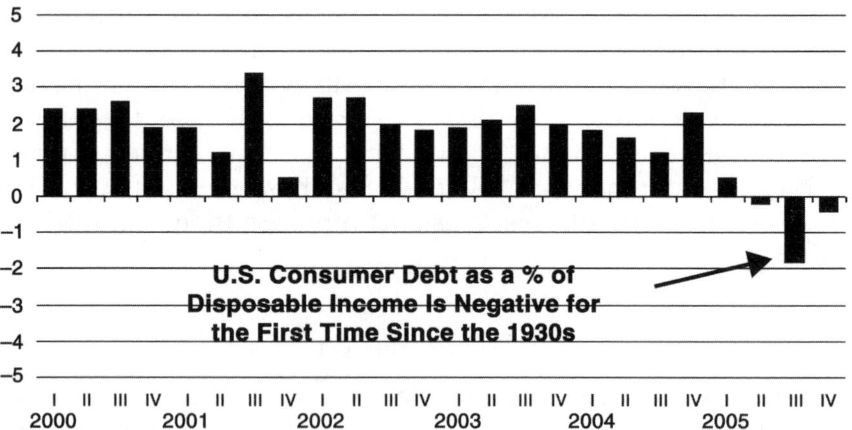

Figure 6.2 Personal savings rate as a percent of disposable income
Source: U.S. Bureau of Economic Analysis

1998. And if you count mortgages, it amounts to more than $10 trillion. According to John Wasik, who writes for Bloomberg, consumer debt has increased over disposable income by an annualized rate of 4.5 percent throughout the decade of the 2000s.[4] The Federal Reserve showed that personal savings had dropped to a mere 2 percent of after-tax income in the first part of 2003. By 2006, it had reached negative territory for the first time since the Great Depression of the 1930s. This is shown clearly by the graph from the U.S. Bureau of Economic Analysis given in Figure 6.2.

The Debt Solutions

So what's the solution? There are several. First, we could be logical and get politicians to stop spending. The government could sell off some of its assets, such as some of its vast reserves of public land, and we might manage to get out of debt. Dr. Kotlikoff, in his report on the U.S. government being bankrupt, suggested a government sales tax of 33 percent, a cut of 50 percent in discretionary government spending, the privatization of Social Security, and a globally budgeted health-care system. Do you think that will happen? If you do, then the politicians you know are different from the ones I know. And since Americans themselves are not logical with regard to debt, how can we expect our elected representatives to be logical?

The second solution is that we could simply default on our debt. What would happen if we did that? Treasury bills would move from being considered "risk free" to being worthless and our Treasury bonds also would be worthless. The U.S. dollar would be worthless, and our country would be bankrupt. Our country would have no credit because no one would lend to us. Thus, solution 2 is not a viable solution.

The third solution is that we could have a massive economic collapse and a big depression. During such scenarios our money becomes worth much more and things become worth less. If our money were worth more, then our $37 trillion debt might seem like $370 trillion and be impossible to pay without a default. This deflationary scenario is not likely at all. Our current Federal Reserve Governor, Ben Bernanke, made the following remarks to the National Economists Club in November 2002:

> The second bulwark against deflation in the United States . . . is the Federal Reserve System itself. The Congress has given the Fed the responsibility of preserving price stability (among other objectives), which most definitely implies avoiding deflation as well as inflation. I am confident that the Fed would take whatever means necessary to prevent significant deflation in the United States and, moreover, that the U.S. central bank, in cooperation with other parts of the government as needed, has sufficient policy instruments to ensure that any deflation that might occur would be both mild and brief.

And the fourth solution is to inflate the debt out of existence. After saying that the Federal Reserve will prevent deflation at all costs, Bernanke then goes on to say this:

> The U.S. government has a technology, called a printing press (or, today, its electronic equivalent), that allows it to produce as many U.S. dollars as it wishes at essentially no cost. By increasing the number of U.S. dollars in circulation, or even by credibly threatening to do so, the U.S. government can also reduce the value of a dollar in terms of goods and services, which is equivalent to raising the prices in dollars of those goods and services. We conclude that, under a paper-money system, a determined government can always generate higher spending and hence positive inflation.

Thus, Bernanke points directly to the most logical solution—we'll inflate our debt out of existence. Inflation really means that our money will become worth less and less.

My mother, who would be over 100 now if she were alive, could remember going to the movies when they cost 5 cents. I can remember, as a child, going to double-feature movies (that is, they actually showed two movies for one price) for 50 cents. All-night drive-ins were even better—you could get four to six movies for a car full of people for a few dollars. Today you could pay $8 to $10 for a single movie ticket, and movie theaters make most of their money off of concessions, not the price of the ticket. Thus, it could easily cost you $20 per person for a movie, popcorn, and a drink. That's inflation.

However, we've seen relatively mild inflation throughout most of America's history. The Federal Reserve actually targets having about 2 percent inflation. But what if inflation ran 100 percent per year as it has in some Central and South American countries? If it did, our debt would soon be worthless, as would the dollar. But we could always start again with a new currency. Such an inflationary scenario would be the most likely solution to the problem of a continually growing American debt. Our debt could be inflated out of existence. And under such circumstances, things would go up in value dramatically.

What would happen to the stock market under such an inflationary scenario? We had relatively high inflation during the 1966 to 1982 bear market. The stock market basically had a lot of volatility, but it was range bound, with the Dow trading between 500 and 1,000 for much of the period. During the entire period, stock prices went up a little, but stock valuations went down a lot and people generally lost money. And that could easily happen. By 1982, the price-to-earnings ratio of the major averages was in the single-digit range.

The fifth solution is that the dollar depreciates relative to other currencies. This solution will make the balance of payments shrink to zero or even become positive assuming that Americans stop spending as foreign goods become more and more expensive. As a result, it should be considered a possibility. This will generally occur as the United States raises interest rates because money moves to where it is treated best. However, high interest rates mean that our debt becomes more and more costly to service. So under that scenario, how would we get rid of the current accumulated debt or even manage it?

And there is a sixth solution and that is for the government to default on its promises of entitlements for Social Security and Medicare. It is a government promise, not a contractual obligation, to pay our Treasury bills and bonds. It would be easy for the government to just change the laws in a way that basically eliminates these entitlements.

What's Your Personal Assessment of Factor 1?

- Do you believe that government, business, and consumers in the United States can continue to spend at current rates without serious consequences?
- Or even if we stopped deficit spending right now, do you believe that we can get out of the current massive debt without serious economic consequences?
- If your answer to the first two questions is no, then what do you think the economic consequences will be? Your answer should be part of the planning you do with respect to the big picture.
- If your answer to the first two questions is yes, then how do you deal with the fact that our gross federal interest payments are now 14 percent of the government's expenses (although they cheat on this and credit about half of it to social security)? If the deficit keeps growing, what will happen?

FACTOR 2. THE SECULAR BEAR MARKET

The U.S. stock market tends to move in large secular cycles, lasting 15 to 20 years. During the bull cycles, stock valuations go up, which means that price-to-earnings (P/E) ratios increase. It also means that equity prices go up. During the bear cycles, stock valuations go down (that is, P/E ratios go down), which usually means that prices go down.[5] Tables 6.1 and 6.2 show the major cycles that have affected the U.S. stock market over the last 200 years.

TABLE 6.1

Primary Bull Markets

Bull Market	Approximate Dates	Real Yearly Returns, %
Good feelings	1815–1835	9.6
Railroad boom	1843–1853	12.5
Civil War and beyond	1861–1881	11.5
Pre–World War I	1896–1906	11.5
Roaring Twenties	1921–1929	24.8
Post–World War II boom	1949–1966	14.1
High-tech boom	1982–2000	14.8

According to market historian Michael Alexander, we have had many such cycles during the last 200 years. Table 6.1 shows a listing of primary bull markets. On the average, these bull markets tend to last about 15 years, and investors who buy and hold the major averages earn about 13.2 percent per year. These bull markets lasted 103 years of this 200-year period.

Unfortunately, for people who believe in buying and holding stocks, primary bull markets tend to be followed by primary bear markets. These are major shakeouts, which tend to correct the excesses of the bull market. The United States is now in such a

TABLE 6.2

Primary Bear Markets

Bear Market	Approximate Dates	Real Yearly Returns, %
Pre–War of 1812	1802–1815	2.8
First Great Depression	1835–1843	−1.1
Pre–Civil War era	1853–1861	−2.8
Banking Crisis era No. 1	1881–1896	3.7
Banking Crisis era No. 2	1906–1921	−1.9
Second Great Depression	1929–1949	1.2
Inflation era	1966–1982	−1.5
War on Terrorism	2000–present	?

primary bear market, which began in early 2000. Table 6.2 shows a listing of primary bear markets.

The average primary bear market lasts 18 years and shows a "real" return of 0.3 percent per year.[6] Thus, stocks may be facing a long period of decline ahead.

At this point, you might be thinking, "This is just someone's theory. You could go into the past and make arguments for all sorts of cycles. And just because cycles may have occurred in the past doesn't mean they'll continue now." But perhaps your thoughts will change if you understand Ed Easterling's "financial physics."

Here are some key points to consider:

- A secular bear cycle doesn't mean that the stock market will go down for 18 years. Instead, it just points out the overall direction of a major cycle within which there will be other bull and bear cycles that could last years. For example, Alexander in 2005 actually commented that we could have a bull cycle that goes into 2007.
- A secular cycle doesn't forecast prices. Instead, it forecasts valuations. For example, in an inflationary atmosphere, prices could go up dramatically but not as much as inflation, meaning that you'd lose real value in the stock market. In addition, stock earnings could go up dramatically while prices rise relatively slowly. This could eventually produce quite low P/E ratios while the stock market continues to go up. During the 1966 to 1982 bear cycle, the Dow Jones Industrial Average bounced off the 1,000 level several times, while P/E ratios continued to erode. During secular bull and bear markets, the number of up versus down days does not vary that much. It's just the results of investing that change because secular bear markets are associated with a high percentage of big down years whereas secular bull markets are associated with a high percentage of big up years.[7]
- Secular bull and bear markets have nothing to do with the economy. For example, from 1966 to 1981 the economy grew at an average rate of 9.6 percent each year while the

Figure 6.3 Change in the P/E ratio since early 2002
Source: Federal Reserve Board

stock market declined. And while the economy grew at a pace of 6.2 percent per year from 1982 through 1999, the stock market grew at a pace of 15.4 percent per year during that time. And ironically, over the last 100 years, economic growth has actually been stronger during secular bear markets when the stock market was weak.

If you've never seen it before, I strongly suggest that you look at Crestmont Research's matrix that shows real returns from the stock market over 20-year periods.[8] What clearly strikes you when you view this chart is that if you invest when P/E ratios are high, you can invest for periods as long as 20 years with a negative return from the stock market. And when the last secular bull market ended, stock market P/E ratios were at historical highs. Even in 2006, they are still way beyond the average at which one can expect reasonable returns. What's the bottom line? The stock market is a dangerous place to be if you just invest and hold onto stocks.

What's the current picture? As of February 1, 2006, the P/E ratio of the S&P 500 was standing at 19.26. This still ranks it in the bottom 10 percent of 10-year groups for expected returns.

Furthermore, it is still way above the historical average for the last 100 years of 15.8.

When the P/E of the S&P 500 is 19 or higher, the average P/E ratio 10 years later is usually around 9. Figure 6.3 shows the change in the P/E ratio of the S&P 500 since the secular bear market started in 2000. Notice that even though 2003 through mid-2006 have not been major down years for the stock market, the P/E ratio has still declined sharply since 2002. And if Easterling is correct about his theory, we could have much more downside.

The next observation that Easterling came up with is that secular bear markets start when dividend yields are very low. The average dividend rate of the S&P 500 over the last 100 years has been around 4.4 percent. Bull markets tend to begin when dividend rates are high, whereas bear markets tend to begin when dividend rates are low. And while today's current dividend rate of the S&P 500 is rising (perhaps due to the impact of favorable taxation on dividends), it is still historically low at 1.48 percent. Bear markets begin at levels this low.

Last, the key element of Ed Easterling's research, in my opinion, is his theory of why P/E ratios change. It all has to do with inflation or deflation. Basically, when inflation is low and stable, the stock market will support P/E ratios in the S&P 500 of 20 or higher. But when inflation starts to grow or deflation sets in, then P/E ratios plummet. And during the end of secular bear markets, P/E ratios are usually in the single-digit range. Furthermore, the worst time to invest, according to Easterling's research is when P/E ratios are high and inflation is relatively stable. Thus, even though Figure 6.3 shows that P/E ratios are generally declining, they are still historically high and inflation is starting to appear.

Easterling believes that U.S. economic growth (real GDP) is relatively stable over time and that U.S. corporate earnings grow consistently with the GDP. Therefore, he believes that an investor needs a perspective only on inflation-deflation to determine future valuations of companies. Under moderate inflation, 1 to 2 percent, we can support high P/E ratios of 20 or higher. But when inflation goes to 3 to 4 percent, P/E ratios will plummet to around 15. At 4 to 5 percent they'll go down to about 13, and at 7 percent and higher they'll go to 10 and below. And under deflationary conditions of any magnitude (that is, –3 percent), they'll also plummet to the single-digit range.

What's Your Personal Assessment of Factor 2?

So what does this mean for you? These are some of the questions you'll have to ask yourself when thinking about the stock market over the long term:

- Do you believe that stock P/E ratios go through cycles?
- Do you believe that during high P/E levels (over 19 percent), long-term returns from the stock market could easily be zero?
- Do you believe that P/E ratios are likely to fall when inflation heats up or deflation enters the picture?
- Do you believe that this pertains to your investing system? In my opinion, the shorter your time frame, the less it pertains to you. However, it would be a mistake to say "I'm a day trader and this doesn't pertain to me" because most day traders could not make it as stock market volatility disappeared during the initial phases of this secular bear market. Generally, as the market goes down, interest in the stock market disappears and market volatility drops.

FACTOR 3. THE GLOBALIZATION OF ECONOMIC FACTORS

An informed investor-trader cannot afford to hide his or her head in the sand of the U.S. markets and not pay attention to what is going on globally. For example, 2003 appeared to be a great year for the U.S. stock market with the S&P 500 going up about 25 percent. But even if you made 25 percent in the U.S. stock market, you still lost money on a worldwide basis because the dollar was down about 40 percent and the U.S. stock market was one of the poorest performing stock markets in the world. In 2003, for example, you could have made 50 percent in Europe, 50 percent in Asia, 38 percent in Latin America, and even 39 percent in Japan, which has been in a major recession-depression for 10 years. A smart investor must look at the entire picture from a global economic standpoint.

So let's look at some of the factors that are influencing the big picture globally. In my opinion, there are three major factors. First, the economies of emerging nations are starting to rise. Second, these emerging economies need raw materials and are thus starting to produce a huge boom in commodity prices. And last, the countries of the world are currently supporting the U.S. dollar because most of the world growth of the 1990s was due to the U.S. consumer. This phenomenon has been called "Bretton Woods II" by some economic commentators.[9]

The first major issue is the growth of emerging countries. China and India, for example, are emerging as major players globally. Many U.S. companies are investing huge amounts of money in China, which is causing its economy to grow. The U.S. companies want access to the market of the billion people that populate China. And these U.S. companies are giving up major concessions in order to gain that access.

While manufacturing tends to be moving to China, the service area tends to be moving to India. India produces many highly trained professionals in business and engineering each year. They will work for a fraction of the cost of their U.S. counterparts; so, many companies are starting to outsource their services to India. For example, if you call up technical support for Microsoft or Dell, chances are you'll end up talking to a technician in India. And according to Forrester Research, by 2015 about 3.3 million U.S. high-tech and service industry jobs will be moved overseas, mostly to India. That represents about $136 billion in lost U.S. wages.[10] In addition, international businesses are replacing their top American executives with executives from India because they are much cheaper and they are as well or better trained.[11]

The second major issue is that the growth of emerging countries is creating a boom in the prices of raw materials. The *Economist* magazine has said that "if China's consumption of raw materials and energy were to rise to rich country levels, the world supply would not have the resources to supply them."[12] Slowly, but surely, however, the Chinese are securing raw materials worldwide. And this suggests that even without inflation, we should have a huge boom in commodities in the next 10 to 15 years.

For example, in late 2004 my friend Steve Sjuggerud was in Argentina. He said that the Chinese were everywhere, and they were doing their best to secure supplies of timber, copper, agricultural products, and whatever raw materials they could get their hands on cheaply. Why do you think the cost of oil has risen to over $70 per barrel in this decade? It's not because oil is becoming scarce. It's because the worldwide demand is increasing, and China is a major source of that demand.

If you look at commodity prices over the last few years, you'll find that they are in a major uptrend. Commodity price increases tend to signal that inflation is increasing but they also signal that the huge worldwide demand for limited commodity resources is also increasing. Figure 6.4 shows a chart that illustrates the basic rise of the CRB (a commodity index). Notice that the trend is clearly up, with prices rising from 280 to about 360—an increase of almost 31 percent in the space of a year.

The third major issue globally is the support of the U.S. dollar by foreign countries, especially Asian countries, so that they can continue to sell to the U.S. consumer. It's estimated that most of the growth of the world economy during the 1990s was due to the insatiable demand for products by the U.S. consumer. Other countries want to continue to sell to the U.S. consumer, and they can do that reasonably only if their currencies remain low in cost compared

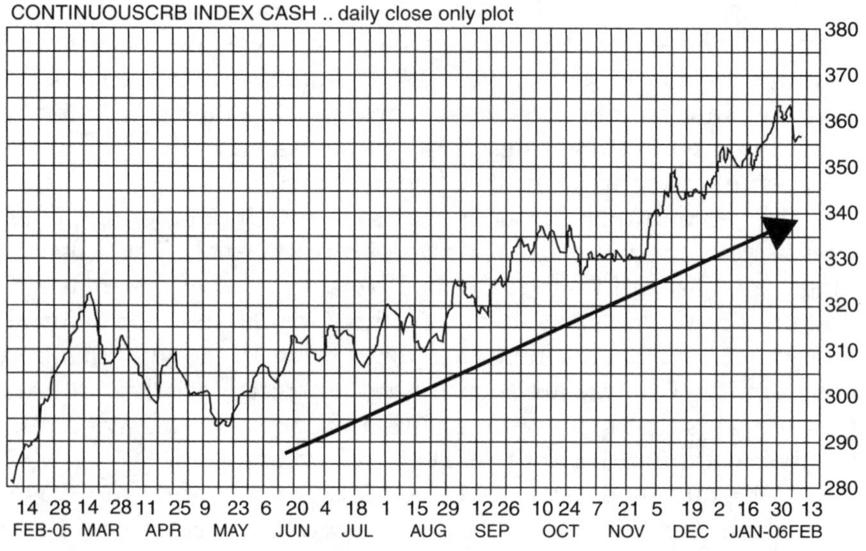

Figure 6.4 The growth in commodity prices (as of February 9, 2006)
Source: Barchart.com

with the U.S. dollar. As a result, an unofficial agreement, known as Bretton Woods II, has sprung up in which foreign countries tend to support the U.S. dollar to keep it from falling (despite the huge deficit in the balance of payments) by purchasing U.S. debt. Foreign countries now own about $3 trillion in U.S. debt, which they maintain by purchasing Treasury bills, notes, and bonds. That debt took more than a decade to accumulate, but it could double within the next three years if our balance of payments does not change.

So what are foreign countries going to do? If they don't continue to support our debt by buying U.S. debt instruments, then the dollar will fall sharply. This will have undesirable effects in that (1) the U.S. consumer will no longer be able to afford their products and (2) they will lose lots of money because they are holding U.S. dollars in the form of debt instruments.

The solution to this problem that many foreign countries have adopted is to slowly move away from supporting the U.S. debt and the U.S. dollar. For example, China is allowing its currency to slowly move up in measured increases. Furthermore, they are using their U.S. dollars to purchase commodity-based products and industries worldwide rather than accumulate U.S. debt.

What's Your Personal Assessment of Factor 3?

In my opinion, when you look at your investment results, you must look at them from a global perspective. If your investments go up, that's great, but what's happening to the major currency in which all of your investments are based? For example, if you make 25 percent on your investment in the U.S. stock market, while the dollar loses 40 percent relative to other currencies, you've basically lost money. If you make 25 percent of your investment but you could have made 50 percent by looking outside of the United States, then your performance is relatively poor.

Thus, when looking at your investment style, you should always consider the global economy by asking yourself the following questions:

- What has my base currency done (relative to other currencies) during the time period I'm considering?
- What has inflation done to the value of my base currency?

- Are my returns reasonable when compared with other markets worldwide in which I could have invested during the same time period?
- How is the global economy moving during this time period, and what is the impact that it will have on my investment strategy?
  - For example, what if commodities continue to escalate at 30 percent per year?
  - What happens if the economy of the country in which I largely invest (for example, the United States) shrinks relative to the economy of other nations in the world?
- What happens if Bretton Woods II disappears and other countries stop supporting the U.S. debt and the U.S. dollar?

FACTOR 4. THE IMPACT OF MUTUAL FUNDS

During most bull markets, people have participated by buying stocks directly. The last bull market was different. Instead, most people were participating through mutual funds. These funds are supposedly managed by a full-time professional manager who could spread his or her risk around and do full-time research for you. In fact, by the peak in the market in 2000, there were nearly as many mutual funds as there were listed stocks. Furthermore, most of these funds were run by fairly young people whose only experience in the market was during the 18-year bull market from 1982 through 2000. They had never seen any sort of bear market of significance.

After the first 30 months of this primary bear market, 566 mutual funds had been absorbed into other funds. In addition, another 414 had been liquidated. This means that 980 mutual funds disappeared in the first 30 months of the bear market.

According to Gregory Baer and Gary Gensler in their book, *The Great Mutual Fund Trap*,[13] most people are much better off in a passively managed index fund than they are in an actively managed mutual fund. Here's why:

- Actively managed mutual funds generally cannot outperform an index fund with no professional management. According to Baer and Gensler, the average annualized performance of actively managed mutual funds that had been around for at least five years trailed the S&P 500 Index by 1.9 percentage points per year. And these figures did not include those funds that failed entirely.

- The financial media is largely supported by the brokerage and mutual fund industries. Consequently, the information that is conveyed to you through that source is biased to support the "bread and butter" of the media. As a result, what you hear is generally not in your best interest. Instead, it is designed to keep you in the market and actively trading.
- People tend to invest in the hot mutual fund. However, these "hot" funds usually underperform the rest of the market once they are advertised to the public.
- The best funds tend to be very small and less than three years old. This is because a mutual fund family can give favorable treatment to a new small fund, giving it preference for new stocks (initial public offerings that they can get at a huge discount) and by allowing it to trade prior to the larger funds in its family. When it becomes hot, the fund family can then advertise it aggressively until it becomes large. Baer and Gensler report that funds that are advertised have had great past track records, but those records seldom continue once they are promoted to the public.
- While a few mutual funds may outperform the market, they usually do so with a lot of variability. One year the fund may make 40 percent, the next year it may lose 15 percent, the next year it might be up 35 percent, and the next year it might be down 30 percent. It might be the best overall performer, but it is doing so with a huge variance in its performance. You probably wouldn't like that sort of performance, especially when you could do much better simply buying an index fund.
- When a mutual fund sells a stock at a profit, it must pass on its tax gains to its shareholders. Thus, you could buy a

mutual fund in November, watch it go down in value, and still have to pay taxes on the gains that the mutual fund incurred by selling stocks at a profit earlier in the year before you invested. This tax is different from the tax you must also pay if you sell the mutual fund at a profit, but it is still your responsibility.

- Mutual funds have more than just management fees, administrative fees, and marketing fees that are passed on to you. They also have trading costs and the costs of having to have a certain amount of its assets in cash. Many mutual funds also have a sales load when you buy or sell your fund. These fees are paid by you. Thus, the costs of investing in funds that are actively managed are huge. According to Baer and Gensler, these fees are the primary reason that actively managed mutual funds cannot outperform a passive fund that simply buys and holds a major stock index.

There are also several drawbacks to mutual funds that Baer and Gensler do not point out:

- First, mutual funds control much of the stock market through their ownership. Most of them tend to invest in the large blue-chip companies of Wall Street, partially because these are the most liquid. In addition, if the fund falls in value, the public is not likely to fault them much if their holdings include giants such as General Electric and Microsoft. However, in the bear market scenarios described in factor 2, there is a huge risk to the market in this sort of strategy. When panic selling sets in, which is almost a certainty in a major market crash, the only way mutual funds can raise cash is by selling their most liquid stocks, those of the major blue-chip companies. When this happens, we will see the major indexes going down very sharply.[14]
- Second, active mutual funds cannot outperform the market indexes because they are generally traded on a model that doesn't expect outstanding performance. Instead, the goal of the average mutual fund is to outperform the market

averages and other mutual funds. This means that if the overall market is down 15 percent on the year and most funds are down 20 percent or more, then a fund manager who is down only 5 percent will be considered a star performer. However, losing money is still losing money!

- In addition, most mutual funds are guided by a charter that shapes their investing. This charter usually requires that they maintain a particular level of commitment to stocks. For example, a mutual fund's charter might require that it be at least 90 percent invested in S&P 500 stocks even in a bear market. Different mutual funds will have different charters, but most of them do not allow the flexibility that would be required to practice the most common risk control techniques that I have been giving to my clients for some time. In other words, they cannot practice proper risk control and position-sizing techniques that you'll learn about later in this book. As a result, it would not surprise me if we had 1,000 or fewer mutual funds remaining by the time this secular bear market is over.
- Last, most retirees have been forced to put their retirement funds into mutual funds because their 401(k) plans do not allow any other form of investment. As a result, when the baby boomers start to retire between 2008 and 2011, we will start to see a massive liquidation of mutual funds. And since these funds basically support the major averages, we will probably see huge falls in the major averages as the retirement funds move out of the market.

This last point is probably the most important point of all. Think about it carefully and decide whether or not you believe it. If it is true, it is one of the major factors that will play itself out before the current secular bear market ends.

However, one aspect of mutual funds has become very helpful to the stock market long term: the development of exchange-traded funds (or ETFs). You can find exchange-traded funds for almost everything—countries, sectors of the market, styles of investing, and even some commodities such as gold and energy. What this basically means is that even though the stock market might not be the best place to be over the long term, you can probably find an ETF that represents some sector of the world economy that is doing very well. In my opinion, this is a huge silver lining. Whenever there is a potential crisis, there is also an opportunity.

What's Your Personal Assessment of Factor 4?

In my opinion, when you look at the big picture, you must look at what institutional money is doing. I've basically laid out my beliefs about how mutual funds affect the market. Right now they shift money around a lot to see if they can get better returns, but it doesn't leave the market and it tends to support the major averages. But you must begin to think about what will happen when retirement funds move out of the market.

In addition, I did not discuss other aspects of institutional money. I believe that institutional traders are among the most inefficient in the world, yet they control a good share of the money in various markets. Banks make markets for foreign exchange, but bank traders (in my opinion) are largely very inefficient and very poorly managed. What impact does this have on you if you are a forex trader?

At minimum, I believe you should ask yourself the following questions:

- What markets will I be trading, and who trades most of the money in these markets?
- What is the system by which the big players operate in my market? Is there some way that their system could totally break down? How and under what condition is it likely to occur?
- How can I monitor what the big traders are doing?
- How will "what the big traders are doing" affect my strategy and my performance?

FACTOR 5. CHANGES IN RULES, REGULATIONS, AND TAXES

Another factor that strongly influences the big picture in trading is any change in the rules, the regulations, and the laws (especially tax laws) affecting the market you wish to trade. These are especially important to keep up with, although it is sometimes difficult to discern exactly what the future effects will be on your markets. However, let me give you a few examples of such changes and how they have impacted the markets. You can then decide for yourself how much you want to keep up with them in the future.

Tax Reform Act of 1986: Wiping Out Many Real Estate Investments and the Boating Industry

When Ronald Reagan tackled tax reform in the 1980s, he dramatically lowered the top tax rates, which, in my opinion, helped to greatly stimulate the economy. However, he also closed many loopholes. Many real estate partnerships, for example, sprang up in the 1980s in order to take advantage of significant loopholes in the tax law. But when those loopholes were closed by the Tax Reform Act of 1986, those partnerships basically went out of business. The net result was a record number of bankruptcies for people involved in those loopholes. It also produced a savings and loan crisis in which the government had to bail out the savings and loan industry to the tune of $125 billion. Here are some of the implications of that tax bill:

- Depreciation on real estate went from 19 to 31 years, effectively making profitable investments unprofitable.
- Real estate losses were denied to passive investors, making real estate partnerships that accumulated real estate for tax savings for their limited partners obsolete overnight.
- In addition, the dividend tax exemption was eliminated, and there was an increase in taxes on the purchase of luxury boats, which caused the boating industry to collapse.

Now ask yourself this question: Had you been involved in any of those businesses that were taking advantage of some major tax loopholes, do you think it might have been to your advantage to do some planning just in case the loopholes were closed? In essence those businesses were a form of arbitrage (taking advantage of loopholes). And in any arbitrage system, you must know when the loophole closes and have a way to get out without getting ruined financially.

Day Trading: Regulations Changed by the SEC

On February 27, 2001, the SEC imposed rules that changed day trading forever. First, they declared that anyone making four or more day trades in five consecutive days was a pattern day trader. The rule itself is ridiculous because you could enter five long-term positions but get stopped out the same day and suddenly you are a day trader.[15]

Second, if you became a day trader, there was one positive benefit: You got your margin increased to four times your equity (but this margin could not be carried overnight). But it also required that you must have a $25,000 account, which immediately eliminated about 80 percent of the day traders at the time. It was a significant move that had a major impact on trading.

It is ironic that my day trading book came out in 2001. Not only did the scope of day trading change dramatically just prior to the publication of the book, but the New York Stock Exchange went to decimalization. Suddenly, the minimum bid-ask spread was no longer a 1/16—it was now a penny. And in an instant, some of the strategies we'd developed for that book were obsolete.

Again, you must ask yourself, what regulations could suddenly change for my selected markets that would totally change how I approach the market? Such regulations can change how you trade and your profitability.

Development of the Roth IRAs

The Taxpayer Relief Act of 1997 established the Roth IRA. Money placed into a Roth IRA was not tax deductible, but money taken out of the Roth IRA was not taxable at all, including accumulated profits. What a short-term windfall for the government! Suddenly, everyone was transferring their funds from traditional IRAs to Roth IRAs. And for every one of these transfers, the government received a tax on the total amount based on the investor's tax bracket. During the late 1990s, the Clinton administration was credited with having a balanced budget. But how much of the balanced budget was due to the massive tax infusion that came from millions of taxpayers transferring all of their IRA contributions into Roth IRAs? While I don't know the answer to this question, the example is a classic one of the government changing a regulation to make the current administration's economic picture look very bright at the expense of future government revenues. By the way, to gain back some revenues, the government could easily change its mind and make the profits from Roth IRAs taxable. In fact, I predict they will. As an example, they said that they'd never tax social security, but that promise certainly changed when money was needed.

Strong Dollar Policy to Weak Dollar Policy

During the Clinton administration, the U.S. government had a strong dollar policy. They supported the U.S. dollar vigorously. And short-term interest rates were high enough that the dollar was an attractive vehicle for foreign money. When the Bush administration took over, the strong dollar policy was dropped as interest rates were lowered dramatically. The results on the dollar of both policies were obvious, although the effects on the economy of such policies have been more subtle.

What's Your Personal Assessment of Factor 5?

To a certain extent assessing factor 5 involves looking at the most recent changes and attempting to determine the long-term effect of those rules, regulations, policy, and law changes. You need to ask yourself the following questions:

- What are the long-term effects of the most recent government changes on my investments and investment strategies?
- Are they fully played out? Are they in progress? Or are they just beginning to impact the markets?
- What will be the effects of proposed legislation on my markets and my strategies?
- What's being proposed, and could it totally ruin my strategy or market?
- Is there any way I can take advantage of these changes?

And last, you need to anticipate things that could change. For example, many of the real estate strategies that were ruined by the Tax Reform Act of 1986 were taking losing real estate deals and making them profitable to investors just because of the tax implications. You can probably state as a rule of thumb that if something costs you money and is worth doing only because of the tax implications, then it is probably a very dangerous strategy.

- Do any of my strategies fall into this category of making sense only because of the tax implications?
- If so, how can I find something that is more effective and makes good money without needing support from the government?

FACTOR 6. HUMAN BEINGS' TENDENCY TO PLAY A LOSING ECONOMIC GAME

The last factor I want to talk about is human inefficiency. When I model some aspect of success, I usually find that most people in general are "programmed" to do exactly the opposite. I can give you a few of these examples here, and I believe they should enter into your long-term planning.

- Some of the best investments you'll ever make are those with real intrinsic value, selling at bargain prices because everyone hates them. This occurs because of the fear and greed cycle that most human beings have. People sell (because of fear) at market bottoms and they buy (because of greed) at market tops.
- If everyone is talking about the investment you are interested in and you hear about it through the media, it's time to sell. In 1999, I can remember the bartender at our hotel saying he didn't need to take my stock market course because he could teach it. And I remember a waiter at a restaurant telling me that this was a "part-time job" because he was a full-time trader and had accumulated nearly $400,000 in trading capital. That's when I get very nervous. And, of course, the secular bull market ended in early 2000, within months of these occurrences.
- The key to making profits in the market is to cut your losses short and let your profits run. However, prospect theory (which won the Nobel Prize for Economics in 2002)

basically says that the average person will take risks with losses and be conservative with profits. In other words, people do the opposite of the golden rule of trading, which I've been saying for more than 20 years.

- The average person thinks that market success is all about picking the right stocks and if you lose money, it's because you picked the wrong stocks. Good traders know it's all about how you sell that really counts. And really successful traders also understand the impact of position sizing and your personal psychology on real success.
- The most important factors in trading are your personal psychology and position sizing. The average person knows little to nothing about either of these topics, and you certainly will not hear the media discussing them. They might discuss the psychology of the market, but not your personal psychology. Furthermore, they might discuss asset allocation, but few people understand that the real advantage of asset allocation is the fact that it tells you "how much" to invest in each asset, including cash.
- An easy way to play the money game is to have passive income that is greater than your expenses. This is what I call financial freedom, and the average person with a plan can achieve financial freedom in five to seven years. However, most people think they win by having a lot of the latest toys, and if the down payments and monthly payments are low enough, they can have those toys now. This idea basically produces financial slavery, and it is why U.S. consumers now have a negative savings rate.

These comments are just a few of the ideas that suggest to me that the average person is doomed to financial failure. The average person is just too full of biases that lead to financial disaster. My solution to this problem is to help people become more efficient in their decision making. However, I believe that you can bank on the fact that most people (including big money institutions) will generally do most things very inefficiently when it comes to money. However, big money institutions have one advantage in that they tend to make the rules that most people follow in their attempt to win the money game.

What's Your Personal Assessment of Factor 6?

Monitoring this factor can also help you generate trading ideas and determine when a potential strategy might stop working because the psychological tide is changing. For example, you should constantly be asking yourself the following questions:

- How am I being inefficient, and how can I make myself more efficient and give myself an edge by working on my personal psychology?
- What are the major trends that the crowd is following? Look at magazine covers and pay attention to the financial media. When the media start to talk about trends, then those trends are probably over with or at least due for a correction.
- What is currently out of favor that has tremendous value? And what happens when I mention these investments to my friends? If they absolutely hate them, then they are probably good investments provided they are not going down in price or (better yet) have started on an uptrend.
- How can I emphasize my personal psychology and position sizing to become a more efficient trader-investor? You'll find ideas on these topics throughout this book.

OTHER AREAS YOU MIGHT CONSIDER

The six factors I've brought up are by no means everything you could (or even should) consider in viewing the big picture. What about global warming? If you believe that global warming is a real, significant trend, then monitor it. Major climate changes over the next 5 to 10 years could have a much greater impact on finances and markets than anything I've mentioned. Look at what's happened with hurricanes recently. What if those hurricanes are just the beginning of the impact of global warming? As the oceans get warmer, hurricanes will get stronger and that's just one of the many potential economic challenges of global warming.

What about the potential for the breakout of major wars in the world? The preceding scenarios that I have mentioned were all based on peaceful world conditions. But what if the War on Terror escalates either because of the actions of the United States or the actions of the terrorists? What impact will that have on your markets or your trading strategies? And what about major hostilities erupting between countries in the world? Perhaps these things are worth planning for and thinking about.

What about major trade wars? What if certain countries stop trading with other countries? What will happen to your markets as a result?

What about the health crisis in America and the world? We currently have a trillion-dollar-a-year industry that feeds America processed foods that destroy our health. And we currently have another trillion dollar industry that is designed to treat the symptoms of eating processed foods, rather than the cause. One doctor in Maryland lost his license by simply giving large doses of vitamins intravenously to his patients. I personally find this treatment to be rejuvenating, but I have to go to Switzerland to get it. I think that health-care trends will also have a major impact on the economy, but, of course, these are just my beliefs.

These elements, along with other major factors that I've probably overlooked, also could become part of your big-picture planning.

HOW WILL YOU MONITOR THE BIG PICTURE?

Let's say that you decide to look at six factors on a monthly basis. It doesn't matter what they are at this point because they could be different for everyone. Everyone's beliefs are different! However, you do need to work out the impact of each factor on your markets and strategies. You also need to understand what conditions would cause you to shift the markets and the types of strategies you use. In addition, you also need to determine how you will measure those factors and how you will keep up with them.

Let me give you several examples of what you could do. I personally write a monthly update on the markets that's published on the first Wednesday of each month in my free e-mail newsletter, *Tharp's Thoughts*.[16] Doing so forces me to keep up with what I think is important and allows me to help others who don't want to do the work themselves.

Ken Long, who teaches a workshop for us on various strategies you can use with exchange-traded funds, writes a weekly commentary on the market that he publishes. That commentary includes a relative weighting of the performance of all of the ETFs that are now traded. Ken's weighted summary looks pretty much like Figure 6.5.

The boxes in Figure 6.5 each represent ETFs for various sectors of the world economy. And with each box is a weighted relative strength number.[17] The idea is to look for sectors of the economy that are much stronger than the S&P 500, which is represented by the SPY box in the center with a rating of 39. Notice that different boxes have different ratings with the strongest being EWZ (Brazil with a rating of 66) and the weakest being bonds (Treasury bonds, TLT, and corporate bonds, LQD, both at 33).[18]

The entire world is represented in this figure. The center nine boxes represent the overall U.S. stock market with big-cap stocks being on the top (DIA, SPY, and QQQQ) and small-cap stocks on the bottom (IJS, IWM, and WT). Value stocks are represented on the left. Growth stocks are on the right. And balanced stocks are in the middle. Thus, at a glance you can tell that the place to be in the U.S. stock market on February 11, 2006, was in small caps (bottom row)

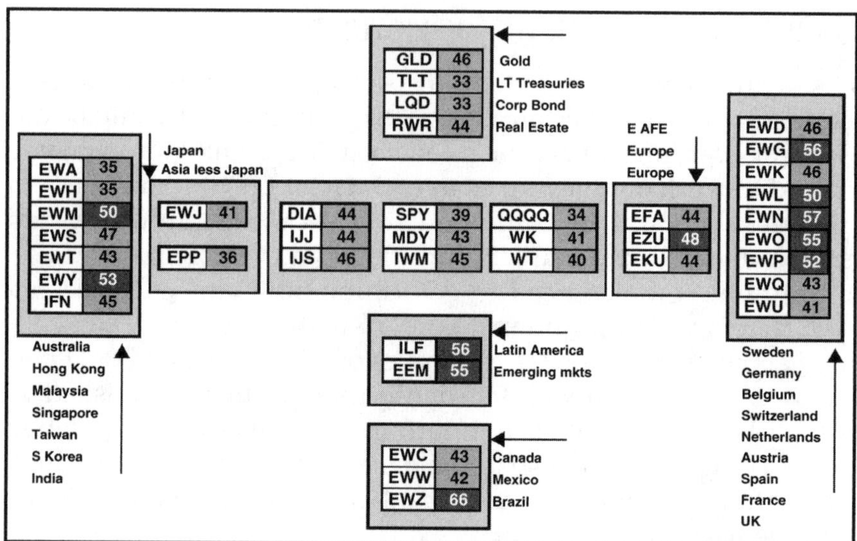

Figure 6.5 A "Tortoise" worldview market model based on ETFs (as of February 11, 2006)

and value stocks (left row). However, those areas are nowhere near the strongest areas on the chart.

You can get a worldview by looking at Asian markets on the left of the page, European markets on the right of the page, and American continent countries at the bottom. Clearly as of February 11, 2006, Latin America (ILF), emerging markets (EEM), Brazil (EWZ), Germany (EWG), Austria (EWO), the Netherlands (EWN), and South Korea (EWY) were the strongest sectors of the world.

The top of the graph also shows other financial markets in the United States, including gold, long-term Treasury bonds, corporate bonds, and real estate. While there are certainly some factors that are not considered in the chart, the chart does give you one of the best pictures of the world markets that I see on a regular basis. And you could either pay for this sort of service from Tortoise Capital[19] or make up a similar chart on your own.

SUMMARY

One method of trading is based on mental scenarios. However, I recommend that all investors do at least a monthly view of the major factors influencing the markets and that they have a way to measure changes and their impact on the way they trade.

A sample view of the factors affecting the major markets of the world was discussed based on my beliefs:

- U.S. debt
- The secular bear market in the United States
- The emergence of countries like China and India with the impact of their consumption patterns on the world's raw materials
- The current mutual fund structure and the problems that will happen when the baby boomers retire
- The impact of rules, regulations, and new laws, especially tax laws
- The fact that most human beings play a losing economic game
- Plus other potential major factors

I strongly suggest that you think about the impact of these potential factors plus any others that you think could be significant. In addition, I strongly recommend that you find a way to measure these factors and their potential impact on your markets and your strategies at least monthly. I have given you several sources of monthly information to begin with.

NOTES

1. Jack Schwager, *Market Wizards* (New York: New York Institute of Finance, 1988), p. 306.
2. U.S. Congressional Record, March 17, 1993, Vol. 33, p. H-1303, Speaker Rep. James Traficant, Jr. (Ohio), addressing the House.
3. John F. Wasik commentary, www.bloomberg.com, January 17, 2006.
4. You can find that study at research.stlouisfed.org/publications/review/06/07/Kotlikoff.pdf.
5. My primary sources for this material are Michael Alexander's book, *Stock Cycles: Why Stocks Won't Beat Money Markets over the Next Twenty Years* (Lincoln, Neb.: Writers Club Press, 2000), and Ed Easterling's fabulous research at www.crestmontresearch.com and his book, *Unexpected Returns: Understanding Secular Stock Market Cycles* (Fort Bragg: Calif.: Cypress House, 2005), pp. 49–52; plus my many years of reading Richard Russell's e-mail commentaries on the Dow Theory. See www.dowtheoryletters.com.
6. "Real" returns are adjusted for inflation. The overall real return for stocks since 1802 is 6.8 percent, according to Alexander, *Stock Cycles*. And two thirds of that return comes from dividends.
7. See Easterling, *Unexpected Returns*, pp. 49–52.
8. This can be viewed at www.crestmontresearch.com/content/Matrix%20Options.htm.
9. I've seen the term "Bretton Woods II" mentioned in both John Mauldin's weekly e-letter (www.JohnMauldin.com) and in William ("Bill") Gross's market commentary, which can be found on the PIMCO Bonds Web site: www.pimco.com.
10. See *Christian Science Monitor*, July 23, 2003.
11. Personal communication with a friend who used to run the Asian division of one of the world's largest corporations.
12. *Economist*, August 19, 2004.

13. Gregory Baer and Gary Gensler, *The Great Mutual Fund Trap: An Investment Recovery Plan* (New York: Broadway Books, 2002).
14. Most of the market decline from 2000 through the end of 2002 was due to individuals selling stock. Mutual fund redemptions still are not that high. If large mutual fund redemptions do not occur, then I would not expect the huge downward scenario described earlier in this book.
15. I'm not a day trader, but I've achieved that status because of being stopped out quickly in my long-term positions.
16. *Tharp's Thoughts* is a free weekly e-mail available by subscription at www.iitm.com. I comment on the overall market on the first Wednesday of each month.
17. While Ken uses a weighted average of the strength, you could also monitor ETFs in terms of efficiency (that is, change in price divided by daily volatility), or you could use risk adjusted strength, or any of a number of other measures based on your beliefs about what is important.
18. Relative strengths tend to change quite rapidly, and this model was already out of date by the time the manuscript was sent to the publisher. However, Ken's strategy is to remain with the strongest ETFs as long as they are outperforming the S&P 500, so he can remain with a position for a long time.
19. Go to www.tortoisecapital.com for more information about Ken Long's weekly updates.

CHAPTER 7

Six Keys to a Great Trading System

He who thinks he knows, doesn't know. He who knows that he doesn't know, knows.

Lao Tse

This chapter is the key to understanding how great traders think in terms of systems. The material is critically important if you want real success as a trader or investor. As a result, I have elected to repeat it through different metaphors many different times. But you have to "get it" only once to really understand the incredible benefits these variables can unleash for you.

In my opinion, there are six key variables that you must understand to develop a successful trading system. Let's explore these six variables and how they impact your profits or losses as a trader or investor:

1. *Reliability or what percentage of time you make money.* For example, do you make money on 60 percent of your investments and lose money on 40 percent of them?
2. *The relative size of your profits compared to your losses when traded at the smallest possible level (that is, one share of stock or one futures contract).* For example, the relative size would be the same if you lost $1 per share on losing trades and made $1 per share on winning trades. However, the relative size would be quite different if you

made $10 per share on winning trades and only lost $1 per share on losing trades.

3. *Your cost of making an investment or trade.* This is the destructive force on your account size whenever you trade. It's your execution costs and your brokerage commissions. These costs can really accumulate over many trades. Day trading used to be prohibitive because of these costs, but even with today's dramatically reduced commissions, they are still a factor that you must consider if you are very active.
4. *How often you get the opportunity to trade.* Now imagine holding the first three variables constant. Their combined effect would then depend on how often you trade. The results will be much different if you make 100 trades each day compared with 100 trades each year.
5. *Your position-sizing model or how many units you trade at one time (that is, 1 share of stock versus 10,000 shares of stock).* Obviously, the amount you win or lose per share is multiplied by the number of shares you trade.
6. *The size of your trading-investing capital.* The effect of the first four variables on your account depends significantly on the size of your account. For example, the cost of trading will have a significantly greater effect on a $1,000 account than it will on a million dollar account. If it costs $20 to trade, then you would take a 2 percent hit on each trade in the $1,000 account before you'd make a profit. As a result, you'd have to average more than 2 percent profit per trade just to cover the cost of trading. However, the impact of the same $20 in costs becomes insignificant (that is, 0.002 percent) if you have a million dollar account. Similarly, a $500 loss will decimate a $1,000 account, but it will have almost no effect (that is, 0.05 percent) on a million dollar account.

Would you want to focus on just one of those six variables? Or do you think that all six of them are equally important? When I ask the question in that manner, you probably agree that all six variables are important.

However, if you were to devote all of your energy into focusing on just one of those variables, which one would it be? Perhaps you think this question is a little naïve since all of them are important. Nevertheless, there is a reason behind this question, so write your answer in the space provided.

ANSWER:

The reason I asked you to focus on one item is because most traders and investors often focus on only one of the six items in their day-to-day activity. Their focus tends to be on the first factor, reliability, or the need to be right. People are obsessed with it to the exclusion of all else. Yet if all six components are important to success, you can begin to understand how naïve it can be to just focus on being right.

The first four variables are part of the topic I call *expectancy*. They are the primary focus of this chapter. The last two variables are part of what I call the *"how much"* factor or *position sizing*. We'll touch on position sizing in this chapter, and we'll focus on it in detail later in this book.

THE SNOW FIGHT METAPHOR

To illustrate the importance of all six variables, let me guide you through a metaphor that might give you a different perspective from one of just thinking about money and systems. Imagine that you are hiding behind a large wall of snow. Someone is throwing snowballs at your wall, and your objective is to keep your wall as large as possible for maximum protection.

Thus, the metaphor immediately indicates that the size of the wall is a very significant variable. If the wall is too small, you can't avoid getting hit. But if the wall is massive, then you are probably not going to get hit. Variable 6, the size of your initial equity, is a little like the size of the wall. In fact, you might consider your starting capital to be a wall of money that protects you. The more money you have, assuming the other variables stay the same, the more protection you will have.

Now imagine that the person throwing snowballs at you has two different kinds of snowballs—white snowballs and black snowballs. White snowballs are a little like winning trades; they simply stick to the wall of snow and increase its size. Now imagine the impact of having a lot of white snowballs thrown at you. They would simply build up the wall. It would get bigger and bigger, and you would have more protection.

Imagine that black snowballs dissolve snow and make a hole in the wall equivalent to their size. You might think of black snowballs as being "antisnow." Thus, if a lot of black snowballs were thrown at your wall, it would soon disappear or at least have a lot of holes in it. Black snowballs are a lot like losing trades—they chip away at your wall of security like losing trades chip away at your equity.

Variable 1, how often you are right, is a little like focusing on the percentage of white snowballs. You would naturally want all the snowballs coming to your wall to be white and add to your wall. It's probably easy for you to see how people who don't focus on the big picture might devote all of their attention into "making" as many snowballs as possible be white.

But let's consider the relative size of the two kinds of snowballs. How big are the white and black snowballs relative to each other? For example, imagine that the white snowballs are the size of golf balls, while the black snowballs are like 6-foot-diameter boulders. If that were the case, it would probably only take one black snowball to break down the wall—even if white snowballs were being thrown at the wall all day. On the other hand, if the white snowball was the size of a 6-foot boulder, then one snowball each day would probably build up the wall enough to protect you from a continual bombardment of black snowballs the size of golf balls. The relative size of the two kinds of snowballs is equivalent to variable 2 in our model—the relative size of profits and losses. Hopefully, by visualizing the snow fight metaphor, you can understand the importance of variable 2.

Variable 3, the cost of trades, is a little like assuming that each snowball has a slight destructive effect on the wall—regardless of whether it is white or black. Each white snowball has a slight destructive effect on the wall, hopefully less than its effect in building up the wall. Similarly each black snowball destroys a little of the wall just by hitting it, and this simply adds to the normal destructive effect of black snow upon the wall. Clearly, the size of this general destructive force could have an overall impact on the outcome of the snowball fight.

Let's assume that our snowballs only come at the wall one at a time. After 100 snowballs have hit the wall, the condition of your wall will depend upon the relative volume of white and black snow hitting the wall. In our model, you can measure the effectiveness of the snowball fight by the condition of the wall. If the wall is growing, it means that the total volume of white snow hitting the wall is greater than the total volume of black snow hitting the wall. And the growing wall is like growing profits. You'll feel more secure as it gets bigger. If the wall is shrinking, then it means that relatively more black, than white, snow is hitting the wall. Eventually, your wall will lose all of its protection, and you will no longer be able to play the game.

When you put the first three variables together, you can calculate the average impact per snowball on your wall. To obtain the total amount of white and black snow that impacted your wall after 100 snowballs hit, you would subtract the effect of the negative impact of the black snow from the positive impact of the white snow. Add to that value the impact of the total destructive power of the snowballs (that is, factor 3). Once you have determined the total effect of the 100 snowballs, divide that value by 100, and you will have the impact of each snowball. If the impact is positive (that is, relatively more white snow), then your wall will grow. If the impact is negative (that is, relatively more black snow), then your wall will shrink. The relative impact of each snowball is our snowball equivalent of what I call "expectancy" in the trading world.

> For those of you who are more mathematically inclined, here is a numerical example:
>
> Let's say 60 white snowballs hit that add 240 cubic inches to the pile
>
> Let's say 40 black snowballs hit that subtract 120 cubic inches from the pile
>
> Let's say the total destructive effect of 100 snowballs is 10 cubic inches
>
> The net impact of 100 snowballs is 240 less 120 less 10 for the destructive effect. The net impact is 110 cubic inches.

> If you divide 110 cubic inches by 100 snowballs, then the net impact is that each snowball adds 1.1 cubic inch to the wall.

In the real world of investing or trading, expectancy tells you the net profit or loss that you can expect per dollar risked over a large number of single unit[1] trades. If the net impact per trade is positive, you can expect your account to grow. If the net impact is negative, you can expect your account to disappear.

Notice that, in the expectancy model, you could have 99 losing trades, each costing you a dollar. Thus, you would be down $99. However, if you had one winning trade of $500, then you would have a net payoff of $401 ($500 less $99)—despite the fact that only one of your trades was a winner and 99 percent of your trades were losers. Let's also say that your cost of trading is $1 per trade or $100 per hundred trades. Thus, you would have a net profit of $301, and your expectancy (that is, the average impact of each trade) would be plus $3.01 per dollar risked. Are you beginning to understand why expectancy is made up of all of the first three variables? And just as the effect on the wall could be predicted by the average impact of a single snowball (that is, snowball expectancy), the effect on your equity can be predicted by the average impact of each trade (that is, trading expectancy).

Now let's continue our snow fight metaphor just a little further. Variable 4 is essentially the frequency at which snowballs are thrown. Let's say that the average impact per snowball is to add 1.1 cubic inches of snow to the wall. If a snowball is thrown once each minute for an hour, the impact will be to add 66 cubic inches to the wall. If two snowballs are thrown each hour, then your wall will only grow 2.2 cubic inches per hour. Obviously the first scenario has 30 times the impact of the second one. Thus, the rate at which snowballs are thrown will have a major impact on the status of the wall.[2]

The frequency of your trades will have a similar effect in the rate of change of your equity. If you make $500 net after 100 trades, then the amount of time it takes you to make those 100 trades will determine the growth of your account. If it takes you a year to make 100 trades, then your account will grow by only $500 per year. If you make 100 trades each day, then your account will grow by $10,000 per month (assuming 20 trading days per month) or $120,000 per year. Which method would you want to trade: one that makes $500 per year or one that makes $120,000 per year? The answer is obvious, but the methods could be exactly alike (that is, in that both have the same expectancy). The only difference is the frequency of trading.

Based on our discussion of the snow fight metaphor, which of the first four variables do you think are most important now? Why? What is the basis of your conclusion? Hopefully, at this time you can see the importance of each variable. These make up the basis for expectancy, and they determine the effectiveness of your trading system.

Variables 5 and 6—the position-sizing variables—are the most important factors in your overall profitability. You should already understand how important the size of the wall (variable 6) is in playing the game. If the wall is too small, then a few black snowballs could destroy it. It must be big enough to protect you.

Let's look at variable 5, the variable that tells you how much. Up to this point we've just assumed that our snowballs arrive at the wall one at a time. But imagine the impact of having snowballs arriving in large numbers at the same time. First, imagine the impact on the wall of one black snowball the size of a golf ball hitting the wall. It would make a single, golf-ball-sized dent in the wall. Now, imagine 10,000 of them hitting the wall simultaneously. It totally changes the impact of your thinking, doesn't it?

The metaphor of 10,000 snowballs simply illustrates the importance of position sizing—that part of your system that tells you how much. We've been talking about 1 unit of size up to now—1 snowball or 1 share of stock. An onslaught of 10,000 black snowballs the size of golf balls could totally demolish your wall unless the wall is massive.

Similarly, you might have a trading method that loses only a dollar per share of stock when it loses. When you purchase your stock in units of 10,000, however, your loss suddenly becomes enormous. It's now $10,000! Again, notice the importance of position sizing. If your equity is $1 million, then a $10,000 loss is only 1 percent. But if your equity is just $20,000, then a $10,000 loss is 50 percent.

Now that you have the perspective of seeing all the key variables involved in the success of your system (or your snowball fight), we can focus in on the details of expectancy. Remember that expectancy is the average impact of a snowball. Similarly, expectancy is the average impact on your account per trade per dollar risked.

LOOKING AT EXPECTANCY UNDER A MAGNIFYING GLASS

One of the real secrets of trading success is to think in terms of reward-to-risk ratios. Similarly, the first key to understanding expectancy is to think of your trades in terms of their reward-to-risk ratio. Ask yourself, "What's the risk on this trade? And is the potential reward worth the potential risk?" So how do you determine the potential risk on a trade? Well, at the time you enter any trade, you should predetermine some point at which you'd get out of the trade to preserve your capital. That point is the risk you have in the trade or your expected loss. For example, if you buy a $40 stock and you decide to get out if that stock falls to $30, then your risk is $10.

I like to call the risk you have in a trade *R*. That should be easy to remember because *R* is short for risk. *R* can represent either your risk per unit, which in the example is $10 per share, or it can represent your total risk. If you bought 100 shares of stock with a risk of $10 per share, then you would have a total risk of $1,000.

Remember that I'm asking you to think in terms of reward-to-risk ratios. If you know that your total initial risk on a position is $1,000, then you can express all of your profits and losses as a ratio of your initial risk. For example, if you make a profit of $2,000 (or $20 per share), then you have a 2*R* profit. If you have a profit of $10,000, then you have a profit of 10*R*.

The same thing works on the loss side. If you have a loss of $500, then you have a 0.5*R* loss. If you have a loss of $2,000, then you have a 2*R* loss. But wait, you say, how could you have a 2*R* loss if your total risk was $1,000? Well, perhaps you didn't keep your word about taking a $1,000 loss and you didn't exit when you should have exited. Perhaps the market gapped down against you. Losses bigger than 1*R* happen all the time. Your goal as a trader (or as an investor) is to keep your losses at 1*R* or less. Warren Buffett, known to many as the world's most successful investor, says the number 1 rule of investing is to not lose money. However, contrary to popular belief, Warren Buffett does have losses. Thus, a much better version of Buffett's number 1 rule would be to *keep your losses to 1*R *or less*.

When you have a series of profits and losses expressed as reward-to-risk ratios, what you really have is what I call an

R-multiple distribution. *As a result, any trading system can be characterized as being an* R*-multiple distribution.* In fact, you'll find that thinking about trading systems as *R*-multiple distributions really helps you to understand your systems and to learn what you can expect from them in the future.

> A much better version of Buffett's number 1 rule would be to keep your losses to 1*R* or less.

So what does all of this have to do with expectancy? When you have an *R*-multiple distribution from your trading system, you need to get the mean of that distribution. And the mean *R* multiple is what I call the system's "expectancy." What expectancy gives you is the average *R* value that you can expect from the system over many trades. Put another way, expectancy tells you how much you can expect to make on the average, per dollar risked, over a number of trades. In the snowball fight, expectancy was the average impact per snowball. In the world of trading and investing, expectancy is the average impact of any given trade relative to the initial risk or *R*.

Let's look at an example. Since a trading system can be represented by its *R*-multiple distribution, I like to simulate trading systems with a bag of marbles. Let's say we have a bag of marbles consisting of 60 blue marbles and 40 black marbles. According to the rules of the game, when you draw out a blue marble, you win the amount you risked (that is, it's a 1*R* winner), and when you draw out a black marble, you lose the amount you risked (that is, it's a 1*R* loser). Each time a marble is drawn out, it is replaced. Now you can easily figure out the expectancy of this game because it represents the mean *R* multiple for the bag. There are 60 1*R* winners and 40 1*R* losers. The net result of all the marbles is plus 20*R*. And since there are 100 marbles (that is, 100 trades), the expectancy of the bag is 20*R* divided by 100, or 0.2*R*. On the average, over many trades, we can expect to make 0.2*R* per trade.

Notice that with expectancy, you can get a rough estimate of how much you'll make over a given number of trades. For example, suppose you risked $2 per marble pull and you did this 1,000 times with each marble being replaced after it's drawn so that the expectancy is the same for each trade. Since your average gain is 0.2*R*, you'd expect to make 200*R* over 1,000 trades. And if you risked $2 per trade (that is, *R* = $2), then you'd expect to make $400.

Now do you see why it's called "expectancy"? It gives you an idea of what to expect from your system on the average (per dollar risked).

Let's say you make 20 trades each month. Your average monthly gain should be 4*R*. But will you make 4*R* each month? No you won't. *The expectancy is your average gain (or loss) stated in terms of* R. *On about half of your months you'll make less money, and on half your months you'll make more money.* In fact, I ran a Monte Carlo simulation of 10,000 20-trade months with this *R*-multiple distribution. That is, I simulated a 20-trade month by using my computer to pull 1 marble out of a bag (and then replace it) 20 times to see what the overall results would be. I repeated this process 10,000 times to determine what I could expect from the system on the average. What I discovered by doing this was that the system would lose money on about 12 percent of the months.

What would happen if our bag of marbles is more complex—as is the market and most games of chance? Let's say you have a number of different possibilities of winning and losing. For example, let's say you have a bag of 100 marbles of different colors. And let's give each color a different payoff according to the matrix given in Table 7.1.

Once again, we'll assume that a marble is replaced in the bag once it is drawn out. Notice that the chances of winning are only

TABLE 7.1

Marble Payoff Matrix

Number and Color of Marbles	Win or Lose	Payoff
50 black marbles	Lose	1:1
10 blue marbles	Lose	2:1
4 red marbles	Lose	3:1
20 green marbles	Win	1:1
10 white marbles	Win	5:1
3 yellow marbles	Win	10:1
3 clear marbles	Win	20:1

36 percent in this game. Would you want to play it? Why or why not? Before you answer this question, remember our discussion of the first four keys to investment success. Based on that, ask yourself, "What's the expectancy of this game? Is it better or worse than the first game?"

To find the expectancy of this game, we need to determine the mean *R* multiple. To do so, we can again find the total of all the *R* multiples and divide by the number of marbles (that is, the definition of a mean). The *R* multiples of all the winning marbles total +160*R*, and the *R* multiples of all the losing marbles total –82*R*. This means that the sum of all the *R* multiples in the bag is +78*R*. Since there are 100 marbles in the bag, our mean value is 0.78*R*. So this bag has a lot better expectancy than the first bag. We could only expect 0.2*R* per trade in the first game, whereas this one gives us 0.78*R* per trade.

Just with these two examples, you should have learned a very important point. Most people look for trading games that have a high probability of winning. Yet in the first game, you had a 60 percent chance of winning but only 0.2*R* expectancy. In the second game, you had only a 36 percent chance of winning, but your expectancy was 0.78*R*. Thus, in terms of expectancy, game 2 is almost four times as good as game 1.

It's important to put in a word of caution here: Variables 5 and 6 are critically important to your profitability. *You can realize your expectancy over the long term only if you size your positions wisely according to how much equity you have.* Position sizing is that part of your system that tells you how much to risk per position. It's a critical portion of your overall system, and we'll discuss it extensively later in this book.

But let's look at one example just to see how position sizing and expectancy go together. Suppose you are playing game 1—the 60 percent marble game. You have $100 in total equity, and you start playing the game. Let's say you start the game by risking your entire $100 on the first draw. You have a 40 percent chance of losing, and you happen to draw a black marble. That can happen and when it does, you will have lost your entire stake. In other words, your position size (that is, bet size) was too large relative to your equity to be safe. You cannot play anymore because you don't have any more money. Therefore, you cannot realize the 0.2*R* expectancy over the long run playing the game.

Let's look at another example with game 1. Suppose you decide to risk 50 percent of your stake on each draw, not 100 percent. Thus, you start out with a $50 bet. You draw a black marble and you lose. Now your stake is down to $50. Your next bet is 50 percent of what's left, or $25. Again, you lose. You now have $25 left. Your next bet is $12.50 and you lose again. You are now down to $12.50. Three losses in a row is quite possible (that is, there is about 1 chance in 10 with three consecutive events) in a system that only wins 60 percent of the time.[3] You must now make $87.50 just to break even—that's an increase of 700 percent. You're not likely to make that much at all with only 1*R* winners. Thus, because of improper position sizing, you've again failed to obtain your expectancy over the long run, and you've ended up losing money.

> Your position size on any given trade must be low enough that you can realize the long-term expectancy of your system.

Remember that your position size on any given trade must be low enough that you can realize the long-term expectancy of your system.

At this point, you might say that you will control your risks by your exits, not your position sizing. However, remember the snow fight metaphor? Risk is essentially variable 2, the size of the wins compared with the losses. That's what you control by your exits. Position size is essentially another variable (that is, variable 5) that you use on top of the relative size of the gains and losses. It tells you how much total risk to take relative to your equity.

OPPORTUNITY AND EXPECTANCY

There's one other variable involved in evaluating your system that's just as important as its expectancy. That factor is opportunity, our fourth variable. How often can you play the game? For example, suppose you could play either game 1 or game 2. However, you are allowed to draw out only one marble during every five minutes of playing game 2; whereas you are allowed to draw out one marble every minute of playing game 1. Under those conditions, which game would you rather play?

Let's look at how the opportunity factor changes the value of the games. Suppose you could play the game for an hour. Since you could draw out a marble every minute in game 1, you'd have an opportunity factor of 60, or 60 chances to play the game. Since you could draw out a marble every five minutes in game 2, you'd have an opportunity factor of 12, or 12 chances to play the game.

Remember that your expectancy is the amount you would win per dollar risked over a large number of opportunities. Thus, the more times you can play a game, the more likely you are to realize the expectancy of the game.

In order to evaluate the relative merits of each game, you must multiply the number of times you can play the game by the expectancy. When comparing the two games over an hour, you'll get the following results:

Game 1. Expectancy of $0.2R \times 60$ opportunities $= 12R$ per hour
Game 2. Expectancy of $0.78R \times 12$ opportunities $= 9.36R$ per hour

Thus, given the opportunity restraints that we arbitrarily imposed, game 1 is actually better than game 2. And when you evaluate expectancy in the market, you must give a similar consideration to the amount of opportunity your system presents you. For example, a $0.5R$ expectancy system (after transaction costs) that gives you three trades per week is much better than a $0.5R$ system (again after transaction costs) that gives you one trade each month.

PREDICTION: A DEADLY TRAP

Let's pause for a moment to discuss a common trap for most traders and investors—the prediction trap. Thinking about the concept of expectancy will allow one to more clearly see why so many people have been tripped up over the years making *predictions* of what a market will do in the future. In fact, most of the trading concepts discussed in Chapter 5 are based on some method of "predicting" what will happen in the future. For example, we might assume that

- Trends will continue.
- Prices will move to the opposite band.
- Fundamentals move prices.
- Prices are a function of what happens in multiple markets.

- Prices move according to historical cycles.
- There's an order to the universe that helps predict prices and turning points.

All these concepts base their prediction algorithms on history—sometimes even assuming that it will repeat exactly. However, extremely successful prediction can even result in losing all of your capital. How? You can have a method that is 90 percent accurate and still lose all of your money trading it.

Consider the following "system" that has 90 percent winning trades with the average winning trade being 1*R* and the average loss being 10*R*. You'd probably say that you can predict well with this system because you'd be right 90 percent of the time. But what's the expectancy of the system?

$$\text{Expectancy} = 0.9(1R) - 0.1(10R) = -0.1R$$

The expectancy is negative. This is a system through which *you get to be right 90 percent of the time and you'll eventually lose all of your money trading it.* There is a strong psychological bias to be *right* about what we do with our investments. For most people, this bias greatly overrides the desire to make a profit overall in our approach, or it prevents us from reaching our true profit potential. Most people have an overwhelming need to control the market. As a result, they end up with the market controlling them.

It should be clear to you by now that it is the combination of the payoff and the probability of winning that allows you to determine whether a method is viable or not. That's why expectancy, the overall impact of each trade per dollar risked, is so important. You also have to consider variable 4 (how often you get to play the game) to determine the relative worth of a system or method.

REAL TRADING APPLICATIONS

So far we've been dealing with bags of marbles. In each bag of marbles, we know the population of marbles, the probability of each marble and its payoff. None of those things is true when we deal with trades in the market.

When you play the market, you don't know the exact probability of winning or losing. In addition, you don't know exactly how much you are going to win or lose. However, you can do historical testing and get some idea (that is, a sample) of what to expect. You also can get large samples of data from real-time trading and investing expressed as *R* multiples. It's not the exact population of trades that your system will generate, but it does give us an idea of what to expect.

Remember that I'm referring to a trade's reward-to-risk ratio as an ***R multiple***—*R* simply being an abbreviation for reward-to-risk. To calculate a trade's *R* multiple, simply divide the total initial risk of the trade into the total profit or loss that you've obtained. Table 7.2 gives you an example of what such data might look like.

You might notice several things about Table 7.2. First, every stock has almost the same initial total risk. This is done through position sizing to make the total risk 1 percent of your equity. In this case, 1 percent of a $50,000 account equals $500 worth of total risk. The amounts differ slightly from trade to trade because of rounding.

The worst-case exits (that is, expressed by entering a stop order) could be different for each of the stocks, but our initial risk remains about the same for each stock. This is because we are making the total risk on each trade equal to 1 percent of our total equity of $50,000, or $500. In other words, we're basically using position sizing to equate our initial risk despite the fact that our stops are different. We'll be talking more about the importance of both setting your initial risk and position sizing later in this book.

Second, real *R* multiples are usually not round numbers as they are in my marble games. Instead, they are expressed with decimal points. In the example in Table 7.2, I've rounded to two

TABLE 7.2

R Multiples from Trade Data

Stock	Initial Risk	Profit or Loss	*R* Multiple
ATI	$509	$1,251	+ 2.46
DLX	$498	−$371	−0.74
GES	$512	−$159	−0.31
MTH	$500	$2,471	+4.94
ORA	$496	$871	+1.76
WON	$521	−$629	−1.21
Totals		$3,434	6.90*R*
Expectancy =			1.15*R*

decimal points. Thus, it is much more difficult with a real system to say that 30 percent of the losses will be 1*R* losses. Instead those losses might be 1.11*R*, 1.21*R*, 0.98*R*, 1.05*R*, 0.79*R*, and so on. This is especially likely since transaction costs need to be taken into account in your profit and loss amounts.

Third, the sample in Table 7.2 is very small—only six trades. The results suggest that we have a great expectancy of 1.15*R*. But the question you must ask yourself is, Can you really understand what your system is going to do based on six trades? No, six trades is too small a sample to be meaningful. The bigger our sample, the more likely we are to know how our system will really perform. I'd recommend a minimum of at least 30 trades just to get an idea of expectancy. However, 100 trades will probably give you a much better idea of what to expect from your system in the future.

Let's look at a sample expectancy problem as it applies directly to playing the market. Suppose you have a trading system that you've traded for two years. It's generated 103 trades: 43 of them winners, and 60 of them losers. The distribution of your trades is shown in Table 7.3 using only the effect of trading one unit per trade (that is, minimal position sizing).

You'll notice from the table that we do not have the initial total risk of each trade. This may be your situation if you've been trading for some time without understanding the concept of *R* multiples. However, even if you don't have data in which you know the initial risk of each trade, you can still estimate your expectancy and your *R*-multiple distribution by using your average loss as 1*R*. This is what we'll do, using the data from Table 7.3:

$$\text{Average profit} = \frac{\text{net profit}}{\text{103 trades}} = \frac{\$10{,}843}{103} = \$105.27$$

$$\text{Expectancy} = \frac{\text{average profit/per trade}}{\text{average loss}} = \frac{\$105.27}{\$721.73} = 0.15R$$

TABLE 7.3

Trades Produced by a Sample System over Two Years

Winning Trades			Losing Trades		
$23	$17	$14	($31)	($18)	($16)
$12	$32	$8	($6)	($23)	($15)
$6	$489	$532	($427)	($491)	($532)
$611	$431	$563	($488)	($612)	($556)
$459	$531	$476	($511)	($483)	($477)
$561	$499	$521	($456)	($532)	($521)
$458	$479	$532	($460)	($530)	($477)
$618	$1,141	$995	($607)	($478)	($517)
$1,217	$1,014	$832	($429)	($489)	($512)
$984	$956	$1,131	($521)	($499)	($527)
$1,217	$897	$1,517	($501)	($506)	($665)
$1,684	$1,501	$1,654	($612)	($432)	($564)
$1,464	$1,701	$2,551	($479)	($519)	($671)
$2,545	$2,366	$4,652	($1,218)	($871)	($1,132)
$14,256			($988)	($1,015)	($978)
			($1,123)	($1,311)	($976)
			($1,213)	($1,011)	($993)
			($876)	($1,245)	($1,043)
			($1,412)	($1,611)	($3,221)
			($1,211)	($945)	($1,721)
Average gain = $1,259.23			Average loss = ($721.73)		

Total profit=$54,147; total loss=$43,304; net profit=$10,843

This is obviously just a rough estimate of expectancy, but it's what you are forced to do when you do not have an initial risk amount for each trade.[4]

Now, let's look at two different trading systems to determine how expectancy might be used to determine the relative merits of each system.[5]

Fred's System

The first system comes from an options trader named Fred. From May 1 through August 31, he completed 21 trades as shown in Table 7.4.

TABLE 7.4

Fred's Options Trading Summary

	Gains	Losses	
	$2,206.86	$143.14	
	$1,881.86	$68.14	
	$3,863.72	$543.14	
	$181.86	$1,218.14	
	$1,119.36	$143.14	
	$477.79	$3,866.57	
	$48.43	$340.64	
	$327.36	$368.14	
	$21.80	$368.14	
		$358.14	
		$493.14	
		$328.14	
Total	$10,129.04	$8,238.61	= $1,890.43
N	9	12	= 21
Average	**$1,125.45**	**$686.55**	**= $90.02**

The system made $1,890.43 over 21 trades during the four-month period. This amounts to an average gain of $90.02 per trade. Since the average loss is $686.55, we'll assume that is equivalent to 1*R*. If we divide $90.02 by $686.55, we get an expectancy of 0.13*R*.

The biggest fault with Fred's system is that it has a giant $3,867 loss that offsets the giant $3,864 gain. Without that one loss, Fred would have an outstanding system. As a result, Fred needs to study that loss and see if similar losses can be prevented in the future. He's probably not trying to limit his losses to 1*R*.

Ethyl's System

Next, let's look at another group of trades that we'll call "Ethyl's system." Ethyl made these stock trades over a two-year period. She had one gain of $5,110 from the purchase of 1,000 shares of stock and a gain of $680 from the purchase of 200 shares of stock; and a loss of $6,375 from the sale of 300 shares of stock. All of the rest were 100-share purchases. As a result, we will enter these gains and losses as if they were each a round lot of 100 shares to eliminate the effect of position sizing.

The system, after our adjustment, made $7,175 over 18 trades during the two-year period. This amounts to an average gain of $398.61 per trade. Remember that Fred's system made only $90 per trade. In addition, Ethyl's system makes money 55.6 percent of the time, while Fred's system makes money only 45 percent of the time. Ethyl obviously has a better system. Or does she?

Let's look in Table 7.5 at the expectancy per dollar risked of Ethyl's system and the opportunity factor. When these factors are considered, who do you think has the better system?

Ethyl's system made $7,175 over 18 trades, which gave it an average profit per trade of $398.61. It has an average loss of $1,527.63, so we must consider this to be her average risk or 1*R*. To get Ethyl's expectancy, we must divide $398.61 by the average loss of $1,527.63. The net result is an expectancy of 0.26*R*. The net

TABLE 7.5

Ethyl's Stock Trading Summary

	Gains	Losses
	$511	$2,125
	$3,668	$1,989
	$555	$3,963
	$1,458	$589
	$548	$1,329
	$3,956	$477
	$340	$1,248
	$7,358	$501
	$499	
	$503	
Total	$19,396	$12,221
N	10	8
Average	**$1,939.60**	**$1,527.63**

result is that Ethyl's expectancy is twice as good as Fred's expectancy.

Remember that Fred's profit was mostly a function of one good trade. Well, the same is also true of Ethyl's profit. Her one profit of $7,358 was bigger than her entire two-year net profit of $7,175. Thus, one trade made her entire profit over the two-year period. This is quite often true of good, long-term systems.

Comparing Fred's and Ethyl's Systems

But how does the opportunity factor influence our evaluation of both systems? Fred's system produced 21 trades in 4 months. In two years, Fred might produce six times as many trades. Let's compare the expectancy times the number of opportunities for a two-year period to really evaluate the systems.

When you look at the two systems in terms of expectancy times opportunity, then Fred appears to have the better system. However, this assumes that both investors have made the maximum use of their opportunities.

The comparison of the two systems brings up an interesting variable with respect to opportunity. Ethyl only made 18 trades in a two-year period. But this did not necessarily mean that she only had 18 opportunities to trade. An investor makes the maximum use of his or her opportunities only under the following conditions: (1) he or she is fully invested when there are opportunities to trade, (2) he or she has an exit strategy and exits the market when that strategy is triggered, and (3) he or she makes full use of other opportunities when cash is available to do so. If any of these three criteria are not met, then the comparison of systems by expectancy and opportunity is not necessarily a valid one.

Fred's System			**Ethel's System**		
Expectancy	Opportunities	Total	Expectancy	Opportunities	Total
0.13*R*	108	14.04*R*	0.26*R*	18	4.68*R*

DETERMINING HOW YOUR SYSTEM WILL PERFORM

Let's assume that we have an adequate sample of trades from our system. We have 200 trades from all sorts of different markets. Thus, we have a pretty good idea of the *R*-multiple distribution that the system is likely to produce. Now, let's pretend that each trade is simply a marble being drawn from a bag as in our previous examples. Once you draw the marble out, you determine its *R* multiple and then replace it into the bag. By simulating trading in this manner, perhaps 100 times or more, we can get an excellent idea of what to expect from our trading system in the future.

First, you'll want to develop a position-sizing algorithm supporting the expectancy, which will help you meet your trading objectives. Furthermore, you'll want that position-sizing algorithm to be linked to the initial risk for each trade and the ongoing account equity. Let's begin by using a simple 1 percent risk model as we did with Table 7.2.

Second, you'll want to consider the potential *distribution* (the order) of the marbles being drawn. The system's winning percentage is inversely proportional to the length of strings of losing trades. Therefore, you need a position-sizing algorithm that will allow you to withstand substantial strings of potential losing trades while being able to exploit the big winning trades. But even a system that's right 60 percent of the time can easily have streaks as long as 10 losses in a row in a series of 100 trades. You need to determine how long such streaks might be, so that you can handle them when they do occur.[6]

Many traders have failed to trade a sound system because (1) they were not prepared for the distribution of trades that the markets presented to them through their method and/or (2) they were overleveraged or undercapitalized. You can estimate the maximum number of losing trades in a row for 1,000 trials given the winning percentage of the system, but you really never know the "true" value. Even flipping a fair coin can yield some lengthy streaks of heads in a row, for example.

Figure 7.1 shows the distribution of trades for one 60-trade sample of a marble game such as the one described with Table 7.1. Remember that this is only one sample, and each sample will

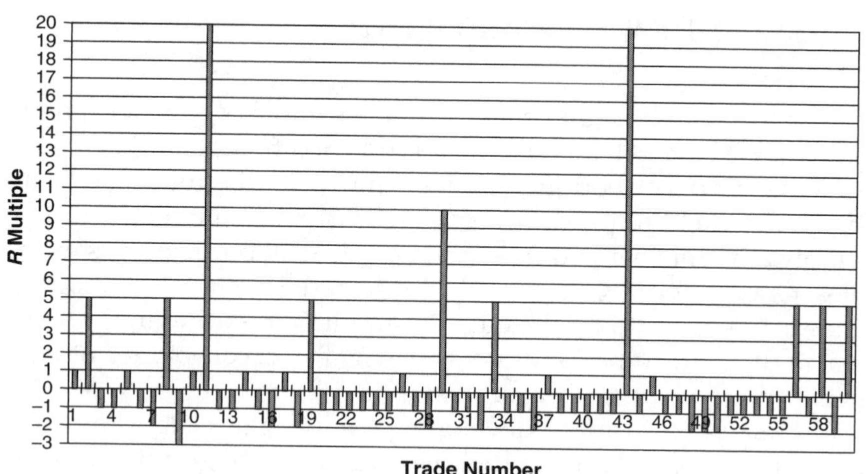

Figure 7.1 Marble game: Successive *R* multiples from our system

probably be different. Note the lengthy losing streak between trades 46 and 55. It's about this time that many people playing the game develop one of two opinions: (1) they believe it's *time* for a winning marble to be drawn, or (2) they decide to bet against the expectancy at some future point in the game so they profit from streaks like these. If the losing streak happens early in the game, option 2 is common. If the losing streak happens late in the game, then option 1 is common. The psychology of some participants forces them to bet bigger the deeper they go into a losing streak since they *know* a winner is just around the corner. I'm sure you can guess the typical results of such a game.

Figure 7.2 shows the equity curves for the above game betting a constant 1.0 percent, 1.5 percent, and 2.0 percent of current equity for each trade (and staying completely calm and detached the whole time). The return for the 60 trials at 1.0 percent was 40.1 percent and the peak-to-trough drawdown was 12.3 percent. There were three significant losing streaks of 5, 6, and 10 trades, respectively. The 2 percent risk doubled the return, but it also doubled the drawdown. And what would happen if you abandoned the system after that big drawdown? In every case in Figure 7.2, the larger position-sizing algorithm outperforms the small ones. However, in many samples, larger position sizing leads to ruin, especially when the losing

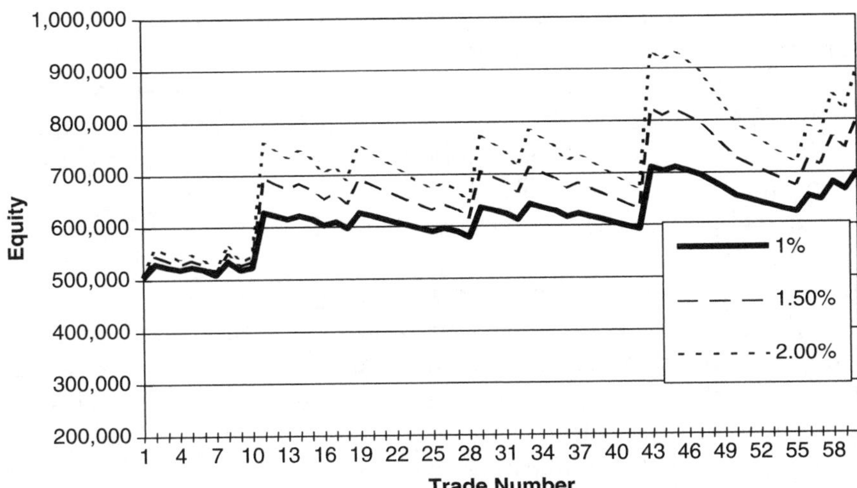

Figure 7.2 Equity curves by risk per trade on marble games according to bet size

streaks come early, whereas smaller position sizing allows you to overcome such streaks, which eventually leads to profits.

Figure 7.3 shows the equity curve betting a constant 1.0 percent of current equity betting against the expectancy. *Betting against the expectancy* means that the big marbles (that is, *R* multiples) go against you. Yes, you get to be "right" 64 percent of the time and

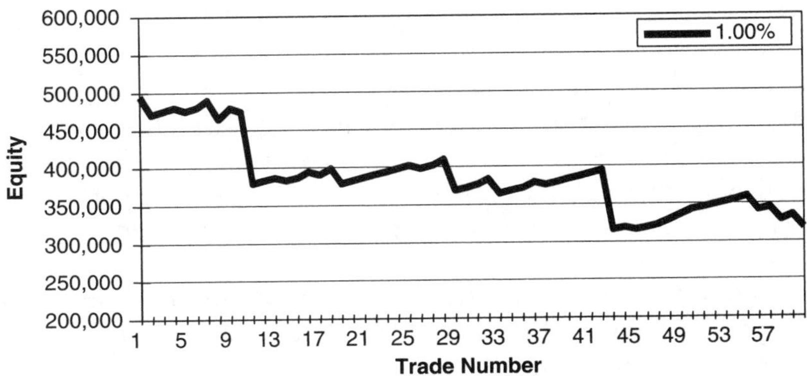

Figure 7.3 Marble game equity curve betting with the probabilities and against the expectancy, 1.0 percent risk per trade

even enjoy a 10-trade winning streak, but you also get to lose 37 percent of your starting equity.

If we were trying to better understand how this system works, we would probably need to evaluate at least 100 such samples. At that point we could make a better decision about the position-sizing algorithm to use. In addition, we would be able to train ourselves better on what to expect from this system in the future. This example was simply to show you what was possible if you treated your system's *R* multiples as a bag of marbles.

If we did 100 or more simulations, as I've suggested, then we could develop mental rehearsals for many scenarios that may occur in the future—rehearsing how we will respond given each outcome. Keep in mind that even with 100 such samples, you don't know *for sure* what the marble bag (or the market) will reveal in the future. And, just as important, you still don't know if there isn't a big *R*-multiple loser out there that you've never seen before. That's why part of your mental rehearsal should include rehearsing how you will respond to an event for which you are not prepared.

SUMMARY

Just as a review, once you have a system, or at least a rudimentary system, you need to calculate its expectancy and look at a number of issues involving expectancy. Here are the steps involved.

The best and most accurate way to calculate the expectancy of your trading system is if you know your *R* multiples for each trade. Your expectancy is simply the mean of your *R* multiples. It's that simple.

If you already have a system that you have been using or have tested, but you don't have your results expressed as *R* multiples, then you can assume that your average loss is equivalent to 1*R*. Thus, you can calculate the expectancy of the system by determining its average profit or loss per trade and dividing it by your average loss.

Last, you need to evaluate your opportunity to obtain your expectancy. How many trades does your system make in a year? Multiply that by your expectancy, and you'll have some idea what to expect per year from your system in terms of *R*.

Once you have a large enough sample to feel as though you have an adequate representation of your trading system's *R*-multiple distribution, consider representing each *R* multiple as a marble in a bag. You can then draw out a year's worth of trades (replacing each marble as it's drawn), noticing (1) how much you'd risk on each trade, (2) the result of the trade on your equity, and (3) your psychological response to each trade. Do this for a year's worth of trading at least 100 times. If you do, then you'll have a fairly good idea of what to expect from your system in the future.

Such simulations still assume that you know the *R* multiples that your system will produce. No matter how well you've sampled, it's probably safe to assume that there is a bigger loser out there than you've ever seen before.

Remember that expectancy and probability of winning are not the same thing. People have a bias to want to be right on every trade or investment. As a result, they tend to gravitate toward high-probability entry systems. Yet quite often these systems are also associated with large losses and lead to negative expectancy. As a result, always take your risk in the direction of the expectancy of the system.

Finally, even with a high positive expectancy system you can still lose money. If you risk too much on a trade and you lose, you can (and probably will) have trouble recovering.

NOTES

1. One share of stock or one futures contract would be a single unit.
2. This would seem to imply that if the cost of trading is factored in, it's better to trade more frequently than less frequently. While this assumption is true, it doesn't take into account the psychological wear and tear that comes from frequent trading.
3. When you make 100 trades in a year, it's virtually certain that you'll have three losses in a row. In fact, in 100 trades, the possibility of seven losses in a row is quite likely.
4. In the first edition of this book, I didn't realize that expectancy was simply the mean *R* multiple. That error was corrected in my more recent books, *Financial Freedom through Electronic Day Trading* and *Safe Strategies for Financial Freedom*. Because of that lack of insight, we used some crude techniques of classifying the trades into bins and using the bins to determine the expectancy in that first edition. The method of using the average loss as being 1*R* and dividing the average profit (or loss) by the average loss to obtain expectancy is still inaccurate.

However, it's much better than the original method used in the first edition of this book.

5. When position sizing is taken into account, there are still better ways to evaluate the quality of a system. However, a discussion of such methods is beyond the scope of this book.
6. Remember the discussion of objectives with Tom Basso; Tom said that he understood and frequently experienced long losing streaks. They simply are a part of trading.

PART THREE

Understanding the Key Parts of Your System

This part is designed to help you construct your system. Note that before you begin this section, you should thoroughly understand Parts One and Two of the book. They form the necessary groundwork that you must have before you begin the actual construction.

Chapter 8 talks about setups. Setups are conditions that are necessary in order for something else to occur. I've put the setups chapter first because most entry and exit systems consist of a setup plus a trigger for action. In Chapter 8, you'll learn about the most common entry setups—both for the stock market and the futures market. These are all setups used by master traders and investors. However, quite often they are promoted as systems all by themselves, and people tend to accept that because of the lotto bias. However, when you understand the material in this book, you'll be able to combine these setups with other critical parts of a system to create something that really is worthwhile.

Chapter 9 discusses entry techniques. Your entry technique essentially controls the reliability of your system—how often it makes money. However, you've learned by now that reliability is not nearly as important as your expectancy in evaluating a system because reliability can be high while expectancy can be negative. In Chapter 9, you'll learn why entry becomes less and less significant to your trading as your time frame becomes longer. Chapter 9 will show you that most entry techniques are not much better than random entry, but it will also give you the few entry systems that seem to produce system reliability that is higher than you might expect from just random entry.

Chapter 10 is about how to define your risk per position (that is, 1*R*) in your system. Every system should have a method of getting out of the market to preserve capital. This is the "disaster stop" part of your system. It's one of the most important criteria of any system. We'll be discussing the purpose behind such disaster stops and the advantages and disadvantages of wide stops and narrow stops.

Chapter 11 is about profit-taking exits. Profit-taking exits are designed to help you maximize the reward-to-risk ratio of your trades and thus improve your expectancy. We'll be discussing the purpose of various exits, various kinds of exits, the advantages of multiple exits, and the importance of simplicity in your exits. You'll learn how to develop exits to improve your expectancy.

The discussion in Chapters 8 through 11 is not exhaustive. Our goal is simply to give you techniques that work and to avoid discussing, except in a general way, the techniques that do not work. My intention is not to give you a complete system. If I did that, it wouldn't be right for you because it wouldn't fit your beliefs. My intentions are to give you the tools to design your own system and to help you overcome your psychological biases so that you can develop a system that's right for you.

We'll also be illustrating the parts of a system by showing you what is commonly known about some well-publicized trading systems. You'll be able to see what parts everyone focuses on and how you can improve them by emphasizing what most people neglect. My goal is in no way to criticize these systems since most of them are well known and they all have some excellent qualities. In fact, if you like one or more of them, I'd encourage you to go to the original source to learn more about them. My goal in these chapters is to review these systems in enough detail so that you can understand their strengths and weaknesses.

CHAPTER 8

Using Setups to Jumpstart Your System

Speculation, in its truest sense, calls for anticipation.

Richard D. Wyckoff

Setups refer to conditions that must occur before other action is taken. They are an essential aspect of most entry and exit portions of any system. I've chosen to discuss them first because they form a foundation for the subsequent discussions on entry and exit techniques.

One of the key uses of setups could be to tell you when conditions are right to use your system. For example, in my "big picture" analysis in Chapter 6, I suggested that we are in a secular bear market that could last until 2020. However, that doesn't mean that we won't have very strong, profitable moves during which being in the stock market could be wise. And to tell you when to activate such a system, all you need is a simple setup.

Many of the ideas presented in Chapter 5, for example, simply have to do with setups for entry. For example, the concept having to do with "order to the market," in most cases, gives you a window of opportunity during which you can expect a substantial move in the market—that window is nothing more than a time setup. It certainly is not an entry signal or a trading system.

For example, I consulted with an expert in Elliott Wave—one of the "there's an order to the universe" concepts. He claimed that he was right on about 70 percent of his ideas, but only 30 percent of his trades. He typically had a very tight stop below his entry point to preserve his capital. Quite frequently, the market would take him right out of a position. Thus, he would have to enter three or four times in order to capitalize on a given idea. In addition, by the time the market went against him three or four times, he was often too nervous to reenter the market and would subsequently miss the move. Other times, he would be right about the idea, but the market would start to move so violently that he felt there was too much risk to take the move. Essentially, this trader's problem was confusing a setup (that is, gauging market conditions with respect to Elliott Wave analysis) with an entire trading system. He had no real entry system (as defined in the next chapter), and he had no way of capitalizing on the great reliability of his idea because he got stopped out too often.

We corrected both problems with ideas that you'll learn about in the next few chapters. However, the critical issue was a problem that most investors and traders have—they confuse setups with a complete trading system. Most investors and traders buy books on their craft that consist of nothing but such setups. If the setups are accompanied by enough best-case examples, then the author can usually convince his or her readers that the book contains the Holy Grail. One of the key points you must take from this book is that a setup is about 10 percent (or less) of your trading system. Most people will place all their emphasis on finding the right setups, but setups are actually one of the least important parts of the system.

> If you learn one critical thing from this book, it should be that a setup is about 10 percent (or less) of your trading system. Most people will place all their emphasis on finding the right setups, but setups are actually one of the least important parts of the system.

Let's look at a concept—fundamental analysis—to help you understand how setups come out of various concepts. Fundamental analysis essentially gives you a number of conditions that, when favorable, suggest the market is ripe for entry on the long or the short side.[1] Those conditions might mean that the market is overvalued or undervalued because of supply-and-demand conditions. However, fundamentals do not give you anything about timing—they simply indicate that conditions are appropriate for an entry at some time in the future. The actual market move might not occur until months later.

To better understand setup conditions, let's talk about the five phases of entry. Generally, every trader or investor should give some thought to each of these five phases.

THE FIVE PHASES OF ENTRY

Appropriate Conditions for Your System

The first phase of entry is to determine if the appropriate conditions are present to warrant the use of a particular system. If the answer is yes, then you move on to the other phases. But if the answer is no, then you must look for other appropriate systems for which today's conditions are a good fit.

Let me give you an example from my book *Safe Strategies for Financial Freedom*. In that book, I presented a bear market mutual fund trading technique. If you elected to use that particular technique as one of your systems, you could commit up to 50 percent of your trading capital to an *inverse mutual fund*, one that goes up when a major index such as the S&P 500 goes down. However, conditions must be right to use that system.

The system is appropriate to use only in secular bear market conditions. And based on my big-picture scenario, we will be in one for the next 10–15 years. However, that system is meant to be used when the market is in what we call *red light mode*. Red light mode requires that two of the following three conditions be met:

1. The market must be overvalued, meaning that the P/E ratio of the S&P 500 must be over 17. That condition has been met for many years.
2. The Federal Reserve must be in the way, meaning that it is raising interest rates or, if the Fed is presently doing nothing, that its last change was to raise interest rates sometime during the preceding six months. As of this writing (in late 2006) the Federal Reserve has increased interest rates 17 consecutive times.
3. The market has to be acting badly. This basically means that the market is above its 45-week moving average.

The market has been in red light condition throughout much of the secular bear market. And I report on this particular indicator once each month in my free monthly update on the market.[2] This type of setup tends to be quite broad because it is really a measurement of the big picture. However, we were in "red light mode" from July 2005 to the present (August 2006) and the markets have just been flat and the bear market mutual fund strategy did not work.

As another example, in the first edition of this book, I talked about the Motley Fool Foolish Four[3] approach to trading and looked at the various parts of this system in the book. However, since this system focuses on only the Dow 30 stocks and holds them for a year, I don't believe this method is appropriate at all under today's stock market conditions. Remember that mutual funds strongly support the major averages they use as their benchmarks. However, when the baby boomers start pulling their retirement funds out of mutual funds, I would expect the major averages to collapse. Thus, any system that relies on holding stocks in the major averages for a year is not appropriate for this market climate. That's an example of using logic to determine when (and when not) to use a system.[4] Furthermore, when the Motley Fool Web site introduced this simple technique to millions of investors, you can imagine what happened: many, many investors were focusing their efforts on just four stocks. But how can the "dogs of the Dow" remain a viable strategy if *everyone* is buying four specific stocks? The answer is that it can't, and that's probably why the strategy no longer works.

Market Selection

The second phase of entry is your selection of what markets you should trade. What qualities must a market have before you want to be a part of it? Give some thought to using one or more of the following criteria:

1. Liquidity How active do you predict the market will be in the future? Basically, the issue is one of liquidity, which has to do with the ease of getting into or out of the market at the bid or asked price—or even within the spread between the bid and asked price. If the market is fairly illiquid, then that spread could be huge and you would have to pay a large price (beyond commissions) just to get in and out of that market.

Liquidity is a major factor in entry. Why? If you have substantial size, then the price might move a significant amount in an illiquid market simply because of your presence. On the other hand, if you are a small trader—who could enter into an illiquid market quite easily—you might want to avoid such markets because a "foolish" large trader might enter into those markets, causing a significant move just because of his or her presence.

Stock market traders, for example, might want to avoid stocks that trade less than 10,000 shares per day. This means that a simple round lot would be 1 percent of the daily activity. That could be a problem for you when you want to get into or out of that market.

2. Newness of the Market Generally, it's best to avoid new markets—whether it's newly created futures contracts or stocks that have just been introduced onto the exchange. A lot of mistakes are made in such new issues because you have little idea of what the underlying product is going to be. If a market has been around at least a year, you'll have a much better idea of what to expect.

Some people specialize in new issues, called initial public offerings, or IPOs. Certainly, in strong bull markets, new stock issues often tend to go up rapidly. They also collapse rapidly. Perhaps your "edge" might be that you keep on top of enough information about new companies that you feel safe investing in them. However, just remember that this is a dangerous area for amateurs.

3. What Exchange Makes a Market for the Underlying Investment, and Do You Know Its Rules of Trading? In essence, who is behind the market you are trading? Who are the market makers? What is their reputation? What can you expect when you deal with these people? Who regulates these market makers? What's likely to happen if you put in a stop order at one of these exchanges—is it something that is executed easily for your benefit, or is it a license to steal from you?

For example, certain stock and commodity exchanges are much more difficult to trade than other exchanges. It's much more difficult to get good fills. If you have experience trading markets on these exchanges and know what to expect, then it's probably okay to trade them. On the other hand, if you are new to the market, then it's probably best to trade only the older, well-established exchanges—the New York Stock Exchange, the Chicago Board of Trade, and the Chicago Mercantile Exchange.

Overseas markets can also be great opportunities or disasters waiting for the uninitiated trader to step in. Find people who have traded the markets you want to trade. Ask them what to expect—what are worst-case scenarios? Make sure that you can tolerate such scenarios before you trade in those types of markets.

In 1992, I married a wonderful woman who was born in Singapore and raised in Malaysia. And in late 1993, we visited her relatives in Malaysia. We traveled all over the country, and everywhere people were talking about how much money could be made buying Malaysian stocks. As a result, due to my belief that when everyone is interested it's a sign that the end is near, I became totally convinced that the Malaysian stock market was doomed for a crash. And in January 1994, it lost 50 percent of its value. However, there were no good ways for me to short that market in 1993.

Today, however, you can broadly trade most foreign markets through exchange-traded funds (ETFs). The worldview chart (given in Figure 6.5) shows examples of various ETFs that you can trade to get a position in various world markets. And today, if I wanted to short the Malaysian stock market, I could simply short the Malaysian ETF, EWM. It's simple to do in the United States and can be done, even though the Malaysian government thinks that the idea of foreigners shorting their stock market is anti-Malaysian.

4. Volatility *Volatility* essentially means how much price movement has occurred within a specific time frame. Day traders, for example, need to trade highly volatile markets. Since they are typically out of a position at the end of the day, they need to trade markets that have enough daily volatility to allow for large profits. Usually, only certain currency markets, the stock indexes, highly liquid stocks, and the bond markets qualify as good markets for day traders.

If you happen to be trading a system that trades turning points in consolidating markets, then you probably need to select markets that have enough volatility to make that sort of trading worthwhile.

Thus, again volatility of the markets would be an important consideration.

For both day trading and consolidation market trading, you need enough volatility that given the size of your initial risk, you can still make a profit that is at least two to three times the size of that initial risk. This should be your most important criterion in selecting your markets.

5. Capitalization Stock traders often select stocks on the basis of capitalization. Yet some investors want only highly capitalized stocks while other investors want only low-capitalization stocks. Let's look at the possible reasons for each criterion.

Typically, speculative investors who are looking for sharp moves in the market want low-capitalization stocks (under $25 million). Research has proven that low-cap stocks account for the majority of stocks that go up by 10 times or more. Generally, as demand for the low-cap stock goes up, the price will rise dramatically because there are only a few million shares outstanding.

On the other hand, conservative investors don't want a lot of price fluctuation. They don't want to see the price rising a point on a 1,000-share order and then falling a point again on another 1,000-share order. Instead, they want slow, smooth changes in price. You are much more likely to see this kind of behavior in highly capitalized stocks with several hundred million shares or more outstanding.

6. How Well Does That Market Follow Your Trading Concept? Generally, no matter what your trading concept is, you need to find markets that fit that concept well. And the less capital you have, the more important this selection process is to you.

Thus, if you are a trend follower, you need to find markets that trend well—be they stocks that show good relative strength or futures markets that typically show good trends several times each year. When the market typically has met your trading concept in the past, it probably will do so again.

The same goes for any other criteria you may be trading. If you follow seasonal patterns, then you must trade markets that show strong seasonal tendencies—agriculture products or energy products. If you follow Elliott Wave, then you must follow those markets for which Elliott Wave seems to work best. If you are a band trader, then you must find markets that produce nice, wide bands consistently. Whatever your trading concept, you must find the markets that best meet them.

7. Select a Portfolio of Independent[5] Markets This topic is somewhat beyond the scope of this introductory book on developing a system. However, I would suggest that you look at the correlation of the various markets you select. You will profit most by selecting markets that are relatively independent because you will be more likely to have at least one market that is in a legitimate profit-making trend than you will if all your markets are correlated. Also you want to avoid having a portfolio of correlated positions that might all move down against you at the same time.

Market Direction

The third phase of entry is market direction. Whether you are trading a market turning point or jumping onboard a fast-moving trend, most people need to assess the predominant direction that the market has been moving in over the last six months. You need to understand what kind of "animal" you are dealing with in today's market. This is the long-term trend of the market.

An old trend follower, who'd made millions trading the market, once told me that he would take a chart of the market, hang it on the wall, and walk to the other side of the room. If the trend of the market was obvious from the other side of the room, then it was a market that he would consider. The old trader's style had a lot of merit in the 1960s and 1970s when there were a lot of long-trending markets. Although the principle behind it is still valid, shorter criteria might be more appropriate now that market trends tend to be shorter.

Generally, people make money in up markets or down markets. However, there are really three directions in which the market can move—up, down, or sideways. Markets tend to trend—move up or down significantly—about 15 to 30 percent of the time. The rest of the time, they move sideways. You need to be able to assess when those conditions occur. For example, a lot of traders have systems that constantly keep them in the market. However, if you accept "sideways" as a condition of the market, then you probably want a system that will keep you out of the market the 70 percent of the time in which you are not likely to make money. You simply need some sort of signal to monitor when "sideways" is occurring. Perry Kaufman has developed an excellent vehicle for doing this that we will explore later in this chapter.

The person who is always in the market is going to spend a lot of time in sideways markets, which could mean losses and high commissions to trend followers. Such markets, if volatile enough, could be good for short-term band traders. Thus, if you are a trend follower, you might want to take a look at avoiding sideways markets as a part of your methodology.

Setup Conditions

The fourth phase of entry consists of your setup conditions. Setup conditions, as mentioned earlier, are conditions that must occur according to your concept before you enter the market. When you have such setup conditions, they generally improve your chances of a significant move in your favor.

Most people make money in the markets because the market moves a significant amount from the entry point. The various concepts discussed in Chapter 5 were mostly designed to detail the conditions under which you can expect a significant market move. Generally, all of these concepts consist of market setups. These concepts were designed to help you "predict" what might happen and to help you select the correct market direction.

Setups might consist of a window of opportunity during which you might expect a turnaround: fundamental conditions that must exist before you enter the market, seasonal situations that might attract your attention, or any of a number of other significant criteria that might be useful.

Setups are not usually criteria for entering the market. Instead, they are necessary criteria that you should expect before you will even consider taking a position in the market.

> Many publicly offered systems, because of the lotto bias described in Chapter 2, consist of nothing but setups.

Different kinds of setups that have proven themselves are the topic of this chapter. We'll be talking about setups that are useful for the stock market and setups that are useful for futures markets, forex[6] markets, options markets, or other speculative areas. In fact, you'll learn that *many publicly offered systems, because of the lotto bias described in Chapter 2, consist of nothing but setups*. But first, let's discuss the last phase of entry—market timing.

Market Timing

The final phase of entry is market timing. Let's say you've selected the markets you want to trade. You understand your concept, and the current market conditions fit your concept for trading. You also have several market setups, and those conditions have also been met. However, one more key criterion should be met before you actually enter the market—the move you are expecting should start. In other words, if you are predicting a large up move in the market—because of fundamentals, a seasonal pattern, an expected turning point date, or any other reason—chances are that your move will not have begun at the time you first predict it. *Profitable traders and investors usually wait for the move to begin before they enter the market.*

Profitable traders and investors usually wait for the move to begin before they enter the market.

As you'll see in the next chapter on entry, very few entry techniques beat a simply random entry—a coin flip at a random time to determine whether to go long or short in the market. Consequently, you need to do whatever you can to improve your odds.

The best way of improving your odds is to make sure the market is moving in the direction you are expecting before you enter the market. This is basically your timing signal. We'll be discussing a number of significant timing signals later in this book.

SETUPS FOR STALKING THE MARKET

Readers who are familiar with my Peak Performance Home Study Course know about the 10 tasks of trading that great traders do on a regular basis. One of the 10 tasks of trading is called *stalking*. It amounts to shortening your time frame to find entry conditions to make your risk even lower. Short-term setups constitute the best stalking tools.

There are many of these, so I will simply present three categories of short-term setups and give an example of each. My comments about these setups simply reflect my own opinion about them. Connors and Raschke have written a book, *Street Smarts*,[7] that covers many different short-term setups for those of you who would like a lot more detail. If you actually plan to trade these patterns, I'd suggest that you study their book.

"Failed-Test" Setups

Test setups are basically failed tests of previous highs or lows. After a particular high or low occurs, many interesting patterns occur. The Ken Roberts method, given below, for example, is based on a failed-test setup.

The reason such tests can work is because they are commonly used as entry signals. These entry signals might set up trades that return big profits, but they are not that reliable. The logic behind using tests as an entry signal is that this method makes use of false breakouts (moving to a new high or low) to set up the trade.

For example, Connors and Raschke have one pattern that they facetiously call Turtle Soup. It's called Turtle Soup because a famous group of traders, called the Turtles, was known for entering the market on 20-day breakouts. In other words, if the market made a new 20-day high, they would enter a long position. Or, in contrast, if the market made a new 20-day low, they would enter into a short position. Today, most of these 20-day breakout signals are false breakouts—in other words, they don't work and the market falls back. Thus, Turtle Soup gets its primary setup from 20-day breakouts that are expected to fail. The Turtles have made a lot of money trading these breakouts (see Chapter 9 for more information on channel breakouts) so be careful here.

Figure 8.1 shows an example of a Turtle Soup pattern. There are several 20-day breakout highs in mid-July on this chart. In each case the breakout high is followed by a substantial (albeit short-term) decline. You could make money with each of them as a short-term trader.

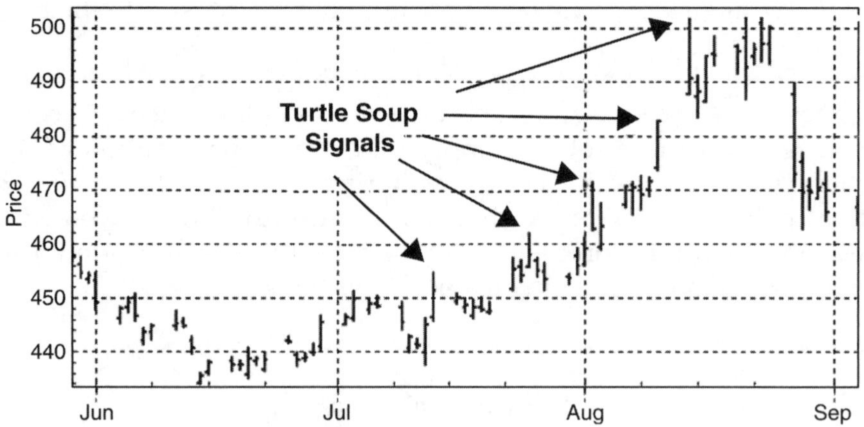

Figure 8.1 Turtle Soup setup

If I showed you enough examples of such patterns working, you'd probably get very excited about them. There are a lot of examples that work and many examples that fail. The pattern is only worthwhile, in my opinion, if you can combine it with the other parts of a trading system—such as exits and position sizing—that are really important to making money in the market.

Another high-probability setup is based on the observation that when a market closes in the top part of its trading range, it has a strong probability of opening higher. The converse is also true. These are extremely high-probability setups with 70 to 80 percent reliability for a more extreme opening in the same direction the next day. This could be used for an exit in a trading system, but it can also be used as a test setup.

Another observation is that even though there is a high probability of the market opening up in the same direction, the probability that it will close in that direction is much less. In addition, when you have a trending day yesterday (that is, the market opening up at one extreme and closing at the other), there is an even greater probability of a reversal. Thus, it might provide a basis for a *test-pattern setup*. What you need in this pattern is some sign of a reversal. Thus, three setups are involved in this "test" pattern as shown in Figure 8.2.

Figure 8.2 shows a pattern beginning on Thursday, December 8. It's a trending day that opens higher and closes lower. That is the first part of the setup.

1. The market has a trending day—opening up at one extreme and closing at another. See December 8 in Figure 8.2.
2. The market opens with another move in the same direction as the close (that is, if it closed lower, then the market opens down even more; if it closed higher, then the market opens up even more). On December 9, the market continues its move by opening down more.
3. The market reverses to yesterday's high (sell signal) or low (buy signal). Notice that as the day continues on December 9, the market reverses and goes above yesterday's low close. This is the last part of the setup (and in this case it is actually the entry signal).

Notice in the figure that the market closes higher and then continues to go up for several more days. Remember that all I did was find a graph here to illustrate the pattern. Don't get too excited about setups because they are only a small part of the equation for making money.

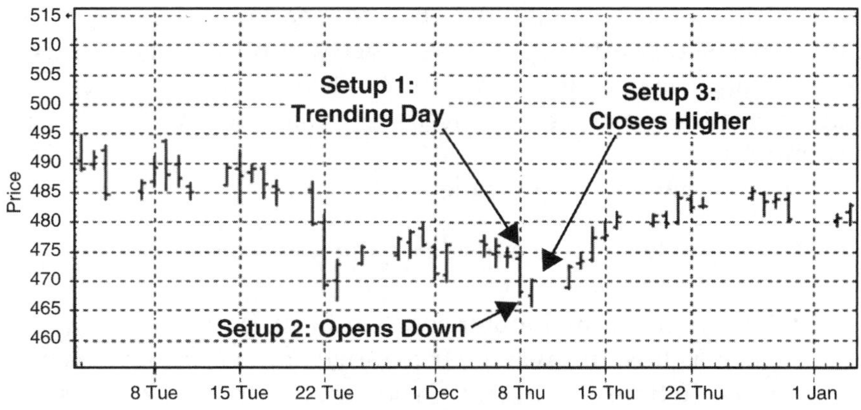

Figure 8.2 Setup of a trending day followed by a more extreme open

If your goal is to do short-term trading, or "swing" trading, then *failed-test setups* are probably what you want to use. Now that you understand the principle involved in failed-test setups—the market tests a new extreme and then falls back—you can design your own related setups without needing to rely on the ideas used by others. Experiment on your own!

Climax Reversals or Exhaustion Pattern Setups

These setups follow the same principle as the failed-test setups except that there is some additional evidence to suggest that the move is an extreme that will not follow through. These setups are typically designed to pick low-risk trades that signal a reversal of trend. They require, as part of the setup, a signal that the market has already reached an extreme, a highly volatile environment, and a move in the direction you want to trade as your entry point. These types of patterns can vary a lot, and many such climax moves are typically chart patterns that are difficult to objectively describe so that they can be computerized. I tend to object to chart patterns because there is strong evidence that many of them might not be real patterns that one can objectively trade. Thus, we'll just confine discussion to one of them, the gap climax move.

Gap Climax Move One sign of a climax move is that of the market gapping to a new extreme but failing to show follow-through. The market then falls back and closes in the direction opposite of the climax move. Another possibility is that the market, on a subsequent day, shows signs of filling the gap. Such setups are based on two observations: (1) gaps to an extreme tend to be filled; and (2) days that reverse from market extremes tend to have follow-through the next morning.

Here's how you might trade such a move:

1. The market gets to a new extreme (that is, this is your climax setup).
2. You might want another setup indicating high volatility such as this: the average true range of the last 5 days is two to three times the average true range of the last 20 days. However, this sort of criterion might not be necessary.

3. The market shows signs of weakness such as (a) closing at the opposite end of the range from the extreme or (b) starting to close the gap on a subsequent day.
4. You would then place an entry signal, expecting a short-term move against the previous trend.

In my opinion, these patterns are dangerous. What you are attempting to do is "stop" a freight train that is going very fast. You are hoping it will reverse a little so that you can get something off of it (that is, some profits), knowing that it could take off again going just as fast as it did before.

Climax setups, in my opinion, are primarily for brave short-term traders. Their primary use for long-term traders would be to become familiar enough with them to avoid entering the market around such moves since they have a high probability for a short-term reversal. If you are interested in such trades, then by all means study the Connors and Raschke book, *Street Smarts*.

Retracement Setups

The next type of setup that you might want to consider in short-term trading (or stalking your long-term trades) is the retracement. Basically, this kind of setup involves (1) finding the longer-term trend of the market; (2) getting some sort of pullback from the trend; and then (3) entering in the direction of the trend based on some third type of signal such as a resumption of the trend with a new high. These are very old trading techniques. For example, Richard D. Wyckoff, a highly successful Wall Street investor in the 1920s, was fond of saying, "Don't buy on breakouts. Wait for the retracement test."

Trend-following signals, once triggered, will usually be followed by some sort of retracement—at least, intraday. That intraday retracement can be used as a low-risk setup for entry. Several such retracements are clearly visible in Figure 8.3.

Figure 8.3 shows clear breakout signals in a trend. These are illustrated by the arrows on top. Each of them is followed by a retracement (bottom arrows). And notice how many opportunities there are.

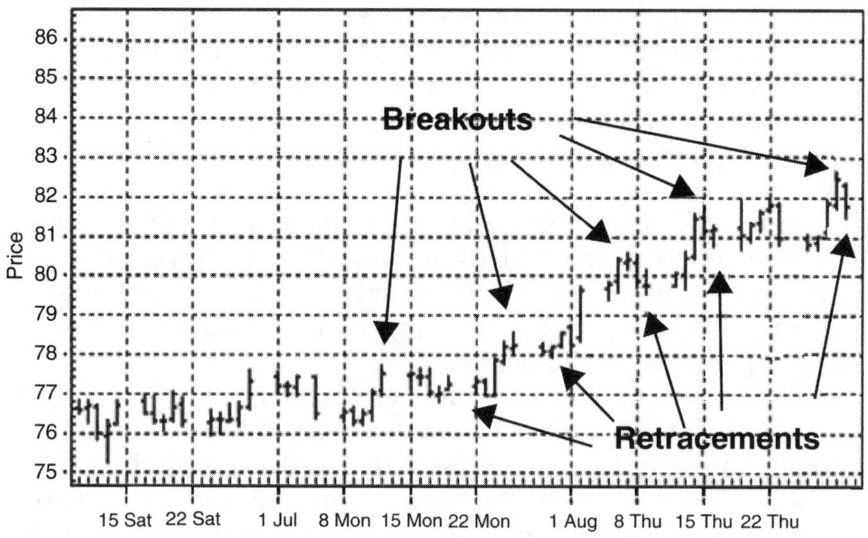

Figure 8.3 An example of a clear trend with numerous retracement setups

Retracement setups are an excellent consideration for trend followers. They have many advantages in that (1) they allow you to place tight stops and thus extract high reward-to-risk trades; (2) you can use them for both short-term "swing" trading or for long-term "position" trading; (3) they give you a way to get into a market that you might have originally missed; and (4) they provide you with an excellent way to get back into a market once you have been stopped out. Consider developing your own methods based on such retracements because some of the best trend-following methods I've ever seen are based on this concept. In fact, my friend Ken Long has developed a great example that he teaches in his ETF workshop.

FILTERS VERSUS SETUPS

A filter is some sort of indicator that must be triggered before your entry occurs. I used to say that filters were one of the 10 critical components of a trading system. Chuck LeBeau, who often is a guest presenter at our System Development workshop, then usually said during his presentation that you should totally avoid filters. Filters might help you predict the market in hindsight, but they wouldn't help you trade the market in the present.

Let me explain Chuck's comment. Because of the lotto bias, people want to know the perfect entry signal to the market so that they can "control" the market prior to entry. When you are looking at past data, the more you can use indicators to fit that data, the more accurately those indicators will seem to perfectly predict every turn in that data.

When you are looking at past data, the more you can use indicators to fit that data, the more accurately those indicators will seem to perfectly predict every turn in that data.

Most trading software will have several hundred indicators. You can use those indicators, almost automatically, to totally curve fit past markets. For example, you can use an oscillator, a moving average, and some cycles to almost perfectly predict what some historical market did at almost any time. The result is that you will probably feel extremely confident about trading, but you will find that your "highly optimized" indicators do not help you at all when trying to trade today's markets.

Some people try to get around this by optimizing over the short term (that is, the last several months) in the hopes that indicators optimized for more recent historical data will accurately reflect today's market as well. The task is usually fruitless because too many indicators are used.

Generally, the simpler your system, the better it will work trading the markets. However, there is one general exception to this rule. Many different indicators will generally help you in trading the market if *each of those indicators is based on a different type of data.*

This really provides us with a critical difference between filters and setups. Filters are typically based on the same data and should be avoided in your system. Setups based on different data are quite useful. As long as your setups are based on different, but reliable, data, more is generally better.

Filters are typically based on the same data and should be avoided in your system. Setups based on different data are quite useful.

By looking at some of the setups you can use, you can see what I mean by different types of data. Here are some of the examples given previously:

Time Setup

You have some idea when a move is supposed to occur because of your various models. Time is different from price data, so such a setup could be very useful. Time filters might include cycles, seasonal data, or astrological influences. Look at Chapter 5 for interesting "time setups" that might be useful in your trading.

Price Data in Sequence

You might require that your price data occur in a specific sequence. The resulting information is usually more valuable than simple price data if it's based on some high-probability relationship that you've observed in the market. For example, retracement setups are based on such a sequence of price data: (1) the market establishes a trend; (2) the market makes a retracement; and (3) the market shows some sort of movement back in the direction of the original trend. These are all price data, but they occur in a specific logical sequence that has some meaning.

Fundamental Data

You have some idea what the supply-and-demand characteristics are for the market you are trading. For example, you might have statistics for the soybean crop and also some statistics about new foreign demand for this market. See the discussion later in this chapter of Gallacher and Buffett for some examples of fundamental setups. Generally, trends supported by the fundamental data are the strongest trends.

Volume Data

The amount of activity in your particular market is quite different from the current price data and could be quite useful. There's a lot written about volume data, especially by stock market experts like Richard Arms. The Arms Index is now given regularly with market updates. It was originally known as the "TRIN trading index." This is the ratio of advances to declines divided by the ratio of up volume to down volume.

Here's how you might use it as a setup. Use a moving average of the Arms Index (typically use about five days). A reading above 1.2 indicates a potential bottom, and a reading below 0.8 indicates a potential top. These are short-term trading opportunities of one to three days. However, these readings should be combined with an entry signal of price moving in the expected direction.

Component Data

If your market consists of a number of items, then you might have some valuable information simply knowing what those various items are doing. For example, in the stock market knowing what the market as a whole is doing is quite different from knowing what each component of the market is doing. How many stocks are advancing? How does the volume of rising stocks compare with the volume of declining stocks?

If you are trading a market index, you can look at what all of the individual stocks are doing. Generally, people who try to trade a market index, such as the S&P 500, without looking at anything but the price data of the index could be at a severe disadvantage compared with all of the experts who are looking at component data.

People who try to trade a market index, such as the S&P 500, without looking at anything but the price data of the index could be at a severe disadvantage compared with all of the experts who are looking at component data.

One example of a composite indicator, given with every market update, is the tick. The *tick* is the difference between all NYSE stocks on an uptick versus those on a downtick. Here's how you might use the tick as a setup. An extreme reading can often predict a market turn—at least in the short term. Thus, an extreme in the tick would be an example of a test setup. You would simply trade some sort of reversal signal that occurs once this extreme was reached.

Volatility

This term refers to the amount of activity in the market, and it is generally defined by the range of prices. It's generally quite useful information that is very different from just price alone.

Several years ago I conducted a computer trading workshop in which the purpose was (1) to become familiar with some trading software and then (2) to develop some systems that, based on historical testing, would return 100 percent per year or more without optimizing. I had assumed that most people would do this through developing a high-expectancy trading system using great exits and then combining it with a position-sizing method that would stretch the system to its limits. Most people did it that way, except for one. The one exception was a person who found that a measure indicating that the market was in a narrow range, when combined with some other parameters, often signaled a potential move of some force. When you combine a narrow range setup with good entry, you have a great chance of a high reward-to-risk trade.

Here are a couple of ideas for narrow-range setups.

1. The market is in a trend as measured by any number of indicators such as being above or below a moving average or having a high ADX value.
2. The market moves into a narrow range, which might be shown by comparing the range of the last 5 days with the range of the last 50 days. The ratio would have to fall below some predetermined value such as the range of the last 5 days being less than or equal to 60 percent of the range of the last 50 days.

This sort of setup can easily add 10 to 15 cents to your expectancy per dollar risked in a long-term trend-following system.

The second narrow-range setup might be something more like the following:

1. The market has an inside day (that is, its price range is contained between the high and low of the previous day).
2. The market has the narrowest range of the previous *X* days.

When you have an inside day of this sort, a breakout in either direction is typically a good short-term trading entry. There are many types of entries described in Chapter 9 that could be used with narrow-range setups.

Business Fundamentals

Most of the setups used by Warren Buffett, as well as some of those used by William O'Neil, are business fundamentals. What are the earnings? What is the yield? What are sales? What are profit margins? What are the owner's earnings? How many shares are outstanding? What is the book value and earnings per share? How has business grown? This sort of information is quite different from price data. We'll be discussing fundamentals such as these in the next section.

Management Information

Who is running your potential investment, and what is their track record? Warren Buffett had several tenets for management. And, whether you buy a stock or a mutual fund, the track record of the person behind your investment is probably critical to the success of that investment.

There are probably other types of data that are also useful. For example, if you can find some data that is reliable and that few other people have access to, then you probably can create some very valuable setups for your trading.

Now that you understand that useful setups come from data other than price data, you have the basis to create your own setups. That might be one of the keys to your Holy Grail system.

Don't get caught up in the importance of setups. They will help you increase the reliability of your winners. However, you can still have a highly reliable system that will give you a negative expectancy if you have some very big losers. Spend at least as much time on your system stops and exits as you do on setups and entry. And spend more time on the position-sizing portion of your system than on all of the rest of your system put together. If you do that, you'll have a good chance to find your Holy Grail that fits you and your objectives.

SETUPS USED BY WELL-KNOWN SYSTEMS

Stock Market Setups

In this discussion of stock market setups, I have no intention of giving you an exhaustive collection of possible setups for use in the stock market. Instead, I think it's much more useful to examine two different approaches that make money in the market. Each method is quite different from the others. And by comparing the setups that are used in each, you'll get a much better understanding of them and be able to invent your own. If any of the systems interest you, I suggest that you study the original source material. All of my comments simply reflect my opinions about the various models.

William O'Neil's CANSLIM Trend-Following Model

One of the most successful and widely followed models for trading has been promoted by William O'Neil and David Ryan—the CANSLIM model. O'Neil has presented the model well in his book *How to Make Money in Stocks*.[8] The model is also promoted through his newspaper, *Investor's Business Daily*, and his chart service, *Daily Graphs*. Many people have also attended workshops that his trainers have given all over the United States. My purpose here is not to present their model or even evaluate their model. Instead, I'll refer you to one of O'Neil's own fine sources for those purposes. My purpose here is to use the CANSLIM model to illustrate the setups involved in a commonly followed model.

CANSLIM is an acronym—with all of the letters standing for entry setups.

C stands for *current earnings per share*, with O'Neil's criterion being an increase of 70 percent over the same quarter a year ago. Therefore, the current earnings per share is the first setup criterion for O'Neil.

A stands for *annual earnings per share*. O'Neil believes that the annual earnings per share over the last five years should show at least a compounded five-year rate of about 24 percent. Again, this is another setup.

N stands for *something new* about the company. This new factor could be a new product or service, a change in management, or even a change in the industry. It also means that the stock has reached a new high price. Thus, N would really be two setups for entry. However, the new high price might actually be the entry trigger signal as discussed in Chapter 9.

S stands for *shares outstanding*. O'Neil did a study of the best-performing stocks and found that their average capitalization was below 12 million shares, with a median capitalization of only 4.8 million shares. Thus, another setup criterion for O'Neil is a small number of outstanding shares—fewer than 25 million.

L stands for *leader*. O'Neil believes in a relative strength model of the market. People who use relative strength typically rank the change in the price of all stocks over the last 12 months. A stock in the top 75 to 80 percent would probably be one to consider. Some people also give more weight to the amount of change that has occurred in the last 30 days. O'Neil's ranking is probably something of that nature. He says to pick only stocks that he rates above 80 percent—so that's another setup.

I stands for *institutional sponsorship*. It usually takes some institutional sponsorship to produce a leading stock. But a lot of sponsorship is not desirable since that would mean a lot of selling if anything went wrong. In addition, by the time all the institutions have found it, it's probably too late to expect a good move. However, some institutional sponsorship is another setup for O'Neil.

M in the formula stands for what the *overall market* is doing. Most stocks—75 percent or more—tend to move in the direction of the market averages. As a result, you want to have positive signs for the overall market as a setup, before you buy your stocks.

I've just given you the entire "O'Neil Acronym," consisting entirely of setup criteria. You know very little about the actual entry into the market except that the N criterion also includes the stock's making a new high. In addition, you know nothing about protective stops, nothing about how to get out of the market, and nothing

> What most people think of as O'Neil's trading system consists of just his setups.

about the most critical part of a system—position sizing. What most people think of as O'Neil's trading system consists of just his setups. Isn't that interesting? We'll talk more about O'Neil's criteria for other parts of the system when we get to them.

The Warren Buffett Value Model

Warren Buffett is perhaps the most successful investor in the world today. Buffett has never really written about his approach to the market, but many books have been written about Warren Buffett and his approach to the market. Some of the better ones include *Of Permanent Value* by Andrew Kilpatrick; *Buffett: The Making of an American Capitalist* by Roger Lowenstein; and *The Warren Buffett Way* by Robert Hagstrom, Jr. The last-named book includes a detailed explanation of the author's understanding of Buffett's philosophy of investing. My favorite Warren Buffett book is actually by Warren Buffett, and it consists of many of his writings, including his annual reports to his investors. That book is called *The Essays of Warren Buffett: Lessons for Corporate America* by Warren Buffett. All of these books are listed in the Recommended Readings list at the end of this book.

Once again, this is not meant to be a detailed discussion of Buffett's strategy but simply an overview of the setups that Buffett appears to use. I'd suggest that you go to Hagstrom's book if you are interested in a detailed account of Buffett's strategy. Buffett was selected simply because he is perhaps America's most successful investor and his methodology is somewhat unique.

Buffett's real strategy is to buy a business—he does not consider that he is buying stock. Most times, when you buy a business, you have no intention of selling it—and Buffett likes to keep the rumor going, in my opinion, that he doesn't sell most of his holdings. Buffett would advise anyone who wants to learn about investing to learn about every company in the United States that has publicly traded securities and store that knowledge in your head in a way so that it is always available. If you are overwhelmed, because there are over 25,000 publicly traded companies, Buffett's advice would be to "start with the A's."

Few people would be willing to do the kind of preparation that Buffett suggests. In fact, most people don't do anything like the research Buffett recommends, even with the few companies they select to actually buy, so you can understand what an advantage Buffett has in finding undervalued companies.

Buffett, according to researcher Robert Hagstrom, has 12 criteria that he looks for before buying any company. Of the 12 criteria, 9 amount to setups, and the remaining 3 might be considered entry criteria. Indeed, the entry criteria might also be considered setups. Buffett really isn't concerned about timing since most of his investments are lifetime investments. However, we will discuss his entry criteria briefly in Chapter 9. In this chapter, we look at the 9 setups used by Buffett.

The first three setups have to do with the nature of the business. Basically, (1) Buffett needs to be able to understand any business he might own, and it must be simple. He's not willing to invest in great high-technology stocks because he does not understand that sort of business or the risks involved. In addition, (2) the company needs to have a consistent operating history. He wants a long-term track record, and he tends to avoid companies that are going through any sort of severe change. Buffett believes that severe change and exceptional returns don't mix.

The last business setup is that Buffett is looking for (3) the companies that can raise prices regularly without any fear of losing business. The only companies that can do this are those that have a product or service that is needed and desired with no close substitute and that have no problems with regulations.

The next three setups that Buffett uses have to do with the management of the company. Running a business, Buffett understands, is a psychological enterprise and depends entirely on the strength of the management. As a result, Buffett demands that (4) management must be honest with the public. Buffett deplores managers who hide weaknesses in their business behind generally accepted accounting principles. In addition, he believes that managers who are not frank with the public are not likely to be honest with themselves. And self-deception definitely leads to sabotage of their leadership and their company.

The most important task that management does, according to Buffett, is allocate capital. Buffett's next criterion is (5) to look for managers who are rational in their allocation of capital. If the company reinvests its capital in the company at less than the average cost of that capital, which is a very common practice among business managers, then it is being completely irrational. Buffett avoids those companies entirely.

Buffett's last management criterion is (6) to avoid managers who tend to be conformists and constantly compare themselves with other managers. These people tend to resist change, develop projects just to use up available funds, imitate peer companies' behavior, and have yes-men working for them who will find reasons to justify whatever their leader wants. Obviously, finding Buffett's setups involves intensive study and research into the workings of the company.

Buffett's criteria for buying a company also include three financial setups. The first financial setup is that the business must (7) achieve good returns on equity while employing little debt. Return on equity is basically the ratio of operating earnings (earnings less unusual items such as capital gains or losses) to shareholder equity where shareholder equity is valued at cost rather than at market value.

Next, Buffett is very concerned about (8) owner earnings. Owner earnings consist of net income plus depreciation, depletion, and amortization less capital expenditures and the working capital necessary to run the company. Buffett says that about 95 percent of American companies require capital expenditures that are equal to their depreciation rates, so that should be considered when estimating owner earnings.

Buffett is very concerned with (9) profit margins. Consequently, he's looking for managers who are in tune with the idea of systematic cost cutting to increase margins. Buffett's market entry is based on the belief that if you purchase something that's undervalued, then the market price will eventually catch up to it. As a result, your returns will be superior. We'll be discussing Buffett's market entry in Chapter 9.

Once again, notice that Warren Buffett is like William O'Neil in that most of his thought process goes into the decision to enter the market. However, since Buffett seldom sells a company, once he buys it, his criteria are justified—and his track record proves that justification.

Futures Market Setups

Now, let's look at some models that have been used for futures trading. The big picture I presented in Chapter 6 suggests that commodities should boom during the next 10 to 15 years, so these methods should do well.

Once again, I have no intention of giving you an exhaustive collection of possible setups for use in the futures market. Instead, we'll examine several different approaches that make money in this market and look at the setups involved in those approaches. For purposes of this discussion, I've selected methods that I believe to be sound, and my comments simply reflect my opinions about these methods.

We'll talk about a method of trading suggested by Perry Kaufman in his book *Smarter Trading*; a fundamental method of trading suggested by William Gallacher in his book *Winner Take All*; and a method of trading that Ken Roberts has been teaching to novice traders all over the world.

Perry Kaufman's Market Efficiency Model

Perry Kaufman, in his book *Smarter Trading*, gives some interesting adaptations to trend-following methods.[9] He says that trading in the direction of the trend is a safe, conservative approach to the markets. But trend following must be able to separate the trend from the *random noise* of the market—that is, the random activity of the market at any given time.

Kaufman argues that longer trends are the most dependable, but they respond very slowly to changing market conditions. For example, long-term moving averages barely reflect a large, short-term price move. Furthermore, when they do provide some sort of signal for action, the price move usually has finished. Thus, Kaufman argues that an adaptive method is necessary for trend following. You need a methodology that speeds up entry when the markets are moving and does nothing when the markets are going sideways. Kaufman's solution to this is to develop an adaptive moving average. I'll refer the interested reader to Perry Kaufman's book (and the brief discussion in Chapter 10 in this book) to learn more about this average. Here, we'll just present his "market efficiency" filter, which probably can be adapted to work with almost any type of entry.

Basically, the fastest "trend" that one can use is limited by the amount of noise that is present in the market. As the market gets more volatile (noisy), one must use a slower trend to avoid getting whipsawed in and out of the market. For example, if the average daily volatility is about 3 points, then a 4-point move is not that significant. It could easily "retrace" back into the noise. In contrast, a 30-point move that might occur over a month or so is very tradable within a daily background noise of 3 points.

However, at the same time, the faster prices are moving, the less significant the factor of noise becomes. If the market moves 20 points in a single day, then a background noise of 3 points per day is not that significant. Thus, you need some measure of market efficiency that includes both noise and the speed of movement in the direction of the trend. A price move that is either "cleaner" or "faster" can take advantage of a short time frame for entry; while a price move that is "noisy" or "slow" must use a longer time frame for entry.

Kaufman's efficiency ratio combines both noise and speed. It essentially divides the net price movement between two time periods by the sum of the individual price movements (with each movement assumed to be a positive number). This is essentially a ratio of the speed of the movement to the noise of the market. Kaufman uses only 10 days in which to constantly update the ratio, but the reader could select a larger number.

Here are the formulas for the efficiency ratio:

$$\text{Movement speed} = \text{close yesterday} - \text{close 10 days ago}$$

$$\text{Volatility} = \Sigma \text{ absolute value [close today} - \text{close yesterday] over the 10 days}$$

$$\text{Efficiency ratio} = \frac{\text{movement speed}}{\text{volatility}}$$

The efficiency ratio essentially is a number that ranges from 1 (no noise in the movement) to 0 (noise predominates throughout the movement). This efficiency ratio is an excellent filter that can be mapped onto a range of speeds for a number of different entry signals. Doing so is slightly tricky. Kaufman gives a great example of how to do so with different moving averages. However, you could simply require that this number be above some particular value (for example, 0.6) as a required setup prior to taking an entry signal.

More details of how Kaufman might trade the markets will follow in subsequent chapters as we explore the effect of other components of a system when added to this method of trading. However, I strongly recommend that you read Kaufman's book if the method interests you.

William Gallacher's Fundamental Trading Method

Gallacher, in his book *Winner Take All*, begins with a scathing critique of system trading.[10] He then goes on to show how someone with a fundamental approach can make a lot of money. Gallacher's methods are not widely used, but a fundamental approach to futures trading is probably useful in today's market climate. Thus, I've elected to include his ideas in this book. In this section, I'll show the setups in Gallacher's fundamental trading methodology.

First, Gallacher says that you must select markets according to value—meaning that they are historically "cheap" or "expensive." He says that this can be done easily for certain markets (that is, a pound of bacon is cheap at $0.75 and expensive at $3.49), but for other markets it's much more difficult. For example, gold has gone from $35 per ounce to $850 per ounce to $280 per ounce and back up to $740 per ounce. With this variability, Gallacher asks, "What is expensive and what is cheap?" Thus, the market selection phase of entry is an important part of Gallacher's methodology.

Second, Gallacher says that the trader must develop a critical eye for what is "important" fundamental information to a particular market. He says that what's important is constantly changing, but he presents his current opinion about important fundamentals for various futures markets.

For example, he says that annual variations in supply are the big movers in corn. Generally, the corn produced in the United States is the main grain for hog production. Most of it is consumed domestically with only about 25 percent being exported. The demand is fairly constant. Thus, variations in supply are the major determinants of value for corn. Gallacher says that previous bad markets were sheltered by large carryover stocks from previous harvests. However, he says that when such carryover is historically low, then a bad crop could push corn prices to very high levels.

Thus, for corn the critical fundamental setups would be "carryover" and the amount of supply in the "new crop."

Gallacher goes on in this manner, covering soybeans, wheat, cocoa, sugar, cattle, pork bellies, precious metals, interest rate futures, stock index futures, and currencies. If you are interested in this type of fundamental information, take a look at Gallacher's book. Also realize that some of his fundamental ideas may be out of date given the stronger demand from countries like China and India for basic commodities and the fact that his book was written some years ago.

My overall conclusion is that it is very difficult to get any precise setups for commodity fundamentals. The only thing you really get is a bias that says (1) be neutral, (2) be bullish, or (3) be bearish. And that bias is based on a lot of information that is different for each market. One's real setup, therefore, is simply the opinion you develop after looking at the data.

Once you develop an opinion, Gallacher still believes in a price entry signal, limiting losses, taking profits systematically, and practicing sound position sizing—all techniques described in later chapters of this book.

Ken Roberts' Method[11]

Ken Roberts has been marketing commodity trading courses to thousands of beginners all over the world. He teaches several systems, but his primary method is based upon a simple 1-2-3 setup that is rather subjective. Essentially, the setups require that the market make a major high or low and then show a reversal hook pattern. You open a position when it's "clear" that the major trend is reversing.

The Major High or Low Essentially, in this method, the first setup is for the market to make a nine-month to one-year high (or low). Thus, if the market produces the highest high of the last nine months or the lowest low of the last nine months, you have the first setup. This is the 1 in the 1-2-3 pattern.

The Market Makes a Hook Reversal The next important setup is for the market to move away from the high or low to what's called point 2. The market then moves back toward the high or low and forms point 3. Points 2 and 3 form the "hook reversal," but point 3 cannot be a new all-time high or low. The market then goes back past point 2, and you have an entry point. Figures 8.4 and 8.5 show some examples of 1-2-3 patterns.

Both setups in the Roberts method seem subjective to me. The major high or low is fairly objective, but the exact time parameters under which it occurs are not. In addition, the exact conditions that

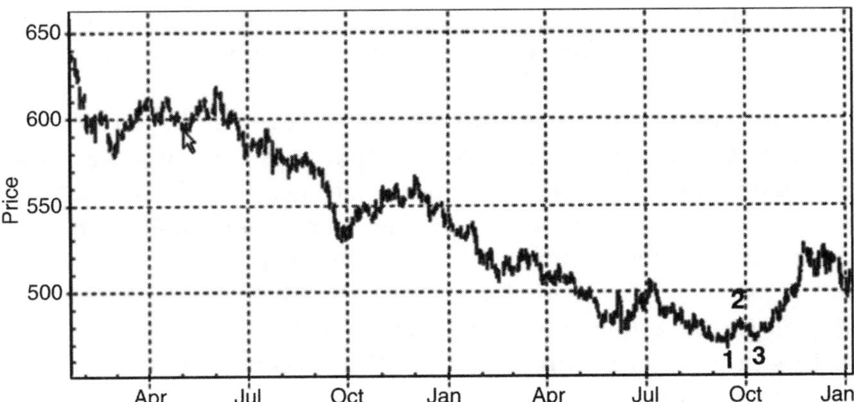

Figure 8.4 Roberts' 1-2-3 pattern in a bear market

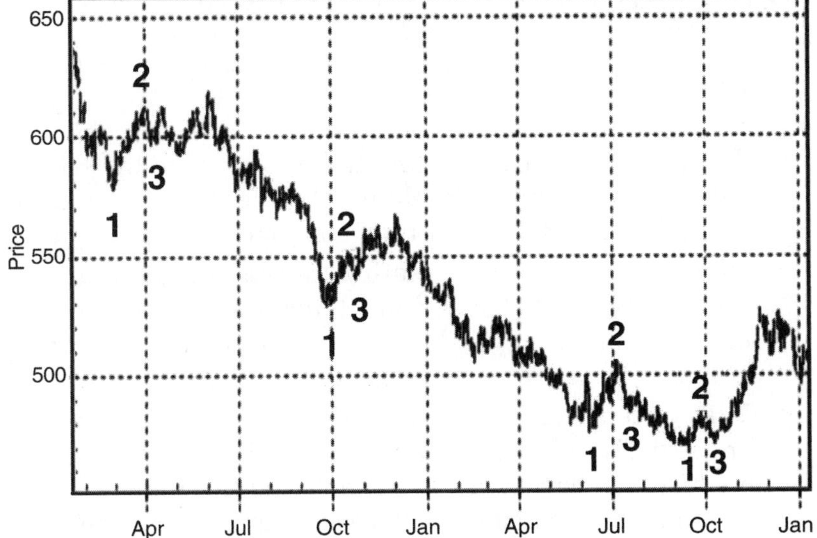

Figure 8.5 Notice the three other 1-2-3 patterns in the same graph as Figure 8.4

define the 1-2-3 pattern are quite subjective. Such patterns occur in the market after almost every high that occurs—at least in a short time frame—and Roberts does not define the exact time conditions under which such a pattern must occur. Thus, there is plenty of room for subjective error.

Figure 8.4 shows a typical long-term 1-2-3 bottom. The low (point 1) comes in mid-September. The market makes a 2 high in October and then falls back to a 3 low (that's not quite as low). Notice that the market then goes on to make new highs about a month later.

The problem with illustrating such setups is that your mind looks at them and gets excited about what might be possible. It does not realize how many false positives can occur with any pattern, especially a subjective one. However, this doesn't mean that you cannot trade such a pattern if you develop proper stops, profit-taking exits, and position-sizing algorithms to go along with it.

Now take a look at Figure 8.5. It is the same as Figure 8.4 except that I've pointed out three other 1-2-3 patterns in the same graph. All of them would have resulted in losses.

Although the setup is somewhat subjective, the overall method still is worthy of some consideration. We will be discussing other components of Ken Roberts' 1-2-3 system in subsequent chapters.

SUMMARY

- Most people give overwhelming importance to the setups in their system. In reality, about 10 percent of your efforts should be devoted to selecting and testing setups.
- There are five phases of entering the market: (1) system selection, (2) market selection, (3) market direction, (4) setups, and (5) timing. The first four phases are all forms of setups.
- Three varieties of short-term trading setups are considered for use in short-term trading or as "stalking tools": (1) tests in which the market hits a new extreme and then reverses, (2) climax or exhaustion patterns as signals to reverse, and (3) retracements that are used as setups for entering with the trend.

- Filters are not very useful additions to trading systems because they just amount to multiple ways of looking at the same data. Such filters will allow you to perfectly predict price changes with historical data but will not be very useful with today's market data. Good setups, in contrast, use other types of data as illustrated below in the next point.
- Setups can be very useful as long as they come from data sets other than price. Such data sets might include (1) time, (2) the sequencing of events, (3) fundamental data, (4) volume data, (5) composite data, (6) volatility, (7) business information, and (8) management data. Each of these data sets could be the basis for some useful setups for traders or investors.
- Trying to trade stock market indexes on price data alone is very difficult because your competition is using much more information from other data sets.
- Two stock market systems are reviewed: William O'Neil's CANSLIM system and Warren Buffett's business purchase model. These systems, as most people know them, are mostly setups.
- Three futures trading systems are reviewed in terms of setups: Perry Kaufman's idea of market efficiency, William Gallacher's fundamental model, and Ken Roberts' model that has been so widely promoted around the world.

NOTES

1. Fundamental analysis for stocks is somewhat different. Here you are looking at the earnings, the book value, the management, and other conditions that tell you about the internal structure of a company.
2. You can subscribe to *Tharp's Thoughts*, my free weekly newsletter, at www.iitm.com.
3. The Motley Fool Foolish Four approach stopped working because it was so widely disseminated by the Motley Fool Web site. Methods of this nature that focus on a few stocks and are widely known cannot possibly continue to work just because they are widely known.

4. This system became ineffective as it became more popular (because everyone was just buying four stocks), and it totally collapsed when the bear market downturn started.
5. I originally used the word "noncorrelated" here. However, Tom Basso was quick to point out that under extreme conditions all markets tend to become correlated. Thus, "independent" is actually a better word.
6. Forex stands for "foreign exchange." This is the big market in currencies that is set up by the large banks all over the world. It's a 24-hour market, and it is the largest market in the world.
7. Laurence A. Connors and Linda Bradford Raschke, *Street Smarts: High Probability Short-Term Trading Strategies* (Sherman Oaks, Calif.: M. Gordon Publishing, 1995). Turtle Soup is a trademark of Connors, Basset Associates.
8. William O'Neil, *How to Make Money in Stocks: A Winning System in Good Times or Bad*, 2d ed. (New York: McGraw-Hill, 1995).
9. Perry Kaufman, *Smarter Trading: Improving Performance in Changing Markets* (New York: McGraw-Hill, 1995).
10. To be fair to system trading, Gallacher presents only a simple reversal method—which despite its shortcomings appears to make a return of 350 percent. However, reversal systems keep you in the market all the time and do not have sophisticated exit techniques. Thus, in my opinion considerable improvement could be made to his "best-efforts" system trading method. Nevertheless, his book is excellent and presents some great ideas that most traders will enjoy. See William R. Gallacher, *Winner Take All: A Top Commodity Trader Tells It Like It Is* (Chicago: Probus, 1994).
11. Ken Roberts, *The World's Most Powerful Money Manual and Course* (Grants Pass, Oreg.: Published by Ken Roberts, 1995). This method was developed and published by William Dunnigan in the 1950s. That book was reprinted in 1997. See William Dunnigan, *One Way Formula for Trading Stocks and Commodities* (London: Pitman, 1997).

CHAPTER 9

Entry or Market Timing

Avoiding mistakes makes people stupid and having to be right makes you obsolete.

Robert Kiyosaki, If You Want to Be Rich and Happy, Then Don't Go to School[1]

The basic purpose of using entry signals, most people assume, is to improve your timing in the market and thus increase the reliability of your system. I would estimate that 95 percent or more of the people who attempt to design trading systems are simply trying to find a "great" entry signal. In fact, traders are always telling me about their short-term systems that have reliability rates of 60 percent or better. Yet in many cases they are wondering why they are not making money. Unless you started with this chapter, you should know that a system with a high percentage of wins can still have a negative expectancy. The key to money making is having a system with a high positive expectancy and using a position-sizing model that will take advantage of that expectancy while still allowing you to stay in the game. Entry plays only a small part of the game of making money in the market. Nevertheless, some energy should be devoted to finding entries that fit your objectives. There are two approaches to doing so.

The first approach is to assume that reliability has some importance and to look for signals that are better than random. In fact, a number of books make the assumption that picking good stocks is all there is to making a fortune in the stock market. They have titles like *How to Buy Stocks the Smart Way, Stock Picking: The Eleven Best Tactics for Beating the Market, How to Buy Stocks, How to Pick Stocks Like a Pro,* and *How to Buy Technology Stocks.*[2] We will also make the assumption in this chapter that reliability can be an important criterion for entry signals and talk about some potentially good signals.

The second approach is to focus not on reliability but on finding entry signals that have the potential to give you high-*R*-multiple winners. This approach is totally different from the first approach because it makes a different assumption about what is important to make big profits. While both approaches are valid, the second approach has the potential to totally change the way people think about trading.

Readers who have studied my Peak Performance Course know the importance of stalking the market. *Stalking* is waiting for exactly the right moment to enter a trade so that the risk is minimized. The cheetah, for example, is the fastest animal in the world. Although it can run extremely fast, it doesn't necessarily need to do so. Instead, the cheetah will wait until a weak, lame, young, or old animal gets very close. When it does, it requires much less energy for the cheetah to make an almost certain kill. That's what you want to do in your entry techniques. For many of you, stalking simply amounts to shifting down to a smaller time frame to determine the most opportune time to "jump on your prey."

I've divided this chapter into four sections. The first section has to do with random entry and with the research designed to increase one's reliability over random entry into the market. The second section discusses some common techniques that meet one of the two assumptions listed above. The third section has to do with designing your own entry signal. Finally, the fourth section continues our discussion of specific systems and gives you some entry techniques that have been used in these well-known systems—both for the stock market and for more leveraged markets.

I've deliberately abstained from showing you many best-case illustrations to convince you of the validity of certain methods. This strategy would appeal to some of your natural biases and psychological weaknesses. However, I consider doing so to be hitting below the belt at best. Consequently, if you use any of the recommendations given in this chapter, I'd suggest that you test them out for yourself. Doing so is part of what it takes to make them yours and give you a feeling of comfort and confidence using them. The only system you can ever trade is one that fits you. Testing it out for yourself is part of the process that some people need in order to make a system theirs.

If you use any of the recommendations given in this chapter, I'd suggest that you test them out for yourself. Doing so is part of what it takes to make them yours and give you a feeling of comfort and confidence using them.

TRYING TO BEAT RANDOM ENTRY

I did a workshop with Market Wizard Tom Basso (see his sections in Chapters 3 and 5) in 1991. Tom was explaining that the most important parts of his system were his exits and his position-sizing algorithms. As a result, one member of the audience remarked, "From what you are saying, it sounds like you could make money consistently with a random entry as long as you have good exits and size your positions intelligently."

Tom responded that he probably could. He promptly returned to his office and tested his own system of exits and position sizing with a "coin flip" type of entry. In other words, his system simulated trading four different markets, and he was always in the market, either long or short, based on a random signal. As soon as he got an exit signal, he'd reenter the market again based on the random signal. Tom's results showed that he made money consistently, even using $100 per futures contract for slippage and commissions.

We subsequently duplicated those results with more markets. I published them in one of my newsletters and gave several talks on them. Our system was very simple. We determined the volatility of the market by a 10-day exponential moving average of the average true range. Our initial stop was three times that volatility

Our random entry system—consisting of random entry, a three-times-volatility trailing stop, and a simple money management system involving 1 percent risk—made money on 100 percent of the runs.

reading. Once entry occurred by a coin flip, the same three-times-volatility stop was trailed from the close. However, the stop could move only in our favor. Thus, the stop moved closer whenever the markets moved in our favor or whenever volatility shrank. We also used a 1 percent risk model for our position-sizing system, as described in Chapter 14.

That's it! That's all there was to the system—a random entry, plus a trailing stop that was three times the volatility, plus a 1 percent risk algorithm to size positions. We ran it on 10 markets. And it was always in each market, either long or short, depending upon a coin flip. It's a good illustration of how simplicity works in system development.

Whenever you run a random entry system, you get different results. This system made money on 80 percent of the runs (that is, with 10 markets over 10 years) when it traded only one contract per futures market. It made money 100 percent of the time when I added a simple 1 percent risk money management system. Although the returns were not very big, making money 100 percent of the time with random entry and the requirement of having to be in the market at all times is pretty impressive. The system had a reliability level of 38 percent, which is about average for a trend-following system.

The LeBeau and Lucas Studies

Chuck LeBeau and David Lucas, in their book *Technical Traders' Guide to Computer Analysis of the Futures Market*,[3] did some marvelous studies with entry. They used various types of entry signals to enter the market when doing historical testing. The only exit they used was at the close of business 5, 10, 15, and 20 days later. Their primary interest in using this approach was to determine what percentage of their trades made money and if the percentage exceeded what one would expect from entering the market at random. Most of the indicators failed to perform any better than random—including all the oscillators and various moving-average crossover combinations that are so popular.[4]

If you have a market entry that has a reliability of 60 percent or more at the end of 20 days, it would seem to be very promising. However, when your only exit is to get out of the position at the close after so many days, you are wide open to catastrophic losses. You must protect yourself from those losses with a protective stop. Yet when you do, you reduce the reliability of your entry signal—some of those signals go below your stop (whatever it is) and then come back and become profitable, except that you're no longer in the market. In addition, whenever you add any sort of trailing stop (to reduce your initial risk and take profits), you are going to further reduce the reliability of your entry. Why? The reason is because some of the stops designed to reduce your initial risk will be hit and take you out at a loss. This is why a good trend-following system usually has a reliability of less than 50 percent.

Since most trend-following systems make money from a few good trades each year, another reason for their low reliability might be that the good systems concentrate on getting high-*R*-multiple trades. Let's look at some common entry techniques that might help you with one or both of these approaches.

COMMON ENTRY TECHNIQUES

Most people trade or invest using only a few categories of entries. In the following section, we discuss some of the most common entry techniques and their usefulness.

Channel Breakouts

Suppose you have a goal, as a trend follower, of never missing a major trend in the market. What kind of entry signal could you use? The classic answer to this question is an entry signal known as the "channel breakout." Basically, you enter the market on either the highest high of the last *X* days on the long side or the lowest low of the last *X* days on the short side. If the market is going to trend up, then it must make new highs. If you enter on one of those new highs, then you will not miss an uptrend. Similarly, if you enter a short position on a new low, then you will not miss a downtrend. Figure 9.1 shows an example of a 40-day channel breakout working in an uptrending market. There are a number of breakouts in this chart, but the clearest one occurs on August 2.

In regard to Figure 9.1, the word "channel" is rather misleading. A channel assumes that the market has been moving along in a

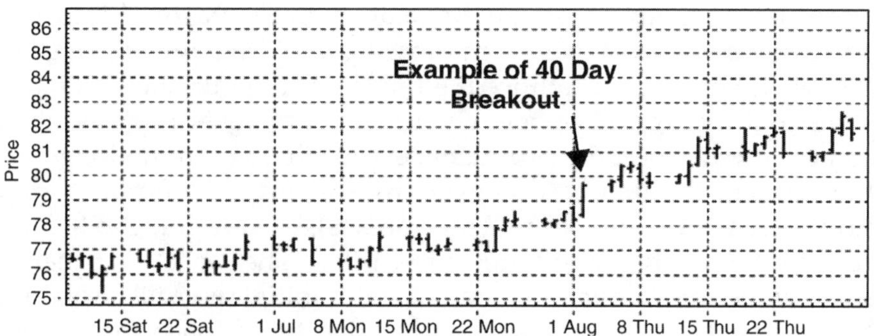

Figure 9.1 A 40-day breakout occurs on August 2 in the chart

narrow range for a number of days and then suddenly "breaks out" on either the upside or the downside. Obviously, this entry technique would capture that type of move quite well. However, you would need to know (1) the length of the channel and (2) when the channel started.

This leads to the most important question having to do with channel breakouts—"How big a trend must be signaled before I get onboard?" The answer to that question determines the number of days needed to produce the high or low at which you'll enter.

The channel breakout technique was originally described by Donchian in the 1960s. It was then popularized by a group of traders known as the "Turtles," who have made billions[5] of dollars trading commodities using this entry technique. They originally entered on 20-day breakouts and were quite successful with it. But as they continued to use the method, eventually 20-day breakouts stopped working as effectively. As a result, they simply moved up to 40-day breakouts.

Today, research seems to indicate that breakouts between 40 and 100+ days still work fairly well. Breakouts involving fewer days are not as good, except when going short. Since bear markets tend to have swift, sharp moves, they may need a much quicker entry signal.

This technique is very simple to apply. You can plot the daily highs or lows. When the market makes a higher high than it has done any time in the last 20 days, you enter a long position. When the market makes the lowest low of the last 20 days, you enter a short position. Table 9.1 shows how this might work. It gives you 60 days of corn prices during early 1995. New 20-day-high prices are shown in boldface. Each boldfaced price is an entry target or an actual entry signal.

Notice that the first 20 days are used for establishing a baseline that ends on January 30, 1995. During the initial 20-day period the market high occurs on January 12 at 170.25. It almost reaches it on February 6 when it hits 170 and that soon becomes the 20-day high. No other prices are that close until March 6 when the market gives a clear entry signal by hitting 171.5. Notice that the market also gives entry signals on March 10, March 13, March 14, and March 15, which are all in bold. These would have set you up for one of the all-time best moves in corn.

In the case of the data given, we would have gotten the same signal if we had been looking for a 40-day channel breakout. The March 6 signal was also a 40-day high.

Now, let's look for downside signals. During the initial 20 days, the lowest price is 161.25, which occurs on January 4. That is not surpassed, and soon the 20-day low becomes the price on January 30 of 162.25. This again is not surpassed. By the end of February, the 20-day low becomes the price 20 days ago, which continues to rise, practically each day. During this entire period, a new 20-day low was not set.

Cole Wilcox and Eric Crittenden have also done some interesting research on channel breakouts with equities.[6] They looked at a huge database of about 2,500 stocks (that is, after filtering out penny stocks and stocks with low liquidity). And they used the ultimate definition of a channel breakout—the stock makes a new all-time high in price. When that occurred, they'd enter at the opening price the next day. They also wanted to make sure that they'd stay with the trend as long as possible so they used a 10-times-ATR trailing stop in which the ATR was defined by the last 45 days.

They did 18,000 trades over a 22-year test period and found that their average trade made 15.2 percent. Winners, on the average, lasted 441 days and made 51.2 percent (that is, they could have made 100 percent and given back 50 percent in highly volatile stocks). Losers lasted 175 days and lost, on the average, 20 percent. They made money on 49.3 percent of their trades—so these were pretty impressive results.

TABLE 9.1

Early 1995 Corn Prices

Date	Open	High	Low	Close
1/3/95	164.5	164.5	161.5	162
1/4/95	162	163	**161.25**	162.25
1/5/95	163.5	164.5	163	164.25
1/6/95	165.25	165.5	163.75	165.25
1/9/95	165.25	166.75	164.25	166.25
1/10/95	165.25	166	165	165.75
1/11/95	166.25	166.25	165.5	166
1/12/95	168.5	**170.25**	167.75	167.75
1/13/95	168	168.5	166.5	167.5
1/16/95	167	168.5	166	168
1/17/95	168.5	170	168	169
1/18/95	169	169	167.75	168.25
1/19/95	167.75	168.25	167	167.75
1/20/95	167.75	168.5	166.25	167
1/23/95	166.25	166.5	165	166.5
1/24/95	166.75	167.25	166	166.75
1/25/95	167	167	166.25	166.75
1/26/95	166.5	167.5	166	166.5
1/27/95	166	166.5	165.5	165.75
1/30/95	165	165	162.25	163
	End of the Initial 20-day Baseline Period			
1/31/95	162.75	164	162.5	163
2/1/95	163	165	162.75	164.5
2/2/95	164	165.75	164	165.25
2/3/95	165.5	166.5	165.5	166
2/6/95	166.25	170	165.75	169.25
2/7/95	168.25	169	167	167.25
2/8/95	167	167.5	166.5	167.25
2/9/95	166	167.5	165	167.25
2/10/95	168	169	167	168
2/13/95	167.75	168	167	167.5
2/14/95	167.25	168.5	167	168.25
2/15/95	168	168.25	166.75	167.75
2/16/95	167.25	167.25	166.5	166.75

(Continued)

TABLE 9.1 *(Continued)*

Early 1995 Corn Prices

Date	Open	High	Low	Close
2/17/95	166.25	166.75	165.75	166.25
2/21/95	165.75	166	164.75	165.75
2/22/95	165.5	167	165.25	166
2/23/95	167	167.75	166.25	167.25
2/24/95	167	167.75	166.75	167.25
2/27/95	167.5	167.5	166.5	167.25
2/28/95	167	168	166.75	167.5
3/1/95	167	168.5	167	168
3/2/95	167.5	168.25	167	167.75
3/3/95	167.5	167.5	165.75	166
3/6/95	165.75	**171.5**	165.75	169.25
3/7/95	169	**171.5**	168.5	170.5
3/8/95	169.75	170.5	169	170
3/9/95	169.75	170.75	169.5	170.25
3/10/95	170.5	**171.75**	169.75	170.75
3/13/95	171.25	**173.25**	171.25	173
3/14/95	172.75	**173.5**	172.25	172.75
3/15/95	173.25	**174.5**	172.25	174
3/16/95	173.25	174.25	172	172.5
3/17/95	172.5	174	172	172.75
3/20/95	172.25	173.5	171.75	172

I would be concerned that a few large *R* multiples at the end of the bull market might have produced most of their results. But that was not the case. Their biggest year for large *R*-multiple trades was actually 2003. Thus, the method seems to work great in bull and bear markets.

I was interested in looking at their results in terms of expectancy. Eric was kind enough to do the work for me, and he put it into Figure 9.2. The chart also shows the distribution of *R* multiples in 0.5*R* increments. In other words, each *R* multiple was calculated and then put into the closest bin corresponding to that value. The expectancy of all the trades was 0.71*R* with a standard deviation of 2.80*R*, so it is an excellent system.

Figure 9.2 shows the R-multiple distribution of an excellent trend-following system. It's a good illustration of my belief that a system is really characterized by its R-multiple distribution. We'll be showing more illustration of this in Chapter 13.

Notice that they had 109 trades that produced 15R gains or better. Furthermore, they had only 91 losses as big as 1.5R and 22 losses as big as, or bigger than, $-2R$. This is an excellent profile. The authors also simulated the method with their proprietary position-sizing techniques and found that it produced a compounded annual return of 19.3 percent.[7]

The above study shows how powerful simple entry techniques can be because you cannot get any simpler than entering when the stock makes a new all-time high. You also cannot get any simpler than their exit, which was a very wide trailing stop.

Most people, however, usually want to combine an entry with some sort of setup. They might ask the simple question, "How can I make sure that I select only the best moving stocks and eliminate all the others because I don't want 1,600 stocks in my portfolio?" This would start you in the direction of more complexity and into the world of setups.

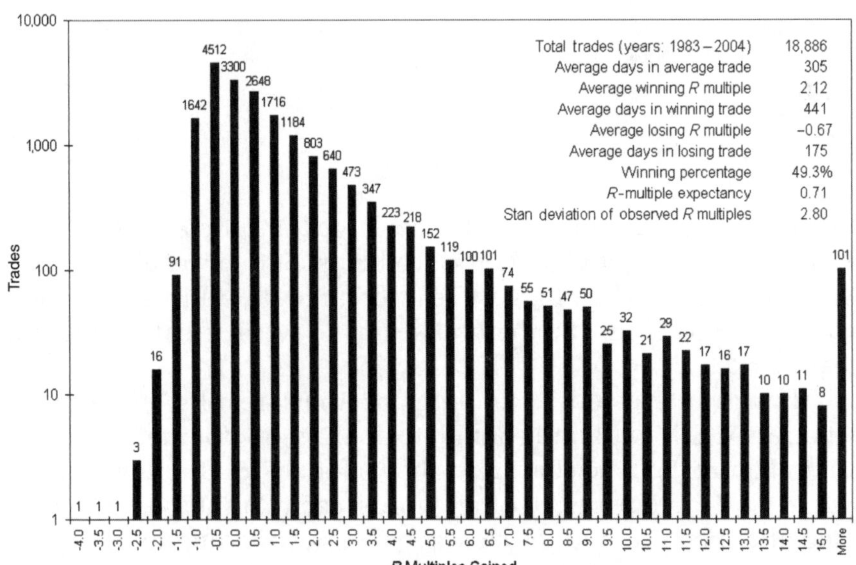

Figure 9.2 An R-multiple distribution for a long-term stock system

The channel breakout can be used with any number of setups, such as those given in Chapter 8 for both stocks and futures. For example, you might decide not to trade it unless you also have strong fundamentals in the item under question. You might require high earnings per share in a stock or a strong sign of demand in the commodity you are considering.

The channel breakout could also be used as a setup. You might look for a breakout and then enter on a retracement, followed by another breakout on a shorter time frame. And your initial stop could actually be placed under the initial retracement so that your initial *R* was quite small rather than 10 times ATR. You could still use 10 ATR as the trailing stop, with it taking over when it moves the stop up from your initial tight exit. This would result in a much lower reliability, but the winning *R* multiples could become huge.

There are thousands of possibilities for using channel breakouts. If you use them as an entry signal, you'll never miss a big move because (1) you'll never get a big trend without a channel breakout, and (2) if you happen to miss a signal, then there will continually be new signals to enter if the trend is a valid one.

There are two major drawbacks with the channel breakout systems. First, they tend to produce large drawdowns. This, of course, is a function of the size of the stops used. For example, if you use another channel breakout as the exit—even if it's a smaller one—you still could give back lots of profits. However, that's more of an exit problem than a problem with the entry.

The second major problem with the channel breakout is that a lot of money is usually required to trade it successfully. We did extensive testing with entering on a 55-day breakout and exiting on a 13-day breakout with various position-sizing algorithms starting with a million dollar portfolio. The results suggested that a million dollars was probably an optimal account size for this sort of system. A $100,000 account, in contrast, could trade only a few markets—as opposed to the 15 to 20 markets that are normally traded with such a system.

In summary, the channel breakout entry is a good entry system that ensures that you will never miss a trending signal. However, it does get whipsawed a lot. As a result, its reliability is not much better than random entry. In addition, it requires a large account size to trade it optimally because it needs to trade at least 15 markets simultaneously.

If you plan to trade a channel breakout, I would make the following recommendations. First, use a setup with the entry that involves a sequential condition with price (that is, something that happens to the price before you are willing to take a breakout signal). For example, you might require (1) a narrow band of volatility before the breakout occurs, (2) an "efficient market" before taking a breakout signal, and/or (3) a clear sign of a trend signaled by a high relative strength in the stock you are considering. Generally, the setups that will help you are those that involve a sequence of price changes prior to the entry or involve some element other than price as discussed in Chapter 8.

Second, most of the problems that are associated with drawdowns or require large accounts in breakout systems can be solved by market selection and a careful selection of your stops and exits. However, those are both topics of other chapters.

Visual Entry Based on Charts

Many experts don't have an exact entry signal into the market. Instead, they visually inspect the charts and act on their gut feelings about what they see.

For example, one great trader told me that his entry technique was to look at a long-term chart of the market he was considering. He'd put the chart, such as the one in Figure 9.3, on the wall and go to the other end of the room and look at it. He said that if the market's trend was obvious from the other side of the room, then he would have no trouble entering that particular market in the direction of the trend.

One of my clients regularly makes a million dollars in profits each year trading stocks for his own account. He uses only visual patterns for entry, although he claims that his visual entries are somewhat intuitive.

This particular type of entry has some real advantages for people with the discipline to follow it. For example, price information is much purer than any summary information you might get from some indicator. If price information indicates a clear trend, then the chances are pretty good—probably as high as 60 percent—that the

Figure 9.3 A clear visual trend

trend will continue for some time. Thus, entry in the direction of the trend is probably much better than a random entry.

Patterns

Many people take the visual interpretation of charts much further. For example, the art of technical analysis focuses on the many types of chart patterns that markets tend to form. Some patterns are described as bullish and others as bearish. Thus, those patterns could give you your entry signals. Types of chart patterns include daily patterns such as gaps, spikes, key reversal days, thrust days, run days, inside days, and wide-ranging days. These patterns are typically used as short-term trading signals.

Other patterns are better described as continuation patterns. These include triangles, flags, and pennants. These have little meaning unless you wish to enter in the direction of the major trend after a breakout from these patterns.

Finally, there are top and bottom patterns. These include double bottoms and tops, head and shoulders patterns, rounded tops and bottoms, triangles, wedges, and island reversals. Obviously, these would tend to be entry signals for top and bottom pickers.

Other charts are composed of candlesticks, where the difference between the open and the close is either "clear" or "filled in" depending on whether the price is up or down, respectively. Books

Figure 9.4 Example of a candlestick chart: Google (GOOG) in early 2006

have been devoted to describing the various patterns that can be made with these candlesticks. The patterns have such obscure names as "doji," the "hammer," and the "hanging man." Figure 9.4 shows a sample candlestick chart of Google (GOOG) in early 2006.

If you are interested in a pattern approach to trading, then read the appropriate chapters of Jack Schwager's book, *Schwager on Futures: Fundamental Analysis.*[8] It has excellent descriptions of all these patterns as well as numerous chart examples. However, such patterns are very difficult to computerize and thus test. In addition, when people do test these various patterns, they do not find any evidence that they increase the reliability of entry signals beyond the 50 percent level. That being the case, I have elected not to spend a lot of effort describing such patterns in this chapter. Most people are much better off just entering in the direction of a major trend than they are looking for a particular pattern in the trend.[9]

Pure Prediction

A number of prediction techniques were discussed in the "there's an order to the universe" section of the concepts chapter—Chapter 5. Prediction techniques include Elliott Wave, Gann, and various forms of countertrend trading that predict tops and bottoms. My belief is that prediction has nothing to do with good trading. Many good forecasters, despite being excellent at their craft, have a great deal of trouble making money in the markets.

I once met a man who described himself as the Michael Jordan of the markets—meaning that he believed that no one was better than he was at trading the markets. He claimed that the markets were perfectly orderly and that he had worked out some "patented secrets" that he wouldn't sell for a million dollars. He showed me some old accounts that he had taken from $5,000 to $40,000 in less than six months to prove his knowledge and skill.

I wasn't particularly interested in his secrets, but I was interested in how he traded. As a result, I watched him trade for about six months. During that time, the account he was trading dropped in value by 97 percent. Just over 22 percent of his trades made money, and the account was never profitable throughout the entire six months.

Be wary of people who claim extensive trading skill. Watch their trading and, in particular, how they size their positions. If they don't practice low-risk position sizing, then don't walk away—run!

One of the reasons his trading accuracy was so dismal, and this is true for most market predictors, was that he always anticipated turning points in the market. For example, in November he anticipated an early freeze in the Midwest that would destroy next year's soybean crop. It didn't happen. Several times he said the market was due for cyclic turns. He said they would be dramatic so he wanted to get into the market early. The turns never happened, or if they did, they were insignificant.

One of the reasons his trading accuracy was so dismal, and this is true for most market predictors, was that he always anticipated turning points in the market.

Prediction is fine if it is accompanied by market confirmation. In other words, if you think you can predict a market bottom or top, fine. But don't trade it until the market shows you some sort of confirmation that it is turning. A good example of such a confirmation is a volatility breakout, as discussed below.

Volatility Breakouts

The next two techniques, volatility breakouts and directional movement, were first described by J. Welles Wilder, Jr., in *New Concepts in Technical Trading Systems*.[10] The techniques are simple and have withstood the test of time.

Volatility breakouts are essentially sudden dramatic price movements in a particular direction. Suppose the average true range is about 3 points. We might define a volatility breakout to be a move of 0.8 times the average true range (from the prior close) in a single day, or 2.4 points. Let's say today's price closed at 35. A volatility breakout would be a move of 2.4 points from the close, either up or down. If the price moved to 37.4, then you'd have an upside volatility breakout and you'd want to buy. If the price moved to 32.6, then you'd have a downside breakout and you'd want to short the market. *This is the general type of entry signal that I would recommend for those of you who have setups that involve market prediction.*

Wilder's system is somewhat different from what is described above. He recommends that the average true range be multiplied by a constant of 3.0 (called the *average true range times a constant*, or ARC). This essentially is used as a trailing stop from the close, and it becomes both an exit point for a current position and an entry point for a new position. In essence, the exit is almost exactly the same as the exit that we use on the random entry system (that is, three times the average true range).

Generally, when the market makes a strong one-day move in some direction, it's a good sign that you may want to be in the market on the side of that move. For example, you may have a strong uptrend, but a solid volatility breakout to the downside would be a good indication that the trend was over and that you need to go with the market in its new direction. At minimum, you probably don't want to go against a strong volatility breakout, so it's always a good exit as discussed in the next chapter.

Figure 9.5 shows an example of a volatility breakout in bonds. Depending on how the volatility breakout is defined, a clear breakout seems to occur on July 24, and an even stronger one occurs on August 2. Notice the large range of prices on the breakout day, and notice how far from the old close the new prices break out.

When you use a volatility breakout, you have some interesting advantages. First, this type of price movement is quite different from the channel breakout—which requires a clear trend when you have a long (40 days plus) channel. However, the examples shown in Figure 9.5 were also both channel breakouts.

Figure 9.5 Examples of volatility breakouts

The volatility breakout could simply signal the end of a trend and the start of a new one. As a result, at least part of the movement in a volatility breakout would have little correlation with a channel breakout. In fact, if the exit is quick enough, there may be no correlation between the profits generated by these two diverse entry signals.

The second advantage, which I've already mentioned, is that volatility breakouts are ideal for people who use various models to predict price movement. Price prediction is very dangerous unless it is accompanied by a sound trading system. Volatility breakouts could help you achieve the entry part of that solid system to trade your "secret knowledge" about how the markets work.

Price prediction is very dangerous unless it is accompanied by a sound trading system. Volatility breakouts could help you achieve the entry part of that solid system to trade your "secret knowledge" about how the markets work.

Directional Movement and the Average Directional Movement

Market technicians for some time have struggled with the concept of "trendiness" in the market. How do you know when a market is really trending?

J. Welles Wilder, Jr. (again from *New Concepts in Technical Trading Systems*), developed two concepts called *directional movement* and *average directional movement*, which for many people define trendiness. For example, Bruce Babcock, before his death, used to publish a book each year called *Trendiness in the Market*.[11] In that book he ranked the various tradable futures markets according to their trendiness. The book was based on the idea that if you trade the markets with the most "history of trending," you're most likely to catch a future trend in those markets. Babcock's measure of trendiness was simply a measure of the profitability of using a 28-day directional movement index (see below) to trade each market. When the net directional movement is up, you go long. When the net directional movement is down, you go short. Profitable markets were deemed to be "trendy," and the most profitable market was deemed to be the "trendiest."

The basic assumptions behind directional movement are the following:

1. When the trend is up, today's high price should be above yesterday's high price. Thus, the difference between the two prices is the up directional movement.
2. When the trend is down, today's low price should be below yesterday's low price. Thus, the difference between the two prices is the down directional movement.
3. *Inside days*, when the high and low of today do not fall outside of yesterday's range, are essentially ignored.
4. *Outside days*, when both the high and low are outside of yesterday's range, will add both an up and down directional movement. However, only the larger value is used.

The directional movement indicator is calculated as follows:

1. Add the up days (Σ DI+) and the down days (Σ DI−) for a predetermined period of days (Wilder suggests 14).
2. Divide each sum by the average true range for the same number of days. The directional movement indicator is then calculated as follows:
3. Determine the difference between the Σ DI+ and the Σ DI− and find the absolute value, that is, DI difference = $|(\Sigma \text{ DI+}) - (\Sigma \text{ DI−})|$.

4. Determine the DI sum: DI sum = Σ DI+ plus Σ DI−.
5. The directional movement index is defined by (DI difference)/(DI sum)×100. Multiplying by 100 normalizes the directional movement index so that it falls between zero and 100.
6. Although Wilder suggests 14 days for your calculations, LeBeau and Lucas report that 14 to 20 days are all good, with 18 days being optimal.

Perhaps the most important extension of the directional movement indicator is the *average directional movement index*, or ADX. The ADX is simply a moving average of the directional movement index. It's usually averaged over the same number of days that was used previously (that is, 14).

LeBeau and Lucas claim that "the proper interpretation of the ADX allows traders to significantly improve their odds of finding good markets and avoiding bad ones." They believe that the ADX actually provides a means to quantify the strength of various trends and claim to have done more work in that area than anyone else. Since I've done many workshops with Chuck LeBeau, I'm also quite familiar with his love of, and use of, the ADX.

Generally, the higher the ADX, the more directional movement there has been in the market. You don't know, however, whether the movement has been up or down. The lower the ADX, the less directional movement there has been in the market. Thus, the size of the ADX tells you the strength of the trend, but it says nothing about the direction of the trend.

According to LeBeau and Lucas, you cannot use the absolute value of the ADX to indicate whether a trend is strong or not. Instead, they make the following observations:

1. As long as the ADX is rising, any level of the ADX above 15 indicates a trend.
2. The greater the increase in the ADX, the stronger the trend. For example, a jump in the ADX from 15 to 20 is probably a better signal than a jump from 25 to 27.
3. Decreases in the ADX mean only that the trend is weakening or that the market is no longer trending.

4. When the ADX is rising, indicators such as overbought or oversold oscillators will not work. Such oscillators work only when the ADX is falling.

Before suggesting ways to use the ADX or directional movement as an entry signal, let's first discuss a few of the problems that tend to occur with the ADX. These include spikes and the lag factor.

When the market changes direction suddenly in the form of a spike, the ADX has a hard time adjusting. For example, when the market suddenly shifts direction, the longer-term ADX, as recommended by LeBeau and Lucas, may suddenly appear to go flat—indicating a trendless market. As a result, a substantial downtrend could be totally ignored by the ADX.

The long-term ADX also has a lag built into it. That is, you won't know that you are in a trending market until the trend is well under way. This is a real disadvantage if you are a short-term trader and you want to get into trends early. On the other hand, if your objective is to get into only strong trends with a clear signal, then the lag in the ADX is not a problem at all.

Now that you understand what directional movement and the ADX are, we can give you some useful entry signals. The following entry signals are only some suggestions for you to ponder:

1. Enter after crosses of the DI+ and the DI−. Long trades would occur after the DI+ goes above the DI− and the high of the previous day is penetrated. Short trades would occur after the DI− goes above the DI+ and the low of the previous day is penetrated. This is Wilder's original use of the indicator, and he believes that the price penetration is an important part of the signal.
2. Enter in the direction of the market movement when the ADX increases more than 4 points in two days.[12] Of course, you'll need a setup (such as a visual inspection of the chart) to tell you whether to go long or short since an ADX rise indicates only a strong trend.
3. Enter when the ADX reaches the highest value of the last 10 days. Once again, you'll need another signal (also a setup) to tell you which direction to go.

Moving Averages and Adaptive Moving Averages

Moving averages are very popular trading indicators because they are simple and easy to calculate. As far as I can tell, they have been used since trading markets were first invented by human beings.

The concept behind such an average is simple: You represent the price over the last *X* days by a single number, an average. It's the sum of the prices over the *X* days, divided by the number of days. That number moves with time. When you get tomorrow's price, you simply drop the price *X* days ago (that is, the number of days in the moving average), add in the new price, and once again divide by the number of days.

One bar is simpler for most people to grasp than, for example, 30 bars might be, even though the 30 bars might give you a lot more information about what the market is really doing. But people feel more control over the market when they transform data in some way. As a result, a lot of traders and investors use moving averages.

If you have a lot of days in your average, then you will have a slow-moving average. If your moving average includes only a few days, then it will move quickly. For example, many stock market followers use one-year moving averages to indicate the overall trend of the market. When the price has been going up consistently, it should be well above the one-year average. When the price drops below the one-year moving average, some people make the assumption that the direction of prices has changed. Colby and Meyers, in their *Encyclopedia of Technical Market Indicators*,[13] found that the strategy of buying stock when the price crossed above the one-year average and selling it when it crossed below that average outperformed a buy-and-hold strategy by a large margin.

The strategy of buying stock when the price crossed above the one-year average and selling it when it crossed below that average outperformed a buy-and-hold strategy by a large margin.

Short moving averages, in contrast, are quick moving. A market does not have to go up too many days for the price to be above its five-day moving average. Similarly, prices could quickly drop below that average.

Donchian was one of the first people to write about a system using moving averages. He used both the 5-day and the 20-day moving averages. When the 5-day average crossed above the 20-day average, you went long. When the 5-day average went down and crossed below the 20-day average, you reversed and went short.

This kind of system works well in pure trending markets. However, it assumes that the market has only two directions, up and down. Unfortunately, markets tend to trend about 15 percent of the time and spend 85 percent of the time consolidating. As a result, during the consolidation periods such a system gets whipsawed continually.

To overcome this problem, traders have decided to use three moving averages. R. C. Allen popularized a method in the early 1970s involving the 4-, 9-, and 18-day moving averages.[14] When the 4-day and 9-day averages have both crossed the 18-day average, you would enter the market—long if they are moving up and short if they are moving down. When the 4-day signal crosses back across the 9, you get an exit signal. However, you don't get a new entry signal until both the 4 and the 9 are on the same side of the 18-day average. Thus, this sort of system gives you a neutral zone.[15]

There are numerous types of moving averages and moving-average systems. For example, you have simple moving averages (as described), weighted moving averages, exponential moving averages, displaced moving averages, and adaptive moving averages. Each type is designed to overcome particular problems of the others, but they also each create their own problems.

Weighted Moving Averages

The simple moving average gives as much weight to the day that drops off as it does to the most recent day. Some people argue that this is not the best way to trade because the newest price is the most important. As a result, weighted moving averages give more weight to the most recent data and less weight to distant data.

Weighted moving averages can get very complex because you can give only the most recent day extra weight or you can give a different weight for each day. For example, you could have a 10-day weighted average that multiplies the first day (most distant) by 1, the second day by 2, the third day by 3, and so on. This is probably nonsense, but some people think that complex calculations make trading more effective. The assumption is wrong, but people do it anyway.

Some people think that complex calculations make trading more effective. The assumption is wrong, but people do it anyway.

Exponential Moving Averages

The exponential moving average weights the most recent data most heavily, and it doesn't drop anything out. For example, a 0.1 exponential moving average (equivalent to about a 20-day average) would multiply the current day's price by 0.1 and add it to yesterday's average. Nothing would be subtracted. This procedure is quite handy for calculations, and it does give more weight to the most recent data.

Displaced Moving Averages

Since a moving average tends to be very close to the prices, the signals can often be too quick. As a result, some people have elected to "displace" their moving averages by moving them into the future a number of days. This simply means that you are less likely to get whipsawed by a moving-average signal.

Adaptive Moving Averages

Adaptive moving averages became quite popular in the mid-1990s. Both Kaufman[16] and Chande and Kroll[17] have various versions of adaptive moving averages. These particular systems change speed according to some combination of market direction and speed.

Think about the amount of noise in the market. The daily price fluctuation is a good measure of the market noise. When there is a lot of noise, the moving average must be very slow to avoid being whipsawed in and out of the market. However, when the market is quite smooth, then fast-moving averages can be used because there is much less chance of a whipsaw. As a result, adaptive moving averages first measure the velocity of market movement against the amount of noise in the market. They then adjust the speed of the average according to the speed and noise factor.

Thus the adaptive moving average must (1) have at minimum some measure of the current efficiency of the market (that is, how much noise exists) and (2) be able to map that scenario onto various moving averages. A specific example of using an adaptive moving average is given under the entry technique designed by Perry Kaufman that is discussed later in this chapter.

Oscillators and Stochastics

Oscillators such as relative strength indicators (RSIs), stochastics, Williams's percent *R*, and so on, are all designed to help people who are trying to pick tops and bottoms. In my opinion, this is a fool's game, and there is no evidence that entry signals based on oscillators have a reliability much better than chance. In fact, in most cases there is no evidence that the market generally meets the assumptions that many oscillators are making. As a result, I've elected not to give a long discussion on something in which I have little faith.

However, there is a way that you can use an "overbought and/or oversold" oscillator—such as Wilder's RSI—to help you trade with narrow stops (see Chapter 11 on protective stops). Here's what you need to do this sort of trading:

1. Wait until the market gives a clear signal of being in a trend. This is a price-based setup.
2. Wait until the market reverses slightly and your oscillator gives a sign that the reaction has probably reached an extreme. This step also is a price-based setup, but it must occur after step 1.
3. Enter the market in the direction of the previous trend when the market gives a signal that it will again move in that direction. An example would be a return of price to the previous high (or low for a short signal) prior to the extreme oscillator signal.

This sort of trading sets up the possibility of a highly reliable trading signal with a very small stop (that is, the extreme of the reaction). In addition, since the risk of such a trade is quite small, it means that the reward-to-risk ratio of the potential trade could be very high. This is actually an example of a retracement setup as discussed in the last chapter, and it is, in my opinion, the best way to use oscillators. In addition, some of the best systems I've ever seen were based upon these concepts.

DESIGNING YOUR OWN ENTRY SIGNAL

The best entry signal for you is probably one that you design for yourself. The best way to design such a signal is to thoroughly reason out the concept upon which your signal should be based. I have designed the following example as an illustration of such thinking—just to give you an example. We'll start out with an idea that is widely used by traders and investors and then go on to something that is not. The ideas suggested are not tested, but feel free to use them if you want to work with them until you find something useful.

Let's design a system around basic ideas behind motion in physics. For example, think about predicting the movement of a car. You have no idea where the car is going (assume you are in a giant parking lot so that there are an infinite number of turns the car could make), but you know where the car has been. You also know its direction, speed (velocity), velocity changes (acceleration and deceleration), and momentum. If you know that information, then under certain conditions you'll have a good idea what the car will do in the near-term future. What you want to determine is when the car will move quickly in the same direction for as long a period as possible.

If the car is moving in a particular direction, it's more likely to continue in that direction than not. It could change directions, but chances are that it will continue in the same direction. Furthermore, if you know more about the car's velocity, velocity changes, and momentum, then there will be certain circumstances when it's even more likely that the car will continue in the same direction.

A car typically has to slow down in order to change directions. Thus, if a car is going fast (fast velocity), it is more likely to continue going fast in the same direction than it is to do something else.

The same is true of the market. If it is moving rapidly in one direction, then it is more likely to continue going fast in that direction than to do something else. Think about it. A quickly advancing market is much more likely to slow down first before there is a major change in direction. Market technicians call this "momentum," which is a really misleading name.[18] The technical indicator known as *momentum* simply measures the change in price (usually the closing price) from one time frame to another. However, we'll use the word *speed* or *velocity* because both are more accurate.

Speed is really stated in terms of distance per unit of time (such as 60 miles per hour). If you use a constant distance (such as 10 days) in your velocity calculations, then you can simply assume that speed is the distance traveled per X-day period, where X is the number of days you pick. *Interestingly enough, more professional traders probably use velocity (which they call* momentum indicators) *in their studies of the market than any other indicator.*

How would you use speed as an entry signal? Zero speed means no movement. The speed indicator tends to be a number that moves back and forth across the zero line from fast up movement to fast down movement or vice versa. *When speed changes direction and begins to accelerate in the opposite direction, you have a potential entry signal.*

When speed changes direction and begins to accelerate in the opposite direction, you have a potential entry signal.

Acceleration and Deceleration

Acceleration and *deceleration* refer to changes in speed. If a car is increasing its speed, then it is even more likely to keep going in the same direction than a car that is simply moving fast. On the other hand, if a car is decreasing its speed, then the chances of it changing direction are much greater.

Although the change in velocity of market movement is not as significant to predicting its future movement as acceleration or deceleration is in predicting the movement of a car, it still is an important factor. However, I have never seen anything that directly looks at acceleration or deceleration in the market. The formula, if it existed, would look something like the following:

$$\text{Velocity change} = \frac{\text{velocity today} - \text{velocity on day } X}{\text{time}}$$

Although we haven't done extensive research on acceleration or deceleration as an entry indicator, we have programmed some data to look at them. Table 9.2 shows the closing prices of the same corn data that we looked at earlier. The table starts after the baseline is completed with day 21. Recall that both a 20-day channel breakout and a 40-day channel breakout occurred on March 6, which is day 46 in the table. Table 9.2 also shows the average rate of change of prices (that is, speed) over 20 days. Decreases in speed are shown in boldface, while increases in speed are in regular type.

Notice that a positive 20-day velocity period actually starts on day 40—7 trading days before the channel breakout on day 46. The last two columns in Table 9.2 show 3- and 5-day accelerations or decelerations (that is, how much speed actually changes over a 3- to 5-day period). The longer-term acceleration (that is, the 10-day) also starts a positive acceleration that becomes negative briefly for only 1 day.

Figure 9.6 shows the three variables on a time graph. Notice that the channel breakout, which actually begins on March 6, starts on day 46. Velocity and acceleration start to move much earlier. However, there is a dip in both velocity and acceleration that occurs just before the breakout, but the numbers still stay positive except for a slight dip of the 10-day acceleration into the negative.

What does this mean? I'm certainly not suggesting that you use a positive velocity or a sign of acceleration (as opposed to deceleration) as an entry system. Instead, I'm just pointing out relationships. Relationships, when you understand them, form the basis for concepts that you can use in your trading.

Remember that money is not necessarily made by being right about entry. Instead, if you can determine an entry that will give you a high probability (say, 25 percent) of a large *R*-multiple trade, you have a good chance of making large, consistent profits. The start of acceleration might give you a low-risk point at which you could place a very narrow stop. This means that *R* is low, so you have the potential of a high-*R*-multiple profit. This, of course, would require extensive testing.

Acceleration might prove to be the perfect tool for a good retracement setup. For example, you might simply need to look for a deceleration right after the channel breakout. As soon as the deceleration turns to acceleration, you could have a perfect signal that

TABLE 9.2

Velocity and Acceleration Study

Date	Close	Velocity −20 day	Acceleration −5 day	Acceleration −10 day
Day 21	166.5	0.225		
Day 22	165.75	0.175		
Day 23	163	**−0.0625**		
Day 24	163	**−0.1125**		
Day 25	164.5	**−0.0875**	**−0.3125**	
Day 26	165.25	**−0.025**	**−0.2**	
Day 27	166	0	0.0625	
Day 28	169.25	0.075	0.1875	
Day 29	167.25	0.0625	0.15	
Day 30	167.25	**−0.025**	0	**−0.25**
Day 31	167.25	**−0.0125**	**−0.0125**	**−0.1875**
Day 32	168	0	**−0.075**	0.0625
Day 33	167.5	**−0.075**	**−0.1375**	0.0375
Day 34	168.25	0	0.025	0.0875
Day 35	167.75	0	0.0125	0.025
Day 36	166.75	**−0.0125**	**−0.0125**	**−0.0125**
Day 37	166.25	**−0.0125**	0.0625	**−0.0875**
Day 38	165.75	**−0.05**	**−0.05**	**−0.1125**
Day 39	166	**−0.0375**	**−0.0375**	**−0.0125**
Day 40	167.25	0.0375	0.05	0.05
Day 41	167.25	0.075	0.0875	0.075
Day 42	167.25	0.2125	0.2625	0.2875
Day 43	167.5	0.225	0.2625	0.225
Day 44	168	0.175	0.1375	0.175
Day 45	167.75	0.125	0.05	0.1375
Day 46	**166**	0	**−0.2125**	0.0125
Day 47	169.25	0	**−0.225**	0.05
Day 48	170.5	0.1625	**−0.0125**	0.2
Day 49	170	0.1375	0.0125	0.1
Day 50	170.25	0.15	0.15	0.075
Day 51	170.25	0.1125	0.1125	**−0.1**
Day 52	173	0.275	0.1125	0.05
Day 53	172.75	0.225	0.0875	0.05
Day 54	174	0.3125	0.1625	0.1875
Day 55	172.5	0.2875	0.175	0.2875
Day 56	172.5	0.3125	0.0375	0.3125

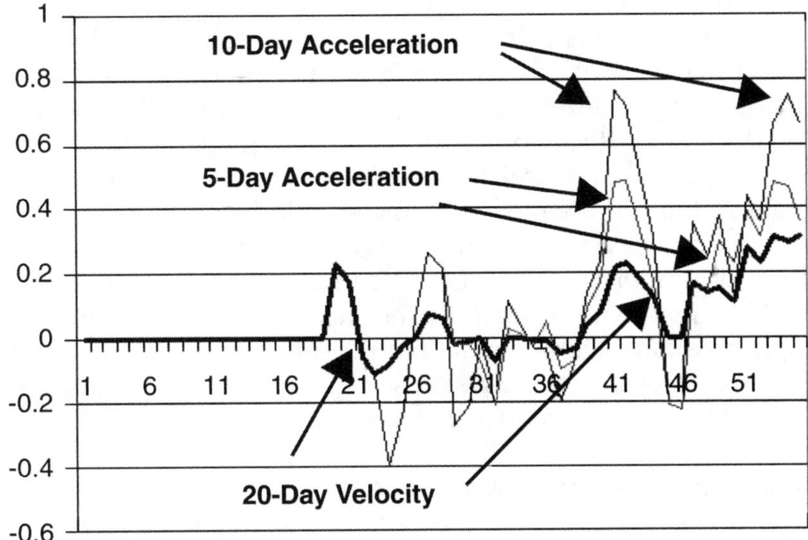

Figure 9.6 Velocity and acceleration in the corn move

would require only a tight stop and give you the potential for a very high *R*-multiple profit. In the example shown, deceleration had started just before the channel breakout.

AN EVALUATION OF ENTRY USED IN SOME COMMON SYSTEMS

Our last task with respect to entry is to review some of the typical entry signals used in some stock market systems and in some systems used in more speculative markets.

Some Stock Market Systems Reviewed

William O'Neil's Stock Market System

The William O'Neil stock market trading system is one that uses the CANSLIM setups as discussed in the previous chapter. Entry is the timing portion of the system that is based on various chart patterns one might find in the stocks under consideration. The key portion of the entry is a price breakout from a consolidation period that has lasted anywhere from 7 weeks to 15 months. Typical patterns would include a cup and a handle, a breakout from a long base, a saucer and a handle, a double bottom, or a double base. However, the first two patterns are by far the most common. William O'Neil presents many examples of these patterns in his excellent book.

The other critical point about entry is that the breakout should be accompanied by a large increase in volume. O'Neil, for example, suggests that the breakout volume should be at least 50 percent above the daily average for that stock. This large increase in volume is the most important aspect of O'Neil's entry that fewer people follow. Most just look for the patterns such as a cup and handle or a simple breakout. Think about volume as the mass of a vehicle. If a heavy truck starts moving fast, it's much more likely to keep going than a tiny car that can turn or stop on a dime.

Warren Buffett's Business Evaluation Model

Buffett's business evaluation model, with all the filters given in the previous chapter, probably does not have an entry technique—although this assumption is somewhat speculation on my part. My guess is that as long as enough money is available, Buffett will buy a new company as soon as he discovers one that meets his criteria. Thus, the discovery of a company that meets all his criteria is probably his entry signal—although I'm not sure any companies would meet his criteria in an overvalued market. Buffett certainly cares little for what the market is doing, as evidenced by the following quote:

> The market is there only as a reference point to see if anybody is offering to do anything foolish. When we invest in stocks, we invest in a business. You simply have to behave according to what is rational rather than according to what is fashionable.[19]

Some Futures Market Systems Reviewed

Perry Kaufman's Adaptive Trading

If you recall from our discussion of Kaufman's adaptive approach in Chapter 8, Kaufman designed an efficiency ratio that was based both on the speed and direction of the market's movement and on the amount of noise in the market. Several examples were given of possible efficiency ratios that one might use.

In the calculations below, we'll assume that you have an efficiency ratio that goes from zero to 1—zero meaning no market movement except for noise and 1 meaning that the market was all movement and no noise. In a very efficient market, the total price movement will be equal to the price movement between the two time periods. The ratio would be 1.0 because there is no noise. For example, if the price moved up 10 points in a 10-day period and the price moved up by 1 point each day, then you'd have a ratio of $10/(10 \times 1) = 1.0$.

In a very inefficient market, there would be a very small total price movement and a lot of daily price movement. The resulting ratio would tend to go toward zero. For example, if the price only moved 1 point over a 10-day period, but the price moved up or down by 10 points each day, then you'd have a ratio of $1/(10 \times 10) = 0.01$. And, of course, if there is no price movement—no matter what the total price movement is—the ratio would be zero.

The next step in calculating the adaptive moving average is to map the efficiency ratio onto a range of moving-average speeds. We could call a 2-day average a fast speed and a 30-day average a slow speed. Kaufman converts the moving-average speed into a smoothing constant (SC) by using the following formula:

$$\mathrm{SC} = \frac{2}{N+1}$$

The smoothing constant for the fast speed is $2/(2+1) = 2/3 = 0.66667$. The smoothing constant for the slow speed is $2/(30+1) = 2/31 = 0.06452$. The difference between these two values, which Kaufman uses in his formula, is 0.60215.

Finally, Kaufman recommends that the formula for mapping the smoothing constants onto the efficiency ratio be as follows:

$$\text{Scaled smoothing constant} = [\text{efficiency ratio} \times (\text{SC difference})] + \text{slow SC}$$

Plugging in our numbers, we get the following:

$$\text{Scaled smoothing constant} = [\text{efficiency ratio} \times 0.60215] + 0.06452$$

Thus if the efficiency ratio were 1.0, our scaled smoothing constant would be 0.66667; and if the efficiency ratio were 0, then our scaled smoothing constant would be 0.06452. Notice how this corresponds to the numbers for 2 and 30 days, respectively.

Since the 30-day number can still produce an effect, Kaufman recommends that you square the final smoothing constant before you apply it. This basically means that you will eliminate trading when the efficiency ratio (ER) is too low.

The formula for the adaptive moving average (AMA) is as follows:

$$\text{AMA} = \text{AMA (yesterday)} + \text{SC}^2 \times [\text{today's price} - \text{AMA (yesterday)}]$$

Let's say that yesterday's AMA is 40. Today's price is 47—a 7-point difference. In an efficient market, this would produce a major change in the average—raise the AMA by nearly 3.1 points—almost half of 7. In an inefficient market, with an ER of about 0.3, the differential would hardly make a dent in the AMA, moving it up about 0.4 point. Thus, you'd be much more likely to get a trade from a movement in the AMA when the market is efficient.

According to Kaufman, the AMA is equivalent to an exponential smoothing and such averages should be traded as soon as they signal a directional change. In other words, you buy the market when the AMA turns up and you sell when the AMA turns down.

However, trading these signals will cause a lot of whipsaws. As a result, Kaufman adds the following filter:

$$\text{Filter} = \text{percentage} \times \text{standard deviation (1-day AMA change over last 20 days)}$$

Kaufman suggests using a small percentage filter for futures and forex trading (that is, 10 percent) and a larger percentage filter (that is, 100 percent) for equity and interest rate markets.

Determine the appropriate filter for the market you wish to trade. Add the filter to the lowest price in a downtrend for a buy signal, and subtract the filter from the highest price in an uptrend for a sell signal. This is basically your adaptive entry.

You probably could map a market efficiency ratio onto many of the techniques we've discussed for entry. For example, you could have an adaptive channel breakout system where the length of the channel is adaptive or an adaptive volatility breakout where the size of the breakout required depends on market efficiency.

William Gallacher's Fundamentals

Recall from Chapter 8 that Gallacher believes in determining the fundamentals of the market as a setup. When the fundamentals are strong, then you can enter in the direction that those fundamentals suggest for the direction of the market. Recall that fundamental data could be different for each market. In addition, recall from LeBeau's discussion of fundamental trading in Chapter 5 that one should defer to experts to determine what the fundamentals are of any particular markets. LeBeau also cautions that you can be right about the fundamentals but terribly wrong about the timing. Thus, you need a good timing system to trade fundamentals.

Gallacher, for the sake of illustration, gives a 10-day channel breakout reversal system to illustrate the folly of technical analysis. While no one that I know of would trade this kind of system, Gallacher suggests that once you know the fundamentals, taking 10-day breakouts in the direction of the market predicted by the fundamentals is a very sound strategy. I personally believe that such a system would lead to many whipsaws. However, a channel breakout of 50 days or more, combined with fundamental support, might be an excellent entry.

Ken Roberts' 1-2-3 Reversal Approach

Ken Roberts recommends the use of two setups before entering the market. The first is that the market must make a 9-month high or low. The second is that the market makes a 1-2-3 reversal. See Chapter 8 for exact details and several illustrations of the market making new 9-month extremes, followed by such 1-2-3 reversals. When you have such setups, what kind of entry should you use?

When these two setups are present, you enter the market when it again moves toward point 2 (as shown in Figure 9.7) and makes a new extreme price. This new extreme price is your entry signal. Figure 9.7 shows a new extreme price after an all-time high and then a 1-2-3 reversal. The line in Figure 9.7 is your entry signal. You could also enter as soon as the price at point 2 is passed in the direction you expect the market to move.

The whole assumption behind this particular method of trading is that after the market has completed a long-term trend and done a 1-2-3-4 pattern, with 4 being a new extreme in the opposite direction, the market will turn around. *Quite often the market doesn't turn around.* Instead, it goes into a long consolidation period that could create many whipsaws. Nevertheless, this method could be traded successfully with the right stops, exits, and position sizing, which will be discussed in subsequent chapters.

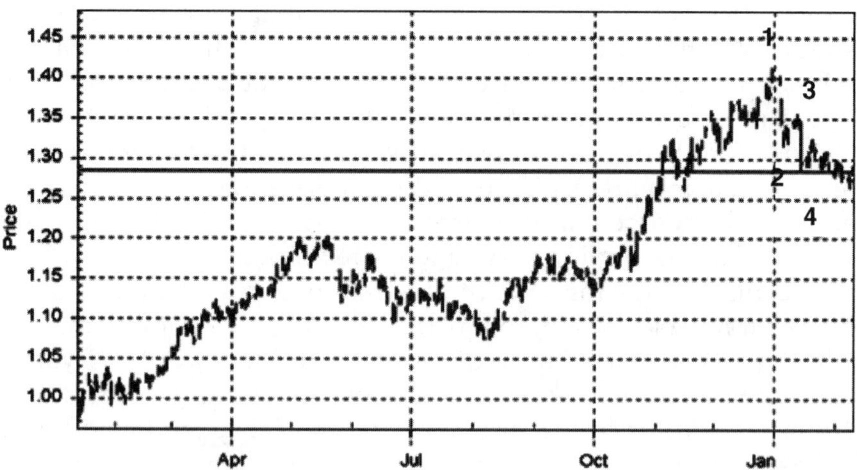

Figure 9.7 A new all-time high (1) occurs in December 1988 in the British pound. This is followed by a sharp decline to point (2), a reversal to point (3), and then another sharp decline on January 11 to a new low (4)—the entry signal. This worked for a few months, and then the market recovered to new highs.

SUMMARY

- Entry receives more attention from most people than any other aspect of a trading system. This attention is largely misplaced and often at the expense of ignoring the most critical aspects of a system. Nevertheless, if good timing can increase the reliability of your trading without changing its reward-to-risk ratio, then entry certainly deserves some of your attention.
- You can make money with a random entry system. In fact, few entry techniques show a reliability that is much better than random—especially over 20 days or more.
- Good entry indicators would include:

  A channel breakout of over 40 days.

  A volatility breakout in a single day that's about 0.8 times the average true range. This is particularly good for market predictors.

A large ADX movement in a single day (or 2-day period) when combined with a clear indication of a trend.

Use of an indicator that shows that velocity is increasing in the direction of the trend.

An adaptive moving average changing direction and moving a predetermined distance based on a predefined filter.

An oscillator that indicates an extreme move against the major trend followed by a clear resumption of the trend.

- Common entry techniques were discussed for various systems. In a few cases, improvements to the techniques were discussed.

NOTES

1. Robert Kiyosaki, *If You Want to Be Rich and Happy, Then Don't Go to School* (Lower Lake, Calif.: Asian Press, 1992).
2. My comment is in no way a reflection on the quality of any of these books. It simply is an observation that people write books to fulfill the biases of people who want to buy them. I suggest that you judge these books for yourself:
   a. Stephen Littauer, *How to Buy Stocks the Smart Way* (Chicago: Dearborn Trade, 1995).
   b. Richard J. Maturi, *Stock Picking: The Eleven Best Tactics for Beating the Market* (New York: McGraw-Hill, 1993).
   c. Louis Engel and Harry Hecht, *How to Buy Stocks*, 8th ed. (New York: Little, Brown, 1994).
   d. Michael Sivy, *Michael Sivy's Rules of Investing: How to Pick Stocks Like a Pro* (New York: Warner Books, 1996).
   e. Michael Gianturco, *How to Buy Technology Stocks* (New York: Little, Brown, 1996).
3. Charles LeBeau and David W. Lucas, *The Technical Traders' Guide to Computer Analysis of the Futures Market* (Homewood, Ill.: Irwin, 1992).
4. It's much easier to find an entry system with a reliability above 50 percent if your time frame is one day or less (that is, such as a planned exit on tomorrow's opening) than it is to find a long-term reliable exit.

5. The success of the Turtles' trading had much more to do with their position-sizing algorithm, as is usually the case, than it did the fact that they traded a channel breakout system.
6. The entire reference that I used can be downloaded at www.blackstarfunds.com/files/Does_trendfollowing_work_on_stocks.pdf.
7. The authors report having as many as 1,500 positions open up at one time, so their position sizing would have to account for that and the risk of multiple, correlated positions. In addition, the fact that the authors are willing to reveal their entry and exit, but not their position sizing, again illustrates the point that I make repeatedly in this book on the importance of position sizing.
8. Jack Schwager, *Schwager on Futures: Fundamental Analysis* (New York: Wiley, 1996).
9. The focus of this research was not on finding a high-*R*-multiple trade or developing a high-expectancy system, as we advocate in the book. The focus of the research was on finding highly reliable entries that most people do because of the lotto bias.
10. J. Welles Wilder, Jr., *New Concepts in Technical Trading Systems* (Greensboro, N.C.: Trend Research, 1978).
11. Bruce Babcock, *Trendiness in the Market* (Sacramento, Calif.: CTCR Products, 1995).
12. Or whatever number your testing suggests that you should use to meet your objectives.
13. Robert W. Colby and Thomas A. Meyers, *Encyclopedia of Technical Market Indicators* (Homewood, Ill.: Dow Jones Irwin, 1988).
14. See LeBeau and Lucas, *Technical Traders' Guide,* for a thorough discussion of this work.
15. Chuck LeBeau told me that they tested every possible combination of moving-average crossover that they could imagine. All of them worked fairly well in trending markets but failed in sideways markets. None of them were much better than random entry.
16. Perry Kaufman, *Smarter Trading: Improving Performance in Changing Markets* (New York: McGraw-Hill, 1995).
17. Tushar Chande and Stanley Kroll, *The New Technical Trader: Boost Your Profit by Plugging into the Latest Indicators* (New York: Wiley, 1994).
18. In physics, *momentum* means mass times acceleration, which might be the market equivalent of acceleration on a large volume of shares of stock.
19. "The Big Bad Bear on Wall Street," *Fortune,* January 4, 1988, p. 8.

CHAPTER 10

Knowing When to Fold 'Em: How to Protect your Capital

Your protective stop is like a red light. You can go through it, but doing so is not very wise! If you go through town running every red light, you probably won't get to your destination quickly or safely.

Richard Harding, speaking at one of our system development workshops

One of the attendees of a workshop I gave was so depressed that he could hardly concentrate on the workshop. He was depressed over his recent stock market losses. During the first part of the prior year, he'd grown his retirement account from $400,000 to $1,300,000. He said that he had planned to attend the workshop partly so he could tell me what a great investor he'd become. However, in the two weeks before the workshop, a number of stocks in his account had fallen dramatically and his account had dropped by 70 percent. He had one stock in his account that had fallen from just over $200 per share to about $50 per share—where he had sold at a loss. That stock was now $60 a share, and he was convinced that he'd gotten out at the bottom.

That story, I hope, is not a familiar one, but I suspect that it happens all too often. People get into the market on a tip or with some hot new entry technique. But once they have a position in the market, they have no idea when or how they will exit. Exits, whether aborting a losing position or taking profits, are the keys to making money in the market. In fact, the golden rule of trading says to:

> Cut your losses short and let your profits run.

That golden rule seems to me like a commentary on exits. In his marvelous book *Campaign Trading*, John Sweeney makes the following observation:

> Just as it was tough when we were children to look under the bed or in a dark closet for night monsters, it's equally tough to look at a loss and acknowledge it. It was easier to hide under the covers back then, and now it's easier to adopt some defense mechanism. (The one I hear most is "Oh, that trading rule doesn't work!" as if the entry strategy caused the loss.)[1]

The important point here is that getting out of a losing trade is critical if you want to be a successful trader. Most people think mostly about entries or setups, and that just doesn't help you become a success. You'll get rich trading through your exits and mastering the art of position sizing.

In my opinion, *you do not have a trading system unless you know exactly when you will get out of a market position at the time you enter it.* Your worst-case exit, which is designed to preserve your capital, should be determined ahead of time. In addition, you should also have some idea about how you plan to take profits and a strategy for letting your profits run. That aspect of exits is reserved for Chapter 11.

> In my opinion, you do not have a trading system unless you know exactly when you will get out of a market position at the time you enter it.

Here's what some other market legends have said about protective stops:

William O'Neil: "The whole secret to winning in the stock market is to lose the least amount possible when you're not right."

Jesse Livermore: "Investors are the big gamblers. They make a bet, stay with it, and if it goes the wrong way, they lose it all."

WHAT YOUR STOP DOES

When you set a stop loss in the market, you are doing two important things. First, you are setting a maximum loss (risk) that you are willing to take. We'll call this initial risk *R* because it is the basis for determining your *R* multiples as discussed in Chapter 7 on expectancy. Every trader or investor, in my opinion, should understand the concept of *R*. Remember, *R* is the amount that you would expect to lose on a trade when you need to get out to preserve your capital. If you haven't predetermined *R* for every position that you take in the market, then you are just gambling your money away.

Remember, *R* is the amount that you would expect to lose on a trade when you need to get out to preserve your capital. If you haven't predetermined *R* for every position that you take in the market, then you are just gambling your money away.

Over many trades, you may find that your average loss is about half of that, or 0.5*R*, depending on your strategy for raising stops. However, sometimes the market will get away from you and your loss will be 2*R* or perhaps even 3*R*. Hopefully, such larger losses are very rare for you.

Let's say that you take a position in corn and you decide to use a stop loss that is three times the daily volatility. The daily volatility is about 3 cents, which when multiplied by 5,000 bushels per contract equals $150. Thus, your stop is three times that amount, or $450 per contract. If your average loss is only half of that, or 0.5*R*, then you'll most likely lose about $225 if the trade doesn't work for you.

Let's look at an example in stocks. Suppose you buy 100 shares of ABCD Company. The stock is trading at $48. The daily volatility is about 50 cents, so you decide to use a stop loss of $1.50 per share. Thus, you will sell the stock if it moves down to $46.50. That's not a big move, and it represents a loss of only $150 per 100 shares.[2]

The second important thing that you do when you enter a stop loss is to set a benchmark against which to measure subsequent gains. Your primary job as a trader should be to devise a plan that will earn profits that are large multiples of *R*. For example, it doesn't take many 10*R* profits or 20*R* profits to make a tremendous trading system. In the case of the corn trade, it would be nice to make a profit of $2,250 or even $4,500. You can tolerate a lot of $225 losses when you make a few profits like that.

I've talked about *R* multiples before in the expectancy chapter. But this topic is so important for your success that it's worth repeating here. So let's look at our stock market example again with this thought in mind. You purchase 100 shares of a $48 stock, and you plan to get out at $46.50. Now, let's say you hold on to the stock long enough for it to appreciate by 20 percent. This would amount to a gain of $9.63 per share, or a price rise to $57.63. Basically, you have taken a risk of $150 per 100 shares for the opportunity of making $963—that's a little more than a 6*R* gain, which is quite possible.

Realistically, commissions and slippage in the stock market, however, could easily represent another $30 in either the loss or the gain, especially if you don't trade through the Internet. If we include costs, we have a possible loss of $180 ($150 + $30 in costs) to produce a gain of $933 ($963 less $30 in costs). That means that your gain is a 5.35*R* gain. Do you understand how this works? Thinking in terms of *R* is one of the most important concepts you need to understand. It will transform the way you approach the markets. I've actually included a new chapter, Chapter 12, to help you start thinking about your potential reward-to-risk ratio every time you think about entering a trade.

Most people think that their entire $4,800 is at stake when they buy 100 shares at $48.[3] That's not the case if you have a clear idea of when to exit the market and the capacity to do so. Your stop loss predefines your initial risk *R*. *But your primary job as a trader should be to devise a plan that will get you profits that are large multiples of* R. Think about the implications of what I've just said: *One of your primary goals as a trader should be to get big-*R*-multiple trades.*

Remember that the first purpose of your stop loss is to set up the initial *R* value that you will tolerate. That *R* value, if small, will make it possible for you to have very large *R*-multiple wins. However, small stops also make your chances of losing on a given trade much higher and will cut down on the reliability of your entry technique. Remember that the reliability of our random entry system was about 38 percent. It should have been 50 percent, but the 12 percent increase in the rate of losses was due to transaction costs and the fact that we had a stop (albeit, a large one). A tighter stop would cut down your reliability even more. It could stop you out of a trade prior to a big move in your favor. You could get right back in on another entry signal, but many such trades would give you very large transaction costs.

As a result, it's important to look at some criteria that might be useful in a stop loss that you might use. These would include (1) assuming that your entry technique is not much better than chance and putting your stop beyond the noise of the market, (2) finding the maximum adverse excursion of all your winning trades and using a ratio of that value as your stop, (3) having a tight stop that will give you high-*R*-multiple winners, and/or (4) using a stop that makes sense based on your entry concept. Let's look at each of these criteria.

Going beyond the Noise

The day-to-day activity of the market could be considered noise. For example, if the price moves a point or two, you never know whether it's because a few market makers were "fishing" for orders or whether there was a lot of activity. And even if there is a lot of activity, you have no idea whether it will continue or not. Thus, it's reasonable to assume that the daily activity in the market is mostly noise. It's probably better for you to place your stop outside of the likely range of any such noise.

But what is a reasonable estimate of the range of noise? Some people like to use trendlines to determine where their stops should be. For example, Figure 10.1 shows a trendline that could be used to determine a reasonable stop level for a short position in the stock. You could also use support and resistance levels to set the stops. For example, a technical trader would say that the stock has a lot of support at $56.50. Something is happening at that price (that is, support) to keep it from falling more. A short-term trader might even go long if the price went above the trendline, and that trader would use the support at $56.50 as a stop level.

But what would happen if prices fell through $56.50? A technical trader would say that there isn't any more support so it could fall a long way. The $56.50 would then become resistance, and they might put their stop to cover a short position at that level.

Figure 10.1 Using charts to set stops in a downtrending market

Figure 10.2 shows the Brazilian ETF that has been in a tremendous uptrend. A trend follower would definitely want to be long in this position, and he or she could have his or her stop at either the trendline or at the theoretical support level on the chart.

However, one problem with this particular strategy is that everyone knows where those stops are. They are at the trendline or at support and resistance levels. Quite often, markets tend to stampede in reverse and fill everyone's stop orders before they quietly return in the direction of the trend.

You might want to consider putting your protective stop at a level that isn't "logical" to the market and that is still beyond the noise. Let's assume that noise is represented by the activity of the day—that is, the whole day's activity is mostly noise. The activity of the day could be represented by the average true range. If you take an average of this activity over the past 10 days (that is, a 10-day moving average), you have a good approximation of the daily noise. Now, multiply the 10-day moving average of the average true range by some constant between 2.7 and 3.4 and you'll have a stop that's far enough away to be out of the noise.[4] This is probably a good stop for most long-term trend followers in the

Figure 10.2 Using charts to determine stocks in an uptrending market

futures market. Stock market traders who want to remain in their positions for a long time might want to use 3 times the weekly volatility or 10 times the daily volatility.

Your response to a stop that far away might be something like: "I'd never want to put that much risk in any one position." However, there's another way to look at it—which you'll understand better after going through the position sizing chapter. Your stop controls your risk per unit. However, your position sizing controls your total risk. Thus, you could have a wide stop of 10 times the average true range (ATR) while using position sizing to make your total risk as low as 0.25 percent of your equity. Thus, a wide stop is not a lot of risk if your position size is small or minimal. And if a minimal unit with that big of a risk seems like a lot of money to you, then you probably should not be trading that particular instrument—either it's not a good opportunity or you are undercapitalized.

Also remember that your initial stop is your worst-case risk, your *R* unit. Most of your losses will probably be less than 1*R* because your exit will move up as the market moves and with the progression of time. To understand this better, go back and look at the distribution of losses shown in the long-term stock trading system that was presented in Figure 9.2.

Maximum Adverse Excursion

John Sweeney, the former editor of *Technical Analysis of Stocks and Commodities*, has introduced the concept of campaign trading.[5] If you understand the concept of *R*, mentioned earlier, you will understand what Sweeney is trying to convey in writing about campaign trading. Campaign trading, in my opinion, is simply understanding that trading success is more a function of price movement once you are in a trade than it is a function of your entry.

Let's think about the idea of *excursion*—what the price does from the point of entry. When you start thinking about price movement from your entry point, it introduces you to several more interesting concepts. The first of these is the *maximum adverse excursion* (MAE). This is the worst intraday price movement against your position that you are likely to encounter during the entire trade. The worst case is usually taken as being the high or low of that particular day depending on whether you are short or long, respectively.

Figure 10.3 shows an example of adverse price excursion from an entry point on the long side. A bar chart is shown, and the dark line illustrates the MAE for the price data on a long signal. In this case the MAE is $812, yet the initial stop (that is, a three-times-ATR stop that is not shown) is $3,582 away. Thus, the MAE is less than 25 percent of the stop value employed.

Figure 10.4 is the adverse price excursion on a losing trade. You enter the position long at 85.35 on September 23 with a stop $5,343 away. The MAE is at 80.9—a potential loss of $2,781.25. However, the stop is still several thousand dollars off that price. Eventually, the price goes up, along with the stop, and you close out the position with a loss of $1,168.75—nowhere near the stop or the maximum adverse excursion of $2,781.25. In the case of the losing

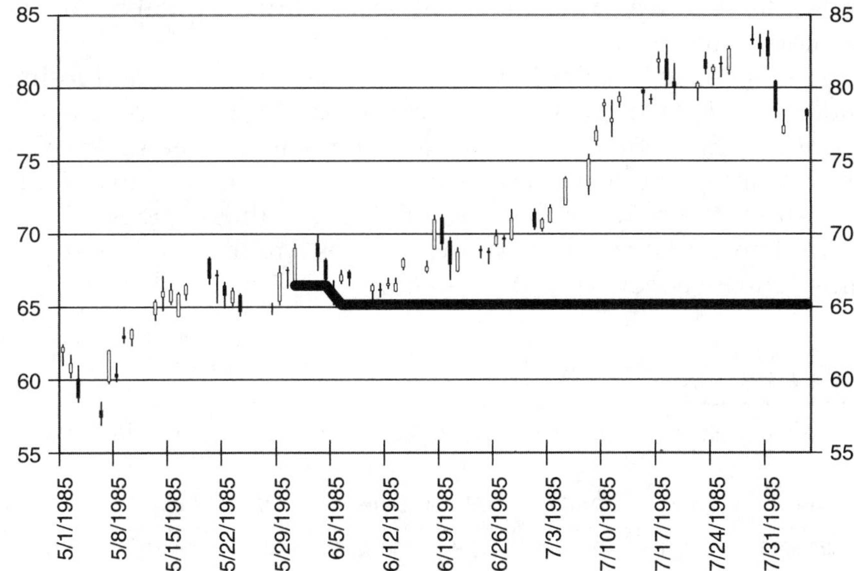

Figure 10.3 Maximum adverse excursion in a winning trade

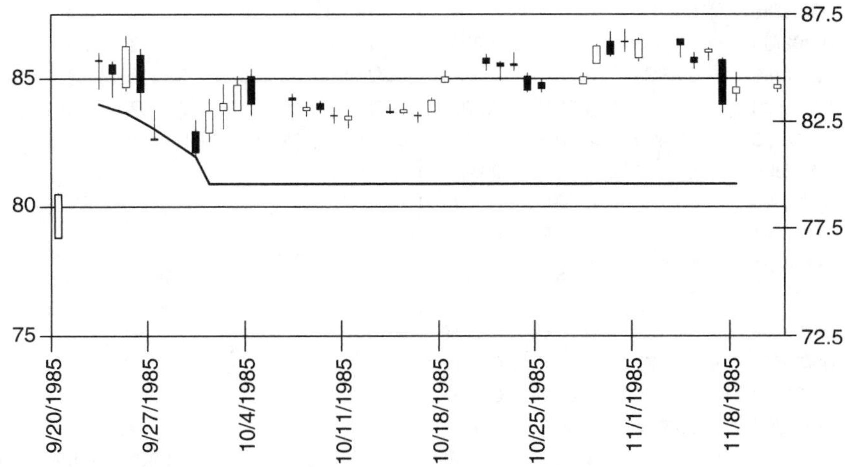

Figure 10.4 Maximum adverse excursion in a losing trade

trade, the MAE was twice the eventual loss, but only half of the initial stop value.

Let's create a table showing the MAE of winning and losing trades. In this case, we looked at British pounds over a seven-year period, using a channel breakout system and a three-times-ATR stop. Winning and losing trades were separated in the table. Table 10.1 shows the profit or loss and the MAE of those trades. Notice how interesting it is to express the MAE as a function of *R*—something John Sweeney has not considered.

TABLE 10.1

Maximum Adverse Excursion in Terms of *R* for Winning and Losing British Pound

Date	1*R*	Profit	MAE	Date	1*R*	Loss	MAE
03/25/85	$6,189	0.70*R*	0.00*R*	**09/23/85**	$5,343	0.22*R*	0.52*R*
05/31/85	$3,582	1.83*R*	0.23*R*	**11/21/85**	$1,950	0.13*R*	0.14*R*
02/24/86	$3,993	0.05*R*	0.33*R*	**01/22/86**	$4,386	2.61*R*	0.33*R*
09/22/86	$2,418	0.44*R*	0.14*R*	**04/17/86**	$3,222	0.22*R*	0.23*R*
12/19/86	$975	5.49*R*	0.13*R*	**05/20/87**	$1,593	1.18*R*	1.18*R*
02/23/87	$1,764	0.36*R*	0.00*R*	**09/01/87**	$2,175	0.43*R*	0.43*R*
10/26/87	$4,593	2.16*R*	0.00*R*	**02/05/88**	$2,532	1.10*R*	1.10*R*
06/28/88	$2,814	2.68*R*	**0.40*R***	**03/02/88**	$2,850	0.09*R*	0.09*R*
10/12/88	$2,244	3.36*R*	0.04*R*	**02/18/88**	$3,582	0.61*R*	0.66*R*
03/01/89	$3,204	0.11*R*	0.10*R*	**01/19/89**	$3,264	0.56*R*	0.59*R*
05/08/89	$2,367	2.54*R*	0.23*R*	**09/15/89**	$6,765	0.47*R*	0.47*R*
12/20/89	$1,839	3.70*R*	0.03*R*	**12/24/90**	$3,804	0.72*R*	0.72*R*
05/15/90	$1,935	4.09*R*	**0.50*R***	**06/12/91**	$2,559	0.03*R*	0.05*R*
07/18/90	$3,420	2.03*R*	0.31*R*	**03/04/92**	$2,859	0.45*R*	0.50*R*
10/05/90	$4,254	0.71*R*	0.02*R*				
01/24/90	$3,759	0.00*R*	0.15*R*				
03/15/91	$3,750	1.46*R*	0.03*R*				
09/06/91	$2,934	0.46*R*	0.13*R*				
11/07/91	$4,794	0.00*R*	0.00*R*				
05/01/92	$1,980	0.73*R*	0.07*R*				
06/05/92	$2,460	1.94*R*	0.06*R*				
08/21/92	$2,850	0.28*R*	0.18*R*				
09/15/92	$6,915	2.89*R*	0.03*R*				
		1.65*R*	**0.14*R***			**0.63*R***	**0.50*R***

This is a small sample and not meant as anything more than an illustration of how to use the technique. Notice the differences between the winning and the losing trades. You don't have any winning trades with MAE greater than 0.5*R* and only 3 of 24 winning trades (that is, 12.5 percent) had a maximum adverse excursion above 0.33*R*. In contrast, 66.7 percent of the losing trades had an MAE above 0.33*R*, and almost half of them were above 0.5*R*. Do you see a pattern here? The mean MAE for winning trades was 0.14*R*, compared with a profit of 1.65*R*. The mean MAE for losing trades was 0.5*R*, compared with an average profit of 0.63*R*.[6]

When you compile such data (and you give yourself a big enough stop), you will find that the MAE of winning trades will seldom go below a certain value. In other words, *good trades seldom go too far against us.*

> Good trades seldom go too far against us.

If you constantly check for what this value is (in case markets change), you will find that you might be able to use much tighter stops than you originally anticipated. The data in Table 10.1 suggests that a 2ATR stop would have been much more effective with these trades than the 3ATR stop was. You would not have been stopped out of any of the winning trades with the tighter stop. You would have had smaller losses in some of your losing trades and all of your *R* multiples would have increased. However, this conclusion comes from looking at the data after the fact which is a form of curve fitting. Generally, however, the advantages of tighter stops include smaller losses (although you may get a few more of them) and bigger *R* multiples on your winning trades.

Tight Stops

Tight stops can be used under certain conditions, such as when we're predicting a major change in the market and the market starts to confirm that prediction. Tight stops can also be used when we are looking at shorter-time-frame data. If your trading methodology will permit tighter stops, and remember that this is also a function of your personal tolerance, then you have some strong advantages going for you. First, you will lose much less money per unit of trading when you abort the trade. Second, because of your small loss, you can make multiple attempts to capture a big move. And third, if you should get such a move, it will give you a much bigger *R*-multiple profit.

However, tight stops have some serious drawbacks as well. First, they will decrease the reliability of your system. You will have to make many more trades in order to make a profit. And if you cannot tolerate a lot of small losses, which many traders and investors cannot, then tight stops will be your downfall.

Second, tight stops dramatically increase your transaction costs because market professionals have developed a system to make sure they profit no matter what you do with your account. Transaction costs are a major part of doing business. Market makers get the benefit of the bid-ask spread. Your brokerage firm gets its commissions. And should you invest in any sort of fund, they get paid a fee based on the size of your investment. In fact, I often see systems that over a number of years produce profits that are not much bigger than the transaction costs they generate. For example, my active trading system generated a 30 percent return in 2004 after transaction costs, but the transaction costs were still about 20 percent of the initial account value. Thus, I got 60 percent of the total profit, while my broker got 40 percent in transaction costs. If you are in and out of the market all the time, then such transaction costs can eat your profits down to nothing. This becomes a major factor if you are trading small size because your cost per trade is very high.

> I often see systems that over a number of years produce profits that are not much bigger than the transaction costs they generate.

Losing much less money when you abort a trade is probably an exciting prospect to most of you. However, the worst thing a trader can do is miss a major move. Consequently, you must be willing to get right back in the position should it again give you a signal. Many people cannot tolerate three to five losses in a row, which this strategy will regularly produce. However, let's say that each exit produces a loss of only $100. You lose on five of these exits in a row, and then the market suddenly gives you the move you expected. A week later you exit with a 20*R* profit of $2,000. You've had five losers and one winner. You've been "right" less than 17 percent of the time—which most people would have problems with—but your total profit from six trades is $1,500 less any commissions and slippage.[7]

In such a situation, you have to understand what is happening. Let's suppose you used a wide stop such as three times the ATR. Let's also suppose that in this situation, the three-times-ATR stop was $600. If you predicted the move correctly, you might not have been stopped out at all. As a result, you would have made only one trade with a 3.33*R* profit of $2,000. But your total profit would be $1,900, including the $100 for slippage and commissions. Remember that in the previous example, you made only $900 after subtracting your losses and your slippage and commissions.

When you have a $600 stop, if it takes two attempts to make the profit, the situation is still a little better than it would have been with a $100 stop. You make $2,000 on the profitable trade, but you lose $600 on the one loss—for a net profit of $1,400. If you subtract $200 for slippage and commissions, you now have $1,200 net profit. This is still better than the first example in which we needed to make six trades to get the profit. However, you might not have concluded that if you had not made the adjustment for slippage and commissions.

With the $600 stop, your profitability drops off dramatically when you have multiple failures. If you are stopped out twice before you get your $2,000 profit, then you will have a net profit of only $500. If you are stopped out three times before you get your $2,000 profit, then you'll have a net loss of $200.

My point in giving you these examples is that your protective loss stop must not be taken lightly. It must be chosen carefully with respect to your objectives and your temperament.

USING A STOP THAT MAKES SENSE

The most important factor in selecting the type of stop to use is to determine if it makes sense given your objectives, the nature of the concept you are trading, and your temperament. You must use something that makes sense. Let's look at some of the other types of protective stops that you might use and examine the issues involved.

Dollar Stops

Many traders advocate the use of dollar stops. These have somewhat of a psychological advantage—you figure out how much you are willing to lose on a trade and set that as a stop beforehand. In addition, they also have several technical advantages. First, such stops are not that predictable. Most people are not likely to figure out where you got into the market, so they are not likely to figure out that your stop is $1,500 or $1,000 away. Second, when such stops are beyond the MAE, they end up being very good stops. Simply determine, in dollars, what your MAE is likely to be in a given contract and set your stop a little beyond that.

However, some people confuse such stops with position sizing and then ignore position sizing. These people believe that if you want to risk 1 percent of your equity and you have $100,000, then just put your stop $1,000 away and call it a money management stop. This is naïve.

If this is how you set your stop, don't confuse it with position sizing. Position sizing is the most important part of your system in determining how much you are likely to make trading the system. Don't give up that most important component of your system by doing something so naïve as to set money management stops.

Percent Retracement

Some people set stops by allowing the price to retrace a certain percentage of the entry price. This is a very common practice among stock traders. For example, you might buy a stock at $30 and sell it if it retraced by 10 percent to $27. Using this same methodology of a 10 percent retracement, you would sell a stock you bought at $10 at $9 and you'd sell a $100 stock at $90.

This practice is fine if your retracement method is based on some sort of MAE analysis. But if you just picked some number out of the air—which is a common practice—then you could be throwing away a lot of potential profits with your stop.

Volatility Stops

Volatility stops are based on the assumption that the volatility, to some extent, represents noise in the market. Consequently, if you set a stop at some multiple of the ATR (we used the example of three times the ATR previously), then you probably have a good stop that is beyond the immediate noise of the market. My experience is that volatility stops are among the best stops you could select.

Dev-Stops

Cynthia Kase coined the term "dev-stop" in her book *Trading with the Odds* and devotes an entire chapter to the topic.[8] If you have a normal distribution of prices, then 1 standard deviation of price change in either direction would account for about 67 percent of the prices. Two standard deviations will encompass about 97 percent of the prices. Market prices are not normal—they tend to be skewed to the right—so some correction is needed in the standard deviation to take into account this skew. This amounts to about a 10 percent correction on the first standard deviation and a 20 percent correction on the second standard deviation.

You might find the standard deviation of the average true range to be quite useful as a stop. Take the average true range for the last 30 days and calculate the standard deviation. The average true range plus 1 standard deviation plus a 10 percent correction factor would be one level of stop. The average true range plus 2 standard deviations plus a 20 percent correction factor would be another level of stop.

Channel Breakout and Moving-Average Stops

Just as the channel breakout and moving-average concepts can be used as entries, they can also be used as stops. My personal bias is that these sorts of stops are not nearly as good as stops based on the average true range or MAE. Nevertheless, they are worthy of a brief discussion for the sake of completeness.

A common entry technique that has been used for many years is the moving-average crossover, which was discussed extensively in Chapter 9. When you have two moving averages, you basically have a reversal exit. When you are in a position and the short average crosses the longer one, you have both a stop to get you out of your current position and a reversal entry signal to go the other way (long or short, depending on the direction of the cross). Of course, the problem with such systems is that you are always in the market and get whipsawed many times.

R. C. Allen popularized the three-moving-averages system in which you get an entry signal when both the shorter averages have crossed the longer.[9] This would mean, by definition, that the shortest average was now on top (or on the bottom). When the shortest signal crosses the medium signal, you now get your stop signal. However, you do not get a reversal signal to enter a short position until both the short and medium averages cross the longer average.

Channel breakouts were also discussed in Chapter 9. You might enter the market, for example, when prices make a new high for the last 40 days. Your stop might also be a channel breakout—when prices make a new low for the last 20 days. This method has the advantage of giving prices a lot of room, being well beyond the noise, and has been used by many well-known traders. However, it has the tremendous disadvantage of giving back a lot of profits because your stop is both the worst-case protective stop and your profit-taking exit.

Time Stops

Many traders and investors say that if a position does not go in your favor fairly quickly, then it probably will not. As a result, another common stop-loss method is the time stop. The time stop simply takes you out of a position after a fixed amount of time if you haven't made a profit (or made a profit above some arbitrary level).

One great trader said that he treated each day in a trade as an entirely new day. If he could not justify getting into that trade on that day, then he would simply close it out. This is effectively a time stop.

The choice to use a time stop is very personal. Don't use one if you are a long-term trader and have no way to get back in the market should your big expected move suddenly occur. Don't use one if you have trouble getting back into a position you have exited. However, if you like short-term trading, then time stops are probably an excellent addition to your arsenal.

Before using time stops, however, check out their effectiveness within the framework of your methodology. A day trader might use a 10-minute time stop, whereas a long-term investor might want a one-month time stop. Let's say, for example, that you decide to use a three-day time stop. Before doing so, you need to determine the effectiveness of such a stop. How often will a position do nothing for three days and then take off? If you find enough examples to suggest that you could miss a major move, then avoid such stops. However, if you find that they generally cut your losses faster or even help you prevent losses, then by all means include them.

Discretionary and Psychological Stops

If you have a good intuitive sense of the market, then you might also consider discretionary stops—of which one might be a time stop. Many of the best professional traders use discretionary stops, but I would not recommend them for the amateur or beginning trader.

The psychological stop, in contrast, is great for most market players. Unless you are in the market for the long haul—that is, you'd like to keep your position for at least a year—then you should consider psychological stops. Long-term trend followers could have a problem with such stops as well since one good trade can make a whole year of trading. Unless you are psychologically well balanced, you'll probably decide it's time to take a vacation or use a psychological stop right about the time the big trade comes along.

There are certain time periods when the most important factor in your trading—you, the human being—is nowhere near 100 percent. These are the times you should just consider getting out of the market. The times that almost predict certain disaster are (1) when you are going through a divorce or separation from a significant person, (2) when a significant person in your life dies or is in the hospital, (3) when a child is born and your lifestyle changes dramatically, (4) when you move your home or office, (5) when you are psychologically exhausted or burned out, (6) when you are involved in legal proceedings, and (7) when you are so excited about the market that you see your position doubling overnight—even when it hasn't moved. These are probably periods when you should just close down all your active positions. These psychological stops are among the most important you can have. So unless you are a long-term trader, I'd strongly recommend that you start using them.

STOPS USED BY COMMON SYSTEMS

Stock Market Systems

William O'Neil's CANSLIM Method

William O'Neil does not promote market-related stops but instead argues that you should never let a stock go against you by more than 7 to 8 percent. This is a version of the "percent retracement" stop discussed earlier. Essentially, O'Neil's 7 to 8 percent refers to a 7 to 8 percent retracement in the price of the stock—it has nothing to do with your equity. Thus, if you buy a stock at $20, you should never let it go against you by more than 7 to 8 percent of $20, or $1.40 to $1.60. If you buy a stock at $100, then you should never let it go against you by more than $7 to $8. O'Neil cautions that 7 to 8 percent should be the maximum loss you should tolerate. He actually recommends that your overall average of all losses be around 5 to 6 percent.

Although O'Neil's guidelines are some of the best provided by anyone recommending methods to trade stocks, in my opinion they can be improved upon. You would be much better off with a market-based stop. Determine your MAE using the O'Neil system. This probably should be calculated with respect to various price ranges. If you find that low-priced stocks, that is, those under $25, seldom move more than $1 against you if they are good purchases, then your stop might be $1. You might find that even $100 stocks seldom move against you by more than $2 if they were good purchases. If that's the case, then your potential for big *R* gains on high-price stocks would be tremendous.

Since O'Neil recommends that you enter when the market breaks out of the base, you probably should exit if it returns to the base—or at least if it goes to the bottom of the base. Another possible exit would be to abort the position if it moves three times the average daily price volatility against you.

Warren Buffett's Approach to Investing

Warren Buffett, according to most of the books on him, considers most of his holdings to be lifetime holdings. He feels that his returns will be large enough over the long term to weather the psychological ups and downs of the market. In addition, he has no desire to pay the transaction costs of getting in and out—to say nothing of the tax consequences. As a result, Warren Buffett considers his main job to be that of buying companies that he is willing to own forever. As a result, Warren Buffett doesn't seem to have any protective stops:

> I never attempt to make money on the stock market. I buy on the assumption that they could close the market the next day and not reopen it for five years.[10]

However, Buffett has been known to sell an investment occasionally. Remember that a protective stop is something that you use in a worst-case scenario to protect your capital. As a result, I'm sure Buffett must go through some regular review of his investments to determine if they still meet his criteria. The more wisely you select your investments, understand how the companies operate, and can evaluate whether or not they are managed well, the more you can use this sort of approach. However, I would strongly recommend that even the most die-hard long-term investor have a worst-case bailout signal for every investment at the time it is purchased. Quite often that solution might be as simple as a 25 percent stop. If the price drops by 25 percent of your entry price, then get out to preserve your capital.

Futures Market Systems

Perry Kaufman's Adaptive Moving-Average Approach

Kaufman, in discussing the nature of stop losses, makes an interesting observation. He says that the size of the erratic price move against you times the number of times that move is likely to occur is always about the same. For example, you might have 20 occurrences of a 5-point move, 10 occurrences of a 10-point move, and 5 occurrences of a 20-point move. All these would add up to 100 points of loss plus slippage and transaction costs. As a result, he argues that larger stops are generally better because they minimize transaction costs.

When Kaufman tests a system in his book, he uses only a few simple ideas with respect to stops. First, a trade is exited at the close if the loss exceeds a preset percentage level. This is much like the O'Neil concept. Second, a trade is exited when a reversal signal is given, including when the trade is losing money.

Many of the concepts discussed in this chapter, in my opinion, would greatly improve the adaptive moving-average system. For example, consider using a volatility stop, an MAE stop, or the dev-stop.

William Gallacher's Fundamental Trading

If you recall, Gallacher is a fundamental trader. He uses fundamentals to trade commodities and enters the market on a 10-day channel breakout when the fundamentals are setups for the market to move in a particular direction. His stop loss is simple. It's a 10-day channel breakout in the opposite direction.

Although many of the ideas behind Gallacher's trading are very sound, readers of this book, in my opinion, would find that many of the stop-loss approaches recommended in this book could greatly improve upon this simple method of trading.

Ken Roberts' 1-2-3 Methodology

Remember that Roberts' setup is that the market makes a 9-month high or low and then makes a 1-2-3 pattern. The entry signal is when the market hits a new price extreme in the opposite direction of the old high or low—in other words, when the market again passes point 2 on the 1-2-3 pattern you enter. The stop loss is simply putting the stop at a logical point on the chart—just beyond point 1.

Once again, in my opinion, users of this approach would be much better off with a stop that was based on a statistical extreme. Several such stops might include (1) three times the ATR, (2) a dev-stop, or (3) an estimate of the MAE in this particular case and a stop put just beyond that.

SUMMARY

- Your protective stop is like a red light. You can go through it, but you're not very likely to do so safely.
- Your protective stop has two main functions: (1) It sets up the maximum loss that you'll likely take in your position (*R*), and (2) it sets a benchmark against which to measure subsequent gains.
- Your primary job as a trader or investor should be to devise a plan that will get you profits that are large multiples of *R*, your initial risk.
- Consider going beyond the noise when you set your stops. This can be done by setting stops that are several times the ATR, by using dev-stops, or by determining the MAE and going beyond that.
- Tight stops have the advantage of creating large-*R*-multiple winners and minimizing losses. However, they have the disadvantage of reducing reliability and greatly

increasing your transaction costs. As a result, you should probably only use tight stops if you have planned your entry very well.

- Other types of stops include dollar stops, percent retracement stops, volatility stops, channel breakout stops, moving-average stops, support and resistance stops, time stops, and discretionary stops. Each has its own particular merit, and selecting the right one for you is part of the job of designing a trading system that is right for you.
- What are your beliefs about stops? You'll only be comfortable trading a system that is compatible with your beliefs about stops.

NOTES

1. John Sweeney, *Campaign Trading: Tactics and Strategies to Exploit the Markets* (New York: Wiley, 1996).
2. This kind of trading is difficult due to the very large commissions charged even by discount stockbrokers. However, discount Internet trading has changed that.
3. The stock exchange promotes this by having margin calls at only 50 percent and teaching people that they could lose it all. Furthermore, they are justified in doing so because most people don't have a plan to trade and are psychologically wired to lose money.
4. Suggested by J. Welles Wilder in *New Concepts in Technical Trading Systems* (Greensboro, N.C.: Trend Research, 1978).
5. Refer to Sweeney, *Campaign Trading*, for more details about maximum adverse excursion (MAE).
6. Notice that losses can be bigger than 1*R* and the MAE because of slippage and commissions. In addition, you can have an MAE that is bigger than your eventual loss if that MAE occurred early in your trade before the stop started moving in your favor.
7. If slippage and commissions are $100 per trade, you have to subtract $600 from your $1,500 profit. It basically makes your 20*R* profit now seem like a 9*R* profit. This is why short-term traders must always consider the transaction cost factor in their trading. It's probably the major factor influencing short-term success.

8. Dev-stop is an indicator copyrighted by Cynthia A. Kase. [See Cynthia Kase, *Trading with the Odds: Using the Power of Probability to Profit in the Futures Market* (Chicago: Irwin, 1996).]
9. Charles LeBeau and David W. Lucas have an excellent discussion of this topic in *The Technical Traders' Guide to Computer Analysis of the Futures Market* (Homewood, Ill.: Irwin, 1992).
10. Warren Buffett, quoted by Jeremy Gain in "The Bull Market's Biggest Winners," *Fortune*, August 8, 1983, p. 36.

CHAPTER 11

How to Take Profits

> You've got to know when to hold 'em; know when to fold 'em; know when to walk away; and know when to run.
>
> *Kenny Rogers, from* The Gambler

One of the great traders featured in Jack Schwager's *Market Wizards*[1] remarked at one of our seminars that if you want to learn how to trade, you should go down to the beach and watch the waves. Soon you'll notice that waves wash ashore and then turn around and go back to sea. He then suggested that you start moving your hands in rhythm with the waves—moving them toward you as the wave approaches and moving them away from you as the wave withdraws. After doing that for a while, you'll notice that you will soon be in touch with the waves. "When you reach that state of being in tune with the flow," he said, "you'll know a lot about what it takes to become a trader." Notice that to be able to get in touch with the waves, it's important for you to know when the wave has finished its movement.

Another man came to visit me from Australia. He'd made millions in the computer software business, and he now wanted to research trading systems. He'd been visiting people all over the United States to learn the essence of trading. We had dinner together, and he carefully explained all his trading ideas to me. When I finished hearing his ideas, which were all good, I was a little perplexed.

All his research had to do with discovering entry techniques into the market. He had done no research into what exits to use or how to control his position size. When I suggested to him that he now needed to spend at least as much time developing his profit-taking exits as he had on entry and an equal amount of time, if not more, on position sizing, he seemed upset because he firmly believed that success in the market was all about picking the right stocks.

People just seem to want to ignore exits—perhaps because they cannot control the market on the exit. Yet for those who want control, exits do control two important variables—whether or not you'll make a profit and how much profit you will make. They are one of the major keys to developing a successful system.

PURPOSE BEHIND PROFIT-TAKING EXITS

There are a lot of problems to solve with exits. If the worst case does not happen (that is, you don't get stopped out), then the job of your system is to allow you to make the most profit possible and give the least amount of it back. Only your exits do this!

Notice that I use the word "exits"—the plural version of the word—because most systems need several exits to do the job properly. As a result, consider using different exit strategies for each of your system objectives. As you design your system, keep in mind how you want to control your reward-to-risk ratio and maximize your profits using the types of profit-taking exits described in this chapter.

There are many different classifications of exits other than your initial stop loss. These include exits that produce a loss but reduce your initial risk, exits that maximize profits, exits that keep you from giving back too much money, and psychological exits. The categories are somewhat overlapping. Several techniques for you to consider are provided with each type of exit. As you peruse each, think about how it could be adapted to your system. Most exit strategies are incredibly accommodating to your system objectives.

Exits That Produce a Loss, but Reduce Your Initial Risk

Your initial stop loss, discussed in Chapter 10, was designed to be your worst-case loss that protects your capital. However, this class of exits will also produce a loss, but these exits are designed to make sure you lose as little as possible.

The Timed Stop

Generally, people enter the market because they expect the price to move in their favor shortly after entry. As a result, if you have a meaningful entry signal, then a potentially useful exit is one that will get you out after a period of time when you are not profitable. For example, such an exit might be "get out of the market at the close in two days if this position is not profitable." Such an exit would cause one to lose money, but not as much as if one's worst-case stop were hit.

Another version of the timed stop occurs when you discover a great new investment idea but you are fully invested. What can you do? You have no more money to invest. However, if you are fully convinced that this opportunity is an excellent one, then I suggest that you find the worst-performing stock in your portfolio and decide that it is "time" to eliminate this one. You can pick one that's losing money or one that just hasn't increased at the rate you had expected.

The Trailing Stop

The trailing stop is one that is adjusted on a periodic basis according to some sort of mathematical algorithm. The random entry system (described in Chapter 9) uses a three-times-volatility trailing stop that is adjusted from the close on a daily basis only when it moves in favor of the trade. For example, after the first day of trading, if the price moves in your favor or if volatility shrinks, then the trailing stop is moved in your favor. It might still be at a loss, but it is moving in your favor. Thus, if the market moves against you enough to stop you out, you will still take a loss, but it will not be as big as your initial stop. Such trailing stops could be based on any number of factors—volatility, a moving average, a channel breakout, various price consolidations, and so on—and each could have any number of different variables controlling them. See the next section for some specific examples.

The important point about trailing stops is that your exit algorithm will continually make adjustments that will move the exit in your favor. That movement might not be profitable, but it will reduce your potential loss.

You must give careful consideration, through testing and examining your results, to whether or not you want to do this. For example, quite often by reducing your initial risk as you move up your trailing stop, you merely give up your chance for a profit. Instead, you just take a smaller loss. Be careful in this area of your system development, and if your system does utilize tight stops, be aware that a reentry strategy can be used.

Exits That Maximize Your Profits

In order to maximize your profits (let them run), you must be willing to give some of them back. In fact, the ironic part of system design is if you want to maximize profits, you must be willing to give back a great deal of the profits you have already accumulated. As a wise and very wealthy trader once said, "You can't make money if you're not willing to lose. It's like breathing in, but not being willing to breathe out." Various types of exits will help you do this (that is, breathe fully), including trailing stops and the percent retracement stop.

The Trailing Stop

The trailing stop also has the potential to help you gain large profits, but it will always give some of your profits back. Let's look at some examples of trailing stops that you might want to use.

The **volatility trailing stop**, which has already been mentioned, is a multiple of the daily volatility of the market. J. Welles Wilder, who first promoted the concept, suggests that it should be a number somewhere between 2.7 and 3.4 times the average true range of the last 10 days. We used 3.0 in the random entry system. The point of the volatility stop is to keep your stop out of the noise of the market, and 3 times the daily volatility certainly does that. Others have looked at the weekly volatility. If you use the weekly volatility, then you probably can get by with a stop somewhere between 0.7 to 2 times the weekly volatility.

The **dollar trailing stop** is another possibility. Here you would decide some number such as $1,500, and keep a trailing stop at that amount behind yesterday's close. Dollar stops are excellent if they have some rational basis. However, using a $1,500 stop in an SP contract, a corn contract, a $150 stock, and a $10 stock is madness. The amount of your dollar stop should be adjusted for what is reasonable for each market. The best way to determine what is reasonable for each market is to check the volatility of that market. As a result, you might as well use a volatility-based stop instead.

A **channel breakout trailing stop** is also quite useful. You might decide that you will get out at the extreme price of the last *X* days (you fill in the number). Thus, in a long position, you might decide to sell if the price hits the low of the last 20 days, whereas in a short position you might decide to sell if the price hits the high of the last 20 days. As the price moves in your favor, this number is always adjusted in your favor.

A **moving-average trailing stop** is another common trailing stop. If the price is moving in any particular direction, then a slow-moving average will trail behind that price and could be used as a stop. However, you will have to determine the number of periods involved in that moving average. For example, a 200-day moving average would have kept you actively involved in the stock market throughout most of the secular bull market from 1982 through 2000.

A 200-day moving average would have kept you actively involved in the stock market throughout most of the secular bull market from 1982 through 2000.

There are many different types of moving averages—simple, exponential, displaced, adaptive, and so on—and all these could be used as trailing stops. Your job is simply to find the one or several that best help you meet your objectives. Different types of moving averages were discussed extensively in the entry chapter, Chapter 9, of this book.

There are also other kinds of **trailing stops based on consolidations or chart patterns**. For example, every time the market moves beyond a consolidation pattern, that old consolidation pattern could become the basis of a new stop. This amounts to a discretionary trailing stop, and it will give back a lot of profits. Nevertheless, it may have some merits in combination with other types of exits.

The Profit Retracement Stop

This kind of stop makes an assumption that you must give back a percentage of your profits in order to allow them to grow. As a result, it just assigns a number to the amount of retracement allowed and makes it part of your system. However, in order to use a profit retracement stop, you must reach a certain level of profitability such as a 2*R* profit.

Here's how this kind of stop might work. Suppose you purchase 100 shares of Micron at $52. You initially assume a 1*R* risk of $6, by assuming that you will get out if the stock drops to $46. Once you obtain a 2*R* profit of $12 by having the stock move up in price to $64, you decide to begin a profit retracement stop. Let's say that you decide to put on a 30 percent profit retracement stop. Since you now have $12, you are willing to give up 30 percent of that, or $3.60.

When the profit moves up to $13, a 30 percent retracement now becomes $3.90. And at $14, a 30 percent retracement becomes $4.20. Since the actual dollar amount as a fixed percent continues to grow as the profit grows, you may want to change the percentage as the profit gets bigger. For example, you might start out at a 30 percent retracement but move the amount down to 25 percent at a 3*R* profit and to 20 percent at a 4*R* profit. You could continue to decrease the amount until you only allow a 5 percent retracement at 7*R*, or you might allow it to remain at 20 percent once you reach 4*R*. This would depend entirely on your objectives in designing your system.

The Percent Retracement Stop

Another very simple stop is a price retracement stop. For example, you could have a 25 percent retracement stop. This means that you initially set your exit at a 25 percent drop in price. However, every time the stock (or whatever you have purchased) makes a new high, then you set a 25 percent retracement of that price as your new stop. And, of course, you always raise your stop, but never lower it.

In 1999 Steve Sjuggerud became the investment director at the Oxford Club, and I was appointed to their advisory panel. Steve had read the first edition of this book, and he immediately instigated a 25 percent stop rule on all the Oxford Club recommendations. It has worked pretty well. I looked at their recommendations when Steve was the investment director from February 1999 through May 2000 when they were stopped out of everything. The expectancy of their trades was an excellent 2.5*R* during that time period, and I believe much of their success was due to their

25 percent stop rule. Other newsletters tried 50 percent trailing stops, but those just did not work because (1) they gave back too much profit and (2) the stock had to move a long way to get back to breakeven when there was a substantial drawdown. Think about it. If you are down 49 percent, you have to make nearly 100 percent just to get back to breakeven. However, if you are down 24 percent, you have to make only a little under 33 percent to get back to breakeven. As a result, I think that the 25 percent trailing stop for stocks is an excellent substitute for the old "buy-and-hold" philosophy. Chapter 13 shows the *R*-multiple distribution of many of the newsletters that I happen to read. Look at Table 13.5 and you'll notice that their expectancy is still excellent.

Exits That Keep You from Giving Back Too Much Profit

If you are managing other people's money, it is more important to minimize drawdowns than it is to produce large returns. As a result, you might want to consider exits that keep you from giving back too much profit. For example, if you have open positions on March 31 that put your client's account up 15 percent in his March statement, then that client is going to be upset if you give back much of that profit. Your client will consider that open profit to be his or her money. As a result, you need some sort of exit that will lock in most of that profit once you reach a particular objective or after a reporting period to the client.

As I mentioned earlier, many of the exit categories overlap. For example, the percent retracement exits combined with a profit-objective exit (see below) is an excellent way to keep from giving back too much profit. However, there are others that also work well.

The Profit Objective

Some people use trading systems that tend to predict profit targets (for example, the Elliott Wave). If you use such a system, then you probably can target specific objectives.

However, there is a second way to target objectives. You might determine, based on historical testing, that your method produces the kind of reward-to-risk ratio you desire if you take a profit at some specific multiple of your initial risk. For example, you might find that four times your initial risk (4*R*) is a great objective. If you can achieve that, then you might want to take your profit or institute a much closer stop at that point. All the methods discussed below can be tightened in some way once a profit objective is reached.

The Profit Retracement Exit

One excellent idea for an exit that was mentioned previously is to be willing to give back only a certain percentage of your profit and to tighten that percentage after some important milestone (such as a report to clients or a profit objective) is reached. For example, after you have a 2*R* profit, you might be willing to give back 30 percent of that profit in order to allow it to grow. When you have a much greater profit, say, 4*R*, you might only be willing to give back 5 to 10 percent of it before you exit.

For example, let's say you bought gold at $400 with a stop at $390. Thus, your initial risk is 10 points, or $1,000 per contract. Gold moves to $420 so that you have a 20-point profit (2*R*). That might be a trigger to allow only a 30 percent retracement of your profit, or $600. If gold moves down to $414, you'll take your profit.

Gold continues to move up and reaches $440, so that you now have a 4*R* profit of $4,000. Until you reached the 4*R* profit, you were willing to give up 30 percent of your profit, which is $1,200 at the $4,000 level. However, the 4*R* level is now your signal to risk only 10 percent of your profit. Your stop is now moved to $436—allowing just over a $400 decline.

My intention is not to suggest specific levels (such as a 10 percent retracement at 4*R*) but merely to suggest a methodology for you to attain your objectives. It is up to you to determine what levels will help you best attain your objectives.

A Large Volatility Move against You

One of the best exits you can have is a large volatility move against you. In fact, this type of move is also a very good entry for a system—commonly known as a *volatility breakout system.*

What you need to do is keep track of the average true range. When the market makes an abnormally large move (let's say two times the average daily volatility) against you, you will exit the market. Let's say you have 200 shares of IBM trading at $145. The average daily volatility is $1.50, and you decide that you will get out if the market moves twice that volatility against you in a single day. In other words, since the market closed at $145 and twice the daily volatility is $3, you'll exit the market if it moves to $142 tomorrow. This would be a tremendous move against you, and you don't want to stay in if this sort of move occurs.[2]

It should be obvious why this cannot be your only exit. Suppose you continue to keep this two-times-volatility stop. The market is at 145 today, so your volatility exit is 142. The market closes down 1 point to 144. Your new volatility exit is now 141. The next day the market closes down 1 point to 143. Your new volatility exit is now 140. This could keep on going until the price goes to zero. Thus, you need some other type of exit—such as your protective stop and some sort of trailing stop—to get you out to preserve your capital.

Parabolic Stops

Parabolic exits were first described by J. Welles Wilder, and they are very useful. The parabolic curve starts out at a previous low point and has an accelerating factor in upward-moving markets. As the market trends, it gets closer and closer to the price. Thus, it does a great job of locking in profits. Unfortunately, it is quite far from the actual price at the beginning of your trade. Also, the parabolic stop may sometimes come a little too close to the prices, and you can get stopped out while the market continues to trend.

There are a few ways of working around these setbacks. One possibility is adjusting the acceleration factor of the parabolic stop to rise faster or slower compared with the true prices of the market. In this way, parabolic stops can be well customized to your particular system and to the market you're trading.

To better control your risk at the start of a trade, you could set a separate dollar stop. For example, if the parabolic stop offers a $3,000 risk at the purchase of the position, you could set a simple $1,500 stop until the parabolic comes within $1,500 of the true contract price; a $3,000 risk might be too much for your particular objectives.

Furthermore, if you are using a parabolic exit, you should consider designing a reentry technique. If the parabolic stop gets too close to the actual price, you might stop out before the end of a certain trend that you are following. You don't want to miss out on the rest of the trend, so you may want to get back into a trade. While parabolic stops may not be as exceptional as other exit techniques for risk control, they are excellent for protecting profits.

Psychological Exits

One of the smartest exits anyone can have is a psychological exit. These depend more on you than on what the markets do. Since you are the most significant factor in your trading, psychological exits are important.

There are certain times in which your probability of losing money in the market goes up greatly—no matter what the markets do. These include periods when you just don't feel well because of health or mental problems, when your stress is high, when you are going through a divorce, when you've just had a new child, when you are moving, and so on. Your chances of doing something that will cause market losses are greatly increased during these periods. As a result, I strongly recommend that you use a psychological exit and pull yourself out of the market.

Another good time for a psychological exit is when you must be away from the market due to business or a vacation. Those also are not good times to remain in the market. Again, I recommend the psychological exit during these periods.

Some people would argue that one trade might make your entire year and you don't want to miss that trade. *I agree with that philosophy if you are disciplined and fairly automated in your trading. However, most people are not.* During any of the periods I mentioned, the average person would lose money despite being in a good trade. Consequently, it is important to know yourself. If it is likely that you will blow out even on a good trade, then you must employ psychological exits.

JUST USING YOUR STOP AND A PROFIT OBJECTIVE

One of your objectives in designing a trading system might be to maximize the probability of high-*R*-multiple trades. You might decide, for example, to use tight stops with the objective of getting a 20*R*-multiple trade. To do so, you might decide to use the break-out-retracement strategy described in Chapter 10 to develop a tight stop. Let's say that your stop is only $1 on a high-priced stock, so you'll only lose $100 on 100 shares. This would be a very tight stop, for example, in a $100 stock undergoing a sharp breakout. You could be stopped out five times in a row with just a $100 loss each time—for a total loss of $500. One $20 move in the underlying stock would give you a $2,000 profit, or a $1,500 net profit. You are "right" one time out of six, but you make a $1,500 net profit,[3] less commissions.

In order for this strategy to work, you must avoid trailing stops, or those stops must be very large. Your only exits will be your initial 1*R* stop and your profit objectives. This will give you the maximum opportunity for a 20*R* profit. You may have to tolerate drops of $1,000 or more in your profit, but never more[4] than a 1*R* loss or $100 to your starting equity. Remember, your goal is a 20*R* profit, which you might achieve regularly.

SIMPLICITY AND MULTIPLE EXITS

Simple concepts work best in system design. Simplicity works because it tends to be based on understanding rather than optimization. It works because one can generalize simple concepts across a number of markets and trading instruments.

However, you can still have multiple exits and make them simple. Don't confuse the two concepts. Simplicity is necessary so that your system will work, while multiple exits are usually necessary to meet your objectives. Each of your multiple exits can be simple, of course.

Let's look at an example. Suppose you have a goal of using a trend-following system, and you'd like to be in the market a long time. You believe that there is nothing magical about your entry signal, so you want to give your position plenty of room. You believe that a large move against you might be a trigger for potential disaster, so you want to get out when it occurs. Lastly, you decide that since your initial risk will be quite wide, you will have to capture as much as possible once you get a 4*R* profit. Consequently, let's design some simple exits based on these beliefs. And notice from this example how important it is to realize what your beliefs are and then build a system that fits your beliefs. That's part of the secret of developing a system that fits you.

First, you want a wide initial stop to give the position plenty of room without whipsawing you out of the market and causing you to have to get in several times with resulting transaction costs. Consequently, you decide to use the three-times-volatility stop that you read about earlier. That will be your worst-case stop, and it will also be your trailing stop because you will trail it from the close each day—always moving it in favor of your position.

Second, you believe that a strong move against you is a good warning sign. Consequently, you decide that whenever the market moves twice the daily volatility from yesterday's close against you in a single day, you will get out. This stop will float on top of the other one.

Last, a 4*R* profit will trigger a much tighter stop so that you will not give back much profit and can be assured of capturing what you already have. As a result, after a 4*R* profit is triggered, your trailing volatility stop moves up to 1.6 times the average true range (that is, instead of 3 times), and it is now your only exit.

Notice that all these stops are simple. They all came out of my head from thinking about what kind of stops would meet the objectives. No testing was involved, so they are not overoptimized. No rocket science is involved—they are simple. You now have three distinct exits that will help meet your trading system goals, but only one of these will be in the market at one time—the one closest to the current price.

WHAT TO AVOID

There is one kind of exit that is designed to get rid of losses, but it totally goes against the golden rule of trading, which, as we've said, is to cut your losses short and let your profits run. Instead, this exit produces large losses and small profits. It is one in which you enter the market with a large position size and then scale out with various exits. For example, you might start with 300 shares and sell 100 of them when you can break even on all 300 shares. You might then sell another 100 shares at a $500 profit and keep the last 100 shares for a huge profit. Short-term traders use this type of strategy frequently. On a gut level, this sort of trading makes sense because you seem to be "insuring" your profits. But if you step back from this sort of exit and really study it, you'll see how dangerous this type of trading is.

What you are actually doing with this sort of exit is practicing the reverse of the golden rule of trading. You are making sure that you will have multiple positions when you take your largest losses. In our example, you'd lose on all 300 shares. You are also making sure that you only have a minimal-sized position when you make your largest gains—100 shares in our example. It's the perfect method for people with a strong bias to be right, but it doesn't optimize profits or even guarantee profits. Does it make sense now?

If it doesn't make sense to you why you should avoid this sort of trading, work out the numbers. Imagine that you only take either a full loss or a full profit. Look at your past trades and determine how much of a difference this sort of trading would have made. In almost every instance when I've asked clients to do this, they become totally amazed at how much money they would have made holding on to a full position.

EXITS USED BY COMMON SYSTEMS

Stock Market Systems

William O'Neil's CANSLIM System

William O'Neil's fundamental profit-taking rule is to take a 20 percent profit whenever you achieve it. Since his stop loss is about 8 percent, this means a 2.5*R* profit. As a result, his fundamental profit-taking exit is an objective.

However, O'Neil then tempers his basic profit-taking rule with *36 other selling rules*. Some of these rules are exceptions to the basic selling rule, while others are reasons to sell early. In addition, he also adds 8 more rules concerning when to hold onto a stock. I'll refer the reader to O'Neil's wonderful book for the specific details since my intention is to explain how various systems fit into the framework outlined in the chapter. It is not my intention to give you every detail of the system.

Warren Buffett's Business Approach

Warren Buffett generally does not sell for two reasons. First, when you sell, you must pay capital gains tax. As a result, if you determine that the company has good returns for the amount you have invested, why sell it? You would automatically be turning over some of your profits to the U.S. government.

Second, why should one sell a company that is fundamentally sound and bringing in excellent returns? If a company has invested its capital in such a way that it is bringing in excellent returns, then you should get an excellent return on your money.

Third, when you do sell, you will also incur transaction costs. Thus, if the market is just going through psychological ups and downs, why sell a good investment?

In my opinion, however, it is more myth than fact that Buffett doesn't sell. That myth is probably created by the fact that Buffett himself has not written about his own investment strategy. Instead, other people, who probably have the typical bias toward emphasizing entry, have tried to decipher what Buffett really does do.

If the business situation in a stock Buffett owned changed dramatically, then he would have to sell. Let me give you an example: Buffett announced in early 1998 that he owned about 20 percent of the world's silver supply. Silver does not pay dividends. If you own as much as Buffett does, you actually have costs involved with storing the commodity and protecting it. If Warren Buffett does not have a planned exit strategy for that silver, then, in my opinion, he could have made one of the biggest mistakes of his investment career.[5] On the other hand, if he does have a planned exit strategy, then I would guess that he has a planned exit strategy for most of his stock purchases as well. When other people have written about him, they have simply reflected their own biases and focused on his entry and setup strategies, while ignoring his exit strategies.

Futures Market Systems

Kaufman's Adaptive Methods

Kaufman cautions that his basic trend-following system should not be confused with a complete strategy. He simply presents it as a sample method with no subtleties in the selection of either entry or exit.

The adaptive moving average was presented in Chapter 9 as a basic entry technique. You simply enter a long position when the moving average turns up by more than the amount of a predetermined filter. You enter a short position when the moving average turns down by more than the amount of a predetermined filter.

Kaufman comments that one should take profits whenever the efficiency exceeds some predetermined level. For example, he states that a high efficiency ratio cannot be sustained, so that it usually drops quickly once a high value is obtained. Thus, Kaufman has two basic exit signals: (1) when there is a change in the adaptive moving average in the opposite direction (perhaps when it exceeds some threshold in the opposite direction) and (2) when the efficiency average hits a very high value such as 0.8.

I think adaptive exits have more potential than any other form of exits. Some of my clients have developed exit strategies that move up with the market, giving the position plenty of room while it moves. However, as soon as the market starts to turn, these exits take you right out. They are incredibly creative and yet simple. And if the market resumes a trend, their basic trend-following system would be able to enter them right back into the market. I would strongly suggest that you spend a lot of time in this area in your system development.

Gallacher's Fundamental Trading

Gallacher's system, as you will recall from Chapter 9, has you entering the market (1) when fundamental setups are in place and (2) when the market makes a new 10-day high (that is, a 10-day channel breakout). The system he uses normally is a reversal system—so it is always in the market. It essentially closes out the position (and reenters in the opposite direction) when the 10-day low is breached (that is, a 10-day channel breakout). However, Gallacher doesn't use it as a reversal system.

Remember that Gallacher takes positions only in the direction of the fundamentals. Consequently, unless the fundamentals change dramatically, he will exit a long position (that is, not reverse it) only on a 10-day low, and he will exit a short position (that is, not reverse it) only on a 10-day high. This is a very simple exit that probably won't get you into a lot of trouble. However, my guess is that this system could be improved dramatically with more sophisticated exits.

Ken Roberts' 1-2-3 Methodology

Ken Roberts' profit-taking approach, in my opinion, is very subjective. It amounts to a consolidation trailing stop approach. If Roberts' method is correct and has gotten one into a long-term move, then Roberts would simply recommend that one raise one's stop and place it below (or above) a new consolidation once it is formed.

This is an old trend-following approach that worked exceptionally well in the 1970s. Its main drawback is that one may give back a lot of profits. It still will work now, but Roberts' methodology would probably work better with many of the exits discussed in this chapter. I would particularly recommend a multiple-exit strategy.

SUMMARY

People avoid looking for good exits because exits do not give them control over the market. However, exits do control something. They control whether you make a profit or a loss, and they control just how big that profit or loss will be. Since they do so much, perhaps they are worthy of a lot more study than most people give them.

We reviewed four general categories of exits—exits that make your initial loss smaller, exits that maximize your profits, exits that minimize how much profit you give back, and psychological exits. Various exit strategies were presented for each category with a great deal of overlap.

The reader would do best to consider simple multiple exits. Simple exits are easy to conceptualize and don't require extensive optimization (if any). Multiple exits are recommended because they will help you most fully meet the objectives that you have stated for your trading system.

We have examined how to set up a high-expectancy system by itself that can return good profits. Chapter 13 will discuss how the opportunity factor interacts with expectancy.

NOTES

1. Jack D. Schwager, *Market Wizards: Interviews with Top Traders* (HarperCollins: New York, 2006).
2. These are hypothetical numbers and not necessarily a recommended exit for IBM. You need exits that meet your own criteria and that you test.

3. Once again this points out the importance of deep discount commissions.
4. Your loss will never be more than 1*R* unless the market gets away from you, which is quite probable from time to time.
5. In Buffett's defense he did buy the silver at an all-time low (that is, about $4 per ounce) and most of it was leased to customers who needed it, so he even found a way to have it earn income. Now because of the way he has handled this investment, I suspect that the future will make him look like even more of a genius than he already seems to be.

PART FOUR

Putting It All Together

The purpose of this part is to help you put it all together. You'll learn how to evaluate your system once you've developed it. You'll learn how great traders think about various market situations. Most importantly, you'll learn how to size your positions to meet your objectives. You will also learn what else you need to think about to complete your system and trade better.

Chapter 12 is designed to help you put it all together. You'll be introduced to seven different traders, each with totally different ideas about the market. You'll watch them analyze five real market situations and see how they perform in those situations over a six-week period. You can decide which trader you most identify with in each situation and see how you would perform.

Chapter 13 is all about opportunity and cost factors—topics that are seldom discussed elsewhere. You'll learn that you don't need to be anywhere near perfect if you have enough trading opportunities. However, cost becomes a very important factor as you trade more. Chapter 13 also discusses the impact of the potential drawdowns that a system will generate. And last, we'll look at the expectancy and opportunity factors that some newsletters have generated over the last two years.

Chapter 14 on position sizing is one of the most critical chapters in the book. Position sizing is really a separate system that you overlay onto your trading system. It's the part of your system that tells you "how much." And once you have a good system with a great expectancy, then you must use position sizing as an add-on to that system to help you meet your objectives. If you really want your system to be a Holy Grail trading system (meaning it's perfect for you), then you must thoroughly understand the topic of position sizing. It's the difference between a ho-hum trading methodology and the world's best methodologies. It's a topic that so few people think about, which is unfortunate because it's the key to meeting your objectives. Chapter 14 is designed to start you heading in the right direction.

Coverage of the topic of position sizing has been very inadequate in the past. Most books on system development don't even cover it at all; you'll learn why in Chapter 14. You'll also learn some ideas with respect to position sizing that are seldom, if ever, applied to the stock market, yet will give exceptional returns when they are used.

Last, Chapter 15 presents my overall conclusions to the book. Here my objective was to briefly cover some of the many topics that are important to trading that have not been addressed previously.

CHAPTER 12

There's Money for Everyone

> You cannot trade the market. Instead, you can only trade your beliefs about the market. However, you can do that successfully if you understand the fundamental concepts behind low-risk ideas, expectancy, and position sizing.
>
> *Van Tharp*

Let's look at five different people, each with different beliefs about how to trade or invest, and see how they would approach some common scenarios. Each of these people is a successful trader-investor who consistently makes money from trading or investing in the markets. These people are similar because they all have 10 qualities (listed below) that help them maintain their success. But they are all different because I've selected people who represent different concepts described in Chapter 5. In this chapter, we'll look at how all five of them approach different trading scenarios. By doing so, you'll understand the following:

- Five different people can each approach the same scenario differently and still have success.
- They make their decisions based on their individual determination on whether an idea has the potential of being a low-risk idea based on their beliefs.
- They each make money in the long run, even though they have entirely different approaches to the market.

Our five investors, although quite different in their beliefs and in the way they approach the market, have the following 10 common traits:

1. They all have at least one tested, well-researched, positive expectancy system that makes money.
2. They all have systems that fit them and their personalities. And they understand that they make money with their system because it does fit them.
3. They all totally understand the concepts they are trading. They know how their concepts generate low-risk ideas.
4. They all know that when they get into a trade or an investment, they must have some idea of when they are wrong about the trade—meaning that the trade is not working out—so they get out and preserve their capital. In other words, they each know what a 1*R* risk means for them for each of their positions in the market.
5. They each evaluate the reward-to-risk ratio of every trade they take. For the more mechanical traders, the reward-to-risk evaluation is a part of their system. The more discretionary traders actually calculate the reward-to-risk ratio before they enter into the position.
6. They all have a business plan to guide their trading-investment approach.
7. They all understand that position sizing is the key to meeting their objectives. Since position sizing is not covered until the end of this book, we won't be covering their position-sizing methods here. However, for the sake of simplicity, assume that one of them has risked 1 percent of his total equity on each position. Thus, a 1*R* loss for him will represent a 1 percent loss in his account and a 3*R* gain will represent a 3 percent gain in his account.[1] Similarly, for someone risking 2 percent per trade, a loss of 1*R* will represent a 2 percent loss, while a gain of 3*R* will represent a 6 percent gain.
8. All of them understand that their performance is totally a function of their own personal psychology, and they spend a lot of time working on themselves.

9. All of them take personal responsibility for the results that they get. This means that they have a goal that stretches them, and when they get off course, they refocus on the goal and examine themselves for how to make improvements and course corrections.
10. They all understand that a mistake means that they didn't follow their system and business plan, and they are constantly learning from their mistakes. Several of them, the top performers, have a coach to help them constantly improve and move closer to their goals.

Each of these five people has a totally different approach to the markets. Yet they all make six-figure salaries from the market. Why? Because what I've just told you about those five people is the essence of good trading and investing. I'd strongly suggest that you also make sure that the 10 common traits, given above, also apply to you. All of these principles should be self-evident by this time. If they are not, then I'd suggest that you reread the appropriate sections of this book until they are.

I've also included two other people, Nancy and Eric, who do not necessarily have the 10 traits. Nancy is a businesswoman who follows newsletter recommendations. She makes money from doing so because she is disciplined and understands many of the 10 traits listed. However, Nancy certainly doesn't take six figures out of the market each year. Eric is an impulsive trader who has no system and just does what feels right to him. He thinks he's a trader, but he consistently loses money because he has none of the 10 traits listed. Perhaps you'll be able to see how these two differ from the others.

HOW SEVEN TRADERS APPROACH THEIR CRAFT

The seven people are Mary, Dick, Victor, Ellen, Ken, Nancy, and Eric. Mary and Dick are both mechanical traders, although one has a long-term orientation and the other a very short term orientation. Both of them put a lot of work and study into developing mechanical systems so that they could be that way. Victor, Ellen, and Ken are all discretionary traders because they put a lot of time and effort into studying each position before they take it. These traders are fictional, but they represent composites of typical traders I know. And finally, Nancy and Eric are discretionary traders who trust their "into wishing" more than their intuition.

Mary—the Long-Term Trend Follower

Mary is a long-term trend follower as described in Chapter 5. She looks to buy what's going up and to sell what's going down. You can look at each chart from a distance and determine the direction in which Mary is likely to be positioned just by seeing whether the long-term trend is up or down. It's that simple. And when it stops doing what it's doing, according to her measurements, she gets out of the position. She uses methods that have already been described. Her entry is a channel breakout. Her initial stop is right below the low of the last 20 days or three times the weekly volatility, whichever is bigger. She also keeps a trailing stop equal to three times the weekly volatility. And when her trailing stop is closer than her initial stop, then the trailing stop becomes her primary exit.

Mary's overall objective is to keep a position for as long as possible, hopefully years. However, she's had trades that exited within a few days of her entry. Sometimes that happens because her initial stop is tighter than her trailing stop. Mary's system is very mechanical; it's all run by her computer. Each evening, her computer does a thorough analysis of the markets and spits out new orders and changes to Mary's stops. However, this process results in a very profitable trading system.

Mary is an engineer by training and has a strong background in computers and programming. She likes to test everything and make everything automatic. And, of course, she does this well.

Dick—the Short-Term Swing Trader

Dick is a short-term swing trader. He has several systems that all work well. One of them is a band trading system. This system sells a position when it touches and then crosses below the upper channel of his proprietary band methodology. It closes the position out when it reaches the opposite band, but under certain conditions it takes partial profits fairly early and moves the initial stop to breakeven. The system also does the reverse—it buys a position when it touches and then crosses above the lower channel of his proprietary band methodology. It closes that position out when it reaches the upper band, but it has certain conditions when he takes partial profits early. This system generates about three trades per day, and the average trade lasts about four days. This system is mostly mechanical, but sometimes Dick uses his intuition to adjust his bands. Nevertheless, Dick's computer generates trades each evening and recalculates all his stops.

Dick also has a short-term trend-following system that kicks in when his band methodology breaks down. This is also a proprietary methodology, but when a position moves outside his bands, Dick calculates the size of the move. When a position moves 2.5 standard deviations beyond his bands, he considers that band to be broken, and he looks to take a position in the direction of that move. In this case, Dick calculates the potential reward to risk of each position, and he will not take the position unless it will give him at least a 3*R* potential profit. This system generates about two trades per week, and these trades last an average of three to four weeks each.

Dick is a former physician. As he ran his practice, he discovered that (1) when he trusted others with his money, he tended to lose it, (2) that he really loved trading the markets himself, and (3) he had the skills to develop some very good systems. He also got really tired of government, HMO, and insurance regulations telling him what he could and couldn't do with his patients. Eventually, he decided that it was time to stop saving the world, especially when others didn't want to be saved, and do something he really enjoyed.

Victor—the Value Trader

Victor is a purely discretionary trader. You might call him a "mental scenario trader." Overall, he has a series of beliefs about the factors that he thinks are influencing the big picture of the markets. He knows that if you asked 10 people to do this, they would all come up with different viewpoints and they might even come up with opposite viewpoints. However, Victor monitors various aspects of the big picture looking at the relative strength of various world sectors along with variability of their performance on a weekly basis. His goal is to have positions in sectors that are the strongest, but he also hopes that by the time they get there, he's had them a long time. However, he liquidates positions that were part of the strongest market sectors as soon as they weaken to a lower level.

Victor might also be called a "fundamentalist" and a "value trader." He likes to buy things with great intrinsic value that everyone hates. He likes to buy those things when they have very little downside potential and a huge upside potential. For example, Warren Buffett bought 129 million ounces of silver when silver was just over $4 per ounce. How much downside risk is there in such a position when you own one-third of the world's supply and you bought it near historical lows? You also know that it will be needed and you'll have to give up some of your store of silver for others to be able to get it. Victor likes to trade that way, but not on the scale of Warren Buffett—at least not yet.

Victor basically buys things that have huge value and minimal downside risk. In addition, he wants the markets to be either (1) sufficiently low that there is no downside risk or (2) already showing some signs of moving in his favor. Victor likes buying things for pennies on the dollar with the idea that they will either return to normal levels (which will give him a significant profit) or they will suddenly be in demand and give him a tremendous profit. That's how Victor gets his low-risk ideas.

Victor has training as an MBA from the Wharton School of Business. He studied many of the great value traders such as Benjamin Graham, and he adopted their way of thinking. He originally learned many of the academic models for investing. He believed in efficient market theory, modern portfolio theory, and the capital asset pricing model. However, the more time he spent working on the markets, the more flaws he found in those ideas. For example, he soon found himself adopting Warren Buffett's idea that *"diversification was a protection against ignorance and that you needed wide diversification only when you didn't know what you were doing."* However, Victor also understood the value of thinking of the reward-to-risk ratio of each trade, and he was familiar with the concepts of *R* multiples, expectancy, and position sizing as described in this book. Victor now runs his own fund, works long and hard at studying the markets and himself, and has the results to prove that his hard work is paying off.

Ellen—There's an Order to the Universe

Ellen understands the world of the esoteric. She's studied the Delta Phenomenon®, and she knows how that method generates market turning points. She knows Gann concepts and Elliott Wave, and she spends a lot of time studying various markets to determine when they might make precise turning points. She also knows about magic numbers and Fibonacci retracement levels.[2] Thus, when she makes a prediction, she usually can set up some pretty precise targets. And, last, she's an expert on seasonal tendencies. She knows when markets are about to take off because of regular cyclic tendencies. Does Ellen use any of these specifically to the exclusion of the others? No, she doesn't. Instead, she studies many, many market situations. And sometimes she finds a situation in which everything seems to line up. She can only do that occasionally, but when it happens, her accuracy is almost uncanny.

Originally, Ellen was a perfectionist about her trading. If she didn't get an exact turning point, she couldn't take it. So she missed many trades. Or sometimes she'd get in a day too early. Nothing would happen so she would get out, only to watch the market take off as she'd predicted the next day.

However, Ellen, by practicing some of the ideas in this book, has solved her problems. First, when she predicts a turning point, she doesn't enter the market until the market proves her right. And once she sees that, she'll enter into a position. Her initial stop-loss points are quite tight because she's very precise in her predictions. Sometimes she'll take several small losses before she'll get a trade right. But her losses are usually about 1*R*, while her gains are usually 10*R* or bigger. And even though her accuracy rate is only about 38 percent, because of these false breakouts, she still makes very good money. And you should be able to understand why at this point.

Ken—the Spreader-Arbitrager

Ken is a private trader, but he is also a member of one of the trading exchanges, and that allows him to make markets and get the bid-ask spread on most of his trades. He also has access to a lot of research, and he is able to find super interesting ideas in various markets.

Sometimes, he'll take a low-risk idea by doing an option spread. Other times, he'll find something that just seems like a loophole. It has no risk as long as the loophole is open. As a result, Ken will jump in with both feet and make a lot of money. Sometimes he only makes 1*R* or 2*R* per position, but when he finds these loopholes, he could make money on most of his trades. However, he's always watching for his loophole to close and has a bailout method should that happen quickly.

Ken liked watching the markets when he was a child, and he always wanted to be a professional trader. Thus, after high school he got a job as a runner at one of the exchanges in Chicago, and eventually he became a clerk and then a trader on the floor. He did that for about five years and noticed that after five years he was one of the few people who'd lasted as long as five years. Most of the others had blown out of their accounts because they hadn't picked up what he understood about risk control and position sizing. And now, although Ken no longer trades on the floor, he still has the insights and knowledge of a savvy floor trader. Ken runs a small trading company with about 10 other traders under his wing. About 35 percent of the company's money belongs to Ken, and the rest belongs to other investors who really appreciate Ken's skills.

The last two traders are not necessarily model traders—Nancy the advice seeker and Eric the impulsive trader. Nancy makes money in the market but not nearly as much as our five great traders-investors listed first. Eric is a perpetual loser.

Nancy—the Businesswoman Who Follows Top Newsletters

Nancy is a senior executive at a large company. She makes a six-figure salary, but she doesn't trust other people to manage her money. She's given her money to others in the past only to discover that others tended to lose her money. In addition, she was very unimpressed by most financial professionals who espoused relative performance (that is, their job was to beat the S&P 500) instead of absolute performance. Those professionals basically charged her high fees and commissions, and they generally said that she should put her money with them, leave it there, and then allow it to grow. She had done that before, only to watch her money shrink.

Nancy, however, didn't have a lot of time to do research on the market because of her busy job. Instead, she chose to subscribe to five newsletters that all had excellent track records.[3] Three of the newsletters concentrated on value, and two concentrated on finding big movers. All of them understood the importance of stop losses, and two of them even told her how big to size her positions—which is something that she believed was a rarity. All of them published their track record each month, which is something she insisted upon. In other words, they showed the recommendation, the entry price at that time, the current price, and the amount of gain or loss. None of them gave their track record in terms of expectancy or *R* multiples, but she knew how to calculate those by herself.[4]

Although Nancy got her ideas from newsletters, she also understood that each of the trades had to fit her. As a result, she looked at charts of each of the recommended trades because she never wanted to buy anything that was going down. Nancy also looked at the arguments behind each of the trades because she wanted to be convinced of the merits of each trade before she invested.[5] Nancy always made sure that she had a clear exit point for each trade, in case it didn't work out. And finally, Nancy thoroughly understood position sizing, and she never risked more than 1 percent of her portfolio on any one idea.[6]

Eric—Mr. Let's Do It Now

Eric has always been described as somewhat impulsive. He thinks he knows everything about the market, when really he just has a few uneducated beliefs about the market. For example, he thinks that the right trading method is simply the skill to pick the right stocks. "After all," he thinks, "aren't great investors successful because they are just good stock pickers?" He sort of believes that there might be a real secret to stock picking, but he thinks that no one who understands it would give it away to someone like him. He also believes that there is a lot of luck involved. Thus, when he loses money in the market, it's just because he got bad advice or was just darned unlucky. Further, Eric loves the action of being in the market and finds it very stimulating to watch his account move 5 percent or more in a day—even if it is down.

HOW OUR TRADERS WOULD LOOK AT FIVE KEY MARKET SITUATIONS

One reason I added this chapter to the new edition of this book is so that you would understand how different systems would generate low-risk ideas and produce unique *R*-multiple distributions. As a result, I picked some "interesting" market situations as they existed at the close of the markets on February 17, 2006. The time or the situation does not really matter. I could have picked any time and any situation because the goal is to analyze how each of our traders-investors would approach each of those market situations to generate a low-risk idea.

Next we'll look at how the ideas turned out six weeks later on March 31, 2006.[7] Six weeks is probably not enough time to determine how some of the ideas turned out for our long-term investors, but it will still give you a number of different perspectives on some key principles that should be common to all of these people: (1) how they generate a low-risk idea; (2) how they determine 1*R* for that trade; and (3) how expectancy might work for them.

Situation 1: Google (GOOG)

So what's been the hottest stock on the U.S. stock market? In 2005 it was Google. Isn't it ironic that the hot stocks of the high-tech boom in the 1990s were Internet stocks? It's now six years later, and the latest hot stock is an Internet stock. New booms are typically not made with the same hot stocks as the old boom, but perhaps that's a commentary on today's market.

So let's look at Google (GOOG). Figure 12.1 shows weekly candlesticks for GOOG since its inception. You'll notice that it was in a very strong uptrend, going to nearly $500 per share. And then it fell back considerably in just a few months. So how would our seven investors deal with this situation?

But before we look at the analysis of our seven investors, ask yourself how would you have reacted to GOOG? Google closed on February 17, 2006, at $368.75—down from its all-time high of $475.11 that occurred about five weeks earlier on January 11, 2006. Is GOOG a great opportunity? Is it waiting for a crash? Or is it a consolidating stock now? And even if you know what happened to

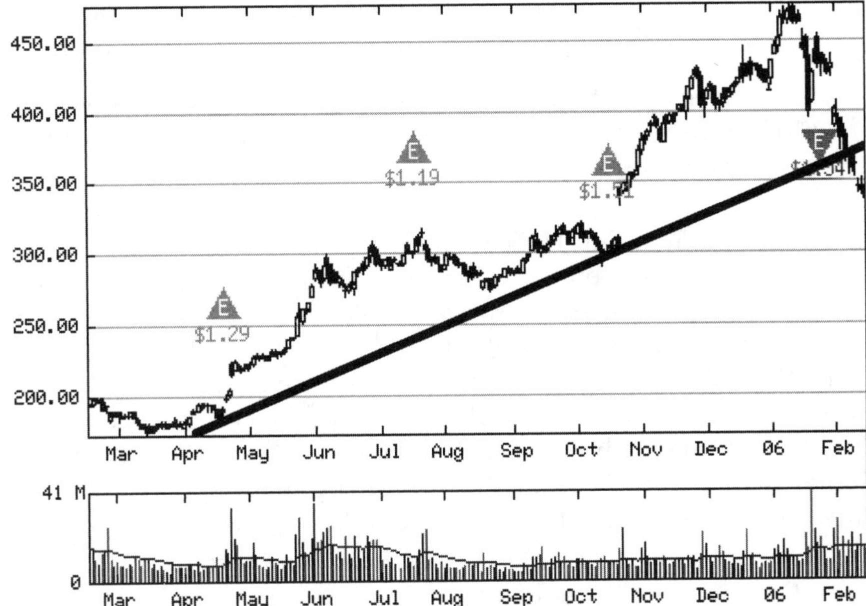

Figure 12.1 The big picture for Google (GOOG)

GOOG since February 17, 2006, pretend that you didn't know. Hindsight is always genius, which is why I wrote this section about what would happen in six weeks before I knew the results. So just ask yourself, "How would you react to Google's chart?"

Would you take a position in this situation?

If you would take a position, would it be a long trade (I expect the market to go up), or a short trade (I expect the market to go down)?

Where would you put your stop-loss order (called *stop* for short)?

Given that stop, what would 1*R* be for you?

How much do you think you could make in this trade in the next six weeks in terms of *R*?

What is your potential reward-to-risk ratio on this trade?

Does taking this trade make sense, assuming there is a 50-50 chance that you might be wrong about the direction of movement on this trade?

How much of your total portfolio would you be willing to risk on this trade? 0.5 percent, 1 percent, 2 percent, more?

Look at the chart and write down your answers before you go on with your reading. And now, let's look at how our seven investors responded to it.

Mary—the Long-Term Trend Follower

Mary actually has been long this stock for over a year because it's been one of the best performers. She has a profit of $153 so far, which is about an 8.4*R* profit. Her stop is a trailing stop of three times the weekly volatility from the all-time high. That puts her stop at $329.31, and that has not been hit yet. Mary is nervous about this stock, but she'll honor her stop. Her initial stop was somewhat tighter with about 18 points of risk, so if she gets stopped out, she'll have a profit of $112, which will be about a 6*R* profit.

Dick—the Short-Term Swing Trader

Dick was actually long this stock in a slightly unusual trading situation for him. He was able to set up a band trade on GOOG, but he saw the potential for a much higher profit than his normal trades. On the previous Monday, there was a negative review of Google in *Barron's* with the weekly paper predicting a 50 percent fall in the stock. That fall resulted in a gap down at the opening on Monday, followed by a consolidation. Dick thought there was a good chance that the gap would be filled before Google started down again, especially when it started a short-term consolidation pattern. This is shown in Figure 12.2.

Dick set up one of his bands to contain the consolidation. And when the price touched the lower band and bounced off, Dick went long on February 15 at $340.80 with a very tight stop at $338.80. His minimum target is the top of the band at $351, which is about a 5*R* move. At that point, he'll take off half of his position and move his stop to break even. He decided there was significant resistance at about $357, so he'd probably take off another half of his position at that point and move his stop up to the top of the band. At that point he would have sold half of his position at a 5*R* profit and a quarter of his position at an 8*R* profit. His goal is then to be able to sell the remaining part of his position at $362, which would be a 10*R* profit.

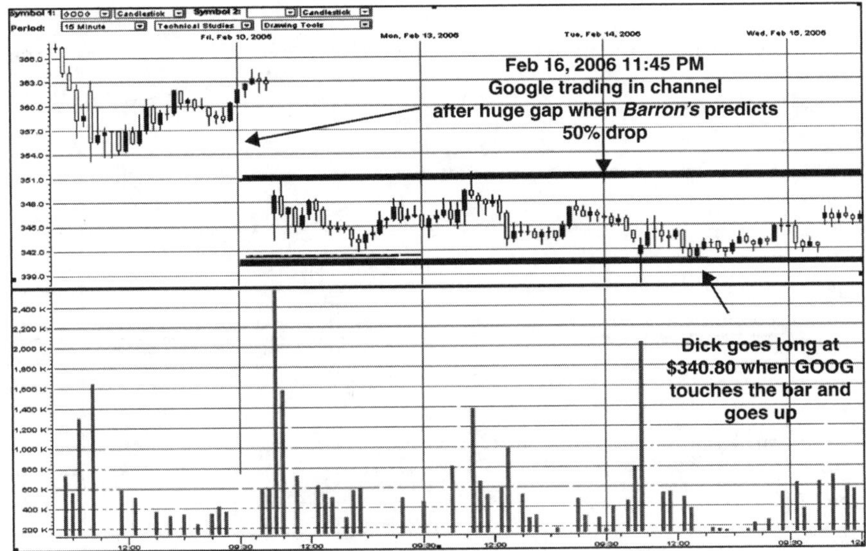

Figure 12.2 Dick's band setup to help him fill the gap

His initial risk was 0.5 percent of his portfolio. Thus, his downside risk with a 1*R* loss is a 0.5 percent.[8] If he fulfills all of his objectives, he could easily have a 7.5R profit in his portfolio in a week or so from this one position.

Dick had met all of his goals by February 16, when Google jumped up to $367. Figure 12.3 shows how the trade worked out for Dick.

By noon on the 16th, GOOG had passed the upper band, so Dick sold half of his position at $352.10 and moved his stop on the rest of the position to break even. See point 1 in Figure 12.3. The stock moved up rapidly to just beyond where Dick thought the resistance would be. As soon as he started to see a significant down bar, he got out of another half of his position at $357.20. See point 2 in Figure 12.3. He then moved his stop to $344.60, just below the support at $346. And finally, Dick was very fortunate because GOOG continued to rise for the rest of the day. As a result, he sold the rest of the position near the close, above his final target, at $366.42. See point 3 in Figure 12.3. The net result was a 5.1*R* profit on half of his position, a 7.15*R* profit on a quarter of it, and a 12.2*R*

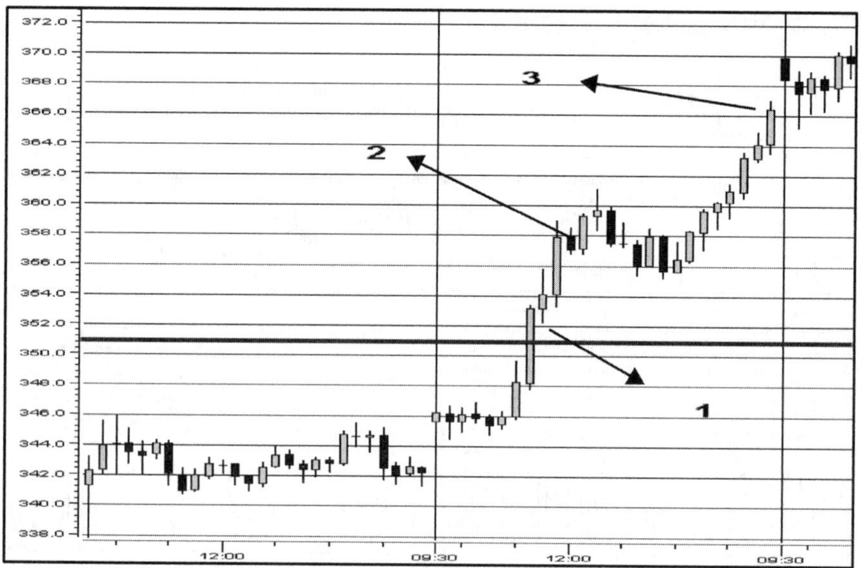

Figure 12.3 Exits on Dick's trades

profit on the remaining quarter. This amounts to a 7.4*R* average profit in three days of trading.

Victor—the Value Trader

Victor doesn't usually like to short the market, but this stock seemed like the perfect candidate. When it hit a price-to-earnings ratio of 100 and a price-to-sales ratio of over 20, he said to himself, "This is ridiculous. It's like 1999 all over again—and it's even an Internet stock. People just don't learn."

Victor decided to short it if it went over $500 or if he saw a clear breakdown in price. It never reached $500, but Victor decided to short it when it clearly began to break down as shown in Figure 12.4. He shorted a large position (about 3 percent of his equity) at about $435. He'd get out of the position if it made new highs again, so his stop was at $477. However, if it went above $500, he would be looking for another point to short it.

Victor doesn't have any particular target on this stock, but he would probably buy back about half the position if it went below

Figure 12.4 Victor shorts Google when it clearly breaks down

$300 per share. He thinks it's possible that in the next major decline in the market that overvalued stocks like GOOG could easily go down to a P/E of 20 or less. A P/E of 20 would put GOOG at about $100 per share where he thinks it might be fairly valued.

At the closing price on February 17 of $368.75, Victor has a profit of $66.25 per share against an initial risk of $42 per share. Thus, his profit so far is about 1.6*R*.

Notice that we've had three different attitudes about GOOG from three different investors or traders. Mary was long and had an open profit of about 8.4*R*. Victor was short and had an open profit of about 1.6*R*. And Dick had already closed out a huge gain of about 7.4*R* for a 3.7 percent gain in his portfolio in a few days. Three people with different beliefs had all found different ways of approaching GOOG, but each set up low-risk ideas and each of them had made money.

Ellen—There's an Order to the Universe

Ellen's approach to GOOG was entirely different. Using some of her magic numbers, she actually predicted that a major turning point in

GOOG would happen on February 16, but she wasn't sure what it would be. It could be a sharp reversal to the upside or a sharp breakdown to new lows. So how could she play that? Figure 12.5 shows you the potential price break and what happened.

Ellen drew some wide bands around the price consolidation between the open on February 13 and the close on February 15. A major price break would either go to the upside and take out the gap or move the stock down significantly. Her gut feeling was that it would go lower, but she was willing to let the market tell her. On February 15 GOOG closed in the middle of the channel at $342.38. It would either break above $352 or break below $338. She'd enter long if it broke above $352 or go short if it broke below $338. And her risk would be at the other side of the band. On February 16, the market clearly broke upward, so Ellen entered into a position at just over $352, with a stop at $339, clearly under the support.

Once she entered into the position, she did a Fibonacci analysis. That is shown in Figure 12.6.

Ellen estimated that her first upside target was at $391. Her second target was at $407, and her final target was $424 where there

Figure 12.5 Ellen believes a major price break (up or down) will occur on February 16

Figure 12.6 Ellen used Fibonacci retracements to set up her targets

was a lot of resistance to any higher movement. Her plan was to sell off her position in thirds at each target level. And on February 17, when the market confirmed her analysis by moving way above the initial entry into the 370 range, she moved her stop to $367.45. She now had locked in a profit of 15 points (that is, 1.2*R*). Her first target of $391 would give her about a 2*R* profit.

Ken—the Spreader-Arbitrager

When Ken noticed the band that GOOG was forming, similar to those shown in Figures 12.2 and 12.5, he believed that GOOG would also fill the gap created on Monday. He bought a GOOG March 340 call for $18.70. That call gave him the right to buy GOOG for $340 until the expiration date in mid-March. He was willing to risk $4 of the $18.70 he spent for the call, so if the call dropped to $14.70, he'd be out quickly. When GOOG closed at $348, he sold a March 350 call for $19.30. That is, Ken has now sold someone else the right to buy GOOG from him for $10 more at $350, and that right expires on the same date that his right expires. He now had a real profit of $0.60 per option contract (that is, the difference between the prices of the two calls) and a good chance to make another $10 per contract if GOOG finished above $350. Thus, he had a guaranteed profit of 0.15*R* and the potential for a 2*R* profit. For example, at expiration at a price of $350, the $350 call (which he was short) would be worth nothing, while the $340 call that he owned would be worth $10. And at any price above $350, he'd make the $10 spread. This was easy money, and if GOOG started to fall below $350, he'd unload the spread and make his $10 less any premium that still remained.

Nancy—the Businesswoman Who Follows Top Newsletters

Nancy was in a pickle on Monday when it came to Google. She didn't own it, but two of her newsletters that she received on Monday had different opinions about it. One of them gave it as an example of a highly overvalued stock that was falling and said that if they recommended shorts, GOOG would probably be one of them. However, a second newsletter recommended GOOG as a long-term holding and said that she should get into it on Monday. What should she do?

This is a typical situation for people who subscribe to multiple newsletters and don't have their own system. However, Nancy decided to analyze the situation. She looked at the graph in Figure 12.1 and decided that she certainly didn't want to own a stock that had already fallen 100 points off of its high. She also didn't want to short a stock that one of her newsletters had just recommended that she buy. As a result, Nancy elected to do nothing with GOOG.

Eric—Mr. Let's Do It Now

Eric was excited about option expirations in GOOG. He'd read the *Barron's* prediction that GOOG shares could fall 50 percent. And on February 16 Google seemed to be going down slowly, and Eric noticed that he could buy the February 360 puts at almost no premium. The March puts had a huge premium, but the February puts, because they were well in the money[9] and only had two days to expiration, had almost no premium. When Eric looked at the charts, he decided that there was a good chance that Google could drop 20 to 30 points within the next two days. And if he bought three of those puts, he could make as much as $9,000 on his $40,000 in two days. That would be great, he thought, and I'll be a market genius. So on February 16, Eric bought three February 360 puts for $15.20, which cost him a total of $4,569.

At the end of the day on the 16th, Eric had lost about $600, but he said, "I've still got one more day to look like a genius." The next day Eric didn't look at the markets until about 10:30 a.m. He was shocked to see that GOOG had jumped up to about $356 and his options were only worth about $4 each. Eric started kicking himself, thinking, "If only I looked at the open, I could have gotten out with perhaps only a $5 per option loss." Next, he decided that he had already lost most of his money, so he would just wait to the end of the day because it might just come back. At the end of the day, Eric did manage to sell the options before they expired at 30 cents each. Eric's total loss, after commissions, was $4,500 or about 11 percent of his account value.

Instead of being a genius, Eric now looked like an idiot. However, Eric didn't follow any of the key principles that we've been taking about in this section.

- First, he had not preplanned a worst-case loss. Thus, we have to consider that Eric's worst-case loss was the full $1,520 that he invested to buy each option contract. Since he lost $1,490, he suffered a 0.98*R* loss.
- Second, Eric didn't look at his reward-to-risk ratio. His dream was to make $9,000 on his account. However, because he didn't preplan any sort of loss, his potential gain was only 2*R*. Almost every trade you take only has about a 50 percent chance of going your way, so taking a trade that only has a 2*R* potential gain is, at its very best, not a wise trade. Your minimum gain should be at least 3*R*.
- Last, Eric didn't risk 1 percent of his account on this trade; he risked over 11 percent of his total account. Yes, he had the chance to be up 20 percent in two days. But, because he didn't practice any of these principles, he was down 11 percent.

So let's see how situation 1 looked on February 17 for our seven people with their different perspectives. This is given in Table 12.1.

TABLE 12.1

Situation 1: GOOG for Our Seven Investor-Traders

Investor-Trader	Action Taken	Result on Close February 17
Mary (long-term trend follower)	Bought at $217.30. 1*R* = 18 pts.	If price falls to her stop, then she'll have a 6*R* profit.
Dick (swing trader)	Bought at $340.80	Closed out position with 7.4*R* profit.
Victor (value trader)	Shorted at $435	Currently at 1.6*R* profit.
Ellen (predictor)	Bought at $352	Currently at 1.2*R* profit.
Ken (spreader-arbitrager)	Bought spread	$0.60 per contract profit plus potential spread profit of $10.
Nancy (newsletters)	No action taken	No result.
Eric (no method)	Bought 3 March 360 puts for $4,569	Took a 1*R* loss, but 1*R* amounted to 11 percent of his account.

Notice that everyone who had their own system had taken action at some point in time on this situation. One of them had already closed out his position for a very large profit. The others all had profits that were protected by stops. Thus, five people with totally different perspectives could all trade this situation and turn it into a low-risk idea.

The two people who didn't have their own systems did not do that well. Nancy could do nothing because she had conflicting input and didn't have any way to handle that sort of situation. And Eric had no understanding of low-risk ideas and lost 11 percent of his account on the remote chance that he could make 20 percent.

Situation 2: South Korean ETF (EWY)

So what's been hot internationally? The South Korean stock market has been pretty good, as evidenced by the performance of EWY, the South Korean ETF as shown in Figure 12.7. Notice that EWY has been in a nice uptrend since August 2004.

Is there a good, low-risk opportunity on February 17? Or is it something that's dangerous and should be avoided? What's your

Figure 12.7 Weekly candlestick chart of EWY, the South Korean ETF. Both long-term trendlines are intact.

reaction to this chart? Would you buy it? Is it too dangerous for you, and, if so, would you short it or just avoid it?

Would you take a position in EWY?

If you would take a position, would it be a long trade (I expect the market to go up) or a short trade (I expect the market to go down)?

Where would you put your stop-loss order?

Given that stop, what would 1*R* be for you?

How much do you think you could make in this trade in the next six weeks in terms of *R*?

What is your potential reward-to-risk ratio on this trade?

Does taking this trade make sense, assuming there is a 50–50 chance that you might be wrong about the direction of movement on this trade?

How much of your total portfolio would you be willing to risk on this trade? 0.5 percent, 1 percent, 2 percent, more?

Look at the chart and write down your answers before you go on with your reading. And now, let's look at how our seven investors responded to it.

Mary—the Long-Term Trend Follower

Mary purchased this ETF in August 2005 and has held it ever since then. She bought it at $36.50, and since then, she has kept a trailing stop of three times the weekly volatility. Currently that stop is at $41.10, so she has locked in a $4.60 profit per share. Her initial risk was about $4.50 per share, so she has a 2*R* profit right now and has locked in a profit of just over 1*R* with her current stop. Although the ETF has been in a consolidation pattern for five weeks, she's hoping the uptrend resumes soon.

Dick—the Short-Term Swing Trader

Dick set up his bands and discovered that there was strong support at $44, so when EWY bounced off of that level on February 13, Dick took a long position at $44.20 with a stop at $43.20. On February 17, EWY closed at $45.73, so Dick had a profit of $1.53 per share (or about 1.5*R*), but none of that profit was locked in because Dick had not yet changed his stop. Dick will take off half of his position at $46.80 and raise his stop to break even, or he will liquidate his entire position by the close on Friday, February 24, if it hasn't gone above $46.80.

Victor—the Value Trader

Victor had no positions in EWY. He prefers to buy individual companies for which he can determine the expected value through his research. Since EWY is a composite of the Korean stock market, he doesn't consider it a low-risk idea.

Ellen—There's an Order to the Universe

Ellen was fascinated at the idea of using her approach on country ETFs. She believes that each stock has a particular energy associated with it, so it is "easy" to predict turning points. However, a country ETF, such as EWY, is a little different because it is a composite of many stocks. Nevertheless, the country also has an energy associated with it, and Ellen decided that her approach might work. Also country ETFs tend to have gap openings because they are trading while the U.S. stock market is closed.

When she did her studies, Ellen concluded that a turning point in the EWY was going to happen on Monday, February 20, 2006. However, there was a problem. South Korea would be active that day, but the U.S. stock market was closed for President's Day, and she wouldn't be able to trade EWY. In addition, she didn't know which direction the turn would make.

Based upon Figure 12.8, Ellen decided that her entry would be any move beyond the resistance at 46.2 or below the support at 44.4. Her bailout point would be the other side of the trade—the support or resistance point. She was really afraid of what would happen on the 20th, but she decided that she was willing to buy within a 1-point range of either of her breakout points. What she was expecting was a breakout to new highs above $48.50 or a breakdown of the trend with EWY falling below $43.50. If EWY broke either point, she'd move her stop to break even.

In this particular case, Ellen could be "right" about her turning point and still have a lot of risk. For example, EWY could move to

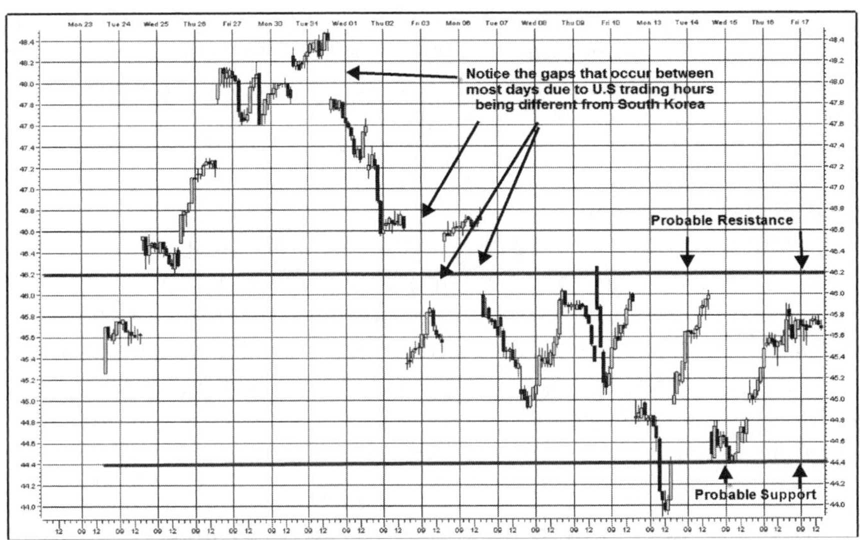

Figure 12.8 Short-term (30-minute) candlestick chart of EWY showing support and resistance

$48.50 in a few days and then bounce back. She might get only a little piece of that move—perhaps at best a 1*R* move. It could also move down to $43.50 and then bounce back—again giving her a very small profit. However, because of the potential of a new breakout or a total breakdown of EWY, which she thought would give her at least a 5*R* move, she decided to take a chance.

EWY opened at $46.35 on February 21, just above her resistance point so she bought there with a stop at $44.20. She decided to sell half her position if EWY hit $48.50 and raise her stop to break even. That would only be a 1*R* profit, but she was nervous about applying her methodology to country ETFs.

Ken—the Spreader-Arbitrager

Ken didn't have any low-risk ideas for this trade. He was exploring the idea of actually trading South Korean stocks against the ETFs, but he had not developed any good low-risk ideas about how to do it yet.

Nancy—the Businesswoman Who Follows Top Newsletters

One of Nancy's newsletters tracked ETFs, and she'd taken a long position in EWY in November 2005 at $41.30. She was keeping a 25 percent trailing stop on this one. She was currently up about 0.6*R*, but she still had the risk of about a 0.5*R* loss.

Eric—Mr. Let's Do It Now

Eric didn't know anything about country ETFs, but when he saw the chart of EWY, he got very excited. EWY was in a nice uptrend and could go to the moon. As a result, he bought 100 shares at $44.54. He had no targets and no stops, so his 1*R* risk was $4,468, including his trading costs. EWY would have to double for him to make a 1*R* return. Furthermore, Eric was risking 12.6 percent of the $35,415 left in his portfolio on this position.

So let's see how situation 2 looked on February 17 for our seven people with their different perspectives. This is shown in Table 12.2.

TABLE 12.2

Situation 2: EWY for Our Seven Investor-Traders

Investor-Trader	Action Taken	Result on Close February 17
Mary (long-term trend follower)	Bought at $36.50	Has 2*R* profit and has locked in 1*R* profit.
Dick (swing trader)	Bought at $44.20	Bought that day, so unknown.
Victor (value trader)	No position	No result.
Ellen (predictor)	No position, but bought later on February 21 at $46.35	No result.
Ken (spreader-arbitrager)	No position; looking at trading South Korean stocks vs. EWY	No result.
Nancy (newsletters)	Bought at $41.30	Has 0.6*R* profit but could still take loss on this position.
Eric (no method)	Bought at $44.54 on Feb 17	Has just entered long position. But a 1*R* risk for him is his entire investment.

Notice again how multiple different approaches, based on totally different beliefs, could all set up positions in the same stock based on different thinking. And since all of them think in terms of *R* multiples (that is, reward-to-risk ratios), they can all be successful in the market with the exception of Eric who will need the stock to double to make a 1*R* profit.

Situation 3: Westwood One (WON)

So let's now switch to a stock that's in a clear downtrend and see how each of our investor-traders would approach the situation. The stock we'll look at is Westwood One, or WON. As Figure 12.9 shows, WON is in a very strong downtrend. Look at the chart and decide what action you would take.

Would you take a position in this situation?

Figure 12.9 Westwood One (WON) candlestick chart showing clear downtrend on February 17, 2006

- If you would take a position, would it be a long trade (I expect the market to go up) or a short trade (I expect the market to go down)?
- Where would you put your stop-loss order?
- Given that stop, what would 1*R* be for you?
- How much do you think you could make in this trade in the next six weeks in terms of *R*?
- What is your potential reward-to-risk ratio on this trade?
- Does taking this trade make sense, assuming there is a 50–50 chance that you might be wrong about the direction of movement on this trade?
- How much of your total portfolio would you be willing to risk on this trade? 0.5 percent, 1 percent, 2 percent, more?

Look at the chart and write down your answers before you go on with your reading. And now, let's see how our seven investors responded to it.

Mary—the Long-Term Trend Follower

Mary had been short WON in 2004, entering the position in April at about $27.40. She got stopped out of her position in December for a small profit. However, she was still very interested in the stock as a short. And when the stock bounced off its long-term trendline in January 2005, Mary again went short this stock at $24.80. She was nearly stopped out during the consolidation between May and September, but her stop was wide enough to protect her. As a result, she was still short at the close on February 17 at $14.30 with her stop $2.10 away at $16.40. Based on her initial risk, she has a 2.5*R* profit with a 2*R* profit locked in place with her stop.

Dick—the Short-Term Swing Trader

Figure 12.10 shows Dick's thinking about WON. Dick set up some hourly bands with the idea of finding a short trade. In this particular case, the long-term downtrend is too strong for Dick to want to go long. However, his bands suggest that a penetration below 13.7

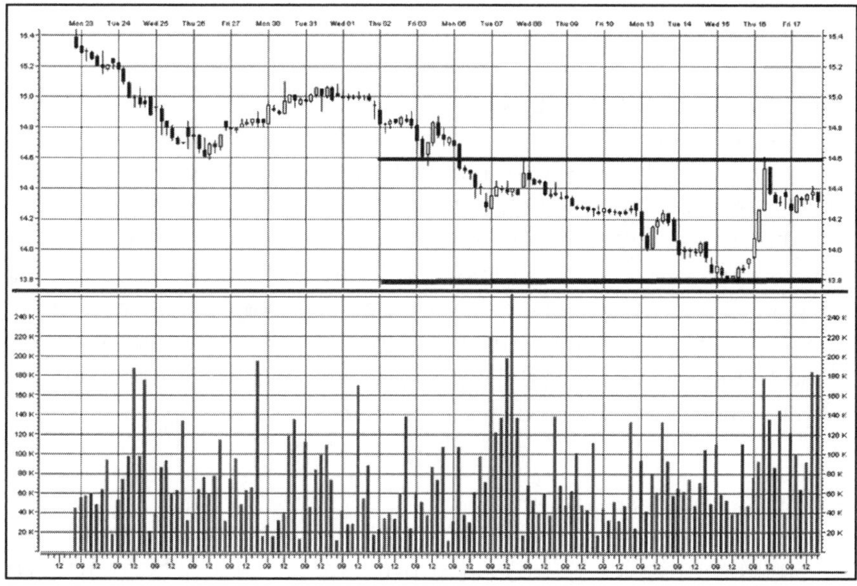

Figure 12.10 Westwood One (WON) hourly candlesticks showing Dick's bands. The chart shows one-day up movement to resistance at $14.60.

will make an excellent entry with a stop at the upper band at 14.6. Dick hasn't taken any action yet, but he will do so when he sees an entry signal.

Victor—the Value Trader

Victor looked at the economic picture behind WON and decided that the management was incompetent and that the stock was highly overvalued. First, the stock is a media provider, and Victor doesn't see that much near-term promise for that industry. Second, the current stockholders' equity is at a negative value of $203 million. Third, insiders sold half of their existing shares within the last six months. Even the people who are running the company don't like their situation! As a result, Victor went short the company in November 2005 at $18.40, with a stop at $21.10. It really wasn't a surprise for Victor when the CEO of WON resigned in December 2005, but it confirmed his thinking about the company. Victor expects the company to fall into single-digit prices by mid-2006. And as of February 17, 2006, he has a profit of $4.10 per share or just over 1.5*R*. He's expecting at least a 5*R* profit out of this short position.

Ellen—There's an Order to the Universe

Ellen expected a sharp move in the stock on February 24. She used her own methods to determine when the sharp move would occur, but was pleasantly surprised to learn that it corresponded to the day that the company was scheduled to announce their fourth-quarter earnings. Again, Ellen wasn't sure if the move would be up or down. And she didn't have enough information to determine what her entry signals would be. However, if WON had not penetrated the $13.80 mark to the downside, she expected that any move below $13.80 would be a move to go short.

Ken—the Spreader-Arbitrager

Ken was also bearish about WON. As a result, he sold the March $12.50 calls for $2.45. To protect himself, he bought the March $15.00 calls for $0.35, and received a credit of $2.10 per spread. If WON finished above $15.00, he'd lose $2.50 per spread less his credit of

$2.10. Thus, his worst-case loss was 40 cents. However, if WON fell below $12.50, then he'd keep his entire credit of $2.10. Ken could potentially make 4.25*R* in this trade if it went his way. He liked this one a lot.

Nancy—the Businesswoman Who Follows Top Newsletters

One of Nancy's newsletters suggested that she short WON at $16.00 with a 20 percent trailing stop at $19.20, so she followed that advice. On February 17, with WON closing at $14.30, she had a profit of $1.70 per share. Her stop was at $15.66, so she still had the potential for a 34 cent loss (that is, about minus 0.1*R*) in this position.

Eric—Mr. Let's Do It Now

Eric looked at the chart and said to himself, "This stock has gone down a lot. It probably can't go down much further. I think I'll buy 400 shares." And when Eric saw the stock going up substantially on the 17th, he bought 400 shares at $14.43. Again, Eric had no preset risk, so a 1*R* risk for Eric was the full $14.43 that he invested in WON. His total risk was $5,800 or 16.8 percent of what was left of his portfolio because Eric didn't understand that there was a significant difference between the amount invested and the amount he should be risking of his investment.

So let's see how situation 3 looked on February 17 for our seven people with their different perspectives. This is given in Table 12.3.

Notice that these different approaches all lead to short positions on this stock, except for Eric whose approach was "let's do it now." And all of them are profitable except Eric because they think in terms of *R* multiples and have the potential for good success in this position.

Situation 4: Toll Brothers (TOL)

So let's look at another stock that is in a downtrend, Toll Brothers, a building company. Building companies did very well for a while until short-term interest rates got high enough (that is, around July

TABLE 12.3

Situation 3: WON for Our Seven Investor-Traders

Investor-Trader	Action Taken	Result on Close February 17
Mary (long-term trend follower)	Short at $24.80	Has 2.5*R* profit and has locked in 2*R* profit.
Dick (swing trader)	Will short at $13.70 if he gets the opportunity	No result.
Victor (value trader)	Short at $18.40	Has 1.5*R* profit.
Ellen (predictor)	No position, but looking for possible drop on February 24	No result.
Ken (spreader-arbitrager)	Bought credit spread on March calls for net credit of $2.10	Maximum risk is a 40 cent loss, with a potential 4.25*R* gain.
Nancy (newsletters)	Short at $16.00	Has 0.5*R* profit but could still take small loss on position.
Eric (no system)	Bought at $14.43	Has 13 cents per share at the close.

2005), and then they started moving down. Toll Brothers is a prime example of such a chart. And Figure 12.11 shows a weekly candlestick chart of the stock. It also shows the stock going through major support at $36.

Would you take a position in this situation?

If you would take a position, would it be a long trade (I expect the market to go up) or a short trade (I expect the market to go down)?

Where would you put your stop-loss order?

Given that stop, what would 1*R* be for you?

How much do you think you could make in this trade in the next six weeks in terms of *R*?

What is your potential reward-to-risk ratio on this trade?

Does taking this trade make sense, assuming there is a 50-50 chance that you might be wrong about the direction of movement on this trade?

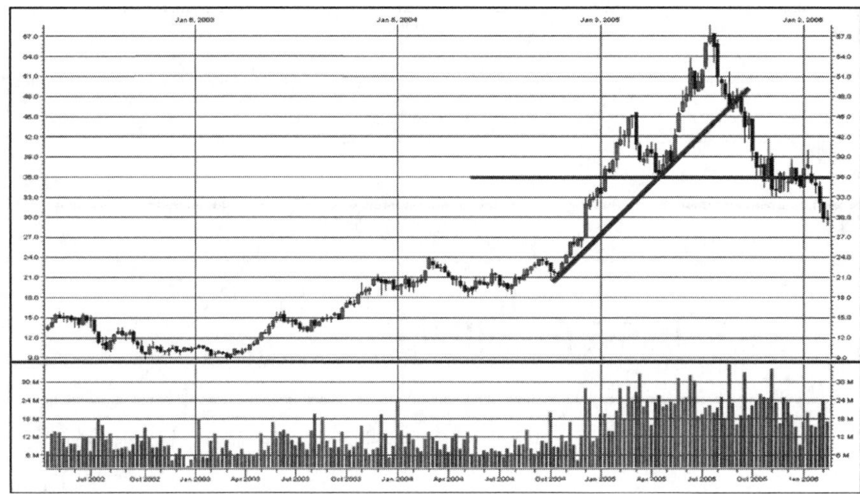

Figure 12.11 Toll Brothers (TOL) weekly candlestick chart

How much of your total portfolio would you be willing to risk on this trade? 0.5 percent, 1 percent, 2 percent, more?

Look at the chart and write down your answers before you go on with your reading. And now, let's see how our seven investors responded to it.

Mary—the Long-Term Trend Follower

Mary saw this one coming. By the time the chart broke its trendline at about $47, Mary had been stopped out of her long position at a nice profit. In addition, by the time the stock hit its support at $36, she was very interested in shorting this stock. And she got her short entry signal at $35.30 with her stop at $44.88. On February 17 the stock closed at $29.75, so she had a profit of about 0.6*R*. Her current stop was at $38.20, so she could still take as much as a 3-point loss on this stock (that is, 0.3*R*).

Dick—the Short-Term Swing Trader

Figure 12.12 shows Dick's thinking about TOL. He'd been short TOL at the upper band, and closed out his position when it penetrated the lower band. However, the strong penetration of the lower band got him into his trend-following mode, and he went short at $31.60.

Figure 12.12 Toll Brothers (TOL) daily candlesticks showing channel breakout

Dick always has stops and targets. So this time his stop is his prior lower band at $33.40. To determine what to expect next, Dick set up some 15-minute candlestick charts. These are shown in Figure 12.13. The chart shows strong price support at $29.60. Since it was close to that level at the close on February 17, Dick sold half of his position at $29.90 for a little less than a 1*R* profit. He hoped to sell the remainder the next day on a breakdown to $28.80 or lower. His current stop on the rest of his position is $30.80, so he has locked in a profit of 80 cents.

Victor—the Value Trader

Victor looked at the economic picture behind TOL, and he was impressed. First, TOL earned $4.78 per share for the last fiscal year, giving it a P/E ratio of 6.97. That alone was enough to get Victor interested in the stock from a value perspective. However, he'd be buying it only if it started to go up.

Victor also looked at the company balance sheet. The current assets of the company[10] were nearly $6 billion, while the company had total liabilities of $3.5 billion. This meant that the company

Figure 12.13 15-minute candlestick chart showing support for TOL

could be liquidated for about $2.5 billion. And with 155 million shares outstanding, that gave it a liquidation value of $15.48 per share. Although Victor liked that number, it wasn't tempting because the stock was selling for nearly twice that price. So TOL was not a super bargain, at least not yet. However, Victor put the stock on his watch list. Should the company start moving up or should it drop another $20 per share, Victor would probably be a buyer.

Ironically, when *Barron's Weekly* came out over the weekend (February 18), they had an article in which they said TOL was highly undervalued and should be expected to outperform the market. Victor didn't like to see his value stocks mentioned in the press. This confirmed to him that it probably was just not time for this stock—at least not yet.

Ellen—There's an Order to the Universe

While Ellen didn't have an expected time frame for a major move in TOL, she thought the stock could easily stop its downside move at the current level and have a significant bounce. The rationale behind Ellen's thinking is shown in Figure 12.14, which shows the decline expected in terms of Fibonacci retracement levels. TOL was just about at the bottom of its retracement. And stocks can sometimes move sharply off of such retracements, especially when they get mentioned in a *Barron's Weekly* story.

When she saw the *Barron's* article on Saturday, she decided to buy TOL at the opening if she could get it under $30. She expected a move to $34 or $35. And since her stop would only be about $1.50 away at $28.50, a $4.50 move to her minimum target of $34 would be a 2.6*R* gain for her.

Ken—the Spreader-Arbitrager

Ken also noticed the Fibonacci retracement levels, and so he purchased March 30 calls when TOL was at $29 on February 14 for $1.10. On February 16, when TOL was almost at $31, he sold March 35 calls for $0.70. The spread cost him $0.40, and it had the potential

Figure 12.14 Long-term candlestick chart of TOL showing retracement levels in clear downtrend but at 0.618 retracement level

to be worth \$5.00 if TOL closed at \$35 or higher at expiration. Thus, his 40-cent risk, which was 1*R*, could turn into a \$4.60 profit or an 11.5*R* profit. Ken really liked this trade.

Nancy—the Businesswoman Who Follows Top Newsletters

None of Nancy's newsletters had mentioned Toll Brothers so the stock had not caught her attention.

Eric—Mr. Let's Do It Now

Eric had been hearing about the potential bubble bursting in the housing market, and when he looked at TOL, it was clearly moving down. Eric had heard about shorting stocks, and he thought the best way to learn about shorting was to do it. He had a margin account that allowed short positions in the market, so he shorted 100 shares of TOL at \$30.15. Since TOL closed on February 17 at \$29.75, he actually had a \$25 profit (after commissions) at the end of the day. Since 1*R* was \$3,030 (because he was risking everything), Eric now had a 0.008*R* profit.

So let's see how situation 4 looked on February 17 for our seven people with their different perspectives. This is given in Table 12.4.

In this example, different ideas lead to different positions. Three people are short and have small profits already. One has a debit spread and will make a huge 11.5*R* profit if TOL closes above \$35 at expiration. Another one is hoping to buy under a certain price at the opening. Two others have no positions, although one of them likes it as a potential value play. Notice how thinking about their trades in terms of *R* multiples gives all of them a chance to make nice profits or suffer only a small loss, except for Eric who is risking his entire investment.

Situation 5: Phelps Dodge (PD)

So let's now switch to a pure commodity stock since the big picture suggests that the next 10 years could be a booming time for commodities. One such stock is Phelps Dodge (PD) shown in Figure 12.15. It's been in a strong uptrend since 2003. What do you think of the chart of PD?

TABLE 12.4

Situation 4: TOL for Our Seven Investor-Traders

Investor-Trader	Action Taken	Result on Close February 17
Mary (long-term trend follower)	Short at $35.30 with 1*R* loss being $9.58	Has 0.6*R* paper profit but still has potential for 0.3*R* loss.
Dick (swing trader)	Short at $31.60 with 1*R* loss being $1.80	Sold half his position at about 1*R* profit. New stop locks in 0.8*R* profit.
Victor (value trader)	Considers TOL to be a potential value play, but not yet	No result.
Ellen (predictor)	Will buy on opening with limit of $30; her 1*R* loss would be $1.50 or less	No result, but her target would give her as much as a 3*R* profit.
Ken (spreader-arbitrager)	Bought debit spread on March calls for $0.40, so 1*R* loss is 40 cents	Has potential gain of 11.5*R* if stock is above $35 at expiration.
Nancy (newsletters)	No ideas about TOL	No result.
Eric (no system)	Shorted TOL at $30.15	Has 0.008*R* profit on position that is risking everything.

Would you take a position in this situation?

If you would take a position, would it be a long trade (I expect the market to go up) or a short trade (I expect the market to go down)?

Where would you put your stop-loss order?

Given that stop, what would 1*R* be for you?

How much do you think you could make in this trade in the next six weeks in terms of *R*?

What is your potential reward-to-risk ratio on this trade?

Does taking this trade make sense, assuming there is a 50-50 chance that you might be wrong about the direction of movement on this trade?

How much of your total portfolio would you be willing to risk on this trade? 0.5 percent, 1 percent, 2 percent, more?

Figure 12.15 Monthly candlestick chart for Phelps Dodge (PD), the commodity company, on February 17, 2006. This chart shows a strong uptrend since the start of 2003.

Look at the chart and write down your answers before you go on with your reading. And now, let's look at how our seven investors responded to it.

Mary—the Long-Term Trend Follower

Mary was currently in Phelps Dodge and had been in the nice trend twice before. Her three trades are shown in Figure 12.16. She purchased the first trade in August 2003 and was stopped out in March 2004 for a 7*R* gain. She purchased the stock again in September 2004, and she was nearly stopped out within the next three months but managed to hang onto the stock until the spring of 2005 when she was stopped out for a small 0.5*R* loss. She made a third trade on July 29, 2005, for $108.20 with her initial stop 12 points away. On February 17, PD closed at $145.02, so Mary had a profit of 37 points or just over 3*R*. Mary's stop is a long way away at $118.77 because the volatility has increased dramatically, but that has kept her in this trade. Thus, her stop so far has locked in only a little less than a 1*R* profit. However, Mary believes this could be a 20*R* trade lasting several years.

Figure 12.16 Mary's trades in Phelps Dodge

Dick—the Short-Term Swing Trader

Figure 12.17 shows Dick's thinking about PD. His hourly bands set up nicely, so Dick bought PD on February 15 at the bottom band (point 1 in Figure 12.17). He sold the position out for a 5*R* profit at point 2. And on February 17, Dick went short at point 3 when the price fell below the upper band. His entry was at $145.90, and his stop is at $147.60. He's expecting PD to go down to the lower band, and he plans to sell at about $140. Thus, a 1*R* loss for Dick is $1.70, and he has a 6-point potential gain or about 3.5*R*. Dick would feel very good about taking over 8*R* in profit (that is, from the previous trade and the current trade) from any of his bands once they are set up. They are usually good for only one to two trades at most.

Victor—the Value Trader

Victor looked at the big picture and is expecting a boom in commodities that could last for a decade or longer. And when the Federal Reserve discount rate got below 2 percent, Victor decided to buy several stocks that emphasized commodities. Phelps Dodge was one of them. He purchased it at $44.50 in 2003. He really didn't have a stop because he could not see himself selling this stock if it

Figure 12.17 Hourly candlesticks for Phelps Dodge with Dick's bands shown at the bottom

went lower. It just had too much value for him. However, when pressed, he said that he was willing to assume that he could lose 50 percent. Thus, we'll say Victor's potential loss was $23 per share.

Even with that large stop, with PD now at $145.20, Victor currently has more than 100 points of profit, which represents about 4*R*. Victor expects to hold on to PD for at least another five years. However, he isn't willing to give back a lot of his current profits so he currently has a stop in at $104, well below some strong support for the stock at $126 and at $108.

Ellen—There's an Order to the Universe

Ellen looked at Fibonacci retracement levels for PD from its high of 167.12. Those are clearly shown in Figure 12.18. When she saw the chart, she felt that the Fibonacci levels were clearly holding the retracement. In addition, it looked to Ellen as if the stock was just about to jump off of the 50 percent level at about 142. Ellen went long the stock early on the 16th at $142.10, with a protective stop at $140.10. Thus, her 1*R* loss was $2.

Figure 12.18 Ellen's Fibonacci retracement levels for PD

As of the close on the 17th, Ellen was up about 3 points, or 1.5*R*. Her goal was a move to at least $150 within the next five days, and her stop was now her entry point at $142.10.

Ken—the Spreader-Arbitrager

Ken was bullish on PD, and he had purchased the March 140 calls at $7.20. Several days later, he was able to sell March 145 calls at $6.20. Thus, he had a debit spread that cost him $1.00. This wasn't as good as his previous debit spread, but he still was happy about it. His worst-case loss was that both calls would expire worthless and he would lose his dollar. Thus, his 1*R* loss was $1.00. However, if PD at expiration were to close above $145, which Ken felt was very likely, then he could collect $5.00 for the spread and make a $4.00 profit. Thus, he was risking $1.00 to make a potential 4*R* profit. Ken also liked this trade.

Nancy—the Businesswoman Who Follows Top Newsletters

One of Nancy's newsletters suggested that she purchase PD at $73 with a 25 percent trailing stop. She liked the trade so she bought it the next morning at $72.80. Her initial stop was 25 percent away, as recommended, so her initial risk was $18.20 per share. On February 17, with PD at $145.02, she had a profit of $72.22, or almost 4*R*. Her stop was then 25 percent away from the most recent high of $167.12, or at $125.34. Thus, if she was stopped out at this point, she'd still have about a 3*R* profit.

Eric—Mr. Let's Do It Now

Phelps Dodge was way too expensive for Eric. He couldn't see himself paying over $100 for a stock. But PD did have options. And PD looked like another stock that was starting to go down.

This time Eric decided to buy the March 145 puts, which were selling at $6.20. So Eric bought two of them for $1,240. Eric would probably let these options expire worthless if they didn't make him money. Therefore, a 1*R* risk for Eric in this trade was $1,255. This time his risk was reasonable, relatively speaking, because it amounted to only about 3.5 percent of his portfolio. That's high risk for most people, but it was low for Eric.

Let's see how situation 5 looked on February 17 for our seven people with their different perspectives. This is given in Table 12.5.

Everyone has a profit on this stock, except Eric, despite the fact that everyone did something a little different. Most of our traders are long, except for Eric and Dick. Again, because all of them think in terms of reward to risk, except Eric, they all have the potential for success.

Before you read the next section, notice how much work our good traders-investors put into analyzing each situation. Great trading requires a time commitment and a thorough understanding of various ideas such as reward-to-risk ratios, expectancy, and position sizing. You must be willing to learn those concepts and put in the time to develop good systems if you want to be successful. You can probably imagine how much time it took for our traders to do their respective analysis of each situation. But what if you had to analyze 100 different situations to find one good one? Would you be willing to do it?

TABLE 12.5

Situation 5: PD for Our Seven Investor-Traders

Investor-Trader	Action Taken	Result on Close February 17
Mary (long-term trend follower)	Long at \$108.20 with 1*R* loss being 12 pts	Has 6.5*R* gains from 2 other trades and 3*R* profit to date on this trade (with 1*R* protected by her stop).
Dick (swing trader)	Short at \$145.90 with 1*R* loss being \$1.70	Has 5*R* gain from prior trade and about 0.5*R* from this one.
Victor (value trader)	Long at \$44.50 with 1*R* loss being \$23	Has 4*R* profit with 3*R* protected by his stop.
Ellen (predictor)	Bounce off of Fibonacci retracement: Long at \$142.10 with 1*R* loss being 2 pts.	Up about 1.5*R*
Ken (spreader-arbitrager)	Bought debit spread in March 140 and 145 PD calls for \$1	Potential \$4 profit against his \$1 loss.
Nancy (newsletters)	Bought at \$72.80 with 1*R* loss equal to \$18.20	Is up 4*R* with 3*R* protected by her stop.
Eric (no system)	Bought 2 March \$145 puts for \$6.20	Closed with \$35 loss on the day.

RESULTS SIX WEEKS LATER

Situation 1: Google (GOOG)

From our entry date in mid-February, GOOG continued up until February 28, reaching a high of \$397.54. It then resumed its downtrend, reaching a low of \$331.55 on March 10. On March 24, the S&P 500 announced to the world that GOOG would become part of the S&P 500 on March 31. It gapped that day and started climbing, reaching a high of \$399 on March 29. It closed on March 31 at exactly \$390 per share. Figure 12.19 shows a daily bar chart of GOOG through March 31.

So let's look at how our investors did with GOOG. For our purposes we'll calculate all the *R* multiples for open positions based on the closing price on March 31 of \$390.

Figure 12.19 Looking at the *R* multiples and expectancy of each trader: Daily candlesticks for Google (GOOG) through March 31, 2006

Mary—the Long-Term Trend Follower

Mary had a long position in GOOG with a trailing stop at $329. She almost got stopped out on March 10 when GOOG reached a low of $331.55, but she was still in it on March 31 when GOOG closed at $390. Mary bought GOOG at $217.30 with an 18-point stop. So with GOOG at $390, she had a profit of $172.70 per share, or 9.6*R*.

Dick—the Short-Term Swing Trader

Dick had already closed out his positions on February 17 at a 7.4*R* profit.

Victor—the Value Trader

Victor did not like GOOG, but he was not that happy with his analysis when he heard that GOOG was going to become part of the S&P 500. This meant that many institutions would now buy GOOG stock, and it would have some support for institutions as long as money was still pouring into mutual funds. As a result, he decided to close his position in GOOG after it gapped up on March 24. He closed his short at $367.40. He had a profit of $67.60, which, since his initial risk was $42, amounted to a 1.6*R* profit. Victor wasn't too unhappy because his 1.6*R* profit amounted to an increase in his account of almost 5 percent in about two months.

Ellen—There's an Order to the Universe

Ellen sold one third of her position when it reached her first target of $390 for a 3*R* profit. The remainder of her position was stopped out at $367.50 for a 1.2*R* profit.

Ken—the Spreader-Arbitrager

Ken had the potential for a 2.65*R* profit if his spread expired above $350. When GOOG reached $380, even though he was about two weeks from expiration, Ken was able to unwind his option position for a 2.5*R* profit because he had too little profit left to risk waiting for expiration and potentially watching his profit disappear.

Nancy—the Businesswoman Who Follows Top Newsletter

Nancy took no action on GOOG because of conflicting ideas from her newsletters.

Eric—Mr. Let's Do It Now

Eric had already taken a 1*R* loss that amounted to 11 percent of his account on this position.

Situation 2: South Korean ETF (EWY)

EWY, the South Korean ETF, basically stopped its uptrend and went into a consolidation pattern for the first quarter of 2006. This meant that a nimble short-term trader could make profits, but a long-term trader had to either exit the position for something better or hope that the trend resumed after the consolidation period was over. On March 31, EWY closed at $46.65, while fluctuating between a low of $43.01 on March 7 and a high of $47.60 on February 27.

Figure 12.20 shows a daily candlestick chart for EWY during the last part of 2005 and the first quarter of 2006. Notice the nice consolidation pattern.

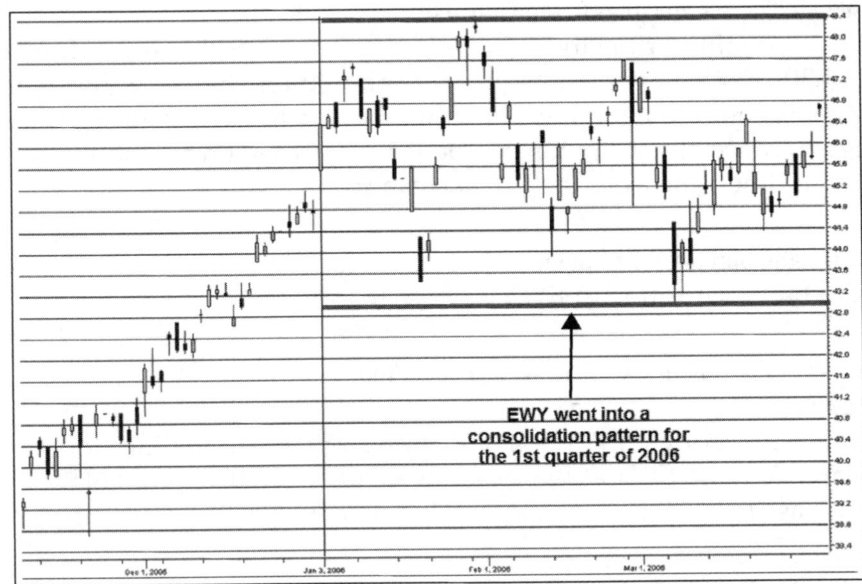

Figure 12.20 Daily candlesticks for EWY, the South Korean ETF through March 31, 2006

So let's look at how our investors did.

Mary—the Long-Term Trend Follower

Mary had a long position in EWY at 41.1. Nothing changed during the consolidation period. So on March 31 she was still long with EWY closing at $46.65. She had about a 2.25*R* profit on March 31.

Dick—the Short-Term Swing Trader

Dick bought at $44.20 with a fairly tight stop. On February 24, his deadline for closing out the position, he was able to take half of it off at $46.80 for 2.6*R* profit. He raised his stop to break even. On February 25, he raised his stop to $46.80 and was stopped out the next day. As a result, he took a 2.6*R* profit on his entire position.

Victor—the Value Trader

Victor had no position in EWY.

Ellen—There's an Order to the Universe

Ellen bought her position on February 20 at $46.35 with a stop at $44.20. EWY never went much higher than that so Ellen was stopped out the next day. She vowed never to trade country ETFs again, especially when her prediction was based on an entirely different time zone from the one she can trade.

Ken—the Spreader-Arbitrager

Ken had no position in EWY.

Nancy—the Businesswoman Who Follows Top Newsletters

Nancy had bought EWY at $41.30 with a 25 percent trailing stop. On March 31, with EWY at $46.65, she was still in it with a profit of $5.35. If we assume that she got out that day, then her profit was about 0.5*R*.

Eric—Mr. Let's Do It Now

Eric had a $211 profit in EWY on March 31. Since his entire investment was at risk, that amounted to a profit of about 0.05*R*.

Situation 3: Westwood One (WON)

WON continued to slide through March 31. In fact, on February 24, just as Ellen predicted, it took a huge plunge.[11] Between February 17 and March 31 the high was $14.66 on February 22 and the low was $10.90 on March 30. The nice downtrend is illustrated by the daily candlestick bars shown in Figure 12.21.

So let's look at how our investors did.

Mary—the Long-Term Trend Follower

Mary had a short position in WON at $24.80. Since WON closed at $11.04 on March 31, she had a nice profit of $13.76 per share. And since her initial stop was about $4, her total profit was about 3.44*R*.

Dick—the Short-Term Swing Trader

Dick was looking for a short opportunity at $13.70. Since WON gapped through that area down to about $12, he never had a chance to enter. As a result, Dick missed this trade opportunity.

Figure 12.21 Daily candlesticks for Westwood One (WON) through March 31, 2006

Victor—the Value Trader

Victor had shorted WON at \$18.40 with a stop \$2.70 away at \$21.10. At the March 31 close price of \$11.04, Victor had a profit of 2.73*R*.

Ellen—There's an Order to the Universe

Ellen predicted a dramatic price change on February 24, but she didn't know the direction. Her gut feeling was that it would be down, and she planned to buy on a move below \$13.80. Just like Dick, she missed the trade because the price gapped down to about \$12. Ellen was really upset because she was right about the position but couldn't trade it. However, that's one of the problems that people who trade through predictions often face.

Ken—the Spreader-Arbitrager

Ken was able to keep his entire credit spread of \$2.10 for a 4.25*R* profit.

Nancy—the Businesswoman Who Follows Top Newsletters

Nancy had shorted WON at $16 with an initial risk of $3.20. At the close on March 31, she had a profit of $4.96, giving her a 1.55*R* profit.

Eric—Mr. Let's Do It Now

Eric, of course, had bought WON. By March 31 he had a total loss of $3.39 per share. However, since his risk was the total purchase amount of $14.43, his loss was 0.23*R*. He had risked 4 percent of his account in this trade so his account was already down 1 percent.

Situation 4: Toll Brothers (TOL)

Toll Brothers had been in a down pattern that ended on February 7, followed by a short consolidation period through February 14. It then started to move up, but it wasn't clear whether the consolidation was becoming a little wider or if a new uptrend was starting. As a result, Toll Brothers was probably the most difficult stock to trade of the five. Three of our traders were looking for downward moves while two of them were long. What actually happened was that TOL started trading in a channel with an upward bias. The channel showed highs on February 23, March 17, and March 27. It showed lows on February 14 and on March 10. And on March 31 TOL closed at $34.63. Figure 12.22 shows the slight upward trend in TOL during this period.

So let's look at how our investors did.

Mary—the Long-Term Trend Follower

Mary had a short position in TOL at $35.30 with a stop at $44.88. As TOL fell, her stop got as low as $38.20. However, when TOL started going up, her stop remained at $38.20. As of March 31, with TOL closing at $34.63, Mary actually still had a small profit of 0.67 per share. If we assume that she closed it out that day, her total profit would be 0.07*R*.

Dick—the Short-Term Swing Trader

Dick had already sold out of half his short position in TOL at a gain of 1*R*. And he had locked in a 0.8*R* profit on the remaining half of

Figure 12.22 Daily candlesticks for Toll Brothers (TOL) through March 31, 2006

his position with his stop at $30.80. And on February 22, he was stopped out of his remaining shares. Thus, Dick's average profit on this trade was 0.9*R*.

Notice that both professionals profited on the short trade even though the stock moved up from March 10 onward.

Victor—the Value Trader

Victor had no position in TOL, but he had thought about it for a future value play.

Ellen—There's an Order to the Universe

Ellen was able to buy the stock at $29.87 on February 17. She was also able to sell the stock at her target price of about $34 on March 23—actually getting $34.20. Since Ellen's risk ended up being $1.87 per share, her profit amounted to a gain of 2.3*R*.

Ken—the Spreader-Arbitrager

Ken was able to capture nearly his entire $5.00 profit target by the time the options expired. His net gain was $4.90. And since his initial risk was the $0.40 on the debit spread, his gain of $4.90 was a 12.25*R* gain.

Nancy—the Businesswoman Who Follows Top Newsletters

Nancy's newsletters did not mention TOL so she did not buy it.

Eric—Mr. Let's Do It Now

Eric, of course, did his first short on TOL. He shorted it at $30.15. Thus, when TOL closed at $34.63 on March 31, Eric had a loss of $4.48 per share. When you compare that with his entire risk of $30.15, his loss was about 0.15*R*. Eric had invested about 12 percent of his portfolio in this stock, so he was down about 1.8 percent on this trade.

Situation 5: Phelps Dodge (PD)

Phelps Dodge did resume its uptrend, but not without making a new low for the quarter of $130.28 on March 8. It resumed its uptrend after splitting two for one on March 13. As of March 13 all of our investors-traders had twice as many shares at half the price. The split price is shown in Figure 12.23, but to avoid confusion, I'll continue to use the presplit price for calculating profits and losses and *R* multiples.

So let's look at how our investors did.

Mary—the Long-Term Trend Follower

Mary's long position on PD came nowhere near her stop at $118.70. As a result, when PD closed at an unadjusted split price of $161.06 on March 31, she had a profit of 4.2*R*. When you combine that profit with her other two gains, she was now up over 10.7*R* in this particular stock.

Dick—the Short-Term Swing Trader

Dick had the misfortune of having PD open up at his stop point the next morning. Thus, he was out immediately at a 1*R* loss on his short position.

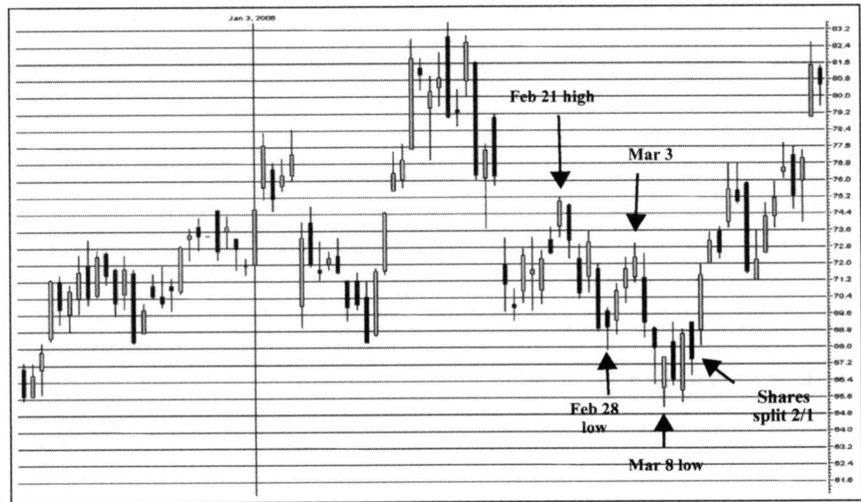

Figure 12.23 Daily candlesticks for Phelps Dodge (PD) through March 31, 2006

Victor—the Value Trader

Victor had a huge profit in this position by the time it closed on March 31. Since he got in at $44.50 and it closed on March 31 at $161.06, his total profit was $116.56 per share on the presplit price. That amounted to a 5.1*R* profit.

Ellen—There's an Order to the Universe

Ellen was long PD at $142.10 with an initial risk of $2. She was able to sell on February 21 at $150.20 for a profit of $8.10. And since her initial risk was $2, she had just over a 4*R* profit. She was very happy about this one.

Ken—the Spreader-Arbitrager

Ken found this to be a difficult trade. By February 28, it looked like he was going to take a loss. However, he held onto the option spread until just before expiration and was able to make his $4 profit. Since his risk was $1, that gave him a 4*R* profit.

Nancy—the Businesswoman Who Follows Top Newsletters

Nancy did very well with PD. She'd bought it at $72.80. It had not reached her large trailing stop; so by the time it closed at $161.06 on

March 31, she had a total profit of $88.26 per share. Since her initial risk was $18.20, that amounted to a 4.85*R* profit.

Eric—Mr. Let's Do It Now

Eric, of course, had bought his first puts on PD. These were March 145 puts, but when PD hit over $150, Eric panicked and sold out for a loss of $480. Since his total investment of $1,240 was at stake, we'll call his loss a 0.4*R* loss.

RESULTS AS *R* MULTIPLES

So let's look at all the results for each investor-trader as a set of *R* multiples and see what it says about their trading. This data is summarized in Table 12.6. Notice that all of them were profitable except Eric, who had no method, no plan, and no stops. Eric's trading was like a doctor's practicing medicine without going to medical school first. You just cannot do it and expect to be profitable, and, of course, Eric's results proved this.

The other traders were profitable despite having totally different ideas in many cases. Some were long on certain positions while others were short, but most of them managed to make money.

TABLE 12.6

Summary Results for All Seven Investors

Investor	GOOG	EWY	WON	TOL	PD	Total
Mary	+9.6*R*	+2.25*R*	+3.44*R*	+0.07*R*	+10.7*R*	+26.06*R*
Dick	+7.4*R*	+ 2.6*R*	No trade	+0.9*R*	−1*R*	+9.9*R*
Victor	+1.6*R*	No trade	+2.73*R*	No trade	+5.1*R*	+9.43*R*
Ellen	+1.8*R*	−1*R*	No trade	+2.3*R*	+4*R*	+7.1*R*
Ken	+2.5*R*	No trade	+4.25*R*	+12.25*R*	+4*R*	+23.0*R*
Nancy	No trade	+0.5*R*	+1.55*R*	No trade	+4.85*R*	+6.9*R*
Eric	−1*R*	+0.05*R*	−0.23*R*	−0.15*R*	− 0.4*R*	−1.73*R*
	(11%)		(1%)	(1.8%)	(2%)	

Mary was up a total of 26.06*R*, *including prior closed out trades in these stocks*. This amounted to well over a year's worth of trading, but she also had many other positions. And if you assume that her risk was about 1 percent per trade, then you can assume that her account was up about 20 percent in these five stocks.

Dick was a short-term trader. He made many, many trades, so those shown in the table are only a few examples. Most of his trades lasted less than a week, yet he was still up 9.9*R*. Even if we assume that he risked only 0.5 percent and made just these few trades, he would still be up over 7 percent over the six weeks. That amounts to a huge annual gain.

Victor's trades could last years and he only took three of the trades. Nevertheless, he was still up 9.43*R* in these trades. And Victor was seldom wrong about his trading so we can assume that his risk on each of these was over 2 percent. Thus, just these trades alone put him up over 19 percent, which was a lot of money considering the size of his portfolio. Furthermore, his GOOG trade amounted to nearly a 5 percent gain in six weeks, which wasn't bad for one he wasn't willing to keep.

Ellen has a loss and was not able to take one trade that she predicted perfectly. Nevertheless, she still had a method she believed in and that had proven itself for her. And she was up 7.1*R* in six weeks. At 1 percent risk per trade, that amounts to a very nice annual gain.

Ken was our star trader. He was up 23*R* in the six weeks from these trades alone and these were only a small sample of his trading.

Nancy wasn't expecting to make six figures from her account, and she didn't spend much time watching the markets. She risked about 1 percent per position so she was up about 7 percent in a year from these stocks. And since these were only a small portion of her yearly trades, she was quite happy with the result.

Contrast that with Eric who had no method and, most important, neither stops nor position-sizing awareness. On the first trade, he lost 11 percent of his account. And these trades totaled to about a 16 percent loss in his account in six weeks. However, trading is a business, and if you don't want to treat it like a business, then your learning expenses will be high indeed.

SUMMARY

Which methods appealed to you the most? The average person would probably say Ellen because of the lotto bias. Ellen can predict so well. But what Ellen does takes a lot of work. It's not any more valid than any of the other methods. And her predictions have nothing to do with making money. All she's doing is predicting the direction of the market. Didn't Mary do a fairly good job of that just by looking at the long-term trend? And notice that Ellen's performance is the weakest of the five professional traders with a total profit of 7.1*R*.

Every successful trader-investor tends to have the 10 traits described: (1) They have a well-researched, positive expectancy system. (2) Their system fits their personality, beliefs, and objectives, and they are comfortable with it. (3) They thoroughly understand the concept they are trading. (4) They understand that they must predefine their worst-case loss before they enter into the trade. (5) They think about each trade to determine the potential reward-to-risk ratio. (6) They have a business plan to guide their investing. (7) They understand that position sizing is the key to meeting their objectives. (8) They spend a lot of time working on themselves and use their trading performance as a benchmark for how they are doing in their self-development work. (9) They take total responsibility for their own trading results. And (10) they learn from their mistakes.

Seven traders were then presented: Mary, the trend follower; Dick, the band trader; Victor, the value investor; Ellen, the predictor; Ken, the spreader-arbitrager; Nancy, the newsletter follower; and Eric, who represents the average trader-investor.

You then learned how each of these traders-investors would approach five different market scenarios. And you then saw how those scenarios turned out six weeks later for each of them.

And you should now begin to understand how each trading system can be represented by the distribution of *R* multiples it generates, with the expectancy being the mean *R* multiple.

NOTES

1. The *amount risked* and the *amount invested* are not the same. For example, if you had a 25 percent stop and you risked $1,000, then your risk would be 25 percent of your total investment. Thus, if you risked

$1,000 in this particular case, your total investment would have been $4,000. If the price goes below your stop, you could lose up to 4*R* if the position suddenly went to zero overnight (that is, a 4*R* loss).

2. These concepts, except for the Delta Phenomenon®, were covered briefly in Chapter 5. The Delta Phenomenon® relates stock market behavior to the behavior of entities such as the sun and the moon.

3. Most newsletters will not give you an accurate track record. They'll tell you about how much you could have made investing in their recommendations, but that is not a track record. For example, a newsletter could say that we recommended ABC and readers watched it go up 400 percent. We also recommended XYZ and it went up 250 percent. People then see their portfolios going up that much—which never happens. In fact, a newsletter could give you some big winners of that nature and still be losing money for their subscribers. Consequently, if you adopt this approach, I recommend that you ask for at least one to two years of back issues and determine the expectancy of their recommendations for yourself. If they gave you at least 30 recommendations and their total expectancy times the number of opportunities they offer in a year is greater than 30*R*, then it's probably worth your consideration in the future.

4. You'll find we did some of that research for you in Chapter 13 just so that you can see the kinds of *R*-multiple distributions that various types of systems generate. What better way to show that than to show you the *R*-multiple distributions of various newsletters espousing various concepts.

5. Requiring that an external source convince you about each trade before you take it is not the sign of a good professional. You should know the expectancy of the method you are trading before you take the trade and that should be enough convincing.

6. Nancy is not an ideal trader-investor, but I included someone with her profile here because so many of the people who read this may be using a newsletter approach to trading. I don't think it's a good idea because you are dealing with someone else's idea of low-risk ideas. You also don't necessarily know whether the person who is making recommendations even understands many of the basic concepts in this book. For example, the only person I know who has given newsletter recommendations and then had the courage to report the results in terms of *R* is my friend, D. R. Barton, who wrote the band trading section of Chapter 5.

7. Six weeks later is not a lot of time. I actually picked all these situations because they seemed "interesting" at the time. When I picked them, I had no idea how they would turn out six weeks later. I was more interested to wear the belief filters of each of these traders to see how they would analyze the situation.

8. Google is a very volatile stock that needs to be watched closely. This price could easily move through his 2-point stop and produce a 2*R* to 3*R* loss or bigger. Since Dick tries to limit his risk in any position to about 1 percent and his initial stop was quite tight, he decided to only take a 0.5 percent risk.

9. A *put* is the right to sell a stock at a particular price. Thus, if Google were currently at $344, then a $360 put (that is, the right to sell GOOG at $360) would be worth $16 per share. So if the option were selling for $16, it would have no premium. And one reason it would have no premium is because that right would expire the next day, so there was only one full day and one partial day in which to make extra profit. However, one could also lose all of the current value in that same time period, so you would still have $16 worth of risk.

10. The *current assets* are what the company would be worth if you sold all of its assets within the next year. One measure of value is when you subtract the total debt of the company from the company's current assets. This gives you a rough idea of the liquidation value of the company, and for most companies this is not even a positive number.

11. These are all fictitious traders, and the magic dates for Ellen were PFA (plucked from air). My intention had been to joke a little about Ellen's predictions, so I was totally floored when there was a huge gap movement down on February 24. However, the irony was that Ellen didn't get to trade it, even though she predicted it, because it gapped through her entry point. I suspect this happens to a lot of people who use magic numbers to predict the market.

CHAPTER 13

Evaluating Your System

> Opportunity is missed by most people because it is dressed in overalls and looks like work.
>
> *Thomas A. Edison*

You have the essence of trading system design in the material covered so far in this book. Most people would be happy with just the material so far because it covers the areas that most people give all their focus to. But the two most important areas involving making money in the market still remain—the opportunity factor (along with the cost per opportunity) and the position-sizing factor.

The material we've covered to this point is really about *R* multiples and expectancy. What does your system look like in terms of *R* multiples? What's the mean *R* multiple? It's expectancy. You need to ask yourself, "How can I get the highest possible expectancy?" It's about how to obtain the most money per trade per dollar risked. Using our snow fight metaphor from Chapter 7, we've shown you how to make sure that the total volume of "white," or winning, snow arriving at any given time (on the average) is larger than the total volume of "black," or losing, snow.

Figure 13.1 shows one possible way of illustrating expectancy. Basically we have created a two-dimensional diagram. The x axis refers to the reliability of trading—the percentage of winning trades. The y axis refers to the size of the average reward compared

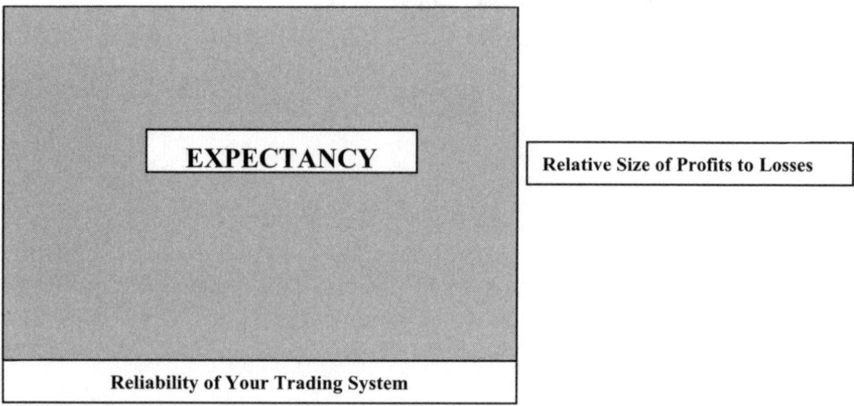

Figure 13.1 Expectancy illustrated as a two-dimensional figure relating the reliability of your system to the relative size of profits and losses. Hopefully, the area is a large positive number.

with the average risk—the size of your average winning trades compared with your average losing trades.

SEVERAL APPROACHES TO TAKE

If you've done a great job absorbing the material in the previous chapters, you should be able to come up with a system that has a positive expectancy. You might take any number of routes to get to that system. Here are some possible examples.

Trader 1: Long-Term Trend Following with a Large-*R*-Multiple Objective

Let's say that you decide you want to be a long-term trend follower and go for big-*R*-multiple trades. You decide to use an 80-day channel breakout as a setup. You then enter after a retracement, putting your stop just below the retracement. You have an initial profit objective of at least 10*R*. This means that either you get stopped out at a loss or you reach your 10*R* profit. Once your 10*R* profit is attained, you then have a 20 percent retracement stop—meaning that you are now willing to give back 20 percent of your profit before you'll get out.

This type of trading means that a 1*R* risk is very small for you. It means that you'll be stopped out frequently (that is, you'll have lots of losses), but that your gains will usually be *R* multiples of 10 or bigger. When you test your system, you will find that you make money on 28 percent of your trades but that your average gain is about 12 times the size of your average loss. These results give us an estimated expectancy of 2.58*R*—an excellent expectancy. However, some critical questions remain: How often will you get one of the 12*R* profits? Will it come once a year or once a week? How often will you be able to trade this system? And when you have a long losing streak, how big will the drawdowns be in terms of *R*?

Trader 2: The Standard Long-Term Trend Follower with a 40 Percent Reliability and 2.5:1 Reward-to-Risk Ratio

Or you might decide that you cannot tolerate the number of losses generated by the high-*R*-multiple approach just described. Instead, you decide to take more of a standard trend-following approach to the market. You decide to use an adaptive moving average as an entry and a three-times-volatility trailing stop—both to protect initial capital and to serve as a profit-taking exit.

In this case, your initial risk is much greater because it is three times the average daily range in prices. However, you discover after a lot of testing that your average loss is only 0.5*R*. You also discover that your average gain is 3.4*R* and that you make money on about 44 percent of your trades. When you work out your expectancy, you discover that your average trade will give you 1.22*R*. Again, you now have some critical questions to answer. How often will you be able to trade this system? How big will the drawdowns be in terms of *R*? And will you be satisfied with those results?

Trader 3: High-Probability, Low-*R*-Multiple Trading

You've decided that you really cannot tolerate the possibility of long losing streaks. Consequently, you need to be "right" at least 60 percent of the time. Furthermore, you are willing to sacrifice the size of your profits in order to be correct more often.

As a result, you decide to use a volatility breakout for an entry. You know that when you get a large move, it's likely to continue for a while. You decide that when the market moves either up or down by 0.7 times the average true range of the last five days, you'll enter.

You also test a lot of such entries, and you notice that the maximum adverse excursion against you is seldom more than 0.4 times the average true range. As a result, you decide to use that as your initial stop. You also are perfectly happy with 0.6 times the average true range as a profit objective because you determine that that objective is reached at least 60 percent of the time. In other words, either you get out at your stop with a loss or you take your profit objective.

When you calculate your expectancy here, you determine that you are likely to make 0.5*R* per trade on the average. However, this is a very active system, and when you subtract transaction costs, you determine that your expectancy is only 0.4*R*. The question you must now ask is, "Can I survive with only a 0.4*R* expectancy?" Do you generate enough trades, compared with the long-term trend followers, to compete with them for investment profits? And what kind of drawdowns can you expect in terms of *R*?

Trader 4: The Market Maker Who Gets the Bid-Ask Edge on Each Trade but Who Occasionally Gets Swept Along by the Market

Our last trader, who represents an extreme, is the market maker. This person tries to get the bid-ask spread on every trade that comes along. Let's say that the bid-ask spread represents a gain of about 8 cents per trade and that our trader gets it about 80 percent of the time. Another 15 percent of his trades are small losses of about 8 cents per trade. However, the last 5 percent of his trades represents the big losses (for him) that he sometimes needs to take when he gets swept along by the market. These losses might amount to 80 cents per trade.

When our last trader calculates his expectancy, he finds that it's about 0.15*R* (where *R* is typically 8 cents). After transaction costs, he clears about 0.11*R*. How does this particular person make a living? He probably does not have much chance compared with the person who knows how to make more than a dollar for every dollar risked. Or does he? And, last, what can our market maker expect in drawdowns in terms of *R*?

EXPECTUNITY: FACTORING IN OPPORTUNITY

Table 13.1 shows our four traders with their various expectancies. Initially, the trader with the largest expectancy seems clearly to be

TABLE 13.1

Expectancy, Cost, and Opportunity Factors for Our Four Traders

	Trader 1	Trader 2	Trader 3	Trader 4
Expectancy	2.58*R*	1.216*R*	0.5*R*	0.15*R*
After costs	2.38	1.02	0.4*R*	0.11*R*
Opportunity	0.05	0.5	5	500
Expectunity	0.119*R*	0.51*R*	2.0*R*	55*R*

the trader that one would expect to have the most success. Indeed, this trader's expectancy is far better than that of most long-term trend followers, so we would expect him to have a great track record. However, as we've shown previously, the opportunity factor clearly changes the element of expectancy. This is also illustrated in Table 13.1 in terms of the number of trades generated per day by the system.

Let's say that Trader 1 generates one trade on the average every 20 days. Trader 2 gets a trading opportunity every other day, while Traders 3 and 4 generate 5 and 500 trades per day, respectively. With that data, we can calculate the average *R* gain per day for each of the traders, as shown in Table 13.1. This is really expectancy times opportunity, which we'll call *expectunity* for short.

With that in mind, we find that the total advantage clearly belongs to the market maker. The market maker, if he is smart, should seldom have a losing day. If the average risk per trade were 0.25 percent of the trader's equity, then Trader 4 could make as much as 13 percent per day, while Trader 1 would make only 0.03 percent on his account each day.

I've had floor traders in my Super Trader program. One of them has never had a losing year and seldom had a losing month. Another turned $100,000 into $1.7 million in trading capital in just over three months. Another made up the entire cost of the Super Trader program in his first month of trading under my supervision. Is that an edge?[1]

Are you beginning to understand how profits are a function of the expectunity, or expectancy times the opportunity? The result is the total *R* profit, on the average, generated for the time period

Figure 13.2 Adding the dimension of opportunity

under consideration. The average total *R* profit, when combined with your position-sizing algorithm, tells you how much money you are likely to make in a given period of time.

Figure 13.2 is the expectancy figure with opportunity, in dark gray, as a third dimension. What you now have, as illustrated in the diagram, is a three-dimensional solid equaling the total *R* value generated by your trading system each day. The resulting profits no longer depend on a two-dimensional surface, but rather on a three-dimensional solid.

THE COST-OF-TRADING OPPORTUNITY

There is a definite cost of trading. The market maker has to get his edge. Your broker has to get her cost. And your profit is what remains, if anything, when these costs are deducted.

The cost per trade is really a part of the expectancy equation, but it is so important that I wanted to add a little more about cost reduction. The fewer trades you make, the less the cost per trade becomes a factor. Many long-term trend followers spend little time thinking about their trading cost because it is so insignificant compared with the potential profit to be made. For example, if you are thinking about making $5,000 per trade, then you probably are not paying much attention to trade costs of $5 to $100 per trade.

However, if you are short term in your orientation and make lots of trades, then trade cost is a bigger consideration for you, or at least it should be. For example, if your average profit per trade were $50, then you would pay much more attention to a $100 trading cost.

Commissions

Unless you need a specific service from your broker, you should pay attention to getting the best possible execution at the lowest possible cost. For example, stock traders can now do unlimited Internet trading for as little as a penny per share. This is a big drop from so-called discount brokers who used to charge $50 just to buy 100 shares of stock plus another $50 to sell those same 100 shares. However, you must be sure that (1) you are getting good execution at a reasonable price and (2) that your Internet broker will be available to you during highly volatile periods when you need to make a trade immediately.

Futures traders have long been able to get great commissions. Typically, a futures broker charges you only one price per *round turn*, which means getting in and getting out of a position. You can typically negotiate rates of $20 and under—sometimes much better depending on your volume of trading.

Execution Costs

Execution costs are the costs of getting into and out of a trade that are beyond the broker's commissions. These are typically the difference between the bid and the ask price (that is, the market maker's edge) and the cost of high volatility. When the market maker isn't sure he can get your position done at a profit (because the market is moving), your cost of execution will typically go up to cover his risk.

Some traders go to great lengths to control execution costs. For example, one of the traders interviewed in Jack Schwager's *The New Market Wizards* needed very low slippage in his trading methodology.[2] Originally, he executed through many brokers and kept track of the slippage he got on each trade through each broker. When the slippage got too high, a broker was typically replaced. Eventually, he decided that he needed to buy his own brokerage company just to be sure his orders were executed correctly.

If you are a short-term trader, then you probably need to give the same sort of attention to execution costs. What does it cost you to execute a trade? How can you lower those costs? Interview your broker carefully. Make sure that anyone who will handle your orders understands exactly what you are trying to accomplish. Proper execution for short-term traders could mean the difference between a solid profit and no profit.

Taxes

There is a third kind of cost on profits—the cost that the government imposes. The government regulates the trading business, and there is a cost of the government's involvement. Thus, there are exchange fees added to each transaction and to the cost of getting data. In addition, there is also the very real cost of the government taxing your profits.

Real estate investors have long been able to avoid some of these taxes on profits by filling out a Form 1031 and then buying another, more expensive piece of property. Furthermore, long-term stock investors (who seldom sell) such as Warren Buffett also avoid these taxes; you don't pay taxes on unrealized profits on your stock. Consequently, a major cost of doing business in the market can be avoided by sticking to real estate or being a long-term stock investor.

However, short-term traders must pay full taxes on their profits, and these taxes can be a significant cost. Futures traders, for example, have their open positions marked to the market at the end of the year and are required to pay taxes on their unrealized profits. Thus, you might have $20,000 on unrealized profits on December 31 that you get taxed on by the government. You later might end up giving back $15,000 of those open profits, but you will not get your taxes back until the next year when your actual profit on that trade is less.

Tax considerations obviously are an important part of the costs of a trading business. The overall topic is way beyond the scope of this book. Nevertheless, it is a real cost and it should go into your planning.

Psychological Costs

So far, we've been focusing on monetary costs, whether from your broker or the government. However, the psychological cost factor can be the most significant factor of all. And the more you trade, the more it comes into play.

Short-term trading, which gives you lots of opportunity, can have a large psychological cost. You always have to be in peak form; otherwise you will fail to open a potentially huge trade, or you will make a mistake that could cost you years of profits.

A number of times short-term traders have said to me, "I'm a day trader. I'm in and out a number of times each day. And I almost always make money each day. It's great! However, yesterday I gave back nearly a year's worth of profits, and I'm really upset." This is definitely a psychological problem. Such mistakes come either from big psychological blunders trading or from the psychological blunder of playing a negative expectancy game that wins most of the time but occasionally has huge *R* multiples against you.

Day trading can be very lucrative, frequently generating double-digit profits each month. But it is also very costly psychologically. If you have not spent a lot of effort working on yourself, then the financial costs of psychological mistakes can be devastating to you as a day trader.

Even long-term traders have a psychological factor to contend with. Long-term traders are usually successful because of a few high-*R*-multiple trades that they make each year. This kind of trader cannot afford to miss those good trades. When you miss your biggest trade of the year, quite often you might not have a profitable year. Again, the psychological factor comes into play!

One of my good friends, who is a professional trader, once told me that psychological factors didn't come into play when he and his partner were trading. They had a game plan worked out, and everything was very mechanical. I said the factors do come into play because you have to execute those trades. He agreed, but he still didn't think psychology was that important for their trading. Several years later, however, his partner got discouraged because they never made money trading the British pound. When a trade came up, they didn't take it. That trade turned out to be the one big trade that would have made their year. Their trading business closed down shortly afterward. The moral is that psychological factors always come into play in any sort of trading.

Let's say you have a system that generates, on the average, 80*R* worth of profits each year. But let's say that every mistake you make costs you 2*R* (this number doesn't come from research—I invented it) and you make one mistake each week. At the end of the year you will have made mistakes costing you 104*R*, which is more than the profit your system could have generated. In my opinion, this is why so many traders and investors lose money.

PEAK DRAWDOWNS

The next thing you need to understand about your system is the peak drawdown that it will generate during a year's worth of trading. When you reach an equity high, what's the biggest drawdown that you can expect to make? Or when you start trading, what's the peak drawdown that you can expect before you begin to make a profit? Hopefully, the latter will not happen. But it can, and if it does, what can you expect? The best way to consider that drawdown is in terms of *R*.

So what does it mean to express a drawdown in terms of *R*? Table 13.2 shows 40 trades from one of our marble games. This is the game with seven 1*R* losers, one 5*R* loser, and two 10*R* winners. Marbles are drawn out one at a time and replaced. Table 13.2 shows the marbles in the order they are drawn out and the drawdowns as they occur.

Since the expectancy of this system is 0.8*R*, we could expect the result of 40 trades to produce 32*R* in profits. Forty trades times 0.8*R* is equal to 32*R*. However, remember that expectancy is only the mean *R*. This means that half of our samples will be better, and half of them will be worse. Let's see how we did with this sample. We got seven 10*R* winners (one less than we might expect on the average). We got five 5*R* losers (one more than we'd expect on the average). And we got twenty-eight 1*R* losers, which is exactly what we might expect on the average. However, the result of having one less 10*R* winner and one more 5*R* loser is huge. The net result is that our total sample produced a result of 7*R*, instead of 32*R*. But remember that this is only one sample. In fact, when I simulated making forty trade samples 10,000 times from this *R*-multiple distribution, I discovered that I'd get a negative expectancy about 15 percent of the time. Thus, if you made forty such trades every month, you could expect 85 percent of your months to be profitable and 15 percent of your months to be losing months.

TABLE 13.2

Peak-to-Trough Drawdown in 40 Trades

Trade Number	*R* Result	Drawdown	Trade Number	*R* Result	Drawdown
1	1*R* loser	−1*R*	21	1*R* loser	−7*R*
2	1*R* loser	−2*R*	22	10*R* winner	
3	1*R* loser	−3*R*	23	10*R* winner	
4	1*R* loser	−4*R*	24	1*R* loser	−1*R*
5	10*R* winner		25	5*R* loser	−6*R*
6	1*R* loser	−1*R*	26	1*R* loser	−7*R*
7	1*R* loser	−2*R*	27	1*R* loser	−8*R*
8	1*R* loser	−3*R*	28	1*R* loser	−9*R*
9	5*R* loser	−8*R*	29	1*R* loser	−10*R*
10	5*R* loser	−13*R*	30	1*R* loser	−11*R*
11	10*R* winner	−3*R*	31	1*R* loser	−12*R*
12	2*R* loser	−5*R*	32	1*R* loser	−13*R*
13	1*R* loser	−6*R*	33	1*R* loser	−14*R*
14	1*R* loser	−7*R*	34	5*R* loser	−19*R*
15	5*R* loser	−12*R*	35	1*R* loser	−20*R*
16	10*R* winner	−2*R*	36	1*R* loser	−21*R*
17	1*R* loser	−3*R*	37	10*R* winner	−11*R*
18	1*R* loser	−4*R*	38	1*R* loser	−12*R*
19	1*R* loser	−5*R*	39	10*R* winner	−2*R*
20	1*R* loser	−6*R*	40	1*R* loser	−3*R*

But now let's look at our drawdowns. Trades 1 through 4 are losers and result in a net 9*R* drawdown. Trades 6 through 10 are also losers, resulting in a much more serious 13*R* drawdown. Trades 12 through 15 result in a net 4*R* drawdown, and trades 17 through 21 result in a 5*R* drawdown. However, notice that winning trades 11 and 16 are not enough to take us out of the drawdown. Thus, trades 6 through 21 are all in a drawdown, and we must be able to survive that. However, that streak of 16 trades is not the worst. The worst drawdown occurs from trade 24 through trade 36 when we experience a total drawdown of 21*R*. The net result is that we must be able to survive a 21*R* drawdown in order to realize the positive expectancy that we eventually get from this sample.

TABLE 13.3

Expected Drawdowns in Terms of *R* for Our System

Drawdown	Probability, %
4*R*	100
12*R*	78
17*R*	50
23*R*	24
29*R*	10
35*R*	5
72*R*	Maximum

I also simulated 40 trades of this system 10,000 times to determine what the worst drawdowns were. Table 13.3 shows the results of that simulation. The median drawdown was 17*R*, so our 21*R* drawdown was a little worse than average. However, notice that we have 100 percent chance of a 4*R* drawdown with this system. And we have a 10 percent chance of getting a drawdown as big as 29*R*, while the maximum drawdown in our 10,000 simulations was 72*R*.

So what does this tell us? Based on the expectancy and the median drawdown, we can estimate that if we risked 1 percent per trade, we'd be up 32 percent at the end of 40 trades, but we might have to tolerate a 17 percent drawdown in order to get it. Don't you think it's valuable information to know what to expect from your system in terms of drawdowns?

Let's look at our four traders presented in Table 13.1 for the drawdowns they might produce in 100 trades. This information is given in Table 13.4.

TABLE 13.4

Expectancy and Drawdowns after 100 Trades for Our Four Traders

	Trader 1	Trader 2	Trader 3	Trader 4
Expectancy	2.58*R*	1.216*R*	0.5*R*	0.15*R*
Drawdown	11*R*	3.5*R*	16*R*	21*R*

Notice here that our day trader has the largest drawdown potential after 100 trades. The larger the drawdown potential, the more you have to be careful of possible ruinous losses.

USING NEWSLETTER RECOMMENDATIONS AS SAMPLE SYSTEMS

To conclude this chapter, I thought you'd find it interesting to look at the recommendations generated by various newsletters as sample trading systems. In doing so, I wanted to (1) determine if newsletters as a whole represented good systems, (2) determine if certain trading ideas were better than others, and (3) give you some information about what you can expect if you follow the recommendations of various newsletters. In order to do this, I approached three groups of newsletters. I told them I would only mention the names of the newsletters if they did well. Two of the groups were eager to cooperate and sent us the data we needed to calculate and analyze their *R* multiples over a large number of years. The head of one group, Porter Stansberry, even said to me, "You can mention the names of all of our newsletters. If we have one that isn't any good, then we'll just close it down." In contrast, another group leader said, "We have no idea what our performance is, and we certainly wouldn't want you to mention the names of our newsletters if we don't look good." These newsletters were all involved in options strategies, and we elected not to even look at them.

Data Analysis

For each newsletter we took the entry date and price and the stop recommended by the newsletter. Most of the newsletters we looked at had 25 percent trailing stops. However, if the newsletter didn't have a stop, we made the assumption that the initial risk was 25 percent of the entry price. Thus, if the stock went to zero, it would present a 4*R* loss, and if the stock doubled in value, it would represent a 4*R* gain. Some of the newsletters make only one recommendation each month (or less), and they tend to hold on to their recommendations. As a result, we assumed that all active positions were closed on June 30, 2006, and we took the closing price on that date as the exit price. For several of them, we only had data through March 31, 2006, so that date was taken as the closing date.

For each newsletter, we calculated several key variables. What was the expectancy of the recommendations for the entire data set we had? How many positions were opened per month on the average? We used that data to determine how many trades to expect in a two-year period so that we could calculate the expectunity of each newsletter. And last, we used a proprietary measure to determine how well one could use position sizing with the recommendations in order to meet one's objectives.

The Newsletters

I generally looked at newsletters published by *Stansberry Research*, the *Oxford Club*, plus two that one of my clients was happy to evaluate for me. Here's some specific information about each one, listed alphabetically.

Blue Chip Growth This newsletter is put out monthly by a portfolio manager. It's designed to give you his best picks, and these are all stock picks that you should hold onto for at least a year. The newsletter was tracked from the end of December 2003 to March 2006. During that time there were 32 recommendations that were closed out. In this case, we didn't look at open positions. This newsletter did not give stops, so we assumed that a 25 percent drop was equivalent to 1*R*. This newsletter also does *not* track its own performance by showing the initial recommended price along with the current price.

Diligence *Diligence* reminds me of a stock analyst's top picks. The editor looks for microstocks that have new products (that is, usually in a research stage) that he believes could have a major impact on the consumer. He holds a monthly conference call with the CEO and other representatives of the company once the stock is recommended. *Diligence* doesn't recommend any stop loss (so we used 25 percent of the entry price to determine 1*R*), and it will hang on to losers for a long time if the editor thinks there is still potential (that is, even after it has dropped a long way). We tracked this newsletter from January 2001 through March 2006. During that time there were

36 recommendations, of which 44.4 percent made money. Of the original recommendations, 22 were still in the portfolio. However, for our calculations we assumed they were closed on March 31, 2006. *Diligence* closed down shortly after we did our analysis.

Extreme Value *Extreme Value* focuses on various value models for picking stocks. The basic investment idea is to find stocks that are extremely undervalued. For example, the editor has found stock that has land selling for thousands of dollars listed on their accounting books at $120 per acre. No stops are given for these stocks, so we assumed that 1*R* was a 25 percent drop in price. We tracked this newsletter from September 2002 through June 2006. During that time the editor made 37 recommendations, and he was still in 21 of them, so we used the June 30, 2006, price to assess the *R* multiples of those trades.

Inside Strategist This newsletter makes the assumption that when insiders of major companies are buying their stock in a big way, then the stock is probably a great buy. We tracked the newsletter from March 2004 through June 2006. During that time there was a trade recommendation each month for a total of 27 positions. We also included the editor's "special holdings" recommendations for an additional 6 positions. This newsletter was still holding on to 58 percent of the recommendations over the two years. Again, we used a 25 percent decrease in price as the initial risk.

MicroCap Moonshots This letter was started by a young man who decided to find efficient stocks that were microcaps. Small stocks tend to move a lot more than large-cap stocks, so this idea has the potential for some real "home run stocks." We followed this newsletter from October 2003 through June 2006. The original editor left on March 18, 2005, with the words, "The choppy market conditions of the last few months could drive a person to drink. Who's with me?" The next week he was replaced with another editor who has been handling the letter since that time. There are clear stops with this newsletter, which we followed in assessing the *R* multiples.

Oxford Club Communiqué This newsletter represents the recommendations of a number of different people, so it is somewhat eclectic.

This was the first newsletter I know of to institute a clear stop-loss policy, using 25 percent trailing stops (on a close-only basis) to control losses and tell them when to take profits. The newsletter has several different portfolios. However, we tracked only one of them, the *Oxford Club Trading Portfolio*. In addition, one of the people who makes regular recommendations to that newsletter always recommends buying a stock and selling a call against it. I don't approve of this strategy because the profits are limited to the amount of money you get from the call, while the downside is the total price of the stock less the cost of the call. As a result, we did not include these trades in our analysis. We tracked 166 recommendations made between September 1999 and June 30, 2006. Of those positions, 27 were still open so we used the price on June 30, 2006, to determine the *R* multiple of those positions.

Porter Stansberry's Investment Advisory (PSIA) Porter's recommendations are mostly momentum stocks that he likes. We tracked his recommendations from July 1998 through June 2006. During that 93-month period, we tracked 175 recommendations, and we included the 12 that were still open at their price on June 30, 2006. Here we used Porter's stops.

True Wealth *True Wealth* is one of the more popular newsletters in the United States with over 70,000 subscribers. The editor is Steve Sjuggerud who was a coauthor with me on *Safe Strategies for Financial Freedom*. I understand Steve's investment strategy quite well because I interviewed him for my own newsletter several years ago. Basically, Steve is looking for investments that everyone else hates and that have limited downside potential and great upside potential. And he's also adopted one of my beliefs in that his recommendations must be moving up before he makes them.

An Expensive Unnamed Newsletter The last newsletter we looked at I won't name, because its track record is terrible. I will say that it is the most expensive newsletter that we tracked, costing more than all the other newsletters combined. It gives weekly trades by e-mail with the idea of going for 100 percent growth or more. The editor who writes it is great at marketing, so if you are on his list, you'll be told that (1) he's got a secret system for picking stocks; (2) while some of his other newsletters might make 100 percent or more, this one is designed to be the best of the best; (3) he's one of the top-ranked newsletter writers in the world according to an independent source. A typical marketing pitch might say, "We're up 50 percent in XYZ, 67 percent in ABC, and 42 percent in QRF!" and go on to claim how excited his subscribers are about his performance. I was actually on a teleconference with him, and I asked him two questions: (1) If your performance is so good, why don't you track it in your newsletter? (2) Why do you sometimes lower your stops from one week to the next? He totally ignored both questions.

The Performance of the Newsletters

Table 13.5 shows the overall performance of the newsletters. It gives the total number of trades, the expectancy, the expectunity of the method over two years, and my proprietary evaluation of how likely you are to be able to meet your objectives using position sizing.[3] With this indicator, a system that significantly makes money at the 0.05 percent level would have a rating of about 1.

TABLE 13.5

Newsletter Analysis

Newsletter	Trades	Win Rate, %	Expectancy	Expectunity (in 2 years)	Proprietary Measures
Blue Chip Growth	32	36.5	0.05	1.37*R*	0.21
Diligence	36	44.4	1.67	22.37*R*	1.17
Extreme Value	37	89.1	1.40	27.06*R*	2.99
Inside Strategist	27	48.1	0.35	8.4*R*	1.47
MicroCap Moonshots	79	49.4	0.28	16.09*R*	1.59
Oxford Club	168	54.2	0.79	38.84*R*	2.17
PSIA	174	48.0	0.61	26.68*R*	1.65
True Wealth	77	67.5	0.68	21.68*R*	2.54
An expensive unnamed newsletter	241	36.5	−0.01	−2.2*R*	−0.05

A rating above 2 is very good, and a rating above 3 is superb. However, at one of our workshops we teach some systems that have ratings above 5.

The two value-oriented newsletters came out with the highest win rates and with our proprietary measure, meaning that you are more likely to meet your objectives with these newsletters with proper position sizing. Both of these newsletters still had a high percentage of active trades—57 percent with *Extreme Value* and 29 percent with *True Wealth*, which we have been tracking much longer.

The *Oxford Club Communiqué* came in with the highest expectunity over two years. It showed a total *R* gain of 38.84*R* over two years. Thus, at 1 percent risk per position, you probably could have easily made 20 percent or more each year with this newsletter.

Diligence showed the highest expectancy at 1.67. This is because it hit a few home runs, as was its intention. However, it also had a number of stocks that lost 50 percent or more and are still in the portfolio. Because of the large performance variability, *Diligence* didn't have very high rankings in any of the other categories. It could be a much better newsletter if some of the techniques suggested in this book were used with it. However, some of the home run stocks might have stopped out before they became home runs had such stops been in place. *Diligence* is no longer an active newsletter as it was closed down shortly after we did the analysis.

These newsletters all represent different types of ideas, and most of them made pretty good profits. The value-oriented newsletters seemed to perform best, but that doesn't mean that value investing is a better concept than trend following. Look at the system of buying stocks that hit all-time new highs described in Figure 9.2. That system produces an expectunity of 429*R* in two years. However, the key problem you'd face is the large number of simultaneous trades. You might be able to risk only 0.1 percent or less on each trade. I've also seen some trend-following systems with systems quality numbers that are off the charts (that is, above 5.0). Thus, I don't think that the newsletter data proves that the value concepts are better than any other concept.

What was quite surprising was the negative expectancy produced by the most expensive newsletter that was evaluated. What can be learned from that? Well, that newsletter did not track its own performance. If you decide to subscribe to a newsletter, be wary of any that don't give you regular performance updates. Incidentally, the expensive newsletter just offered a promotion in which they "guaranteed" that you'd get your money back after a year if you didn't make $1 million trading their recommendations over the next year (that is, 2007). Given their track record over the 241 trades, what do you think the odds are of making $1 million? By the way, I tried three times to get my money back from them in 2005 and hit a roadblock each time.

Conclusions

If you want a newsletter-following system, you still must find a newsletter with trading concepts and an overall strategy that fit your beliefs. I'd also recommend that you do the same kind of analysis that I did here for each newsletter you plan to follow. This means that (1) they must make back issues available to you and (2) they must track their own performance. If you talk to a newsletter editor and he or she doesn't even know his or her track record (that is, it is not likely that they'll tell you that), then run for the hills. Better yet, see if the newsletter publishes a list of their past recommendations along with the entry price, the initial risk, and the exit price. You can determine the *R* multiples and expectancy on your own from that.

If you do decide to follow the recommendations of any newsletter, remember that most of them will not tell you about position sizing (see Chapter 14), and none of them can tell you about the impact of your psychology on the trading. If the newsletter can produce 20*R* worth of profits each year, but you make 10 mistakes that cost you 2*R* each, then you won't make any money following that advice.

SUMMARY

Most of this book has been about developing a high-expectancy trading system. Expectancy is a two-dimensional surface related to the reliability of your trading system and the relative size of profits and losses.

Opportunity to trade makes a third dimension that gives volume to your dollars in profits or losses. You must multiply the opportunity factor by the expectancy factor to get your potential volume of dollars that you could reap each day. Thus, a high expectancy doesn't necessarily translate into a high dollar volume each day if you don't make many trades.

Last, there is a cost to trading that must be subtracted from the dollar volume each day. This cost is usually figured into the expectancy. However, there are a number of costs to trading, and each should be given some consideration. Reducing any one of them could have a major effect on your bottom line. The four major types of costs are brokerage commissions, execution costs, tax costs, and psychological costs. Each was discussed briefly.

In this chapter we also reinforced the idea that a trading system is a distribution of *R* multiples, described by its expectancy. To do so, we evaluated the recommendations of nine different newsletters, each representing a different trading concept. We showed you the performance of each in terms of expectancy, expectunity over two years, and how good the system was for meeting your particular objectives through position sizing. The newsletter analysis shows, as I have suggested throughout this book, that there are many good ways to make money in the markets.

NOTES

1. Most floor traders never make it. They go bankrupt (or at least lose their capital) within a year or two because they don't understand what their edge is or they don't know how to capitalize on it. In addition, they are seldom risking 0.5 percent of their total equity per trade.
2. Jack Schwager, *The New Market Wizards* (New York: HarperCollins, 1992).
3. While I don't wish to reveal my proprietary indicator in this book, it is highly correlated with the Sharpe Ratio. Furthermore, our research shows that the higher the ranking with this indicator, the easier it is to use position sizing to meet your objectives.

CHAPTER 14

Position Sizing—the Key to Meeting Your Objectives

When I get a 30 percent profit, I take a third. When I get a 50 percent profit I take another third. When I get a pattern to the reverse, I'll take the rest of the profit.

Quoted from a lecture on money management at a seminar on stock trading

The most important aspect of system development, other than psychology, is the topic of how much to invest in any given position. Yet most books that talk about trading or system development completely neglect the topic. And when they do talk about it, it's usually called *money management* or *asset allocation*. Yet most of the time, when these two terms are used, they mean something other than "how much." That says to me that the majority of "experts" on the market really don't understand one of the most important aspects of success in the market.

Look at the quote at the start of this chapter. The instructor made that statement at a stock market seminar to train brokers, with the title "Money Management," telling me that the quote described his formula for money management. However, in my opinion, what he said has nothing to do with money management. Instead, it has everything to do with exits.[1] Later, after the seminar, I approached him to ask him what he meant by money management. His response was, "That's a very good question. I think it's how one makes trading decisions."

Portfolio managers tend to talk about "asset allocation" as being important for their success. Now think about the words *asset allocation*. What do they mean to you? Chances are, you think they mean what asset class to select for your assets. This is what it means to most portfolio managers because by charter they must be fully (at least 95 percent) invested. Thus, they think of asset allocation as a decision about which asset class to select. Was this your definition?

Brinson and his colleagues defined *asset allocation* to mean how much of one's capital was devoted to stocks, bonds, or cash.[2] When they defined it that way, they discovered that asset allocation, and not the what-to-buy decision, accounted for 91.5 percent of the performance variability of 82 pension plans over a 10-year period. As a result, portfolio managers and academics have started to stress the importance of asset allocation. Although Brinson and his colleagues found that stock selection and other types of decisions were not that significant to the performance, the lotto bias causes many people to continue to think that asset allocation means selecting the right asset class. Yet what's important is the how-much decision, not the investment selection decision.

Let me reemphasize that what's important about money management or asset allocation is not any of the following:

- It is not that part of your system that dictates how much you will lose on a given trade.
- It is not how to exit a profitable trade.
- It is not diversification.
- It is not risk control.
- It is not risk avoidance.
- It is not that part of your system that tells you what to invest in.

Instead, what's important about money management or asset allocation is that it is the part of your trading system that answers the question "How much?" throughout the course of a trade. "How much" essentially means how big a position you should have at any given time throughout the course of a trade. Furthermore, it is the key

> What's important about money management or asset allocation is that it is the part of your trading system that answers the question "How much?" throughout the course of a trade.

variable in determining whether or not you'll meet your objectives as a trader. And to avoid any confusion, I've been calling it "position sizing" throughout this book.

In the process of answering the question "How much?" you may have to consider some of the issues mentioned above, but those issues are not your position-sizing algorithm. For some of you, elements like risk control may seem more important than deciding how much.[3] But the question of "how much" accounts for most of the variability in the performance of various professional traders.

In 1997, I traveled for Dow Jones giving lectures in major cities throughout Asia on position sizing and psychology to hundreds of professional traders. We played a game in which I illustrated the importance of position sizing. This was a marble game in which marbles, representing the *R* multiples of a trading system, were randomly pulled out of a bag and replaced. Seven marbles were 1*R* losers, one was a 5*R* loser, and two of them were 10*R* winners. The game has an expectancy of 0.8*R*, even though it loses 80 percent of the time. The audience is given $100,000 in play equity and told to risk whatever they thought was appropriate on each marble pull over 40 trades. In other words, they all get the same trades, the same marbles that are randomly pulled out of the bag. Yet at the end of the game, each member of the audience usually has a different ending equity. And those equities might range from bankrupt to over $1 million (that is, up 1,000 percent in 40 trades). This confirms the observations of Brinson and his associates that the how-much factor accounts for over 90 percent of the variance of performance because the only factors involved in this game were how much and the personal psychology of the participants. And I've repeated these results hundreds of times.

My demonstration usually convinces the people in the audience that position sizing is important. Yet when I suggested to the Asian traders that a reasonable solution on how to effectively use position sizing was to base the position sizes on their equity, I discovered that *none* of these professional traders knew how much money they were trading. They were simply trading the "firm's" money, and they had no idea how much it was. As a result, I then asked, "So how much money would you have to lose to lose your job?" Basing position sizing on the amount of money they would have to lose to lose their jobs was another reasonable way to do it, but I discovered that only about 10 percent of my audience of professional traders even knew how big a loss they could make before they lost their job. This meant that thousands of professional traders had no means upon which to base their position sizing. Yet each of them was probably trading millions of dollars. And I observed the same finding in city after city and lecture after lecture.

About three years ago, I gave similar lectures to hedge fund managers and portfolio managers all over the world. I discovered that most of them, at least those who were portfolio managers or who had come into the hedge fund world as a former portfolio manager, had no prior education in position sizing. In fact, many of them thought that position sizing was an insignificant factor because they believed that they needed to be at least 90 percent invested in the market at all times.

Although position sizing and your personal psychology are the two key factors you must master if you want success in the market, let me stress how little they are emphasized by Wall Street, Main Street, or Academia.

- If you are trained as a broker for any major brokerage company, you will have no training on position sizing or in the psychology of trading the markets. Most of your training will be in regulations of the stock exchanges, what products the firm offers, and how to sell those products to customers or potential customers. For example, you have to pass a Series 7 exam to become a licensed broker, but none of the information on the exam has to do with position sizing or the psychology of trading.
- If you become a certified financial planner (CFP), you'll again have no training in personal psychology or in position sizing.

Notice that the last two categories are people that the public believes are experts in the market. These are the people that they go to for advice. So who else could you turn to for advice?

- If you get an MBA from a top university with a specialty in how the markets work, you'll have no training on position sizing and very little training in the psychology of trading.
- If you get a Ph.D. in finance from a top university, you'll again have no training on position sizing. You might have some training in behavioral finance, but even that has little to do with the impact of your personal psychology on your trading results.
- If you become a certified financial analyst (CFA), you'll receive no training in position sizing or in the effect of your personal psychology on your trading performance. Most analysts don't even know how to trade the market because their training is designed to help them figure out whether or not a company will do well in the future.
- And if you get trained to be a professional trader for a bank or a major firm, the same is true. Yes, you guessed it: you'll receive no training in position sizing and little advice on the effect of your personal psychology on your success in the market. In fact, as I mentioned above, most traders don't even know how much money they'd have to lose before they would lose their jobs.

Thus, it is not surprising that most books on investing and almost all the exposure you'll get from the media on successful investing will ignore the critical topics of position sizing and personal psychology.

You've already heard how position sizing accounts for most of the variability of performance of professional traders. But just in case you are not yet convinced, let's look at position sizing logically. Remember the snow fight model described in Chapter 7? Well, position-sizing models include two factors from that metaphor. Those factors are the size of the initial protection (that is, the size of the snow wall or your starting equity) and the number of snowballs that come at the wall at one time (that is, how many positions you have on at one time).

Figure 14.1 gives an illustration of how position sizing adds one more step in determining the total dollar volume that you must consider. Recall that Figure 13.2 created a three-dimensional box that added opportunity to expectancy. Figure 14.1 shows that with

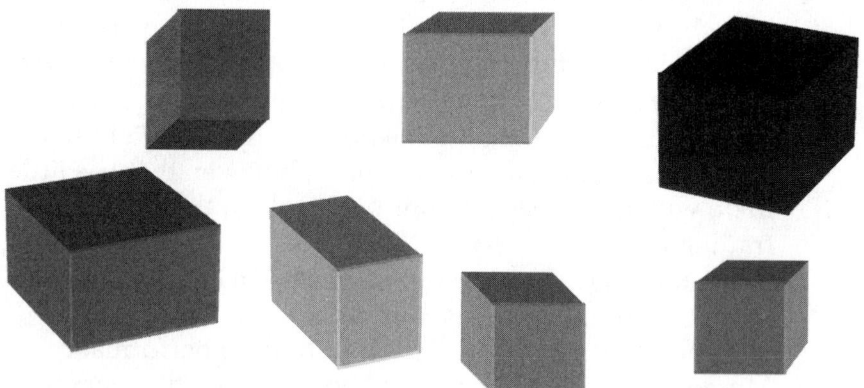

Figure 14.1 Position sizing has the effect of adding many simultaneous three-dimensional boxes to a situation at one time

position sizing, a fourth dimension must be added—the dimension of multiple, simultaneous positions in the market. Since drawing four dimensions is rather difficult, Figure 14.1 illustrates the effect of position sizing by showing that you can have many three-dimensional boxes affecting your position at one time. Expectancy gives you a two-dimensional square. Opportunity gives you a three-dimensional cube, or box. But position sizing gives you multiple boxes all coming at you at once. That's how important it is.

Just in case you are not yet a believer, let's look at one more illustration of the importance of position sizing to one's trading performance. Remember the Ralph Vince study described in Chapter 2? In that study, 40 Ph.D.s played a position-sizing game with a positive expectancy. However, 95 percent of them lost money. Why? The reasons had to do with their psychology and with poor position sizing.

Let's say you had a total of $1,000 and started the game risking $100. In fact, you do that three times in a row and you lose all three times—a distinct possibility in this game. Now you are down to $700, and you think, "I've had three losses in a row, so I'm really due to win now." That's the gambler's fallacy; your chances of winning are still just 60 percent. Anyway, you decide to bet $300 because you are so sure you will win. However, you again lose, and now you only have $400. Your chances of making money in the game are slim now because you must make 150 percent just to break even. Although the chances of four consecutive losses are slim in a 60 percent game—0.0256—it still is nearly certain to occur at least once in a 100-trial game.

Here's another way the Ph.D.s could have gone broke. Let's say they started out betting $250. They have three losses in a row totaling $750. They are down to $250. They now must make 300 percent just to get back to even, and they probably won't be able do that before they go broke.

In either case, the failure to profit in this easy game occurred because the person risked too much money. The excessive risk occurred for psychological reasons—greed, failure to understand the odds, and, in some cases, even the desire to fail. However, *mathematically their losses occurred because they were risking too much money.* For example, if 10 black snowballs that are collectively bigger than the wall are thrown at the wall simultaneously, then the wall will be destroyed. It does not matter how favorable the ratio of white to black snow is—10 black snowballs collectively bigger than the wall will destroy the wall.

The size of your equity is equivalent to the size of the wall in the snow fight metaphor. What typically happens is that the average person comes into most speculative markets with too little money. An account under $50,000 is small, but the average account is only $1,000 to $10,000. As a result, many people are practicing poor position sizing just because their account is too small. *Their mathematical odds of failure are very high just because of their account size.*

Look at Table 14.1. Notice how much your account has to recover from various-sized drawdowns in order to get back to even. For example, losses up to 20 percent require only a moderately larger gain (that is, no more than 25 percent bigger) to get back to even. But a 40 percent drawdown requires a 66.7 percent gain to break even, and a 50 percent drawdown requires a 100 percent gain. Losses beyond 50 percent require huge, improbable gains in order to get back to even. As a result, when you risk too much and lose, your chances of a full recovery are very slim.

BASIC POSITION-SIZING STRATEGIES

Professional gamblers have long claimed that there are two basic position-sizing strategies—martingale and anti-martingale.

TABLE 14.1

Recovery after Drawdown

Drawdowns, %	Gain to Recovery, %
5	5.3
10	11.1
15	17.6
20	25.0
25	33.0
30	42.9
40	66.7
50	100.0
60	150.0
75	300.0

Martingale strategies increase one's bet size when equity decreases (during a losing streak). *Anti-martingale strategies*, in contrast, increase one's bet size during winning streaks or when one's equity increases.

If you've ever played roulette or craps, the purest form of martingale strategy might have occurred to you. It simply amounts to doubling your bet size when you lose. For example, if you lose $1, you bet $2. If you lose the $2, then you bet $4. If you lose the $4, then you bet $8. When you finally win, which you will eventually do, you will be ahead by your original bet size.

Casinos love people who play such martingale strategies. First, any game of chance will have losing streaks. And when the probability of winning is less than 50 percent, the losing streaks could be quite significant. Let's assume that you have a streak of 10 consecutive losses. If you had started betting $1, then you will have lost $2,047 over the streak. You will now be betting $2,048 to get your original dollar back. Thus, your win-loss ratio at this point—for less than a 50:50 bet—is 1 to 4,095. You will be risking over $4,000 to get $1 in profits. And to make matters worse, since some people might have unlimited bankrolls, the casinos have betting limits. At a table that allows a minimum bet of $1, you probably couldn't risk more than $100. As a result, martingale betting strategies generally do not work—in the casinos or in the market.

If your risk continues to increase during a losing streak, you will eventually have a big enough streak to cause you to go bankrupt. And even if your bankroll were unlimited, you would be committing yourself to reward-to-risk strategies that no human being could tolerate psychologically.

Anti-martingale strategies, which call for larger risk during a winning streak, do work—both in the gambling arena and in the investment arena. Smart gamblers know to increase their bets, within certain limits, when they are winning.[4] And the same is true for trading or investing. Position-sizing systems that work call for you to increase your position size when you make money. That holds for gambling, for trading, and for investing.

Position sizing tells you how many units (shares or contracts) you are going to put on, given the size of your account. For example, a position-sizing decision might be that you don't have enough money to put on any positions because your allocation is too big for your account. It allows you to determine your reward and risk characteristics by determining how many units you will allocate to a given trade within the context of your portfolio. It also helps you equalize your trade exposure in the elements in your portfolio. Last, certain position-sizing models equate a 1*R* risk across all markets.

Some people believe that they are doing an adequate job of position sizing by having a "money management stop." Such a stop would be one in which you get out of your position when you lose a predetermined amount of money—say $1,000. However, *this kind of stop does not tell you "how much" or "how many," so it really has nothing to do with position sizing.* Controlling risk by determining the amount of loss if you are stopped out is not the same as controlling risk through a position-sizing model that determines how many or if you can even afford to hold one position at all.

There are numerous position-sizing strategies that you can use. In the remainder of this chapter, you'll learn different position-sizing strategies that work well. Some are probably much more suited to your style of trading or investing than others. Some work best with stock accounts, while others are designed for a futures account. All of them are anti-martingale strategies in that they are all based on your equity. What makes them anti-martingale strategies is that the formula they use for determining how much increases your position size as your account size grows. But remember that many professional traders who work for banks and various corporations don't even know how much money they can lose before their jobs are in jeopardy, much less how much money they are trading.

The material on position sizing is somewhat complex. However, I've avoided the use of difficult mathematical expressions and given clear examples of each strategy. As a result, you simply need to read the material carefully and reread it until you understand it thoroughly.

The System Used

In presenting the results of all these strategies, I've elected to use a single trading system: trading the same commodities over the same time period. The system is a 55-day channel breakout system. In other words, it enters the market on a stop order if the market makes a new 55-day high (long) or a new 55-day low (short). The stop, for both the initial risk and profit taking, is a 21-day trailing stop on the other side of the market.

To illustrate, let's say crude oil hits a 55-day high, and you go long. Now you stay in the position until the market makes a 21-day low. If that occurred quickly, then you would probably be stopped out and you would take a 1*R* loss. However, if the price goes up for 100 days and then backs off to hit a 21-day low, then you would probably have made a substantial profit. On the other side, if the market makes a 55-day low, you would go short. If you are short and the market makes a new 21-day high, you'd exit your position.

This 21-day channel breakout stop is recalculated each day, and it is always moved in your favor so as to reduce risk or increase your profits. Such breakout systems produce above-average profits when traded with sufficient money.

This system was tested with $1 million in start-up equity with a basket of 10 commodities over a 10-year period. Whenever futures data is presented in this chapter, it is based on this same 55-/21-day breakout system tested over the same commodities over the same years. The only difference between the tables is the position-sizing model used. However, every system and every data set chosen would probably produce different results for the different models.

This system was chosen for the purposes of this discussion because it was simple to program and convenient to use to illustrate the differences in the models.

MODEL 1: ONE UNIT PER FIXED AMOUNT OF MONEY

Basically, this method tells you "how much" by determining that you will trade 1 unit for every *X* dollars you have in your account. For example, you might trade 1 unit (for example, 100 shares or one contract) per $50,000 of your total equity.

When you started trading or investing, you probably never heard about position sizing for the reasons indicated earlier in this chapter. Consequently, your most logical thought was probably something like "I can afford only 1 unit." If you knew something about position sizing, your knowledge probably came from some book by an author who didn't understand the subject well. Most books that discuss money management, or asset allocation, are not about position sizing. Instead, they tell you about diversification or about optimizing the gain from your trading. Books on systems development or technical analysis don't even begin to discuss position sizing adequately. *As a result, most traders and investors have no place to go to learn what is probably the most important aspect of their craft.*

Thus, armed with your ignorance, you open an account with $20,000 and decide to trade one contract of everything in which you get a signal to trade (an equity investor might just trade 100 shares). Later, if you're fortunate and your account moves to $40,000, you decide to move up to two contracts (or 200 shares) of everything. Notice that your account had to double for you to increase your position sizing. As a result, most traders who do practice some form of position sizing use this model. It is simple. It tells you how much in a straightforward way.

The 1-unit-per-fixed-amount-of-money method has one "advantage" in that you never reject a trade because it is too risky. Let me give you an example of an experience of two traders I know. One of them trades one contract per $50,000 in equity. The other uses model 3, the percent risk model, and risks a very aggressive 3 percent of his equity, but he won't open a position in which his exposure is more than 3 percent of his account. Each trader saw an opportunity to trade the Japanese yen by his respective trend-following system. The person trading one contract no matter what took the trade. The subsequent move in the yen was tremendous, so this person was able to produce the biggest monthly gain that he'd ever experienced—a monthly 20 percent gain.

In contrast, the second trader couldn't take the trade. His account size was $100,000, but the risk involved exceeded his 3 percent limit if the trade went against him. The second trader did not have a profitable month.

Of course, this factor of always taking a trade also works in reverse. The first trader could have taken a huge (20 percent or more) loss if the yen trade had gone against him, which the second trader would have avoided.

Table 14.2 shows the results with this system using the first position-sizing model. Notice that the system breaks down at one contract per $20,000 in equity. At $30,000, you'd have to endure an 80 percent drawdown, and you'd have to have at least $70,000 if you wanted to avoid a 50 percent drawdown. What if your goal was to avoid big drawdowns and you decided that you would stop trading if you had a drawdown greater than 20 percent? You'd stop

TABLE 14.2

55-/21-Day Breakout System with 1 Contract per $X in Equity (starting equity is $1 million)

1 Contract per $X in Equity	Profits	Rejected Trades	Annual Gain, %	Margin Calls	Maximum Drawdown, %
$100,000	$5,034,533	0	18.20	0	36.86
$90,000	$6,207,208	0	20.20	0	40.23
$80,000	$7,725,361	0	22.30	0	43.93
$70,000	$10,078,968	0	25.00	0	48.60
$60,000	$13,539,570	0	28.20	0	54.19
$50,000	$19,309,155	0	32.30	0	61.04
$40,000	$27,475,302	0	36.50	0	69.65
$30,000	$30,919,632	0	38.00	0	80.52
$20,000	($1,685,271)	402	0	1	112.00

trading with all of the values shown in the table and end up with a loss. Therefore, it doesn't seem like a great model, but to really evaluate this position-sizing method, you'll have to compare it with the tables developed from the other models (see Tables 14.4 and 14.6).[5]

Despite its advantage of allowing you to always take a position, I believe that the 1-unit-per-fixed-dollars type of position sizing is limited because (1) not all investments are alike, (2) it does not allow you to increase your exposure rapidly with small amounts of money, and (3) you'll always take a position even when the risk is too high. This form of position sizing is dangerous! And last, the units-per-fixed-amount model, with a small account, amounts to minimal position sizing. Let's explore these reasons.

Not all investments are alike, but model 1 treats them that way. Suppose you are a futures trader and you decide you are going to be trading up to 20 different commodities with your $50,000. Your basic position-sizing strategy is to trade one contract of anything in that portfolio that gives you a signal. Let's say you get a signal for both bonds and corn. Thus, your position sizing says you can buy one corn contract and one bond contract. Let's assume that T-bonds are at $112 and corn is at $3.

With T-bond futures at $112, you are controlling $112,000 worth of product. In addition, the daily range at the time (that is, the volatility) is about 0.775, so if the market moved three times that amount in one direction, you would make or lose $2,325. In contrast, with the corn contract you are controlling about $15,000 worth of product. If it moved three daily ranges with you or against you, your gain or loss would be about $550. Thus, what happens with your portfolio will depend about 80 percent on what bonds do and only about 20 percent on what corn does. Obviously, this particular position-sizing model has nothing to do with total risk.

One might argue that corn has been much more volatile and expensive in the past. That could happen again. But you need to diversify your opportunity according to what's happening in the market right now. Right now, based on the data presented, one corn contract would have about 20 percent of the impact on your account that one bond contract would have.

Model 1 does not allow you to increase your exposure rapidly. The purpose of an anti-martingale strategy is to increase your exposure when you are winning. When you are trading one contract per

$50,000 and you have only $50,000, you will have to double your equity before you can increase your contract size. As a result, this is not a very efficient way to increase exposure during a winning streak. In fact, for a $50,000 account it amounts to almost no position sizing.

Part of the solution would be if you had a minimum account size of $1 million. If you did that, your account would have to increase by only 5 percent before you moved from 20 contracts (1 per $50,000) to 21 contracts.

With model 1 you'll always take a position, even when the risk is too high. The 1-unit-per-*X*-dollars model will allow you to take 1 unit of everything. For example, you could buy one S&P contract, controlling $125,000 worth of stock with a $15,000 account.[6] Let's say the daily volatility in the S&P is 10 points and you have a three-times-volatility stop, or 30 points. Your potential loss is $7,500, or half your equity. That is tremendous risk for just one position, but you could take that risk with the 1-unit-per-$*X* model of position sizing.

One reason to have a position-sizing strategy is to have equal opportunity and equal exposure across all the elements in one's portfolio. You want an equal opportunity to make money from each element of your portfolio. Otherwise, why trade those elements that are not likely to give you much profit? In addition, you also want to spread your risk equally among the elements of your portfolio.

Having equal opportunity and exposure to risk, of course, makes the assumption that each trade is equally likely to be profitable when you enter into it. You might have some way to determine that some trades are going to be more profitable than others. If so, then you would want a position-sizing plan that gives you more units on the higher-probability-of-success trades—perhaps a discretionary position-sizing plan. However, for the rest of this chapter, we're going to assume that all trades in a portfolio have an equal opportunity of success from the start. That's why you selected them.

The units-per-fixed-amount-of-money model, in my opinion, doesn't give you equal opportunity or exposure. But most good position-sizing methods do allow you to equalize the elements of your portfolio. These include model 2—equating the value of each element in the portfolio; model 3—equating the amount of risk (that is, how much you would lose when you got out of a position in order to preserve capital) in each element of the portfolio; and model 4—equating the amount of volatility of each element in the portfolio. Model 3 also has the value of equating what 1*R* means to each market despite the fact that you could set different risk levels for different positions.

MODEL 2: EQUAL VALUE UNITS FOR STOCK TRADERS

The *equal units model* is typically used with stocks or other instruments that are not leveraged or have minimal leverage. The model says that you determine how much by dividing your capital up into 5 or 10 equal units. Each unit would then dictate how much product you could buy. For example, with our $50,000 capital, we might have 5 units of $10,000 each. Thus, you'd buy $10,000 worth of investment A, $10,000 worth of investment B, $10,000 worth of investment C, and so forth. You might end up buying 100 shares of a $100 stock, 200 shares of a $50 stock, 500 shares of a $20 stock, 1,000 shares of a $10 stock, and 1,428 shares of a $7 stock. The position-sizing model involved in this strategy would be to determine how much of your portfolio you might allocate to cash at any given time. Table 14.3 shows how many shares would be purchased of each of the 5 stocks, each with a $10,000 investment.

Notice that there is some inconvenience in this procedure. For example, the price of the stock may not necessarily divide evenly into $10,000—much less into 100-share units. This is shown with stock E in which you end up buying 1,428 shares. This still does not equal $10,000. Indeed, with this example, you might want to round to the nearest 100-share unit and purchase 1,400 shares.

In futures, the equal units model might be used to determine how much value you are willing to control with each contract. For example, with the $50,000 account you might decide that you are willing to control up to $250,000 worth of each futures contract. And let's say you arbitrarily decide to divide that into 5 units of $50,000 each.

If a bond contract is worth about $112,000, then you couldn't buy any bonds under this position-sizing criterion because you'd be

TABLE 14.3

Distribution of Funds in Equal Units Model (each unit represents $10,000)

Stock	Price per Share	Total Shares	Total Dollar Amount
A	$100	100	$10,000
B	$50	200	$10,000
C	$20	500	$10,000
D	$10	1,000	$10,000
E	$7	1,428	$9,996

controlling more product than you can handle with 1 unit. On the other hand, you could afford to buy corn. Corn is traded in units of 5,000 bushels. A corn contract, with corn at $3 per bushel, is valued at about $15,000. Thus, your $50,000 would allow you to buy 3 units of corn, or $45,000 worth. Gold is traded in 100-ounce contracts in New York, which at a price of $490 per ounce gives a single contract a value of $49,000. Thus, you could also trade 1 gold contract with this model.

The equal units approach allows you to give each investment an approximate equal weighting in your portfolio. It also has the advantage in that you can see exactly how much leverage you are carrying. For example, if you are carrying five positions in your $50,000 account, each worth about $50,000, you would know that you had about $250,000 worth of product. In addition, you would know that you had about 5-to-1 leverage since your $50,000 was controlling $250,000.

When you use this approach, you must make a decision about how much total leverage you are willing to carry before you divide it into units. It's valuable information, so I would recommend that all traders keep track of the total product value they are controlling and their leverage. This information can be a real eye-opener. However, leverage does not necessarily equate to the volatility of movement or to risk, so be careful here.

The equal units approach also has a disadvantage in that it would allow you to increase "how much" only very slowly as you make money. In most cases with a small account, equity would again have to double to increase your exposure by 1 unit. Again, this practically amounts to no position sizing for the small account.

Some professional stock traders not only use an equal value model to control their initial position size, they also use a form of it throughout their trading. Namely, they advocate that one periodically rebalance the portfolio so that all positions continue to be equally balanced. This means that you sell off your winners (at least to the point of rebalancing your shares) and add to your losers. In my opinion, this is using position sizing to make sure that you do *not* follow the golden rule of trading. Basically, you are periodically cutting your winners and adding to losers with this strategy. Several of the newsletters, evaluated earlier in the book, used this form of position sizing. In addition, many mutual fund portfolio managers, who have had no training in position sizing, also use this approach.

MODEL 3: THE PERCENT RISK MODEL

When you enter a position, it is essential to know the point at which you will get out of the position in order to preserve your capital. This is your *risk*. It's your worst-case loss—except for slippage and a runaway market going against you. It's what I've been calling a 1*R* risk throughout this book.

One of the most common position-sizing systems involves controlling your position size as a function of this risk. Let's look at an example of how this position-sizing model works. Suppose you want to buy gold at $380 per ounce. Your system suggests that if gold drops as low as $370, you need to get out. Thus, your worst-case risk per gold contract is 10 points times $100 per point, or $1,000.

You have a $50,000 account. You want to limit your total risk on your gold position to 2.5 percent of that equity, or $1,250. If you divide your $1,000 risk per contract into your total allowable risk of $1,250, you get 1.25 contracts. Thus, your percent risk position sizing will only allow you to purchase 1 contract.

Suppose that you get a signal to sell short corn the same day. Gold is still at $380 an ounce, so your account with the open position is still worth $50,000. You still have $1,250 in allowable risk for your corn position based on your total equity.

Let's say that corn is at $4.03, and you decide that your maximum acceptable risk would be to allow corn to move against you by 5 cents to $4.08. Your 5 cents of allowable risk (times 5,000 bushels per contract) translates into a risk of $250 per contract. If you divide $250 into $1,250, you get 5 contracts. Thus, you can sell short 5 corn contracts within your percent risk position-sizing paradigm.

CPR Model for Risk

Some people get confused at this point. If *R* is the risk per share, then what is the total risk? Don't you sometimes call the total risk *R*? The answer is that when you use the percent risk model for position sizing, your risk per share and your total risk have the same ratios. Thus, you can use your total initial risk and your total profit or loss to determine what *R* is for you. To help you understand it even more, let's call the risk per unit *R*. Let's call the total risk *C* for cash. And let's call position sizing *P*. These variables have an easy relationship, which I call *CPR* for traders and investors.[7]

Let's say you want to buy a stock for $50 per share, and you decided that you'll get out of the position if the stock drops $2 per share to $48. Thus, *R* is now $2. Let's also say that you are using a percent risk model for position sizing, and you decide to limit your total risk to 1 percent of your $50,000 portfolio, or $500. Thus, your total risk (or *C*) will be $500. To determine your position size, you will use the following formula:

$$\text{Formula 14.1: } P \text{ (position size)} = \frac{C \text{ (cash)}}{R \text{ (risk per share)}}$$

Let's apply the formula to our example. We don't know the position size, but we do know that $R = \$2$ and $C = \$500$. Thus,

$$P = \frac{\$500}{\$2}$$
$$= 250 \text{ shares}$$

Our position-sizing formula for model 1 has us buying 250 shares of our $50 stock. Notice that our total investment will be $12,500, or 25 percent of our account. However, our risk per share is only $2, and our total risk is only $500 or 1 percent of our account.

Now let's say that our stock goes up to $60 per share. We now have a profit of $10 per share. Since our initial risk was only $2 per share, our total gain is 5 times that or 5*R*. However, we could just as easily compare the total profit, $2,500 (that is, $10 times 250 shares) with the total initial risk of $500. Here we still see that we have a 5*R* profit. Thus, both the total risk and the risk per share could be used to determine your *R* multiples.

Notice that our 5*R* profit amounted to a 5 percent gain. Thus, if you have a system that produces an average profit of 80*R* after 100 trades, you could expect to make 80 percent (or more with compounding) using a 1 percent risk model.

Comparison of Models

Table 14.4 shows the same 55-/21-day breakout system with a position-sizing algorithm based upon risk as a percentage of equity. The starting equity is again $1 million.

Notice that the best reward-to-risk ratio occurs at about 25 percent risk per position, but you would have to tolerate an 84 percent drawdown in order to achieve it. In addition, margin calls (*which are set at current rates and are not historically accurate*) start entering the picture at 10 percent risk.

If you traded this system with $1 million and used a 1 percent risk criterion, your bet sizes would be equivalent to trading the $100,000 account with 10 percent risk. Thus, Table 14.4 suggests that you probably should not trade this system unless you have at least $100,000, and then you probably should not risk more than about 0.5 percent per trade. And at 0.5 percent, your returns with the system would be very poor. Essentially, you should now understand why you need at least $1 million to trade this system with ten commodities.

Just how much risk should you accept per position with risk position sizing? Your overall risk using risk position sizing depends on the quality of your system and your objectives. However, some general guidelines might be to use 1 percent risk or less if you are trading other people's money; 0.5 to 2.5 percent for your own money, depending on your objectives and the quality of your system; and over 2.5 percent if you are looking for huge returns and are willing to risk a high probability of ruin.

Most stock market traders don't consider a percent risk model at all. Instead, they tend to think more in terms of the equal units model. But let's look at one more equity example.

Let's say you want to purchase IBM and you have a $50,000 account. Suppose IBM's price is about $141 per share. You decide

TABLE 14.4

55/21 System with Percent Risk Model

Risk, %	Net Profits	Rejected Trades	Gain per Year, %	Margin Calls	Maximum Drawdown, %	Ratio
0.10	$327	410	0.00	0	0.36	0.00
0.25	$80,685	219	0.70	0	2.47	0.28
0.50	$400,262	42	3.20	0	6.50	0.49
0.75	$672,717	10	4.90	0	10.20	0.48
1.00	$1,107,906	4	7.20	0	13.20	0.54
1.75	$2,776,044	1	13.10	0	22.00	0.60
2.50	$5,621,132	0	19.20	0	29.10	0.66
5.00	$31,620,857	0	38.30	0	46.70	0.82
7.50	$116,500,000	0	55.70	0	62.20	0.91
10.00	$304,300,000	0	70.20	1	72.70	0.97
15.00	$894,100,000	0	88.10	2	87.30	1.01
20.00	$1,119,000,000	0	92.10	21	84.40	1.09
25.00	$1,212,000,000	0	93.50	47	83.38	1.12
30.00	$1,188,000,000	0	93.10	58	95.00	0.98
35.00	($2,816,898)	206	0.00	70	104.40	0.00

that you would get out of this position at $137, or a drop of $4 per share. Your position-sizing strategy tells you to limit your risk to 2.5 percent, or $1,250. When we use our formula $P = C/R$, we divide $4 risk per share into the total risk of $1,250, and we get 312.5 shares.

If you bought 312 shares at $141, it would cost you $43,392—over 80 percent of the value in your account. Again, notice that your total investment has nothing to do with your initial risk. You could do that only two times without exceeding the marginable value of your account. This gives you a better notion of what a 2.5 percent risk really means. In fact, if your stop was only a $1 drop to $140, you could purchase 1,250 shares based on the model. But those 1,250 shares would cost you $176,250—which you couldn't do even by fully margining your account. Nevertheless, you are still limiting your risk to 2.5 percent. The risk calculations, of course, were all based on the starting risk—the difference between your purchase price and your initial stop loss.

The percent risk model is the first model that gives you a legitimate way to make sure that a 1*R* risk means the same for each item you are trading. Let's say that you are trading a $1 million portfolio in the stock market and are willing to use full margin. You are using a 1 percent risk model, and thus you are risking $10,000 for each position. Table 14.5 shows how this is done.

The stop shown is arbitrary and represents a 1*R* risk. You might think that the stops are tight for such high-priced stocks, especially the $0.20 for TXN. However, they might not be if you were going for big-*R*-multiple trades. Table 14.5 shows that we can't even buy 5 stocks because the dollar value of the stocks exceeds our $2 million margin limit. Nevertheless, our risk is only $10,000 per position if we are able to rigidly follow our predetermined stops. Thus, our total portfolio risk on a $1 million portfolio is only $50,000 plus slippage and costs. If you are an equity trader, study Table 14.5. It might change the way you think about trading a portfolio of stocks.

But what if you continually got new signals to buy stocks, despite being fully margined after purchasing only a few stocks? Well, you'd have only a few possible solutions. First, you could limit new purchases. Second, you could eliminate your worst-performing position before adding a new one. Third, you could make your position sizing much smaller in order to continue purchasing more shares. And last, you could do some combination of the first three ideas.

TABLE 14.5

Using a 1 Percent Risk in a Stock Portfolio

Stock	Price	Stop (1*R* Risk)	Number of Shares with $10,000 Risk	Equity Value
GOOG	$380.00	$10.00	1,000	$380,000
INTC	$21.00	$2.00	5,000	$105,000
TXN	$32.00	$0.20	50,000	$1,600,000
SUNW	$4.50	$0.50	20,000	$90,000
VLO	$63.00	$3.20	3,125	$196,875
Total				$2,271,875

MODEL 4: THE PERCENT VOLATILITY MODEL

Volatility refers to the amount of daily price movement of the underlying instrument over an arbitrary period of time. It's a direct measurement of the price change that you are likely to be exposed to—for or against you—in any given position. If you equate the volatility of each position that you take, by making it a fixed percentage of your equity, then you are basically equalizing the possible market fluctuations of each portfolio element to which you are exposing yourself in the immediate future.

Volatility, in most cases, is the difference between the high and the low of the day. If IBM varies between 141 and 143.5, then its volatility is 2.5 points. However, using an average true range takes into account any gap openings. Thus, if IBM closed at 139 yesterday, but varied between 141 and 143.5 today, you'd need to add in the 2 points in the gap opening to determine the true range. Thus, today's true range is between 139 and 143.5—or 4.5 points. This is basically Welles Wilder's average true range calculation as shown in the Glossary at the end of the book.

Here's how a percent volatility calculation might work for position sizing. Suppose that you have $50,000 in your account and you want to buy gold. Let's say that gold is at $600 per ounce, and during the last 20 days the daily range is $3. We will use a 20-day simple moving average of the average true range as our measure of volatility. How many gold contracts can we buy?

Since the daily range is $3 and a point is worth $100 (that is, the contract is for 100 ounces), that gives the daily volatility a value of $300 per gold contract. Let's say that we are going to allow volatility to be a maximum of 2 percent of our equity. Two percent of $50,000 is $1,000. If we divide our $300 per contract fluctuation into our allowable limit of $1,000, we get 3.3 contracts. Thus, our position-sizing model, based on volatility, would allow us to purchase 3 contracts.

Table 14.6 illustrates what happens with our 55/21 system in our portfolio of 10 commodities over 11 years when you size positions based on the volatility of the markets as a percentage of your equity. Here volatility was defined as the 20-day moving average of the average true range. This is the same system and the same data described with the other models. The differences between the results in Tables 14.2, 14.4, and 14.6 are due to the position-sizing algorithm.

Notice in Table 14.6 that a 2 percent volatility position-sizing allocation would produce a gain between 67.9 and 86.1 percent per year and drawdowns of 69.7 to 85.5 percent per year. The table suggests that if you used a volatility position-sizing algorithm with the system, you probably would want to use a number somewhere between 0.5 and 1.0 percent per position, depending on your objectives. The best reward-to-risk ratio in this system occurs at a 2.5 percent allocation, but few people could tolerate the drawdown of 86 percent.

If you compare Table 14.4 with Table 14.6, you'll notice the striking difference in the percentages at which the system breaks down. These differences are the result of the size of the number that you must take into consideration before using the equity percentages to size positions (that is, the current 21-day extreme against you versus the 20-day volatility). Thus, a 5 percent risk based on a stop of the 21-day extreme appears to be equivalent to about 1 percent of equity with the 20-day average true range. These numbers, upon which the percentages are based, are critical. They must be considered before you determine the percentages you plan to use to size your positions.

TABLE 14.6

55/21 Breakout System with Volatility-Based Position Sizing

Volatility, %	Net Profits	Rejected Trades	Gain per Year, %	Margin Calls	Maximum Drawdown %
0.10	$411,785	34	3.30	0	6.10
0.25	$1,659,613	0	9.50	0	17.10
0.50	$6,333,704	0	20.30	0	30.60
0.75	$16,240,855	0	30.30	0	40.90
1.00	$36,266,106	0	40.00	0	49.50
1.75	$236,100,000	0	67.90	0	60.70
2.50	$796,900,000	0	86.10	1	85.50
5.00	$1,034,000,000	0	90.70	75	92.50
7.50	($2,622,159)	402	0.00	1	119.80

Volatility position sizing has some excellent features for controlling exposure. Few traders use it. Yet it is one of the more sophisticated models available.

THE MODELS SUMMARIZED

Table 14.7 gives a summary of the four models presented in this chapter, along with their respective advantages and disadvantages. Notice that the model with the most disadvantages is the one that most people use—the units-per-fixed-amount-of-money model. Let's reemphasize those disadvantages because they are so important.

First, assume that you are opening an account with $30,000. That's probably not enough to trade futures with unless you just trade a few agricultural markets. However, many people will do it. In that account, you could probably trade a corn contract, an S&P contract, and a bond contract—although the margin requirements might prevent you from doing them simultaneously. However, the model has some flaws because it does allow you to trade all of them. A percent risk model or a percent volatility model, in contrast, might reject both the S&P and the bond trades because they were too risky.

Second, this model would allow you to buy one of each of the contracts. That's ridiculous because you would be giving all your attention to the S&P contract because of its volatility and risk. All investment units are not alike, and one should probably reject any sort of position-sizing algorithm that does treat them alike. This model does because you have 1 unit of each.

Third, if your position-sizing model is to take 1 contract per $30,000, then you would have two problems. If your account dropped by $1, you couldn't take any positions. Most people wouldn't follow this because they would assume that they could take 1 contract per "however much money was in their account." In addition, if you were lucky enough for your account to go up, the account would have to double in size before you could take another contract. That's basically no position sizing!

Notice that the last three models do a much better job of balancing your portfolio. Why not select one of them?

TABLE 14.7

Four Position-Sizing Models Compared

Model	Advantages	Disadvantages
Units per fixed amount of money	You don't reject a trade because it's too risky. You can open an account with limited funds and use this model. It gives you minimum risk per trade.	It treats unequal investments alike. It cannot increase exposure rapidly for small units. Small accounts could be overexposed.
Equal units model	It gives each investment an equal weighting in your portfolio.	The small investor would be able to increase size only slowly. Exposure is not necessarily alike for each unit. Investments frequently do not divide well into equal units.
Percent risk model	It allows both large and small accounts to grow steadily. It equalizes performance in the portfolio by the actual risk.	You will have to reject some trades because they're too risky. The amount risked is not the actual risk because of slippage, and Gallacher would say that the exposure is unequal.
Percent volatility model	It allows both large and small accounts to grow steadily. It equalizes performance in the portfolio by volatility. You can use it to equalize trades when using tight stops without putting on large positions.	You will have to reject some trades because they are too risky. The daily volatility is not the actual risk.

One could invent as many position-sizing algorithms as people have entry algorithms. There are millions of possibilities, and we have touched only the surface of the topic in this chapter.[8] Nevertheless, if you are beginning to understand the impact of position sizing, then I have accomplished my objective.

POSITION SIZING USED BY OTHER SYSTEMS

The performance of the world's greatest traders, in my opinion, has been driven by position sizing. However, let's look at the systems we've been discussing throughout this book and at the position sizing that they use. In most cases that will be quite easy because they don't even talk about position sizing.

Stock Market Models

William O'Neil's CANSLIM Method

William O'Neil does not address the issue of how much to own in any given position. He addresses only the issue of how many stocks to own. He says that even a multimillion-dollar portfolio should own only six or seven stocks. People with a portfolio of $20,000 to $100,000 should limit themselves to four or five stocks. People with $5,000 to $20,000 should limit themselves to three stocks, while people with even less should probably only invest in two.

This discussion sounds like the equal units approach with a slight twist. It suggests that you divide your capital into equal units, but that the number of units should depend on the amount of money you have. A very small account should probably only have two units of perhaps $1,500 each or less. When you have about $5,000, then move to three units. Now you want each unit to grow to approach at least $4,000 per unit (that is, you could afford to buy 100 shares of a $40 stock). When you can do this with five units ($20,000), then do so. At this point, you keep the same number of units until you can grow the size of a unit to about $25,000 to $50,000. At $50,000, you might want to move to as many as six or seven units.

The Warren Buffett Approach to Investing

Buffett is interested in owning only a few of the very best businesses—those that meet his exceptional criteria. He wants to own as much of those few businesses as he can, since it should give him excellent returns and he never plans to sell. Now that he has billions of dollars at his disposal, he can afford to own multiple companies. As a result, he simply adds more companies to his portfolio as they meet his criteria.

This is a rather unique style of position sizing. However, Buffett is the richest professional investor in the United States (and the second-richest man, after Bill Gates). Who can argue with that kind of success? Perhaps you should consider this style of position sizing!

Futures Market Models

Kaufman Adaptive Moving-Average Approach

Kaufman doesn't really discuss position sizing in his book *Smarter Trading*. He does discuss some of the results of position sizing such as risk and reward, using the academic definitions of the terms. By *risk* he means the annualized standard deviation of the equity changes, and by *reward* he means the annualized compounded rate of return. He suggests that when two systems have the same returns, the rational investor will choose the system with the lower risk.

Kaufman also brings up another interesting point in his discussion—the 50-year rule. He says that levees were built along the Mississippi River to protect them from the largest flood that has occurred in the last 50 years. This means that water will rise above the levee, but not very often—perhaps once in a lifetime. Similarly, professional traders who design their systems properly may be faced with a similar situation. They may design their system carefully, but once in a lifetime they may be faced with extreme price moves that have the potential to wipe them out.

Safety, as we have indicated by the various position-sizing models, relates directly to the amount of equity you have and the amount of leverage you are willing to risk. As your capital grows, if you diversify and deleverage, then your capital will be safer. If you continue to leverage your profits, then you risk the chance of a complete loss.

Kaufman suggests that you can control your worst-case risk by looking at the standard deviation of your risk when testing at the selected leverage level. For example, if you have a 40 percent return and the variability of your drawdowns suggests that 1 standard deviation is 10 percent, then you know that in any given year:

- You have a 16 percent chance (1 standard deviation) of a 10 percent drawdown.[9]

- You have a 2.5 percent chance (2 standard deviations) of a 20 percent drawdown.
- You have a 0.5 percent chance (3 standard deviations) of a 30 percent drawdown.

These results are excellent, but if you believe you will be in serious trouble if you lose 20 percent or more, Kaufman suggests that you trade only a portion of your funds.

Kaufman also talks about asset allocation, which he defines as "the process of distributing investment funds into one or more markets or vehicles to create an investment profile with the most desirable return-risk ratio." Asset allocation may simply amount to trading half of your capital with one active investment (that is, a stock portfolio) while the rest of your capital is in short-term yield-bearing instruments such as government bonds. On the other hand, asset allocation may involve combining many investment vehicles in a dynamic approach—such as actively trading stocks, commodities, and the forex market. This is another example of "asset allocation" being used for, and somewhat confused with, the topic of "how much."

It's clear from Kaufman's discussion, although he doesn't state it directly, that he is used to using the first position-sizing model—the 1 unit per so much capital. His form of reducing risk is simply to increase the capital required to trade 1 unit.

Gallacher's Fundamental Trading

Gallacher actually has an extensive chapter on position sizing in his book *Winner Take All.* He says that risk is directly related to exposure in the market and he appears to detest the percent risk model presented here because it does not control exposure. For example, 3 percent risk on any size account could be 1 unit or 30 units depending on where your stop is. There is no way, Gallacher argues, that the risk with 1 unit is not less than the risk in 30 units. For example, he states, "An account trading one contract of a commodity and risking $500 is a much less risky proposition than an account trading two contracts of that same commodity and risking $250 on each." Gallacher's statement is true, and everyone accepting the percent risk model should understand it. The stop is only the price at which your broker is told to turn your order into a market order.

It does not in any way guarantee that price. This is one reason we recommend the percent volatility model for anyone who wants to trade tight stops.

Gallacher also points out that your risk increases not only with exposure but also with time. The longer you trade the market, the greater the opportunity you have to be exposed to a tremendous price shock. A trader, trading 1 unit with all the money in the world, could eventually lose everything, Gallacher believes. That belief probably is true for most traders, but not all traders.

Trading different investments, Gallacher contends, only speeds up the effects of time. He argues that trading *N* positions for 1 year is the same as trading 1 position for *N* years in terms of the potential equity drawdown.

Gallacher recommends that you find the *largest expected equity drop* (LEED) that you will tolerate—perhaps 25 percent or perhaps 50 percent. He asks that you assume that this LEED will occur tomorrow. It probably won't, but you need to assume that it will occur.

He goes on to calculate a distribution of potential drawdowns by using the system's expectancy and the possible distribution of daily ranges for various commodities. He then recommends a minimum trading amount for various commodities so as not to experience a 50 percent drawdown. In other words, Gallacher is recommending a version of the typical 1 unit per so much equity in your account, but that amount varies depending on the daily volatility of the investment.

The amount needed per unit of trading also differs depending on whether you are trading 1, 2, or 4 simultaneous units. For example, he would recommend 1 unit per $40,000 for each $1,000 in daily range traded if the instrument is traded by itself. He recommends 1 unit per $28,000 for each $1,000 in daily range traded if the instrument is traded with one other. And, last, he recommends 1 unit per $20,000 for each $1,000 in daily range when traded with three other instruments.

Let's look at an example by looking at corn. Suppose the current price of corn varies by 4 cents per day. This amounts to a daily price variation of $200 (since 1 unit is 5,000 bushels). Based on Gallacher's model, since $200 is 20 percent of $1,000, you could trade 1 unit with 20 percent of $40,000 or 1 unit per $8,000. If you were trading corn with one other instrument, you could trade 1 unit per $5,600. And if you were trading with three other simultaneous instruments, you could trade 1 unit per $4,000.

Gallacher's method is an excellent variation of the 1-unit-per-so-much-equity model because it equates the various instruments according to their volatility. Thus, his method overcomes one of the basic limitations of that model. It does so by adding some complexity, but nevertheless it's an interesting way to trade.

Ken Roberts' 1-2-3 Methodology

Roberts' first position-sizing principle is that you don't need much money to trade commodities.[10] He answers the question of how much by saying to trade only one contract. Unfortunately, he's catering to people who have only $1,000 to $10,000 in their account. Thus, the primary position-sizing rule is to trade only one contract.

Roberts does say that one shouldn't take any risk over $1,000, which means that he avoids certain commodities like the S&Ps, various currencies, and perhaps even coffee—because the risk involved would typically be greater than $1,000. This statement makes Roberts sound conservative. Roberts does not include a position-sizing algorithm in his system. This can be dangerous, in my opinion, because you might still take a position in the market when most position-sizing algorithms would indicate that you should not do so.

SUMMARY

In my opinion, the most significant part of any trading system design is the part that has to do with how much to put into each position. Both *money management* and *asset allocation* have been used to describe how much, but these terms have also been misused over the years. Thus, these terms are at best confusing. As a result, I've elected to use the term *position sizing* in this book to eliminate the confusion.

Position sizing basically adds a fourth dimension to the dimensions of reliability, reward-to-risk ratio, and opportunity. It dramatically adds to the potential profits or losses that can occur throughout the course of trading. In fact, position sizing, in my opinion, accounts for most of the variation in performance of various money managers. In essence, expectancy and opportunity form a solid that determines your volume of profits. Position sizing determines how many solids contribute to your profits at one time.

Position sizing also points out the importance of your underlying equity. With large amounts of equity, you can do a lot with position sizing. With small amounts of equity, it is very easy to get wiped out.

Anti-martingale systems in which you increase your bet size as your equity increases are the primary models that work. Several anti-martingale position-sizing models were given, including the following:

Units per fixed amount of money. This model allows you to take one position per so much money. It basically treats all investments alike and always allows you to take one position.

Equal units model. This model gives an equal weighting to all investments in your portfolio according to their underlying value. It's commonly used by investors and equity traders.

The percent risk model. This model is recommended as the best model for long-term trend followers. It gives all trades an equal risk and allows a steady portfolio growth.

The percent volatility model. This model is best for traders who use tight stops. It can provide a reasonable balance between risk and opportunity (expectancy).

NOTES

1. It's not even a good exit methodology, as explained in the exit chapter, because you take losses with a full position and you take your maximum profits with only a partial position.
2. Gary Brinson, Brian Singer, and Gilbert Beebower, "Determinants of Portfolio Performance II: An Update," *Financial Analysts Journal* 47 (May–June 1991): 40–49.
3. One of the best methods of position sizing is to use a percent risk algorithm, such as risking 1 percent of your total equity on a given position so that position sizing does control your total risk. However, you can use algorithms that have little to do with risk for position sizing.

4. See William Ziemba, "A Betting Simulation, the Mathematics of Gambling and Investment," *Gambling Times* 80 (1987): 46–47.
5. The data presented with the 55-/21-day system presents you with 10 years of data, and thus seems quite reliable. However, the system gives you one set of *R* multiples. And even if you assume that the sample of trades it generates adequately represents what this system will do, it still represents only one iteration of the data. There are many sequences in which the same *R* multiples might be expressed, all of which would give you different results. And, who knows, there might be a number of large-*R*-multiple losses out there that you have not yet seen with this system. Thus, we can draw only very rough conclusions from the data presented in the tables in this chapter.
6. A full S&P contract is worth $250 per point. Thus, if the S&P 500 is valued at 1,000, then the contract is worth $250,000. The example also assumes that your broker would allow you to trade this contract in that small of an account.
7. I want to thank my friend Ron Ishibashi for first coming up with the idea of CPR for traders and investors.
8. For a much more thorough discussion of how to use position sizing to meet your objectives, see Van Tharp's *The Definitive Guide to Position Sizing and Expectancy* (Cary, N.C.: International Institute of Trading Mastery), which is available through the Web site www.iitm.com. This is a full-length book on these topics that goes way beyond the scope of this book.
9. You can figure it this way: 68 percent of the variability falls between +1 and –1 standard deviations, so 32 percent remains. This also means that there is 16 percent (half of 32 percent) beyond 1 standard deviation of 10 percent. In the same way, 95 percent of the returns falls between +2 and –2 standard deviations. Thus, half of 5 percent leaves 2.5 percent outside of –2 standard deviations. Last, 99 percent falls between +3 and –3 standard deviations. Thus, by the same logic, only 0.5 percent of the results will be worse than –3 standard deviations. However, Kaufman is making the assumption that returns are normally distributed. Since market prices are not, returns may not be either.
10. In my opinion, this assumption allows a lot of people to trade and makes it seem as if there is little risk involved. Readers of this book should be able to judge the risk of this assumption for themselves at this point.

CHAPTER 15

Conclusion

> In the very long run, your results at the poker table will approach the sum of all your opponents' mistakes, less the sum of your mistakes.
>
> *Dan Harrington,*
> *1995 World Series of Poker (WSOP) Champion*

If you understand the psychological foundation for system design, then I've accomplished one of my major objectives in writing this book. The source of the Holy Grail is inside you. You must assume total responsibility for what you do and for what happens to you. You must determine what you want from a system based on your beliefs and then detail a plan with the appropriate objectives.

My second objective was to help you understand that any system can be characterized as a distribution of *R* multiples. That distribution, in turn, can be described by its expectancy (that is, the mean *R*), the nature of its distribution, and the opportunity factor that it gives you. Let me repeat that! Systems are distributions of *R* multiples with certain characteristics. In fact, when someone describes a trading system to you, you should try to visualize what its *R*-multiple distribution looks like. When you do so, you will really begin to understand trading systems.

Furthermore, in order to obtain a positive expectancy, you must have a way to "cut your losses short and let your profits run," which is accomplished through exits. Exits are a major part of developing a high, positive expectancy system. And most importantly, you must understand position sizing well enough to be able to meet your objectives.

My third objective was to help you understand that you achieve your objectives through position sizing. Thus, making money in the markets is all about making sure that your position size is at a low enough level that you can achieve the long-term expectancy of the system. For example, if your system has a 0.8 expectancy and gives you 100 opportunities in a year, then you should be able to make about 80*R* in a year. However, you also discover that some time during the year, you'll experience an average drawdown of 30*R*. If you risk 0.5 percent per trade, you should probably be able to make at least 40 percent per year and probably not experience a drawdown bigger than 15 percent. Most people would be very happy with that. If you risked 1 percent per trade with this system, you might be able to make 100 percent per year, but you could have some serious drawdowns in the process. And if you start out with a 30 percent drawdown, which is possible when risking 1 percent, then you might give up on this system. And last, if you risk as much as 3 percent with this system, you could have a huge gain (for example, 300 to 500 percent), but you could also experience a drawdown early in the year that's big enough to cause you to abandon trading. If you understand the importance of position sizing, then I've accomplished my third major objective in writing this book.

I remember consulting with a trader, and we started working on his position sizing. When I saw what he was doing, which was imposed on him by his firm, I asked to speak to his boss. I told his boss that if his firm kept doing what they were doing with position sizing, they'd soon be out of business. His boss laughed and said, "We know what we are doing." And six months later the firm was out of business. Perhaps if they had paid me a small fraction of what they lost, they would have listened to my advice and still have been in business.

My fourth objective in writing this book was to help you understand the impact of your own personal psychology on system development. Psychology is important because (1) you create the results you get; (2) you can trade only a system that fits you psychologically; and (3) if you don't solve your major psychological issues before attempting to develop a system, then you will simply bring those issues into your system. For example, if you have trouble taking a trade because conditions are never right, then you probably have an issue with perfectionism. If you try to develop a system without solving this issue first, then you will simply bring your issue of perfectionism to the task of building a system and your system will never be good enough.

If you understand the six key elements of making money in the market and their relative importance, then I've met a fifth objective in writing this book. Those six key elements include (1) system reliability, (2) reward-to-risk ratio, (3) cost of trading, (4) your trading opportunity level, (5) the size of your equity, and (6) your position-sizing algorithm. You should understand the relative importance of each of these factors and why successful trading isn't about "being right" or "being in control" of the market.

Last, if you have a good plan in mind about how to develop a trading system that will meet your objectives, then I've met my final key objective in writing this book. You should understand the parts of a trading system and the role that each part plays. If not, then review Chapter 4. You should know how setups, timing, protective stops, and profitable exits combine to create a high-expectancy system. You should understand the key role that opportunity plays and how it relates to trading cost. And most importantly, you should understand the importance of your trading equity size and how it relates to various anti-martingale position-sizing algorithms.

AVOIDING MISTAKES

If you understand those key concepts, then you have a wonderful start. However, I'd like to point out the quotation at the beginning of this chapter by Dan Harrington because it's quite appropriate for trading and investing. However, I'll rephrase it for you: *Your net results as a trader and investor, over the very long run, will be a function of the expectancy of your system less any mistakes that you make.* Let me explain this definition so that it is clear.

> Your net results as a trader and investor, over the very long run, will be a function of the expectancy of your system less any mistakes that you make.

First, you need to understand that a mistake occurs when you don't follow your rules. If you haven't gone through some of the processes suggested by this book to develop a plan, a system, and a set of rules to guide your behavior, then everything you do is a mistake. Trading without a plan to guide you and a system to guide your trading is making one giant mistake.

One of the aspects of poker that Dan Harrington points out is that your job is to cause your opponents to make mistakes and your opponents' job is to cause you to make mistakes. In trading, however, we don't need to have others cause us to make mistakes because our natural inclination is to make lots of mistakes. In addition, big money has developed a system in which (1) they win when you pay fees based on just having money with them regardless of their performance, and (2) they win every time you make a move in the market because you must pay commissions and execution costs.

Second, you need to understand what the most common sources of mistakes are for traders and investors. These include the following:

- Concentrating on investment or trade selection rather than the potential reward-risk ratio of the trade. For example, Eric bought a Google option because he saw the potential for a big gain, but he didn't consider that he could lose as much as (if not more than) he could gain.
- Jumping on a trade because it seems exciting rather than using a well-thought-out plan.
- Taking a trade because you hear a recommendation without understanding the reward-risk potential of the trade. This is particularly dangerous if you think your method of trading is to follow the recommendations of one or more newsletters.
- Needing to be right and taking a profit quickly in order to do so.
- Needing to be right and not taking a loss in order to do so.
- Not having a bail-out point when you take a trade—in other words, not knowing your 1*R* loss when you enter into a market position.
- Risking too much on any given position.
- Allowing your emotions to overrule your rules in a trade.
- Having too many positions in a portfolio, causing you to not pay enough attention to something critical.

- Repeating the same mistakes over and over again because you don't assume responsibility for the results you are getting.

There are many other mistakes, but I think you get the idea. Imagine that every mistake you make costs you something like 3*R*.[1] You have a system with an expectancy of 0.8*R* that generates 100 trades each year. You should make about 80*R* each year on the average. But let's say you make two mistakes every month. Suddenly you've got 72*R* in mistakes. The net result is that you've turned a fairly good system into a very borderline system. And if your system goes into a typical drawdown, when you add the mistake factor into it, you'll probably find that you end up abandoning a perfectly good system. Mistakes are that critical. However, if you concentrate on the "you factor" in your trading, then you have a real chance to get that 80*R* that your system will give you each year. Is it beginning to make sense? This is why working on yourself to eliminate mistakes is so critical. Don't be like the trader I mentioned earlier who said, "Psychology doesn't impact our trading! We're totally mechanical." He eventually lost his business because he ignored this all-important factor.

WHAT'S LEFT NOW: AN INTERVIEW WITH DR. THARP

There is still much to learn in your trading journey that is beyond the scope of this book. As a result, I want to provide a brief overview of some of those areas in this final chapter. Since there is so much material to cover, I've elected to cover it in a question-and-answer format, which allows me to be extremely focused and to the point.

So if someone understands everything covered in this book, then what's left? What you've covered seems quite extensive.

A number of areas remain. We've talked about what's involved in a trading system and the relative importance of each element. However, we haven't extensively discussed data, software, testing procedures, order execution, portfolio design, and managing other people's money. We've touched on those topics, but not in depth. We've also touched on position sizing, but a thorough treatment of the topic of how to use position sizing to meet your objectives is way beyond the scope of this book. Most importantly, we haven't discussed the process of trading at all, nor have we discussed all of the psychological elements that are involved with discipline and the day-to-day details of trading or investing.

Okay, so let's take each of those topics one by one. Where can readers get more information, and what information do they need to know? Let's start out with data.

The topic of data is a broad one and could fill a book of its own. First of all, you must understand that data only represents the market. The data is not the actual market. Second, data may not really be what it appears to be. By the time the average person gets market data, there are usually a number of sources of potential errors. Consequently, if you get data from two different vendors and run the exact same system over the exact same markets and years, you can come up with different results. The reason will be differences in the data. Obviously, this affects both your historical testing and your day-to-day trading.

There are basically two conclusions you will eventually make about data. First, nothing in this business is that exact. Second, you need to find reliable vendors and be certain that they stay reliable.

Okay, what about software? What should people look for in software?

Unfortunately, most software is designed to appeal to people's psychological weaknesses. Most of it optimizes results to make you think that you have a great system when you may not even have a profitable system. The software typically tests one market at a time over many years. That's not the way professionals trade. But it will allow you to get very optimistic results because those results can be curve-fitted to the market.

I would strongly recommend that you at least be aware that this is what most of the software does. It's not the fault of software vendors because they are just giving people what they want.

Last, you need software that will help you concentrate on the more important elements of trading or investing—such as position sizing. There is some software out there that will help, such as *Trading Blox, Trading Recipes,* and *Wealth Lab,* but none of them are designed to work on helping you make decisions over time as you would in a portfolio. That software really doesn't exist unless you are willing to develop it yourself.

What about testing? What do people need to know about testing?

Testing is not exact. We used a well-known software program and ran a simple program that entered the market on a two-day breakout and exited after one day. The program was really simple because we were just looking at the accuracy of collecting online data. However, we were using some well-known, very popular software to do the data collection and run the simple system. Yet when that software was run in real time, it got one set of results. When that software was run again in an historical mode on the same data it had collected, it produced a different set of results. That shouldn't happen, but it did. And in my opinion, that's quite scary.

If you approach the world of trading and investing as a perfectionist, you will be frustrated over and over again. Nothing is exact. You can never know how it will really turn out. Instead, trading is very much a game of discipline, of being in touch with the flow of the markets, and of being able to capitalize upon that flow. People who can do that can make a lot of money in the markets.

The issue of testing usually arises because some people need to test extensively in order to feel comfortable enough to trade a system. But testing is not exact. Most software has errors built into it, so I'd count on at least a 10 percent error factor due to your software. You'll also feed that software with data that may have significant errors in it. Try testing your system with two different sets of data (that is, from different vendors), and you might be surprised how different the results might be. In addition, you can test only one historical data set, but that doesn't tell you what the market is going to do in the future. However, if you need to do some sort of testing to feel comfortable trading a system and you know about all these sources of error, then by all means test.

That sounds very pessimistic. Why test at all?

So you can get an understanding of what works and what doesn't work. You shouldn't believe everything I've told you. Instead, you need to prove to yourself that something is true. When something seems reasonably true, then you can develop some confidence in using it. You must have that confidence or you'll be lost when you are dealing with the markets. Testing and developing confidence in a system, even if it isn't exact, is part of what many people need to feel comfortable trading a system.

What would you recommend doing?

First, determine what your criteria are for feeling comfortable trading a system. Does it fit who you are? Does it fit your beliefs? Do you understand it? Does it fit your objectives? Most people test before they even assess these things. But if it does all of that, then you must ask yourself, "Do I still need more empirical data to prove to me that it does what I think it will do?" What are your criteria for feeling comfortable?

Personally, I'd want a system that fits my beliefs, my objectives, and who I am. I want to really understand how that system works. That's usually enough for me to trade it with very small position sizing. And through real trading, I can collect *R* multiples and determine the qualities of the *R*-multiple distribution I'm getting. When I understand that, then I'll develop a great position-sizing algorithm to make sure that the system will meet my objectives.

You probably can never be exact. But no science is exact. People used to think that physics is exact, but now we know that the very act of measuring something changes the nature of the observation. Whatever it is, you are a part of it. You cannot help that because it is probably the nature of reality. And it again illustrates my point about the search for the Holy Grail system being an inner search.

Okay, let's talk about order execution.

Order execution is important from the viewpoint of communication. If execution is an important part of how you trade, then you must have a broker who understands what you want and what you are trying to do. When you can communicate that, you will get help in accomplishing what you are trying to do.

So what does that mean?

Well, first you must know your system inside out. You must understand your concept: how it works and what to expect from it in different kinds of markets. Then you must convey what you are doing to your floor broker and what you expect from him or her. For example, if you are a trend follower and you are trading breakouts, you will want to trade real breakouts. Communicate that to your broker. You can find someone who will act with a little discretion on your order. If the market is really moving, your order will be executed. But if a few traders are just testing new high prices, then you don't want your order to be executed because the market won't have any follow-through. If you communicate that to your broker, you can get the kind of service that will put you only in the kind of markets you want. If you don't communicate what you want, you won't get that kind of service.

Your broker also needs to know what you will pay for execution. What I just talked about is great for a long-term trend follower, but it is terrible for a day trader. A day trader needs just good execution with a minimum of cost and a minimum of slippage. However, you will never get minimum costs unless you communicate that to your broker, while still giving your broker fair compensation.

What about portfolio testing and multiple systems?

Again, we have a potential topic for a whole book. But think about the opportunity factor that we've discussed in this book. You have a chance, when you trade a portfolio of markets, to open up many more trading opportunities. That means you will get your big trade—perhaps several of them in a year. It means you might have enough opportunity to never have a losing quarter or perhaps a losing month.

Multiple systems give you the same advantage—more opportunity. Multiple systems can be particularly good if they are noncorrelated. It means that you will always have some winners. Your drawdowns will be less or nonexistent. And if that occurs, you will have a much greater capital base to work from (for position sizing) when a giant winner comes along.

I think that people who understand these principles can easily make 50 percent per year or more. I've worked with many traders who are doing much better than that. Furthermore, if you understand how a system can be characterized as an *R*-multiple distribution and how to size the position to meet your objectives, then you should understand how this is possible. However, one of the keys to making all this happen is having sufficient funds. If your snow wall is too small, you'll get wiped out by the first big black snowball that comes along. And that will occur no matter how good your system is or how well prepared you are.

But many professionals would argue that just outperforming the market averages on a regular basis is almost impossible.

First, you have to remember where most of them are coming from: (1) They don't understand risk as I've presented it—your initial stop in any given position in the market. (2) They don't understand expectancy and that it's produced by cutting losses and letting profits run. (3) They don't understand the impact of position sizing on helping you meet your objectives. (4) They don't understand that the key to making all of this work is having the inner strength and discipline to do so, plus the understanding that you really do produce your own results. Those are the main points of this book, yet they just are not taught anywhere else.

But most mutual funds fail to outperform the market averages.

There are two important things about what you just said. Mutual funds are designed to have long positions in the market at all times. Their goal is to outperform a benchmark, such as the S&P 500, and the only way that they can guarantee that they are not too far off is to basically own the stocks in that index. Thus, 85 percent of the fund might be the S&P 500. Now, if you own the index and charge management fees and do trade in and out of the market so you incur trading expenses as well, then you are not likely to outperform your benchmark index.

In this book, I've advocated absolute performance. And that's a whole different story. Let's say you have a system that makes 100 trades a year. It has an expectancy of 0.7*R*, meaning that on the average you should make 70*R* each year. Well, if you risk 1 percent on each trade, you should come close to making 100 percent per year with compounding. And 0.7*R* per year with a 100-trade system is not an unachievable expectancy.

However, size is a major factor. A day trader who makes 20 trades a day could make 50 percent per month. Most don't because their systems stop working or they make big psychological mistakes, but it's possible for them to do that. Imagine that the day trader's system has an expectancy of 0.4*R*. At 200 trades a month, that trader could easily be up 80*R* at the end of the month. And if he or she trades 0.5 percent risk per position, then you can see how he or she could be up 50 percent.

Swing traders who make 20 trades per month could easily make 10 to 15 percent per month. Let's say these swing traders have a system with an expectancy of 0.6*R*. That means they'd make 12*R* per month on the average. If they risk 1 percent, then they could easily make 15 percent. However, most short-term traders will make one mistake per month that could wipe out a whole month's worth of profits.

And let's look at a long-term position trader who makes 50 trades per year. Let's say this trader has a system that has an expectancy of 1.3*R*. At the end of the year, she could easily be up 65*R*. And if she risks 1 percent per trade, then she could make 75 percent per year. However, one or two psychological mistakes could easily destroy that whole return.

I know some people from the academic world want to test out these ideas to see if they really work. Does position sizing really work in the real world? Do the people who position size adequately make good returns? Well, I can answer that already. You need to find people who understand expectancy, how to position size to meet their objectives, and how to control themselves. The first two qualities are rare, but when you add the third factor, we're probably talking less than 1 percent of the traders and investors in the world.

Doesn't your account size also enter into it?
Absolutely, size is important. If your account is too small, then you are likely to trade too big and wipe your account out easily.

However, if you are trading under, let's say, $10 million, then the numbers I've suggested are realistic. However, when your size gets bigger, let's say, $50 million to $1 billion, then you are going to have some execution problems. Some of the big hedge funds that have $5 billion under management are really good if they can make 20 percent per year. But in these cases, moving size tends to ruin the expectancy.

And for most mutual funds, $5 billion is very small. They have huge problems with getting in and out of the market without moving it significantly. Imagine the impact of trillions of dollars trying to trade the ideas I've presented in this book. They probably could not do it. That's why they need to convince you that the secret to making money is to "buy and hold." And that's why they go for relative performance, trying to outperform their benchmark, which they seldom can do.

Okay, what about discipline and process of trading?
This is the area I first modeled over 20 years ago. If you understand this area, you have a real chance of success. But if you don't understand it, then you have little chance of success.

I first started the process of finding out about good trading by asking a lot of good traders what they did. My assumption was that the common answers were the "real" secrets of success.

Give us a synopsis. How about some steps people could follow on a regular basis to be more disciplined in their trading?
Most traders would tell me something about their methods. After interviewing 50 traders, I had 50 different methodologies. As a result, I concluded that methodology wasn't that significant to trading success. These successful traders all had low-risk ideas, but there were a lot of different types of low-risk

ideas, and that was just one of the keys. I would now express that in terms of having a high positive expectancy, with lots of opportunity and with plenty of understanding of how to use position sizing to realize that expectancy over the long run. However, doing that requires a lot of discipline. I've developed a complete course on peak performance trading, and there is very little overlap between that course and this book.

Okay, **step 1** is to have a trading plan and test it. You should know how to do most of that from the information contained in this book. Your basic goal is to develop confidence and a strong understanding of the concept you are trading. If you want more information on developing a trading plan, please visit our Web site at www.iitm.com.

Step 2 would be to assume total responsibility for everything that happens to you. Even if someone runs off with your money or a broker rips you off, assume that you were somehow involved in creating that situation. I know that sounds a bit strong. But if you do that, you can correct your role in what happens. When you stop committing the same mistakes over and over, you have a chance to be successful.

The biggest mistake I ever made was to trust one of my top clients who turned out to be a con artist. Doing so cost me a lot of money and probably some loss of reputation. However, if you follow this philosophy, as I do, then you have to ask yourself, what did I do to attract someone like this into my life? What mistakes did I make? And once you understand that, you can take steps to make sure that this never happens again. If you don't do that, then you tend to repeat your mistakes ad nauseam.

Step 3, find your weaknesses and work on them. I have several coaches to help me as a businessperson. In addition, I act as a coach for a number of people in our Super Trader program. And the key to that program is (1) to develop a strong business approach to trading and (2) to find weaknesses and eliminate them. Develop a diary of what happens to you. You are producing those emotions, so be "at cause" for what happens to you, rather than a victim of external circumstances.

Step 4 is to do some worst-case contingency planning. Make a list of everything that could go wrong in your business, and determine how you will respond to those situations. That will be the key to your success—knowing how to respond to the unexpected. For everything you can think of that might go wrong, develop several courses of action. Rehearse those action plans until they become second nature to you. This is a critical step to success.

Step 5, on a daily basis, analyze yourself. You are the most important factor in your trading and investing. Doesn't it make sense to spend a little time analyzing yourself? How are you feeling? What is going on in your life? The more aware you are of these issues, the less control they will have over your life. Also ask yourself, "Am I committed to trading success?" Without commitment nothing will work, but with commitment, anything is possible.

Step 6 is to determine what could go wrong in your trading at the beginning of the day. How will you react to that? Mentally rehearse each option until you have it down pat. Every athlete does extensive mental rehearsal, and it is important for you to do the same.

Step 7, at the end of the day, do a daily debriefing. Ask yourself a simple question: Did I follow my rules? If the answer is yes, then pat yourself on the back. In fact, if you followed your rules and lost money, pat yourself on the back twice. If the answer is no, then you must determine why! How might you get yourself into a similar situation in the future? When you find that similar situation, then you must mentally rehearse the situation again and again to make sure you know how to respond appropriately in the future.

Those seven steps should have a gigantic influence on anyone's trading.

What is the most important thing that traders or investors can do to improve their performance?

That's an easy question, but the solution is not easy. Take total responsibility for everything that happens to you—in the market and in your life. I've already said it many times. Be at cause for what happens to you, rather than a victim of external circumstances.

I've already mentioned the example of the con artist who cost me a lot of money. A critical step in making sure that doesn't happen again is not to blame that person but instead to figure out what I did to create that person coming into my life and to make sure that I never do it again. Some people who lost money in the incident were just looking for other people to blame and take to court. However, when you do such things, you learn nothing, and you tend to attract the same thing into your life again because you have not changed. For example, the local paper reported that some of the investors with this particular con artist had been duped by as many as three other con artists before this person.

And if that example is difficult for you, then let me give you another example from one of the marble games we play at seminars. Let's say the audience has $10,000 in play equity, and the audience members can risk any amount of that on each marble that is drawn (and replaced). Let's also say 60 percent of the marbles are losers, and one of them loses 5 to 1 (that is, it's a 5*R* multiple). The game goes on for 100 draws so that some large losing streaks will occur. In 100 draws, we'll probably have 10 or 12 losses in a row at some point. Moreover, that losing streak might include the 5-to-1 loss.

I'm a little sneaky. When someone draws out a losing marble, I ask that person to continue drawing until he or she eventually draws a winning marble. That means that someone in the audience will draw the entire long losing streak.

By the end of the game, usually half the audience has lost money, and many of them have gone broke. When I ask them, "How many of you think this person [that is, the person who pulled the losing streak] is responsible for your losses?" many of them raise their hands. If they really believe that, it means that they didn't learn anything from the game. They went bankrupt because of poor position sizing, but they'd rather blame it on someone else (or something else) such as the person who picked the losing marbles.

The most astute traders and investors are the ones who learn this lesson early. They are always looking to themselves to correct mistakes. This means they will eventually clear out the psychological issues that prevent them from making a lot of money. As a result, they will also continue to profit from their mistakes.

Thus, my first advice to anyone is to look to yourself as the source of everything that happens in your life. What are the common patterns, and how can you fix the ones that aren't working well? When you do this, your chances of success go up dramatically. Suddenly, you are in charge of your life.

Any last words of wisdom?

I talked about beliefs earlier in this book, but I'd like to repeat myself because I think they are so important. First, you cannot trade the markets—you can trade only your beliefs about the market. As a result, it is important for you to determine your exact beliefs.

Second, certain key beliefs, which have nothing to do with the market, will still determine your success in the markets. Those are your beliefs about yourself. What do you think you are capable of doing? Is trading or success important to you? How worthy of success do you believe yourself to be? Weak beliefs about yourself can undermine trading with a great system.

At this point, I'd like to mention something that will help you to move to the next step. We have a game you can download from our Web site at www.iitm.com. That game gives you a positive expectancy and emphasizes only position sizing and letting your profits run. What I'd suggest that you do is use that game as a training ground for your trading. See if you can make money playing the game. You can play the first three levels of the game for free. Develop a plan for getting through those three levels without taking a lot of risk. It's possible. See if you can get through the entire game without taking a lot of risk. Getting through the game will help you understand the principles I've been talking about in this book. Play the game a lot because (1) you will learn about different scenarios that you'll have to deal with as a trader; (2) you'll learn a lot about yourself; and (3) you'll learn a lot about position sizing by trying different things. And remember that the first three levels of the game are free.

Prove to yourself that you can do it. Games reflect behavior. If you cannot do it in our game, then you have no chance in the market. You will also have most of the psychological issues playing the game that you will have when you face the market. The game is an inexpensive place to learn.

As my final words of advice, I'd suggest that you read this book over four or five times. My experience is that people filter things according to their belief systems. There is probably a lot of material that you've overlooked if this is your first time through it. A second reading may reveal some new gems for you. And multiple readings will make this information second nature.

NOTES

1. Our preliminary research suggests that the average mistake people make costs them between 2*R* and 5*R*. However, this is just our preliminary research into the *R* value of mistakes.

GLOSSARY

adaptive moving average A moving average that is either quick, or slow, to signal a market entry depending on the efficiency of the move in the market.

algorithm A rule or set of rules for computing, that is, a procedure for calculating a mathematical function.

anti-martingale strategy A position-sizing strategy in which position size is increased when one wins and decreased when one loses.

arbitrage The taking advantage of discrepancies in price or loopholes in the system to make consistent low-risk money. This strategy usually involves the simultaneous purchase and sale of related items.

asset allocation The procedure by which many professional traders decide how to allocate their capital. Due to the lotto bias, many people think of this as a decision about which asset class (such as energy stocks or gold) to select. However, its real power comes when people use it to tell them "how much" to invest in each asset class. Thus, it is really another word for "position sizing."

average directional movement (ADX) An indicator that measures how much a market is trending. Both bullish and bearish trends are shown by positive movement.

average true range (ATR) The average over the last *X* days of the true range, which is the largest of the following: (1) today's high minus today's low; (2) today's high minus yesterday's close; or (3) today's low minus yesterday's close.

band trading A style of trading in which the instrument being traded is thought to move in a range of price. Thus when the price gets too high (that is, overbought), you can assume that it will go down. And when the price gets too low (that is, oversold), you can assume that it will probably move up. This concept is discussed in Chapter 5.

bearish Of the opinion that the market will be going down in the future.

best-case example A situation that represents the best of possible outcomes. Many books show you illustrations of their key points about the market (or indicator) that appear to perfectly predict the market. However, most examples of these points are not nearly as good as the one that is selected, which is known as a "best-case example."

bias The tendency to move in a particular direction. This could be a market bias, but most of the biases discussed in this book are psychological biases.

bid-ask spread The spread market makers offer to potential investors who want to open a position with them. Typically, this spread is how the market makers make their profit. If you want to sell, you'll get the lower price (that is, the market maker's bid price), and if you want to buy, you'll get the higher price (that is, the market maker's ask price).

blue-chip companies Top-rated companies.

breakout A move up from a consolidation or band of sideways movement.

bullish Of the opinion that the market will be going up in the future.

call An option that gives you the right to buy the underlying instrument at a particular price until the expiration date. It is a right to buy, but not an obligation.

candlestick A type of bar chart, developed by the Japanese, in which the price range between the open and the close is either a white rectangle (if the close is higher) or a black rectangle (if the close is lower). This type of chart has the advantage of making the price movement more obvious visually.

capitalization The amount of money in the underlying stock of a company.

channel breakout See *breakout*.

chaos theory A theory that physical systems generally move from stability to chaos. This theory has recently been used to explain explosive moves in the markets and the nonrandomness of the markets.

climax reversal A sharp price decline following a sharp price increase. When a position is moving up, it will often move up dramatically at the end of the move; this is called a *climax move*. It's usually followed by a drop in price, which is called a *climax reversal*.

commodities Physical products that are traded at a futures exchange. Examples of such products are grains, foods, meats, and metals.

congestive range See *consolidation*.

consolidation A pause in the market during which prices move in a limited range and do not seem to trend.

contract A single unit of a commodity or future. For example, a single unit or contract of corn is 5,000 bushels. A single unit of gold is 100 ounces.

credit spread An options trading strategy by which an investor buys one instrument and sells another related instrument and receives money for the transaction. This is called a *credit spread* because the investor received money to make the transaction.

debit spread An options trading strategy by which an investor buys one instrument and sells another related instrument and pays money to make the transaction. This is called a *debit spread* because it costs the investor money to make the transaction.

degree of freedom A statistical term used to describe the quantity that equals the number of independent observations less the number of parameters to be estimated. More degrees of freedom generally help in describing past price movement and hurt in predicting future price movement.

delta phenomenon A theory developed and trademarked by Jimmy Sloman and marketed by Welles Wilder that purports to predict the movement of the markets by what happens in our solar system.

dev-stop A stop-loss criterion developed and copyrighted by Cynthia Kase that depends on the standard deviation of price movement.

directional movement An indicator attributed to J. Welles Wilder using the largest part of today's range that is outside of yesterday's range.

disaster stop A stop-loss order to determine your worst-case loss in a position. See *stop-loss order*.

discretionary trading Trading that depends on the instincts of the trader as opposed to a systematic approach. The best discretionary traders are those who develop a systematic approach and then use discretion in their exits and position sizing to improve their performance.

divergence A term used to describe two or more indicators failing to show confirming signals.

diversification Investing in independent markets to reduce the overall risk.

drawdown A decrease in the value of your account because of losing trades or because of "paper losses" that may occur simply because of a decline in value of open positions.

Elliott Wave A theory developed by R. N. Elliott that holds that the market moves in a series of five up waves followed by a series of three correction down waves.

entry That part of your system that signals how or when you should enter the market.

equal units model A position-sizing model in which you purchase an equal dollar amount of each position.

equities Stocks secured by ownership in the company.

equity The value of your account.

equity curve The value of your account over time, illustrated in a graph.

exit That part of your trading system that tells you how or when to exit the market.

expectancy How much you can expect to make on the average over many trades. Expectancy is best stated in terms of how much you can make per dollar you risk. Expectancy is the mean *R* of an *R*-multiple distribution generated by a trading system.

expectunity A term used in this book to express expectancy multiplied by opportunity. For example, a trading system that has an expectancy of 0.6*R* and produces 100 trades per year will have an *expectunity* of 60*R*.

false positive Something that gives a prediction that then fails to happen.

Fibonacci retracements The most common levels used in retracement analysis, which are 61.8 percent, 38 percent, and 50 percent. When a move starts to reverse the three price levels are calculated (and drawn using horizontal lines) using a movement's low to high. These retracement levels are then interpreted as likely levels where countermoves will stop. Fibonacci ratios were also known to Greek and Egyptian mathematicians. The ratio was known as the *Golden Mean* and was applied in music and architecture.

filter An indicator that selects only data that meets specific criteria. Too many filters tend to lead to overoptimization.

financial freedom A financial state that occurs, according to Van Tharp, when your passive income (income that comes from your money working for you) is greater than your expenses. For example, if your monthly expenses total $4,000 and your money working for you brings in $4,300 per month, then you are financially free.

floor trader A person who trades on the floor of a commodities exchange. Locals tend to trade their own account, while pit brokers tend to trade for a brokerage company or a large firm.

forex The foreign exchange. A huge market in foreign currencies made by large banks worldwide. Today there are also much smaller companies that allow you to trade forex, but they take the side of the bid-ask spread opposite from you.

fundamental analysis Analysis of the market to determine its supply-and-demand characteristics. In equities markets, fundamental analysis determines the value, the earnings, the management, and the relative data of a particular stock.

futures A contract obligating its holder to buy a specified asset at a particular time and price. When commodity exchanges added stock index contracts and currency contracts, the term *futures* was developed to be more inclusive of these assets.

gambler's fallacy The belief that a loss is due to occur after a string of winners and/or that a gain is due to occur after a string of losers.

Gann concepts Various concepts for predicting market movements. These concepts were developed by the famous stock market forecaster W. G. Gann. One of the concepts is a *Gann square*, which is a mathematical system to find support and resistance based on the extreme high or low price for a given period. The attainment of a particular price level in the square, according to Gann, tells you the next probable price peak.

gap An area on a price chart in which there are no trades. Normally this occurs after the close of the market on one day and the open of the market on the next day. Lots of things can cause this, such as an earnings report coming out after the stock market has closed for the day.

gap climax A climax move that begins with a gap at the opening.

hit rate The percentage of winners you have in your trading or investing. Also known as the *reliability of your system*.

Holy Grail system A mythical trading system that perfectly follows the market and is always right, producing large gains and zero drawdowns. No such system exists, but the real meaning of the Holy Grail is right on track: it suggests that the secret is inside you.

indicator A summary of data presented in a supposedly meaningful way to help traders and investors make decisions.

inside day A day in which the total range of prices falls between the range of prices of the prior day.

intermarket analysis The use of the price moves of one market to predict what will happen to another market. For example, the price of the dollar might change depending on what happens with Treasury bonds, British pounds, gold, and oil.

investing Refers to a buy-and-hold strategy that most people follow. If you are in and out frequently or you are willing to go both long and short, then you are trading.

judgmental heuristics Shortcuts that the human mind uses to make decisions. These shortcuts make decision making quite quick and comprehensive, but they lead to biases in decision making that often cause people to lose money. A number of these biases are discussed in Chapter 2.

largest expected equity drop (LEED) A term used by Gallacher to describe a person's risk limits. It refers to the largest drop in equity that a trader or investor can tolerate.

leverage A term used to describe the relationship between the amount of money one needs to put up to own something and its underlying value. High leverage, which occurs when a small deposit controls a large investment, increases the potential size of profits and losses.

limit move A change in price that reaches the limit set by the exchange in which the contract is traded. Trading usually is halted when a limit move is reached.

limit order An order to your broker in which you specify a limit as to how much you want to buy or sell a position for. If your broker cannot get this price or better, the order is not executed.

liquidity The ease and availability of trading in an underlying stock or futures contract. When the volume of trading is high, there is usually a lot of liquidity.

long Owning a tradable item in anticipation of a future price increase. Also see *short.*

low-risk idea An idea that has a positive expectancy and is traded at a risk level that allows for the worst possible situation in the short term so that one can realize the long-term expectancy.

MACD See *moving average convergence divergence.*

marked to market A term used to describe the fact that open positions are credited or debited funds based on the closing price of that open position during the day. If you have an open position, it's considered to be worth whatever the closing price is at the end of the day.

market maker A broker, bank, firm, or individual trader that makes a two-way price to either buy or sell a security, currency, or futures contract.

market order An order to buy or sell at the current market price. Market orders are usually executed quickly, but not necessarily at the best possible price.

martingale strategy A position-sizing strategy in which the position size increases after you lose money. The classic martingale strategy is where you double your bet size after each loss.

maximum adverse excursion (MAE) The maximum loss attributable to price movement against the position during the life of a particular trade.

mechanical trading A form of trading in which all actions are determined by a computer with no additional human decision making.

mental rehearsal The psychological process of preplanning an event or strategy in one's mind before actually doing it.

mental scenario trading A trading concept in which the trader uses his or her macro assessment of what is going on in the markets to develop trading ideas.

modeling The process of determining how some form of peak performance (such as top trading) is accomplished and then the passing on of that training to others.

momentum An indicator that represents the change in price now from some fixed time period in the past. Momentum is one of the few leading indicators. Momentum as a market indicator is quite different from *momentum* as a term in physics to express the quantity that equals mass times velocity.

money management A term that has been frequently used to describe position sizing but that has so many other connotations that people fail to understand its full meaning or importance. For example, the term also refers to (1) managing other people's money, (2) controlling risk, (3) managing one's personal finances, and (4) achieving maximum gain.

moving average A method of representing a number of price bars (that is, showing the high, low, open, and close in a specific period of time) by a single average of all the price bars. When a new bar occurs, that new bar is added, the last bar is removed, and a new average is then calculated.

moving average convergence divergence (MACD) A technical indicator developed by Gerald Appel that follows the difference between a series of moving averages. The indicator has two lines, the MACD line and a signal line. A buy signal is generated when the MACD line rises above the signal line. A sell is generated when the MACD line falls below the signal. Because the MACD is generated from moving averages, it has a unique ability to capture wide-swinging moves in markets. Divergence, trendlines, and support can also be applied to the MACD to generate additional signals.

negative expectancy system A system in which you will never make money over the long term. For example, all casino games are designed to be negative expectancy games. Negative expectancy systems also include some highly reliable systems (that is, those with a high hit rate) that tend to have occasional large losses.

neuro-linguistic programming (NLP) A form of psychological training developed by systems analyst Richard Bandler and linguist John Grinder. It forms the foundation for the science of modeling excellence in human behavior. However, what is usually taught in NLP seminars are the techniques that are developed from the modeling process. For example, we have modeled top trading, system development, position sizing, and wealth building at the Van Tharp Institute. What we teach in our workshops is the process of doing those things, not the modeling process itself.

opportunity See *trade opportunity*.

optimize To find those parameters and indicators that best predict price changes in historical data. A highly optimized system usually does a poor job of predicting future prices.

option The right to buy or sell an underlying asset at a fixed price up to some specified date in the future. The right to buy is a *call option*, and the right to sell is a *put option*.

options spread A trading strategy by which one opens two options positions at the same time and profits from the difference in the price of the two positions. See *debit spread* and *credit spread*.

oscillator An indicator that detrends (normalizes) price. Most oscillators tend to go from 0 to 100. Analysts typically assume that when the indicator is near zero, the price is *oversold*, and that when the price is near 100, it is *overbought*. However, in a trending market, prices can be overbought or oversold for a long time.

parabolic An indicator that has a U-shaped function, based on the function $y = ax^2 + bx + c$. Because it rises at an increasing rate over time, it is sometimes used as a trailing stop that tends to keep one from giving back much profit. In addition, a market is said to be parabolic when it starts rising almost vertically as many high-tech stocks did in 1999, sometimes doubling each month.

passive income Income that occurs because your money is working for you.

peak-to-trough drawdown A term that is used to describe one's maximum drawdown from the highest equity peak to the lowest equity trough prior to reaching a new equity high.

percent risk model A position-sizing model in which position sizing is determined by limiting the risk on the position to a certain percentage of your equity.

percent volatility model A position-sizing model in which position sizing is determined by limiting the amount of volatility (which is usually defined by the average true range) in a position to a certain percentage of your equity.

position sizing The most important of the six key elements of successful trading. This term, invented in the first edition of this book, refers to the part of your system that really determines whether or not you'll meet your objectives. This element determines how large a position you will have throughout the course of a trade. In most cases, algorithms that work for determining position size are based on one's current equity.

positive expectancy A system (or game) that will make money over the long term if played at a risk level that is sufficiently low. It also means that the mean R value of a distribution of R multiples is a positive number.

postdictive error An error that is made when you take into account future data that you should not know. For example, if you buy on the open each day, if the closing price is up, you will have the potential for a great system, but only because you are making a postdictive error.

prediction A guess about the future. Most people want to make money through guessing future outcomes, that is, prediction. Analysts are employed to predict prices. However, great traders make money by "cutting losses short and letting profits run," which has nothing to do with prediction.

price/earnings (P/E) ratio The ratio of the price of a stock to its earnings. For example, if a $20 stock earns $1 per share each year, it has a price/earnings ratio of 20. The average P/E of the S&P 500 over the last 100 years has been about 17.

price-to-sales ratio The ratio of the price of a stock to its sale. For example, if a stock sells for $20 and has $1 per share in total sales, then it has a price-to-sales ratio of 20.

proprietary methodology A methodology that a trader keeps to himself because (1) he doesn't want to share its secrets or (2) he doesn't want to answer questions about what he does.

put option An option that gives someone the right to sell the underlying instrument at a predetermined price up to a specific expiration date. It is the right to sell but not the obligation.

***R* multiple** A term used to express trading results in terms of the initial risk. All profits and losses can be expressed as a multiple of the initial risk (*R*) taken. For example, a 10*R* multiple is a profit that is 10 times the initial risk. Thus, if your initial risk is $10, then a $100 profit would be a 10*R*-multiple profit. When you do this, any system can then be described by the *R*-multiple distribution that it generates. That distribution will have a mean (expectancy) and standard deviation that will characterize it.

***R* value** A term used to express the initial risk taken in a given position, as defined by one's initial stop loss.

random An event determined by chance. In mathematics, a number that cannot be predicted.

relative strength index (RSI) A futures market indicator described by J. Welles Wilder, Jr., that is used to ascertain overbought and oversold conditions. It is based on the close-to-close price change.

reliability How accurate something is or how often it wins. Thus, "60 percent reliability" means that something wins 60 percent of the time.

resistance An area on a chart up to which a stock can trade but cannot seem to exceed for a certain period of time.

retracement A price movement in the opposite direction of the previous trend. A retracement is usually a price correction.

reward-to-risk ratio The average return on an account (on a yearly basis) divided by the maximum peak-to-trough drawdown. Any reward-to-risk ratio over 3 that is determined by this method is excellent. It also might refer to the size of the average winning trade divided by the size of the average losing trade.

risk The difference in price between the entry point in a position and the worst-case loss that one is willing to take in that position. For example, if you buy a stock at $20 and decide to get out if it drops to $18, then your risk is $2 per share. Note that this definition is much different than the typical academic definition of *risk* as the variability of the market in which you are investing.

round turn A term that refers to the process of both getting into and exiting a futures contract. Futures commissions are usually based on a round turn as opposed to being based on charges for both getting in and getting out.

scalping A term that refers to the actions, usually of floor traders, who buy and sell quickly to get the bid and ask prices or to make a quick profit. The *bid price* is what they will buy it for (and what you'll get as a seller), and the *ask price* is what they'll sell it for (and what you'll get as a buyer).

seasonal trading Trading based on consistent, predictable changes in price during the year due to production cycles or demand cycles.

secular (bull or bear) market A term that refers to long-term tendencies in the market to increase valuations (*bull*) or decrease valuations (*bear*). Secular tendencies can last for several decades, but they say nothing about what the market will do in the next few months or even the next year.

setup A term that refers to a part of your trading system in which certain criteria must be present before you look for an entry into the market. People used to describe trading systems by their setups. For example, CANSLIM is an acronym for the setup criteria of William O'Neil.

short Not actually owning an item that you are selling. If you were using this strategy, you would sell an item in order to be able to buy it later at a lower price. When you sell an item before you have actually bought it, you are said to be *shorting* the market.

sideways market A market that moves neither up nor down.

slippage The difference in price between what you expect to pay when you enter the market and what you actually pay. For example, if you attempted to buy at 15 and you end up buying at 15.5, then you have a half point of slippage.

specialist A floor trader assigned to fill orders in a specific stock when the order has no offsetting order from off the floor.

speculating Investing in markets that are considered to be very volatile and thus quite "risky" in the academic sense of the word.

spreading The process of trading two related markets to exploit a new relationship. Thus, you might trade Japanese yen in terms of British pounds. In doing so, you are trading the relationship between the two currencies.

stalking A term that refers to the process of getting ready to get into a position. This is one of the Ten Tasks of Trading from Dr. Tharp's model.

standard deviation The positive square root of the expected value of the square of the difference between some random variable and its mean. A measure of variability that has been expressed in a normalized form.

stochastic An overbought-oversold indicator, popularized by George Lane, that is based on the observation that prices close near the high of the day in an uptrend and near the low of the day in a downtrend.

stop (stop loss, stop order) An order you put with your broker that turns into a market order if the price hits the stop point. It's typically called a *stop* (or *stop-loss order*) because most traders use it to make sure they sell an open position before it gets away from them. It typically will stop a loss from getting too big. However, since it turns into a market order when the stop price is hit, you are not guaranteed that you'll get that price. It might be much worse. Most electronic brokerage systems will allow you to put a stop order into their computer. The computer then sends it out as a market order when that price is hit. Thus, it does not go into the market where everyone might see it and look for it.

support The price level that historically a stock has had difficulty falling below. It is the area on the chart at which buyers seem to come into the market.

swing trading A term that refers to short-term trading designed to capture quick moves in the market.

system A set of rules for trading. A complete system will typically have (1) some setup conditions, (2) an entry signal, (3) a worst-case disaster stop loss to preserve capital, (4) a profit-taking exit, and (5) a position-sizing algorithm. However, many commercially available systems do not meet all of these criteria. A trading system might also be described by the *R*-multiple distribution it generates.

tick A minimum fluctuation in the price of a tradable item.

timing technique A trading technique that attempts to assist people in entering the market just before an up move or in selling just before a down move.

trade distribution A term that refers to the manner in which winning and losing trades are achieved over time. It will show the winning streaks and the losing streaks.

trade opportunity One of the six keys to profitable trading. It refers to how often a system will open a position in the market.

trading Opening a position in the market, either long or short, with the expectation of either closing it out at a substantial profit or cutting losses short if the trade does not work out.

trading cost The cost of trading, which typically includes brokerage commissions and slippage, plus the market maker's cost.

trailing stop A stop-loss order that moves with the prevailing trend of the market. This is typically used as a way of exiting profitable trades. The stop is only moved when the market goes in your favor. It is never moved in the opposite direction.

trend following The systematic process of capturing extreme moves in the market with the idea of staying in the market as long as the market continues its move.

trending day A day that generally continues in one direction, either up or down, from the open to the close.

trendline A line connecting the tops (or bottoms) of rising or falling markets. This line is believed to reflect the market trend. Market technicians tend to believe that when the price "breaks" the trendline, then the trend is probably over. However, it often means that they simply have to draw a new trendline.

Turtle Soup A trademarked entry technique that is based on the assumption that markets typically reverse after 20-day channel breakouts.

units per fixed amount of money model A position-sizing model in which you typically buy one unit of everything per so much money in your account. For example, you might buy one unit (that is, 100 shares or one contract) per $25,000.

validity A term that indicates how "real" something is. Does it measure what it is supposed to measure? How accurate is it?

valuation An exercise in giving some value on the price of a stock or commodity based on some model for determining value. See *value trading*.

value trading A term that refers to a concept in which positions are opened in the market because they have good value. There are numerous ways to measure value. However, a good way of thinking about it is that if the assets of a company are worth $20 per share and you can buy the company for $15 per share, then you are getting a good value. Different value traders will have different ways to define *value*.

volatility A term that refers to the range of prices in a given time period. A high-volatility market has a large range in daily prices, whereas a low-volatility market has a small range of daily prices. This is one of the most useful concepts in trading.

volatility breakout An entry technique that calls for entering the market when it moves a specific amount from the open, based on the previous daily ranges of the market. For example, a "1.5 ATR volatility breakout" would call for entering the market when it moved (up or down) more than 1.5 times the average true range of the last X days from today's open.

RECOMMENDED READINGS

Alexander, Michael. *Stock Cycles: Why Stocks Won't Beat Money Markets over the Next Twenty Years.* Lincoln, Neb.: Writer's Club Press, 2000. Interesting analysis of a 200-year history of the stock market that shows the tendency for long secular bull and bear cycles.

Balsara, Nauzer J. *Money Management Strategies for Futures Traders.* New York: Wiley, 1992. Good money management book, but it is more about risk control than position sizing.

Barach, Roland. *Mindtraps*, 2nd ed. Cary, N.C.: International Institute of Trading Mastery (IITM), 1996. Good book about the psychological biases we face in all aspects of trading and investing. Nearly out of print. Call 1-919-466-0043 for more information.

Buffett, Warren E. *The Essays of Warren Buffett: Lessons for Corporate America*, 1st rev. ed. The Cunningham Group, 2001. This is a self-published book by Dr. Lawrence Cunningham who was able to compile some of Buffett's original writings into a book. Great reading.

Campbell, Joseph (with Bill Moyers). *The Power of Myth.* New York: Doubleday, 1988. One of my all-time favorite books.

Chande, Tushar. *Beyond Technical Analysis: How to Develop and Implement a Winning Trading System.* New York: Wiley, 1997. One of the first books to really go beyond just emphasizing entry.

Colby, Robert W., and Thomas A. Meyers. *Encyclopedia of Technical Market Indicators.* Homewood, Ill.: Dow Jones Irwin, 1988. Excellent just for its scope.

Connors, Laurence A., and Linda Bradford Raschke. *Street Smarts: High Probability Short Term Trading Strategies.* Sherman Oaks, Calif.: M. Gordon Publishing, 1995. Great book of short-term trading techniques.

Covel, Michael. *Trend-Following: How Great Traders Make Millions in Up and Down Markets*, new expanded edition. Upper Saddle River, N.J: Financial Times Prentice Hall, 2005. Probably the best overall book available on the concept of trend following.

Easterling, Ed. *Unexpected Returns: Understanding Secular Stock Market Cycles.* Fort Bragg, Calif.: Cypress House, 2005. In this self-published book, Ed Easterling presents a masterful job of helping people get a major perspective on why the market may do what it's going to do. If you want to understand the big picture, then this book is a must read.

Gallacher, William R. *Winner Take All: A Top Commodity Trader Tells It Like It Is.* Chicago: Probus, 1994. One of the systems mentioned in the text comes from this witty and straightforward book.

Gardner, David, and Tom Gardner. *The Motley Fool Investment Guide: How the Fool Beats Wall Street's Wise Men and How You Can Too.* New York: Simon & Schuster, 1996. Simple investment strategies most people can follow.

Graham, Benjamin. *The Intelligent Investor: The Classic Text on Value Investing.* New York: Harper, 2005. If you are interested in value investing, then this book is a must read.

Hagstrom, Robert, Jr. *The Warren Buffett Way: Investment Strategies of the World's Greatest Investor*, 2nd ed. New York: Wiley, 2004. Probably the best book on Buffett's strategy. However, this is not Buffett writing about his strategy, and the author seems to have all the normal biases that most people have—it makes it seem as if all Buffett does is pick good stocks and hold on to them.

Kase, Cynthia. *Trading with the Odds: Using the Power of Probability to Profit in the Futures Market.* Chicago: Irwin, 1996. I believe there is more to this book than even the author knows.

Kaufman, Perry. *Smarter Trading: Improving Performance in Changing Markets.* New York: McGraw-Hill, 1995. Great ideas and contains another of the systems discussed throughout this book.

Kilpatrick, Andrew. *Of Permanent Value: The Story of Warren Buffett.* Birmingham, Ala.: AKPE, 1996. Fun reading.

LeBeau, Charles, and David W. Lucas. *The Technical Traders' Guide to Computer Analysis of the Futures Market.* Homewood, Ill: Irwin, 1992. One of the best books ever written on systems development.

Lefèvre, Edwin. *Reminiscence of a Stock Operator.* New York: Wiley Investment Classics, 2006. New edition of an old classic first published in 1923.

Lowe, Janet. *Warren Buffett Speaks: Wit and Wisdom from the World's Greatest Investor.* New York: Wiley, 1997. Fun reading with great wisdom.

Lowenstein, Roger. *Buffett: The Making of an American Capitalist.* New York: Random House, 1995. A good book to round out your Buffett education.

Mitchell, Dick. *Commonsense Betting: Betting Strategies for the Race Track.* New York: William Morrow, 1995. A must for people who really want to stretch themselves to learn position sizing.

O'Neil, William. *How to Make Money in Stocks: A Winning System in Good Times and Bad*, 2nd ed. New York: McGraw-Hill, 1995. A modern classic that includes one of the systems reviewed in this book.

Roberts, Ken. *The World's Most Powerful Money Manual and Course.* Grant's Pass, Oreg.: Published by Ken Roberts, 1995. Good course and good ideas. However, be careful if you don't have enough money. Call 503-955-2800 for more information.

Schwager, Jack. *Market Wizards.* New York: New York Institute of Finance, 1988. A must read for any trader or investor.

———. *The New Market Wizards.* New York: HarperCollins, 1992. Continues the tradition, and it again is a must read. William Eckhardt's chapter alone is worth the price of the book.

———. *Schwager on Futures: Fundamental Analysis.* New York: Wiley, 1996. Great book for anyone who wants to understand fundamentals in the futures market.

———. *Schwager on Futures: Technical Analysis.* New York: Wiley, 1996. Solid background on many topics related to learning about markets.

Sloman, James. *When You're Troubled: The Healing Heart.* Raleigh, N.C.: Mountain Rain, 1993. Call 1-919-466-0043 for more information. Great book about helping yourself through life. The author calls this book his life's purpose, and I tend to agree.

Sweeney, John. *Campaign Trading: Tactics and Strategies to Exploit the Markets.* New York: Wiley, 1996. Great book that emphasizes the more important aspects of trading.

Tharp, Van. *The Peak Performance Course for Traders and Investors.* Cary, N.C.: International Institute of Trading Mastery (IITM), 1988–1994. Call 1-919-466-0043 for more information. This is my model of the trading process, presented in such a way as to help you install the model in yourself.

———. *How to Develop a Winning Trading System That Fits You, CD Course.* Cary, N.C.: International Institute of Trading Mastery (IITM), 1997. Call 1-919-466-0043 for more information. This is our original systems workshop, which is great information for all traders and investors.

———. *The Definitive Guide to Expectancy and Position Sizing.* Cary, N.C.: International Institute of Trading Mastery (IITM), 2007. Call 1-919-466-0043 for more information.

Tharp, Van, D. R. Barton, and Steve Sjuggerud. *Safe Strategies for Financial Freedom.* New York: McGraw-Hill, 2004. This book presents some new rules for the money gain, discusses the big picture, and then goes on to lay out specific strategies that fit the big picture. All of those strategies work, and this book describes all of the strategies that I use personally.

Tharp, Van, and Brian June. *Financial Freedom through Electronic Day Trading.* New York, McGraw-Hill, 2000. While many of the specific strategies in this book are out of date, there are nearly 100 pages on how to develop a business plan for your trading, which is information that is not found in any of my other books.

Vince, Ralph. *Portfolio Management Formulas: Mathematical Trading Methods for the Futures, Options, and Stock Markets.* New York: Wiley, 1990. Difficult reading, but most professionals should tackle it.

———. *The New Money Management: A Framework for Asset Allocation.* New York: Wiley, 1995. An improvement from *Portfolio Management Formulas* and again a book that most professionals in the field of investing and trading should read.

Whitman, Martin J. *Value Investing: A Balanced Approach.* New York: Wiley, 2000. Marty Whitman has been making consistent phenomenal returns through value investing for many, many years. In this book he talks about some of his strategies, and I consider it another must read for value investors.

Wilder, J. Welles, Jr. *New Concepts in Technical Trading.* Greensboro, N.C.: Trend Research, 1978. One of the classics of trading and a must read.

Wyckoff, Richard D. *How I Trade and Invest in Stocks and Bonds.* New York: Cosimo Classics, 2005. Reprint of the original 1922 edition.

INDEX

ABOUT THE AUTHOR

Van K. Tharp, Ph.D., is an internationally known consultant and coach to traders and investors, as well as the founder and president of the Van Tharp Institute. He is the author of multiple bestselling books on trading and investing, including *Safe Strategies for Financial Freedom* and *Financial Freedom through Electronic Day Trading.* Tharp is a highly sought-after speaker who develops courses and seminars for large banks and trading firms around the world. He has published numerous articles and has been featured in publications such as *Forbes, Barron's Market Week,* and *Investor's Business Daily.*

A Personal Invitation from Van K. Tharp

Join the Van Tharp community by visiting my Web site at www.vantharp.com, where you can read my newsletter, *Tharp's Thoughts;* test yourself to learn where you fit on the Tharp Trading Scale; and download a free trading simulation game to practice position sizing.

Here's more information:

Free Trading Simulation Game

We believe that the best way to learn position sizing is to practice using it to meet your objectives. And to help you do so, we've developed a 10-level game. The first three levels are free, and you can download them from our Web site, www.vantharp.com. Try it today!

What Type of Trader Are You?

Test yourself on the Tharp Trading Scale. Visit www.vantharp.com for more information.

Free *Tharp's Thoughts* Newsletter

Subscribe to *Tharp's Thoughts*, my free e-mail newsletter, and receive tips, articles, market updates, and more information on systems development, position sizing, *R* multiples, and many other trading topics.

The Van Tharp Institute
(International Institute of
Trading Mastery, Inc.)

102-A Commonwealth Court
Cary, NC 27511

Phone: 919-466-0043
or
800-385-IITM (4486)
Fax: 919-466-0408
E-mail: info@iitm.com